Lecture Notes in Computer Science

Commenced Publication in 1973
Founding and Former Series Editors:
Gerhard Goos, Juris Hartmanis, and Jan van Leeuwen

Louis Marinos   Ioannis Askoxylakis (Eds.)

Human Aspects of Information Security, Privacy, and Trust

First International Conference, HAS 2013
Held as Part of HCI International 2013
Las Vegas, NV, USA, July 21-26, 2013
Proceedings

 Springer

Volume Editors

Louis Marinos
ENISA - European Network and Information Security Agency
Science and Technology Park of Crete
Vassilika Vouton
70013 Heraklion, Crete, Greece
E-mail: louis.marinos@enisa.europa.eu

Ioannis Askoxylakis
Foundation for Research and Technology - Hellas (FORTH)
Institute of Computer Science (ICS)
Telecommunications and Networks Laboratory (TNL)
N. Plastira 100, Vassilika Vouton
70013 Heraklion, Crete, Greece
E-mail: asko@ics.forth.gr

ISSN 0302-9743   e-ISSN 1611-3349
ISBN 978-3-642-39344-0   e-ISBN 978-3-642-39345-7
DOI 10.1007/978-3-642-39345-7
Springer Heidelberg Dordrecht London New York

Library of Congress Control Number: 2013941408

CR Subject Classification (1998): H.5, K.6.5, H.1, C.2.0, K.4, J.1, H.3, H.4

LNCS Sublibrary: SL 3 – Information Systems and Application,
incl. Internet/Web and HCI

Typesetting: Camera-ready by author, data conversion by Scientific Publishing Services, Chennai, India

Printed on acid-free paper

Springer is part of Springer Science+Business Media (www.springer.com)

Foreword

The 15th International Conference on Human–Computer Interaction, HCI International 2013, was held in Las Vegas, Nevada, USA, 21–26 July 2013, incorporating 12 conferences / thematic areas:

Thematic areas:

- Human–Computer Interaction
- Human Interface and the Management of Information

Affiliated conferences:

- 10th International Conference on Engineering Psychology and Cognitive Ergonomics
- 7th International Conference on Universal Access in Human–Computer Interaction
- 5th International Conference on Virtual, Augmented and Mixed Reality
- 5th International Conference on Cross-Cultural Design
- 5th International Conference on Online Communities and Social Computing
- 7th International Conference on Augmented Cognition
- 4th International Conference on Digital Human Modeling and Applications in Health, Safety, Ergonomics and Risk Management
- 2nd International Conference on Design, User Experience and Usability
- 1st International Conference on Distributed, Ambient and Pervasive Interactions
- 1st International Conference on Human Aspects of Information Security, Privacy and Trust

A total of 5210 individuals from academia, research institutes, industry and governmental agencies from 70 countries submitted contributions, and 1666 papers and 303 posters were included in the program. These papers address the latest research and development efforts and highlight the human aspects of design and use of computing systems. The papers accepted for presentation thoroughly cover the entire field of Human–Computer Interaction, addressing major advances in knowledge and effective use of computers in a variety of application areas.

This volume, edited by Louis Marinos and Ioannis Askoxylakis, contains papers focusing on the thematic area of Human Aspects of Information Security, Privacy and Trust, and addressing the following major topics:

- Novel Authentication Systems
- Human Factors in Security
- Security and Privacy Policies
- User Centric Security and Privacy

The remaining volumes of the HCI International 2013 proceedings are:

- Volume 1, LNCS 8004, Human–Computer Interaction: Human-Centred Design Approaches, Methods, Tools and Environments (Part I), edited by Masaaki Kurosu
- Volume 2, LNCS 8005, Human–Computer Interaction: Applications and Services (Part II), edited by Masaaki Kurosu
- Volume 3, LNCS 8006, Human–Computer Interaction: Users and Contexts of Use (Part III), edited by Masaaki Kurosu
- Volume 4, LNCS 8007, Human–Computer Interaction: Interaction Modalities and Techniques (Part IV), edited by Masaaki Kurosu
- Volume 5, LNCS 8008, Human–Computer Interaction: Towards Intelligent and Implicit Interaction (Part V), edited by Masaaki Kurosu
- Volume 6, LNCS 8009, Universal Access in Human–Computer Interaction: Design Methods, Tools and Interaction Techniques for eInclusion (Part I), edited by Constantine Stephanidis and Margherita Antona
- Volume 7, LNCS 8010, Universal Access in Human–Computer Interaction: User and Context Diversity (Part II), edited by Constantine Stephanidis and Margherita Antona
- Volume 8, LNCS 8011, Universal Access in Human–Computer Interaction: Applications and Services for Quality of Life (Part III), edited by Constantine Stephanidis and Margherita Antona
- Volume 9, LNCS 8012, Design, User Experience, and Usability: Design Philosophy, Methods and Tools (Part I), edited by Aaron Marcus
- Volume 10, LNCS 8013, Design, User Experience, and Usability: Health, Learning, Playing, Cultural, and Cross-Cultural User Experience (Part II), edited by Aaron Marcus
- Volume 11, LNCS 8014, Design, User Experience, and Usability: User Experience in Novel Technological Environments (Part III), edited by Aaron Marcus
- Volume 12, LNCS 8015, Design, User Experience, and Usability: Web, Mobile and Product Design (Part IV), edited by Aaron Marcus
- Volume 13, LNCS 8016, Human Interface and the Management of Information: Information and Interaction Design (Part I), edited by Sakae Yamamoto
- Volume 14, LNCS 8017, Human Interface and the Management of Information: Information and Interaction for Health, Safety, Mobility and Complex Environments (Part II), edited by Sakae Yamamoto
- Volume 15, LNCS 8018, Human Interface and the Management of Information: Information and Interaction for Learning, Culture, Collaboration and Business (Part III), edited by Sakae Yamamoto
- Volume 16, LNAI 8019, Engineering Psychology and Cognitive Ergonomics: Understanding Human Cognition (Part I), edited by Don Harris
- Volume 17, LNAI 8020, Engineering Psychology and Cognitive Ergonomics: Applications and Services (Part II), edited by Don Harris
- Volume 18, LNCS 8021, Virtual, Augmented and Mixed Reality: Designing and Developing Augmented and Virtual Environments (Part I), edited by Randall Shumaker

- Volume 19, LNCS 8022, Virtual, Augmented and Mixed Reality: Systems and Applications (Part II), edited by Randall Shumaker
- Volume 20, LNCS 8023, Cross-Cultural Design: Methods, Practice and Case Studies (Part I), edited by P.L. Patrick Rau
- Volume 21, LNCS 8024, Cross-Cultural Design: Cultural Differences in Everyday Life (Part II), edited by P.L. Patrick Rau
- Volume 22, LNCS 8025, Digital Human Modeling and Applications in Health, Safety, Ergonomics and Risk Management: Healthcare and Safety of the Environment and Transport (Part I), edited by Vincent G. Duffy
- Volume 23, LNCS 8026, Digital Human Modeling and Applications in Health, Safety, Ergonomics and Risk Management: Human Body Modeling and Ergonomics (Part II), edited by Vincent G. Duffy
- Volume 24, LNAI 8027, Foundations of Augmented Cognition, edited by Dylan D. Schmorrow and Cali M. Fidopiastis
- Volume 25, LNCS 8028, Distributed, Ambient and Pervasive Interactions, edited by Norbert Streitz and Constantine Stephanidis
- Volume 26, LNCS 8029, Online Communities and Social Computing, edited by A. Ant Ozok and Panayiotis Zaphiris
- Volume 28, CCIS 373, HCI International 2013 Posters Proceedings (Part I), edited by Constantine Stephanidis
- Volume 29, CCIS 374, HCI International 2013 Posters Proceedings (Part II), edited by Constantine Stephanidis

I would like to thank the Program Chairs and the members of the Program Boards of all affiliated conferences and thematic areas, listed below, for their contribution to the highest scientific quality and the overall success of the HCI International 2013 conference.

This conference could not have been possible without the continuous support and advice of the Founding Chair and Conference Scientific Advisor, Prof. Gavriel Salvendy, as well as the dedicated work and outstanding efforts of the Communications Chair and Editor of HCI International News, Abbas Moallem.

I would also like to thank for their contribution towards the smooth organization of the HCI International 2013 Conference the members of the Human–Computer Interaction Laboratory of ICS-FORTH, and in particular George Paparoulis, Maria Pitsoulaki, Stavroula Ntoa, Maria Bouhli and George Kapnas.

May 2013
Constantine Stephanidis
General Chair, HCI International 2013

Organization

Human–Computer Interaction

Program Chair: Masaaki Kurosu, Japan

Jose Abdelnour-Nocera, UK
Sebastiano Bagnara, Italy
Simone Barbosa, Brazil
Tomas Berns, Sweden
Nigel Bevan, UK
Simone Borsci, UK
Apala Lahiri Chavan, India
Sherry Chen, Taiwan
Kevin Clark, USA
Torkil Clemmensen, Denmark
Xiaowen Fang, USA
Shin'ichi Fukuzumi, Japan
Vicki Hanson, UK
Ayako Hashizume, Japan
Anzai Hiroyuki, Italy
Sheue-Ling Hwang, Taiwan
Wonil Hwang, South Korea
Minna Isomursu, Finland
Yong Gu Ji, South Korea
Esther Jun, USA
Mitsuhiko Karashima, Japan

Kyungdoh Kim, South Korea
Heidi Krömker, Germany
Chen Ling, USA
Yan Liu, USA
Zhengjie Liu, P.R. China
Loïc Martínez Normand, Spain
Chang S. Nam, USA
Naoko Okuizumi, Japan
Noriko Osaka, Japan
Philippe Palanque, France
Hans Persson, Sweden
Ling Rothrock, USA
Naoki Sakakibara, Japan
Dominique Scapin, France
Guangfeng Song, USA
Sanjay Tripathi, India
Chui Yin Wong, Malaysia
Toshiki Yamaoka, Japan
Kazuhiko Yamazaki, Japan
Ryoji Yoshitake, Japan
Silvia Zimmermann, Switzerland

Human Interface and the Management of Information

Program Chair: Sakae Yamamoto, Japan

Hans-Jorg Bullinger, Germany
Alan Chan, Hong Kong
Gilsoo Cho, South Korea
Jon R. Gunderson, USA
Shin'ichi Fukuzumi, Japan
Michitaka Hirose, Japan
Jhilmil Jain, USA
Yasufumi Kume, Japan

Mark Lehto, USA
Hiroyuki Miki, Japan
Hirohiko Mori, Japan
Fiona Fui-Hoon Nah, USA
Shogo Nishida, Japan
Robert Proctor, USA
Youngho Rhee, South Korea
Katsunori Shimohara, Japan

Michale Smith, USA

Kim-Phuong Vu, USA

Tsutomu Tabe, Japan

Tomio Watanabe, Japan

Hiroshi Tsuji, Japan

Hidekazu Yoshikawa, Japan

Engineering Psychology and Cognitive Ergonomics

Program Chair: Don Harris, UK

Guy Andre Boy, USA

Joakim Dahlman, Sweden

Trevor Dobbins, UK

Mike Feary, USA

Shan Fu, P.R. China

Michaela Heese, Austria

Hung-Sying Jing, Taiwan

Wen-Chin Li, Taiwan

Mark A. Neerincx, The Netherlands

Jan M. Noyes, UK

Taezoon Park, Singapore

Paul Salmon, Australia

Axel Schulte, Germany

Siraj Shaikh, UK

Sarah C. Sharples, UK

Anthony Smoker, UK

Neville A. Stanton, UK

Alex Stedmon, UK

Xianghong Sun, P.R. China

Andrew Thatcher, South Africa

Matthew J.W. Thomas, Australia

Rolf Zon, The Netherlands

Universal Access in Human–Computer Interaction

Program Chairs: Constantine Stephanidis, Greece, and Margherita Antona, Greece

Julio Abascal, Spain

Ray Adams, UK

Gisela Susanne Bahr, USA

Margit Betke, USA

Christian Bühler, Germany

Stefan Carmien, Spain

Jerzy Charytonowicz, Poland

Carlos Duarte, Portugal

Pier Luigi Emiliani, Italy

Qin Gao, P.R. China

Andrina Granić, Croatia

Andreas Holzinger, Austria

Josette Jones, USA

Simeon Keates, UK

Georgios Kouroupetroglou, Greece

Patrick Langdon, UK

Seongil Lee, Korea

Ana Isabel B.B. Paraguay, Brazil

Helen Petrie, UK

Michael Pieper, Germany

Enrico Pontelli, USA

Jaime Sanchez, Chile

Anthony Savidis, Greece

Christian Stary, Austria

Hirotada Ueda, Japan

Gerhard Weber, Germany

Harald Weber, Germany

Virtual, Augmented and Mixed Reality

Program Chair: Randall Shumaker, USA

Waymon Armstrong, USA
Juan Cendan, USA
Rudy Darken, USA
Cali M. Fidopiastis, USA
Charles Hughes, USA
David Kaber, USA
Hirokazu Kato, Japan
Denis Laurendeau, Canada
Fotis Liarokapis, UK

Mark Livingston, USA
Michael Macedonia, USA
Gordon Mair, UK
Jose San Martin, Spain
Jacquelyn Morie, USA
Albert "Skip" Rizzo, USA
Kay Stanney, USA
Christopher Stapleton, USA
Gregory Welch, USA

Cross-Cultural Design

Program Chair: P.L. Patrick Rau, P.R. China

Pilsung Choe, P.R. China
Henry Been-Lirn Duh, Singapore
Vanessa Evers, The Netherlands
Paul Fu, USA
Zhiyong Fu, P.R. China
Fu Guo, P.R. China
Sung H. Han, Korea
Toshikazu Kato, Japan
Dyi-Yih Michael Lin, Taiwan
Rungtai Lin, Taiwan

Sheau-Farn Max Liang, Taiwan
Liang Ma, P.R. China
Alexander Mädche, Germany
Katsuhiko Ogawa, Japan
Tom Plocher, USA
Kerstin Röse, Germany
Supriya Singh, Australia
Hsiu-Ping Yueh, Taiwan
Liang (Leon) Zeng, USA
Chen Zhao, USA

Online Communities and Social Computing

Program Chairs: A. Ant Ozok, USA, and Panayiotis Zaphiris, Cyprus

Areej Al-Wabil, Saudi Arabia
Leonelo Almeida, Brazil
Bjørn Andersen, Norway
Chee Siang Ang, UK
Aneesha Bakharia, Australia
Ania Bobrowicz, UK
Paul Cairns, UK
Farzin Deravi, UK
Andri Ioannou, Cyprus
Slava Kisilevich, Germany

Niki Lambropoulos, Greece
Effie Law, Switzerland
Soo Ling Lim, UK
Fernando Loizides, Cyprus
Gabriele Meiselwitz, USA
Anthony Norcio, USA
Elaine Raybourn, USA
Panote Siriaraya, UK
David Stuart, UK
June Wei, USA

Augmented Cognition

Program Chairs: Dylan D. Schmorrow, USA, and Cali M. Fidopiastis, USA

Robert Arrabito, Canada
Richard Backs, USA
Chris Berka, USA
Joseph Cohn, USA
Martha E. Crosby, USA
Julie Drexler, USA
Ivy Estabrooke, USA
Chris Forsythe, USA
Wai Tat Fu, USA
Rodolphe Gentili, USA
Marc Grootjen, The Netherlands
Jefferson Grubb, USA
Ming Hou, Canada

Santosh Mathan, USA
Rob Matthews, Australia
Dennis McBride, USA
Jeff Morrison, USA
Mark A. Neerincx, The Netherlands
Denise Nicholson, USA
Banu Onaral, USA
Lee Sciarini, USA
Kay Stanney, USA
Roy Stripling, USA
Rob Taylor, UK
Karl van Orden, USA

Digital Human Modeling and Applications in Health, Safety, Ergonomics and Risk Management

Program Chair: Vincent G. Duffy, USA and Russia

Karim Abdel-Malek, USA
Giuseppe Andreoni, Italy
Daniel Carruth, USA
Eliza Yingzi Du, USA
Enda Fallon, Ireland
Afzal Godil, USA
Ravindra Goonetilleke, Hong Kong
Bo Hoege, Germany
Waldemar Karwowski, USA
Zhizhong Li, P.R. China

Kang Li, USA
Tim Marler, USA
Michelle Robertson, USA
Matthias Rötting, Germany
Peter Vink, The Netherlands
Mao-Jiun Wang, Taiwan
Xuguang Wang, France
Jingzhou (James) Yang, USA
Xiugan Yuan, P.R. China
Gülcin Yücel Hoge, Germany

Design, User Experience, and Usability

Program Chair: Aaron Marcus, USA

Sisira Adikari, Australia
Ronald Baecker, Canada
Arne Berger, Germany
Jamie Blustein, Canada

Ana Boa-Ventura, USA
Jan Brejcha, Czech Republic
Lorenzo Cantoni, Switzerland
Maximilian Eibl, Germany

Distributed, Ambient and Pervasive Interactions

Program Chairs: Norbert Streitz, Germany, and Constantine Stephanidis, Greece

Human Aspects of Information Security, Privacy and Trust

Program Chairs: Louis Marinos, ENISA EU, and Ioannis Askoxylakis, Greece

Julien Touzeau, France
Theo Tryfonas, UK
João Vilela, Portugal

Claire Vishik, UK
Melanie Volkamer, Germany

External Reviewers

Maysoon Abulkhair, Saudi Arabia
Ilia Adami, Greece
Vishal Barot, UK
Stephan Böhm, Germany
Vassilis Charissis, UK
Francisco Cipolla-Ficarra, Spain
Maria De Marsico, Italy
Marc Fabri, UK
David Fonseca, Spain
Linda Harley, USA
Yasushi Ikei, Japan
Wei Ji, USA
Nouf Khashman, Canada
John Killilea, USA
Iosif Klironomos, Greece
Ute Klotz, Switzerland
Maria Korozi, Greece
Kentaro Kotani, Japan

Vassilis Kouroumalis, Greece
Stephanie Lackey, USA
Janelle LaMarche, USA
Asterios Leonidis, Greece
Nickolas Macchiarella, USA
George Margetis, Greece
Matthew Marraffino, USA
Joseph Mercado, USA
Claudia Mont'Alvão, Brazil
Yoichi Motomura, Japan
Karsten Nebe, Germany
Stavroula Ntoa, Greece
Martin Osen, Austria
Stephen Prior, UK
Farid Shirazi, Canada
Jan Stelovsky, USA
Sarah Swierenga, USA

HCI International 2014

The 16th International Conference on Human–Computer Interaction, HCI International 2014, will be held jointly with the affiliated conferences in the summer of 2014. It will cover a broad spectrum of themes related to Human–Computer Interaction, including theoretical issues, methods, tools, processes and case studies in HCI design, as well as novel interaction techniques, interfaces and applications. The proceedings will be published by Springer. More information about the topics, as well as the venue and dates of the conference, will be announced through the HCI International Conference series website: http://www.hci-international.org/

General Chair
Professor Constantine Stephanidis
University of Crete and ICS-FORTH
Heraklion, Crete, Greece
Email: cs@ics.forth.gr

Table of Contents

Security and Privacy Policies

User Centric Security and Privacy

Part I
Novel Authentication Systems

Evaluating the Usability of System-Generated and User-Generated Passwords of Approximately Equal Security

Sourav Bhuyan, Joel S. Greenstein, and Kevin A. Juang

Clemson University
sbhuyan@g.clemson.edu, {iejsg,kjuang}@clemson.edu

Abstract. System-generated and user-generated text-based passwords are commonly used to authenticate access to electronic assets. Users typically have multiple web accounts ranging from banking to retail, each with a different password, creating a significant usability problem. The passwords authenticated by these applications may vary in usability and memorability depending on the type of password generation, composition and length. Researchers have compared the usability of different user-generated password composition schemes. The passwords created using different composition schemes in these studies achieved different levels of minimum security, making comparisons across them difficult. This research compares the usability and memorability of three password generation schemes that each exceed a specified minimum entropy for the sake of security.

Keywords: passwords, usability, security.

1 Introduction

The earliest passwords were generated by a computer system and assigned to the employees to ensure overall security [1] [2]. However, as they were composed of apparently random characters having no meaning for the users, they were more difficult to remember than user-generated passwords [3]. This high degree of complexity caused users to externalize them by writing them down, leading to potential breaches in security [3]. It led to user-generated passwords becoming widely used [1] even though system-generated ones are more difficult to guess [3]. To enhance the security of user-generated passwords, they can be created using a large domain of character sets, giving them the appearance of being randomly generated [3]. However, password guidelines that encourage users to do this, though they may help to create passwords that are more difficult to crack, also become difficult to use [4]. The limitations associated with restrictions on user-generated passwords include the time needed to generate an acceptable one, the guidelines that result in less memorable ones than those generated without them and the additional restrictions that may cause more entry errors and lengthen the login procedure [5]. This issue concerning password generation is made more complex because users also tend to form their own mental models of good passwords regardless of the instructions provided, favoring memorability

L. Marinos and I. Askoxylakis (Eds.): HAS/HCII 2013, LNCS 8030, pp. 3–12, 2013.
© Springer-Verlag Berlin Heidelberg 2013

over security [6]. As a result, users circumvent password guidelines when given a chance, meaning that their passwords are still subject to being breached by brute force attacks. In such attacks, the intruder uses a computer to systematically attempt all possible combinations using a standard US keyboard of 94 characters [7]. In order to protect against such attacks, password guidelines recommend the use of all character sets and longer passwords [7].

The increased use of the Internet has led to an increase in the number of password applications [4]. Users now have multiple web accounts ranging from banking to retail, each with a different password [4], creating a significant usability problem [8]. To improve security and usability of user-generated passwords, proactive password checking is frequently implemented to ensure that user-generated passwords satisfy the composition guidelines [5]. These composition guidelines generally constrain user-generated passwords with respect to length, composition of character sets and inclusion in a dictionary [9].

More recently, researchers have compared the usability of different user-generated password composition schemes. However, the passwords created using different composition schemes in these studies achieved different levels of minimum security, making comparisons across them difficult. To expand on this research, this study compared passwords satisfying NIST Level 2 [10] security requirements that were either assigned by the system or created by the user using two different composition schemes.

2   Related Studies

To compare the usability and preferences of user-generated passwords and randomly assigned passwords, Zviran et al. [3] had 103 participants create two user-generated passwords in addition to being assigned an eight-character random password. One of the user-generated passwords was a maximum of 8 characters long and the other was an alphanumeric passphrase of up to 80 characters. After three months, the participants' recall success rate was the highest for the 8-character user-generated passwords, followed by assigned random passwords and finally the 80-character passwords. These results were supported by the data obtained with a subjective questionnaire in which the participants ranked the 8-character user-generated passwords highest in appeal and ease of recall. These passwords were further analyzed to determine the characteristics affecting their recall. The results revealed that 92% were composed of only lower case letters, suggesting better memorability of passwords of this composition.

To understand the effect of various composition schemes and additional guidelines or restrictions on password usability, Proctor et al. [5] conducted an experiment involving 24 participants. For the first condition, the participants created a password of at least 5 characters, and for the second, passwords incorporated the additional guidelines of having at least one member from all the character sets on a keyboard, at most one character from the username and no consecutive repeated characters. The results indicated that the passwords with additional composition restrictions were significantly harder to generate and remember than those based on the minimal requirements. However, it was observed that the passwords with minimal requirements were weaker than the ones with additional requirements after all the passwords were subjected to password cracking software.

Using a similar procedure, Proctor et al. [5] conducted a second experiment which required a minimum length of at least 8 characters for the passwords. Similarly, the results of the second experiment found a statistically significant difference between the time taken to generate and recall minimal condition passwords and those requiring additional guidelines. Also similarly to the first experiment, the qualitative data found that passwords with additional guidelines were significantly harder to generate and remember compared to passwords with only a length restriction. The results concerning the breached passwords from both experiments suggested that the increase in the minimum length of minimal condition passwords from 5 to 8 characters led to passwords that were as resistant to password cracking software as the minimum 8-character password incorporating additional guidelines.

A more recent study investigating various user-generated password construction schemes was conducted by Vu et al. [11]. They investigated the number of attempts and the time required to generate passwords. They also evaluated the number of login errors and the time required to recall these passwords after a short and long duration of time. Results of the experiments conducted in the study indicated that user-generated passwords composed of initial letters of at least six words of a meaningful sentence were significantly easier to generate compared to similarly composed passwords that additionally included a number and a special character. The results also indicated a statistically lower number of login errors and login times for the passwords composed only of letters. However, the minimally restricted passwords were significantly weaker than the passwords that included a number and a special character.

Komanduri, Shay, Kelley, Mazurek, Bauer and Christin [12] compared passwords created by 5,000 participants, each assigned to one of five conditions across two sessions. The minimum length of these passwords ranged from at least 8 characters to 16 characters. Depending on the password condition, these passwords were either composed of only letters of varying lengths or included at least one character from each of the four character sets of a standard US keyboard. The results from the study indicated that participants took significantly more attempts to create restricted passwords of at least 8 characters than unrestricted passwords of varying character length. Compared to the shorter unrestricted passwords, the participants rated restricted passwords as significantly more difficult to recollect followed by the longer unrestricted passwords. Approximately 25 percent of the participants completely failed to create acceptable passwords in the restricted condition. However, the completion failure rates for participants in the other conditions were significantly lower: all under 19 percent.

3   Method

This study compared the usability of three types of text-based passwords of approximately equal minimum security:

1: An assigned 6-character system-generated password selected randomly from any of the 36 alphanumeric characters available on a standard QWERTY keyboard.

2: A user-generated password of at least 8 characters, with at least one lower case letter, one upper case letter, one number and one special character. This password must also pass a dictionary check.

3: A user-generated password of at least 16 characters with no additional restrictions. This password must also pass a dictionary check.

3.1   Study Participants

The study involved 54 participants, equally divided into three groups, with 18 in each password policy condition. The study took place over two sessions, with a period of 5-7 days in between them. In the first session, depending on the password policy condition, the participants were either assigned or they created a password and entered it into the password application (see Figure 1). If the password entered by a participant was entered incorrectly or failed to comply with the password composition policy, the application prompted the participant to re-enter a password. The participants were then asked to recall their passwords in the same session and after 5-7 days in the second session. The NASA task load indices [13] and the System Usability Scale (SUS) questionnaires [14] were administered at the end of each task: 1st session creation, 1st session recall and 2nd session recall (see Figure 2).

Fig. 1. 6-character alphanumeric password creation

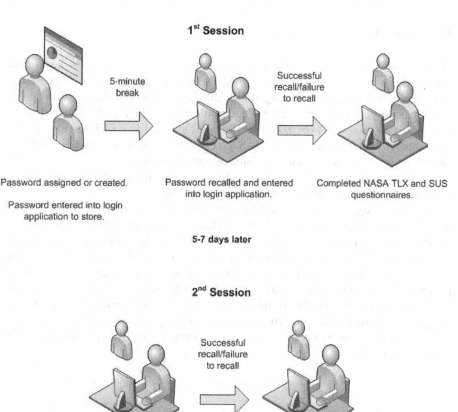

Fig. 2. Procedural flow for first and second sessions

3.2 Experimental Design

The three password policy conditions were compared with respect to the following dependent variables: the time taken to create the password account, the password creation error rate, the time taken to recall the password and recall error rate for both sessions, the number of unrecoverable passwords in the second session and the subjective ratings for the NASA task load indices and the SUS questionnaire for both sessions.

The experiment was considered to be a two-factor design. The first independent variable investigated the password composition scheme at three levels: the three types of password composition policies. The second independent variable of the study was task session. Although the main effect of task session was significant, this result was not a focus of the study.

4   Results

The results showed that it took less time to create an account with the system-generated password than with either of the two user-generated password conditions (see Figure 3). There were also significant differences between the password policy conditions for password creation error rate (p=0.002) (see Figure 4) and the time taken to recall the passwords (p<0.001) (see Figure 5). A post-hoc analysis revealed that the temporal demand index of the NASA-TLX questionnaire was higher for the 8-character user-generated passwords than for system-generated passwords (p=0.012) (see Figure 6). There were no significant differences for recall error rate and unrecoverable passwords between the password policy conditions.

The results suggest that the overall performance of the 8-character user-generated password was weaker than that of the 16-character user-generated and 6-character system-generated passwords. A Pareto chart analysis of the comments made by participants (see Figure 7), as well as additional analysis of the user-generated passwords, suggest that participants were most familiar with the 8-character password policy condition. However, this familiarity did not translate into better memorability of 8-character passwords. The results suggest that the less familiar 6-character system-generated password and 16-character user-generated password composition schemes result in passwords that are at least as easy to recall, while imposing lower temporal demand.

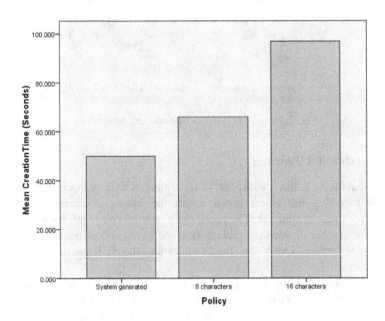

Fig. 3. Mean password account creation time (seconds)

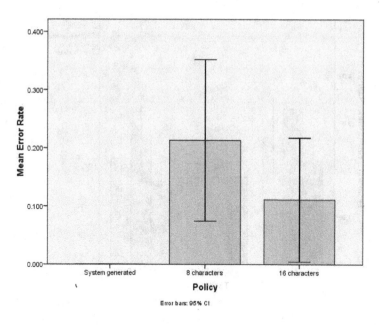

Fig. 4. Mean error rate during creation of password accounts

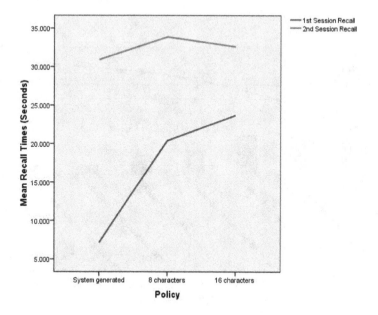

Fig. 5. Mean time taken to recall (seconds)

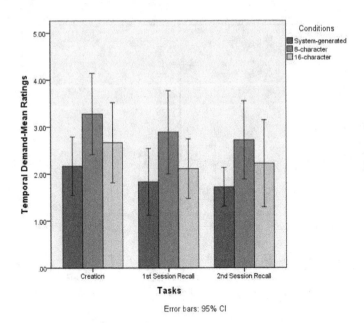

Fig. 6. Mean rating for temporal demand

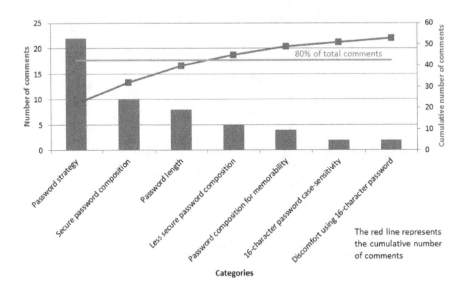

Fig. 7. Distribution of comment categories

5   Conclusions and Recommendations

This study compared the usability of three password conditions that assigned or helped users to generate passwords of approximately equal security, evaluating the trade-off between the length and the complexity of the passwords. The most important conclusion of this study is that the performance of the 8-character passwords was weaker than that of the system-generated passwords during the creation of password accounts and was weaker than the 16-character passwords in terms of long-term recall. Compliance with the restrictions associated with 8-character passwords strengthens security but creates passwords that are complex in composition. Thus, with the increase in applications requiring 8-character password accounts, a user may experience cognitive load when recalling a password from among competing passwords of similar composition. However, if 16-character passwords are created from a meaningful combination of preferably lower case letters, they may be more memorable than 8-character passwords subject to multiple restrictions.

Currently, the designers of password applications put most of the responsibility for creating a secure password on the users, forcing them to comply with a variety of restrictions. The complexity of such passwords may increase their security, but such security can also be achieved by increasing the minimum length of passwords and lowering the complexity of these passwords, thereby reducing the cognitive load on users. Thus, efforts should be taken to educate users on the trade-off between the length and complexity of user-generated passwords. A simpler and longer password can be as secure as a shorter but more complex one.

Designers should consider developing applications that aid users in creating longer but more meaningful passwords to reduce cognitive load. These applications could implement methods to produce 16-character passwords with meaningful combinations of letters, making these passwords more memorable to users. However, care should be taken by the designers to avoid explicitly restricting users to lower case letters only.

This study is a first step in exploring usable password conditions of approximately equal security. Below are suggestions for future research:

- Field studies involving participants belonging to a wider range of demographics.
- Studies involving the use of smartphones or tablets as password input devices.
- Studies on the effect of educating participants on the security of longer passwords composed of lower case letters.
- Studies involving a longer time period between creation and recall tasks to validate the results of the long-term recall of passwords across conditions.

References

1. Adams, A., Sasse, M.A., Lunt, P.: Making passwords secure and usable. Paper Presented at the Proceedings of HCI on People and Computers XII, pp. 1–19 (1997), http://portal.acm.org/citation.cfm?id=646684.702633 (retrieved from)
2. Adams, A., Sasse, M.A.: Users are not the enemy. Commun. ACM 42(12), 40–46 (1999), doi: http://doi.acm.org/10.1145/322796.322806

3. Zviran, M., Haga, W.J.: A comparison of password techniques for multilevel authentication mechanisms. Computer Journal 36(3), 227–237 (1993)
4. Conklin, A., Dietrich, G., Walz, D.: Password-based authentication: A system perspective. Paper Presented at the Proceedings of the 37th Annual Hawaii International Conference on System Sciences, pp. 10 (2004)
5. Proctor, R.W., Lien, M., Vu, K., Schultz, E.E., Salvendy, G.: Improving computer security for authentication of users: Influence of proactive password restrictions. Behavior Research Methods, Instruments, & Computers 34(2), 163–169 (2002)
6. Forget, A., Chiasson, S., Biddle, R.: Helping users create better passwords: Is this the right approach?, Pittsburgh, Pennsylvania. Paper Presented at the Proceedings of the 3rd Symposium on Usable Privacy and Security, pp. 151–152 (2007), doi: http://doi.acm.org/10.1145/1280680.1280703
7. Allendoerfer, K., Pai, S.: Human factors considerations for passwords and other user identification techniques part 1: Field study, results and analysis (DOT/FAA/TC-05/20). Federal Aviation Administration William J. Hughes Technical Center, Atlantic City International Airport (2005)
8. Brostoff, S., Sasse, M.A.: Are passfaces more usable than passwords? A field trial investigation. Paper Presented at the Proceedings of HCI (2000), http://hornbeam.cs.ucl.ac.uk/hcs/people/documents/Angela%20Publications/unsorted/hci2000.pdf
9. Herley, C.: So long, and no thanks for the externalities: The rational rejection of security advice by users, September 8-11. Paper Presented at the New Security Paradigms Workshop 2009, NSPW 2009, pp. 133–144 (2009), http://dx.doi.org/10.1145/1719030.1719050
10. Burr, W.E.: National Institute of Standards & Technology. In: Burr, W.E., Dodson, D.F., Polk, W.T. (eds.) Electronic authentication guideline [electronic resource]: Recommendations of the National Institute of Standards and Technology/ (Version 1.0.2. ed.) U.S. Dept. of Commerce, Technology Administration, National Institute of Standards and Technology, Gaithersburg, MD (2006)
11. Vu, K.L., Proctor, R.W., Bhargav-Spantzel, A., Tai, B., Cook, J., Schultz, E.E.: Improving password security and memorability to protect personal and organizational information. International Journal of Human-Computer Studies 65(8), 744–757 (2007), http://dx.doi.org/10.1016/j.ijhcs.2007.03.007
12. Komanduri, S., Shay, R., Kelley, P.G., Mazurek, M.L., Bauer, L., Christin, N., et al.: Of passwords and people: Measuring the effect of password-composition policies, Vancouver, BC, Canada. Paper Presented at the Proceedings of the 2011 Annual Conference on Human Factors in Computing Systems, pp. 2595–2604 (2011), doi: http://doi.acm.org/10.1145/1978942.1979321
13. Hart, S.: NASA-Task Load Index (NASA-TLX); 20 years later, October 16-20. Paper Presented at the 50th Annual Meeting of the Human Factors and Ergonomics Society, HFES 2006, pp. 904–908 (2006)
14. Brooke, J.: SUS: a quick and dirty usability scale. In: Jordan, P.W., Thomas, B., Weerdmeester, B.A., McClelland, A.L. (eds.) Usability Evaluation in Industry. Taylor and Francis, London (1996)

Multicriteria Optimization to Select Images as Passwords in Recognition Based Graphical Authentication Systems

Soumyadeb Chowdhury, Ron Poet, and Lewis Mackenzie

School of Computing Science, University of Glasgow, UK
{soumc,ron,lewis}@dcs.gla.ac.uk

Abstract. Usability and guessability are two conflicting criteria in assessing the suitability of an image to be used as password in the recognition based graphical authentication systems (RGBSs). We present the first work in this area that uses a new approach, which effectively integrates a series of techniques in order to rank images taking into account the values obtained for each of the dimensions of usability and guessability, from two user studies. Our approach uses fuzzy numbers to deal with non commensurable criteria and compares two multicriteria optimization methods namely, TOPSIS and VIKOR. The results suggest that VIKOR method is the most applicable to make an objective state-ment about which image type is better suited to be used as password. The paper also discusses some improvements that could be done to improve the ranking assessment.

Keywords: image password, TOPSIS, VIKOR, multiple criteria analysis.

1 Introduction

Recognition-based graphical authentication systems are an alternative type of me-chanism where images are used as passwords. The decision making process to select the most suitable image type to be used as passwords in RBGSs has to consider sever-al conflicting criteria (usability and guessability). There has been no existing research to quantify and rank the different image types suitable to be used as pass-words in RBGSs. In this paper we propose a new approach that effectively integrates a series of techniques and concepts so that the decision makers can obtain a comprehensive and consistent evaluation result. Our approach combines: (1) multi criteria decision mak-ing (MCDM); (2) fuzzy set theory and fuzzy numbers; (3) a multi criteria optimiza-tion method.

MCDM [1, 2] usually helps decision makers quantify and evaluate each criterion as well as rank all the alternatives. The main steps of the decision making process involve: (1) Establishing the evaluation criteria; (2) Consider the alternatives; (3) Assessing the alternatives in terms of criteria; (4) Employing multi criteria analysis technique; (5) Accepting one alternative as an optimal choice.

This research incorporates fuzzy set theory [3] in the performance measurement. The main contribution of fuzzy set theory is its ability to represent vague data. In a deci- sion making process each criterion is measured with a different scale, which

L. Marinos and I. Askoxylakis (Eds.): HAS/HCII 2013, LNCS 8030, pp. 13–22, 2013.
© Springer-Verlag Berlin Heidelberg 2013

makes the judgments unbalanced and imprecise. Fuzzy numbers help to deal with the imprecise and uncertain values of each criterion [4]. Each fuzzy number is associated to a linguistic variable as shown in fig 1 [5].

Fuzzy number	Linguistic term
$\tilde{1}$	Very poor
$\tilde{3}$	Poor
$\tilde{5}$	Ordinary
$\tilde{7}$	Excellent
$\tilde{9}$	Very excellent

Fig. 1. Fuzzy numbers with linguistic variables defining them

Multicriteria optimization is the process of determining the most feasible alternative of all taking in to account each of the established criteria. An approach to determine a final solution as a compromise was introduced in [6]. In this context, the VIKOR method [7, 8, 9] is a multicriteria ranking approach developed to help solve the decision problems with conflicting and noncommensurable criteria. It determines the compromise solution for a problem with conflicting criteria. A compromise solution is a feasible solution that is closest to the ideal which is agreed by mutual concessions. Another multicriteria ranking approach, Technique for Order of Preference by Similarity to Ideal Solution (TOPSIS) [10, 11] uses a distance based MCDM approach to choose an alternative that has the shortest geometric distance from the ideal solution and the longest geometric distance from the negative ideal solution. The ideal solution is the best performance value exhibited by any alternative for each criteria and negative ideal solution is the worst performance value.

The rest of the paper is structured as follows. In Section 2 we discuss the usability and guessability study conducted by us. In Section 3 we describe the ranking framework and compare the TOPSIS and VIKOR method with an illustrative example. The data for the example is obtained from the user studies discussed in Section 2. Finally, in Section 4 we discuss the results and scope for future improvements

2   User Study

We developed four RBGSs (online website which used images as passwords). Each of them used a different image type as the password: (1) Mikon; (2) Doodle; (3) Art; (4) Object. We conducted a usability study with independent measures (between subjects) style of experimental design having four conditions namely Mikon, doodle, art and objects. The participants in the Mikon condition created four passwords (each password comprising of 4 Mikon images) and authenticated using them. The same procedure was followed in other conditions too. This study was conducted for eight weeks with 100 participants. The dependant variables were:

Memory: It examined the *average/mean successful login percentage (S)* for each of the conditions calculated as,

$$S = \frac{Total\ number\ of\ successful\ login\ in\ the\ condition}{Total\ number\ of\ login\ in\ the\ condition} \times 100$$

Time: It examined the average/mean registration time (Reg time), and aver-age/mean login time of successful login (Log time). The average registration time for each condition was calculated as,

$$\frac{1}{4}\sum_{i=1}^{4} Registration\ time\ for\ password\ (i), \quad where\ i\ denotes\ password\ 1,2,3,4$$

The average time of successful login for each condition was calculated as given below, z represents total number of successful login

$$\frac{1}{z}\sum_{n=1}^{z} Login\ time\ for\ successful\ login\ (n)$$

Exp-Use: This dimension had two parameters: (1) Sat-use i.e. the satisfaction scores; (2) Str-use i.e. the stress scores. Sat-use was assessed from the ratings (1- 5, 1 being highly dissatisfied to 5 being highly satisfied) given by the participants to the different aspects in the post study questionnaire- (sat1) Ease to register; (sat2) Ease to authenticate; (sat3) Meaningfulness/nameability of the image; (sat4) satisfaction with the type of image used as password. Similarly, str-use was assessed from the ratings (1- 5, 1 being least stressful to 5 being highly stressful) given by the participants: (str1) level of mental stress; (str2) level of physical stress; (str3) amount of effort required to choose images during registration; (str4) amount of effort required to suc-cessfully login.

A guessability study (70 participants) was conducted with the repeated measure protocol having 4 conditions for a period of 8 weeks: (1) login using Mikon passwords; (2) login using doodle passwords; (3) login using art passwords (4) login using object passwords. Each participant had to guess 4 passwords in each condition using the verbal descriptions of the image passwords given to them. Each condition was performed on a different day and participants were randomly assigned to the conditions. The parameters used to measure this criterion were:

Guessing: It examined the mean successful login percentage for each participant

Quality of the Descriptions (descriptions): The participants were asked to rate some aspects on a scale of 1 to 5 (1 being low rating and 5 being high rating): q1-was the description easy to understand; q2-was the description adequate to identify the image; q3-was the description meaningful; q4-was the description useful.

Exp-Guess: This dimension had two parameters: (1) Sat-Guess i.e. the satisfaction scores; (2) Str-Guess i.e. the stress scores. For Sat-Guess, the participants were asked to rate on a scale of 1 to 5 (1 being lowest satisfaction and 5 being highest satisfaction): sat1- Ease to guess the passwords; sat2- Satisfaction of individual performance; sat3- Level of success in guessing the image; sat4- Efficiency to complete the task. In the case of Str-Guess, they were asked to rate on a scale of 1 to 5 (1 being lowest stress/effort and 5 being highest stress/effort): str1- Level of mental stress; str2- Level of physical stress; str3- Level of temporal stress; str4- Amount of effort required to guess.

3   Ranking Framework

Step1: Decision Matrix (Fig 2) - Calculate the mean value for each criterion in each alternative from the experiments. They are represented in the decision matrix as: mean value of the alternative A_i, where i ≤ n (n being the total number of alternatives) with respect to criteria C_j, where j ≤ m (m being the total number of criteria). Here the alternatives are the image types used as password.

Image types	Memory	Log time	Reg time	Sat-Use	Str-Use	Guessing	description	Sat-Guess	Str-Guess
Mikon	74.1	19.52	72.8	13.25	12.12	59.06	13.1	12.81	14.68
Doodle	67.04	22.16	75.4	12	13.12	74.28	14.6	14.84	12.35
Art	54.9	24.56	84.4	9.2	14.66	48.55	10.44	12.2	13.8
Object	77.3	18.28	70.6	13.91	11.87	87.32	16.44	15.9	8.27

Fig. 2. Mean scores for each dimension obtained from the experiments

Step 2: Judgement Matrix (Fig 5) - Each fuzzy number represents an interval for each criterion which is decided by the experimenter (Fig 3). Higher values are considered to be the best in the case of memory, sat-use, description and sat-guess, whereas lower values are considered to be the best in the case of guessing, reg time, log time, str-use and str-use. Then each in the decision matrix is replaced by the corresponding fuzzy number. Each fuzzy number is converted to a triangular fuzzy number T_{ij} using the membership function shown in Fig 4. Finally, the matrix is normalized using eq (1)

$$D_{ij} = \frac{T_{ij}}{\sqrt{\sum_{i=1}^{n} T_{ij}}} \qquad (1)$$

Fuzzy number	Memory	Reg time	Log time	Sat-Use	Str-Use	Guessing	description	Sat-Guess	Str-Guess
1	<45	≥ 90	>30	≤ 8	≥ 15	≥80	≥ 16	≥ 15	≤ 8
3	45-59	81-89	26-30	9-10	13-14	70-79	14-15	13-14	9-10
5	60-69	76-80	22-25	11-12	11-12	60-69	12-13	11-12	11-12
7	70-79	71-75	19-21	13-14	9-10	45-59	10-11	9-10	13-14
9	≥80	≤ 70	<19	≥ 15	≤ 8	<45	<10	≤ 8	≥ 15

Fig. 3. Interval values associated to fuzzy numbers in each criterion

Thus the judgement matrix (**D**) is obtained, which gives the overall judgement scores for each of the alternatives (A_i) with respect to criteria (C_j) without taking into account the relative weight between each criterion.

Fuzzy number	Membership Function
1	(1,1,3)
x̄	(x-2,x,x+2)
9̄	(7,9,9)

Fig. 4. Membership function to convert singular to triangular fuzzy

	Memory	Time	Exp-Use	Guessing	description	Exp-Guess
Mikon	(0.64,0.61,0.58)	(0.55,0.54,0.55)	(0.66,0.61,0.58)	(0.69,0.67,0.64)	(0.16,0.32,0.39)	(0.66,0.64,0.6)
Doodle	(0.38,0.43,0.45)	(0.44,0.46,0.49)	(0.33,0.4,0.43)	(0.13,0.28,0.35)	(0.5,0.54,0.54)	(0.03,0.43,0.45)
Art	(0.13,0.26,0.32)	(0.22,0.31,0.37)	(0.41,0.3,0.36)	(0.69,0.67,0.64)	(0.83,0.76,0.7)	(0.66,0.64,0.6)
Object	(0.64,0.61,0.58)	(0.66,0.62,0.55)	(0.66,0.61,0.58)	(0.13,0.09,0.21)	(0.16,0.11,0.23)	(0.16,0.1,0.22)

Fig. 5. Judgement Matrix (D) with judgement scores for each image type

Step 3: Criteria Weights (Fig 6) - Determine the importance of each criterion by setting the criteria weights. This is done by the experimenter using subjective judgments. We assigned equal weights to usability and guessability (50% in each case).

Criteria	L	M	U
Memory	0.125	0.25	0.5
Time	0.075	0.15	0.3
Exp-Use	0.05	0.1	0.2
Guessing	0.125	0.25	0.5
Description	0.075	0.15	0.3
Exp-Guess	0.05	0.1	0.2

Fig. 6. Weights assigned to each criteria, L= (M/2) and U = (Mx2)

Step 4: Intermediate Performance Matrix (Fig. 7) - Each criterion weight is multiplied to the corresponding criterion score in the judgement matrix i.e. D_{ij} x W_j. The result is (F_{ij}), the performance score for each of the alternatives corresponding to the specified criteria.

Image type	Memory	Time	Exp-Use	Guessing	description	Exp-Guess
Mikon	(0.08,0.15,0.29)	(0.04,0.08,0.16)	(0.03,0.06,0.11)	(0.08,0.16,0.32)	(0.012,0.048,0.12)	(0.03,0.06,0.12)
Doodle	(0.04,0.1,0.22)	(0.03,0.07,0.14)	(0.01,0.01,0.08)	(0.01,0.07,0.17)	(0.037,0.08,0.16)	(0.001,0.04,0.09)
Art	(0.01,0.06,0.16)	(0.01,0.04,0.1)	(0.02,0.03,0.07)	(0.08,0.16,0.32)	(0.06,0.11,0.21)	(0.03,0.06,0.12)
Object	(0.08,0.15,0.29)	(0.05,0.09,0.16)	(0.03,0.06,0.11)	(0.01,0.02,0.1)	(0.01,0.016,0.07)	(0.008,0.01,0.044)

Fig. 7. Intermediate performance matrix with performance scores as triangular fuzzy numbers

Step 5: Defuzzification: First, the interval performance matrix (F^α) as in Fig 8 is obtained using the alpha cut method on the intermediate performance matrix (F). Each score is worked upon using eq. 2 and 3 to form an interval [F_{ijl}^α , F_{ijr}^α]. The value of α (0-1) denotes the experimenter's degree of confidence while evaluating the scores and criteria weights in the process. A larger value expresses stronger degree of confidence. Here, we set up the value to 0.85 because we are confident about the criteria weights chosen (equal distribution between usability and security).

$$F_{ijl}^\alpha = L_{ij} + \alpha \left(M_{ij} - L_{ij} \right) \qquad (2)$$

$$F_{ijr}^\alpha = U_{ij} + \alpha \left(U_{ij} - M_{ij} \right) \qquad (3)$$

	Memory	Time	Exp-Use	Guessing	description	Exp-Guess
Mikon	0.136 0.178	0.072 0.096	0.054 0.07	0.144 0.192	0.04 0.06	0.054 0.072
Doodle	0.088 0.124	0.062 0.084	0.034 0.048	0.058 0.09	0.07 0.09	0.032 0.05
Art	0.014 0.08	0.034 0.052	0.028 0.038	0.144 0.192	0.046 0.13	0.054 0.072
Object	0.136 0.178	0.082 0.104	0.054 0.07	0.018 0.036	0.015 0.021	0.01 0.016

Fig. 8. Interval performance matrix (F^α) obtained by applying $\alpha = 0.85$

The risk index β (0-1) represents the experimenter's positive/ negative view point about their experimental evaluation. A lower value represents positive optimism. Here we choose its value to be 0.15 because we are highly optimistic about our experimental evaluation, since it is reliable (can be reproduced) and valid (gives us significant results). The risk index is used together with the interval per-romance matrix to calculate the final performance matrix using eq. 4.

	Memory	Time	Exp-Use	Guessing	description	Exp-Guess
Mikon	0.17	0.091	0.066	0.182	0.05	0.068
Doodle	0.115	0.079	0.045	0.083	0.08	0.046
Art	0.066	0.048	0.036	0.182	0.11	0.068
Object	0.17	0.099	0.066	0.032	0.02	0.014

Fig. 9. Final performance matrix (F_β^α) obtained by setting $\beta = 0.15$

$$F_{ij\beta}^\alpha = \beta F_{ijl}^\alpha + (1-\beta)F_{ijr}^\alpha \qquad (4)$$

Step 6: Ideal and negative ideal solution (Fig. 10) - Determine the best value (f^*) and the worst value (f^-) for each criterion, using eq. 5 and 6 respectively.

$$f^* = \{\max f_{ij}\} \quad (5) \qquad f^- = \{\min f_{ij}\} \quad (6)$$

	Memory	Time	Exp-Use	Guessing	description	Exp-Guess
Ideal	0.17	0.099	0.066	0.182	0.11	0.068
Non Ideal	0.066	0.048	0.036	0.032	0.02	0.014

Fig. 10. Ideal and negative ideal solution for each criterion obtained from (F_β^α)

For VIKOR Ranking: Compute the utility measure (S_i) eq. 7, regret measure (R_i) eq. 8 and the VIKOR index (Q_i) eq. 9. Rank all the alternatives, sorting by the values utility measure, regret measure and Vikor index in decreasing order. The results are three ranking lists as shown in Fig 11.

$$S_i = \sum_{j=1}^{q} \frac{(f_j^* - f_{ij})}{(f_j^* - f_j^-)} \quad (7) \qquad\qquad R_i = Max \frac{(f_j^* - f_{ij})}{(f_j^* - f_j^-)} \quad (8)$$

$$Q_i = v \frac{S_i - S^*}{S^- - S^*} + (1-v) \frac{R_i - R^*}{R^- - R^*} \quad (9)$$

$S^* = Min\ (S_i),\ \ S^- = Max\ (S_i),\ \ R^* = Min\ (R_i),\ \ R^- = Max\ (R_i)\ \ and\ v\ is\ set\ to\ 0.5$

The alternative with the minimum VIKOR index is best ranked if it satisfies the following two conditions:

Condition 1: Acceptable advantage

$$Q\ (rank:2) - Q\ (rank:1) \geq Z\ ,where\ Z = \frac{1}{j-1}$$

$$0.49 - 0.027 = 0.473 \geq 0.33\ \textbf{(Satisfied for Mikon)}$$

Condition 2: Acceptable stability in decision making- The alternative with rank 1 must also be best ranked by S or/and R. **(Satisfied for Mikon)**

	Utility measure	Rank list 1	Regret Measure	Rank list 2	Vikor Index	Rank list 3
Mikon	0.82	1	0.66	1	0.027	1
Doodle	2.98	2	0.7	2	0.49	2
Art	3	3	1	3	0.5	3
Object	3	3	1	3	0.5	3

Fig. 11. Three ranking lists produced by the VIKOR method

For TOPSIS ranking, compute the ideal separation S_i^+ (eq. 10), negative ideal separation S_i^- (eq. 11) and the relative closeness C_i (eq. 12). Then rank according to as shown in Fig 12.

$$S_i^+ = \sqrt{\sum_{j=1}^m (F_{ij} - F_{ij}^+)^2}\ (10) \qquad S_i^- = \sqrt{\sum_{j=1}^m (F_{ij} - F_{ij}^-)^2}\ (11)$$

$$C_i = \frac{S_i^-}{S_i^+ + S_i^-}\ (12)$$

	Distance from ideal	Distance from negative ideal	Relative closeness to ideal	Rank list
Mikon	0.06	0.2	0.76	1
Doodle	0.12	0.10	0.45	3
Art	0.11	0.18	0.60	2
Object	0.18	0.11	0.39	4

Fig. 12. Ranking list for relative closeness to ideal in TOPSIS method

4   Discussion and Concluding Remarks

The approach presented in the paper is the first work in the field of RBGSs (Human computer interaction-Security) to obtain a comprehensive and consistent evaluation result, while making a decision that considers two conflicting criteria, usability and guessability. The ranking given by VIKOR and TOPSIS are different. In case of TOPSIS, Mikon is ranked 1, followed by art, doodle, and object. This method considers the distance of an alternative from the ideal and negative ideal solution, without the relative importance of the distances, which is a major concern in the decision making process. Being far away from the negative ideal solution is not an essential advantage in decision making process and hence the importance of the separation (distance) has to be considered. This is evident from Fig 9, where art has the best scores for guessability parameters, which is higher than the best scores of usability parameter for objects as well as doodles. Hence TOPSIS ranks art higher than doodles and objects. In case of VIKOR, the ranking is based on closeness to the ideal solution, which integrates the maximum group utility for the majority (eq. 7), and minimum individual regret for the opponent (eq. 8), together with acceptable advantage and stability. Here, Mikon is ranked 1 followed by doodle; objects (highest usability and highest guessability) are ranked the same as art (lowest guessability and lowest usability).

So the results suggest that a distance based ranking method may not always produce a solution which is closest to the ideal, especially when conflicting variables are being considered, which makes the ranking uncertain as well as unsuitable. But the VIKOR method has a very useful applicability in ranking the image types to be used as passwords in RBGSs, especially when a lot of conflicting variables are being considered for the decision making process. It is interesting to note that inclusion or exclusion of an alternative could affect the VIKOR ranking because the value of the VIKOR index depends on the ideal solution. In our ongoing work we are looking into various approaches to fix the ideal solution by defining some standards. In terms of improvement, the assessment of the criteria weights can be improved by integrating several expert's judgement and evaluate its degree of consistency.

References

1. Saaty, T.L., Cho, Y.: The Decision by the US Congress on China's Trade Status: A Multi-criteria Analysis. Socio-Economic Planning Sciences 35, 243–252 (2001)
2. Lee, H.-S., Chou, M.-T.: A Fuzzy Multiple Criteria Decision Making Model for Airline competitiveness Evaluation. In: Gabrys, B., Howlett, R.J., Jain, L.C. (eds.) KES 2006. LNCS (LNAI), vol. 4252, pp. 902–909. Springer, Heidelberg (2006)
3. Zimmermann, H.J.: Fuzzy Set Theory and its Applications, 4th edn. Springer, New York (2005)
4. Mikhailov, L.: Deriving Priorities from Fuzzy Pairwise Comparison Judgments. Fuzzy Sets and Systems 134, 365–385 (2003)
5. Saaty, T.L.: The Analytic Hierarchy Process. McGraw-Hill, New York (1980)
6. Zeleny, M.: Compromise Programming. In: Cochrane, J.L., Zeleny, M. (eds.) Multiple Criteria Decision Making. University of South Carolina Press, Columbia (1973)
7. Opricovic, S.: Multicriteria Optimization of Civil Engineering Systems. Technical report, Belgrade (1998)

8. Tzeng, G., Teng, M., Chen, J.J., Opricovic, S.: Multicriteria Selection for a Restaurant Location in Taipei. International Journal of Hospitality Management 21(2), 171–187 (2002)
9. Tzeng, G., Lin, C., Opricovic, S.: Multicriteria Analysis of Alternative fuel Buses for Public Transportation. Energy Policy 33, 1373–1383 (2005)
10. Hwang, C., Yoon, K.: Multiple Attributes Decision making Methods and Application: a state-of-the-Art Survey. Springer, Heidelberg (1981)
11. Chu, T.: Selecting Plant Location via a Fuzzy TOPSIS Approach. International Journal of Advance Manufacturing and Technology 20, 859–864 (2002)

Investigating an Intrusion Prevention System for Brain-Computer Interfaces

Saul D. Costa, Dale R. Stevens, and Jeremy A. Hansen

Norwich University, Northfield, VT 05663, USA
{saulcosta18,voltechs}@gmail.com, jeremyhansen@acm.org

Abstract. Neurosecurity focuses on the security of the increasingly intimate coupling of human brains and computers, addressing issues surrounding modern computer security and how they relate to brain-computer interfaces (BCIs). Although several elements of this field are not yet relevant in today's society, the goal is to examine what can be done to avoid the post-patch-just-in-time security solution seen in today's computer architectures and networks. Modern computer security has been the unfortunate result of afterthought; patched on out of necessity, often just-in-time at best.

1 Introduction

Neuroscience, the field of study relating to the brain's structure and nervous system functionality, has received increased attention in recent years as educational institutions and government organizations are realizing the potential in precisely interacting with the brain through technology. Researchers and developers of technology are beginning to explore ways to interface with a brain using devices such as prosthetic limbs [10]. In the past, researchers have recorded the electrical charges discharged across the scalp by a brain by employing brain-computer interfaces (BCIs) such as electroencephalogram (EEG) headsets [12]. BCI-enabled technological devices expose critical security vulnerabilities not only for the device, but the physical brain as well. Neurosecurity is a new field of study of vulnerabilities in the brain and BCI-enabled devices [4]. The objective of this research paper is to apply intrusion prevention methods used in computer networks to devices and neurological systems enabled with a BCI in a device agnostic manner.

Until recently, the idea of a brain susceptible to attack via a technological interface has not been considered. This oversight is due to previously limited BCI-enabled devices such as cochlear implants and those that aided the restoration of sight, which lacked the ability to affect the state of a brain [14]. The aforementioned devices have been described as invasive, and because of the complexity of implanting such a device, their danger to the user and inability to stimulate specific areas of the brain; they have not seen widespread deployment.

L. Marinos and I. Askoxylakis (Eds.): HAS/HCII 2013, LNCS 8030, pp. 23–28, 2013.

A new technology called optogenetics has enabled the activation of individual neurons within a brain in a manner that is safe to the subject [8]. Considering there are on average over eighty billion neurons in the human brain, optogenetics is far ahead of similar technologies [13]. Optogenetics works by infecting specific neurons with light-sensitive algae infused with genes such as channelrhodopsins and activating them with ultraviolet blue light [3]. Using other genes and wavelengths of light, researchers have also been able to inhibit activity within specific neurons, which prove extremely effective in the research and treatment of epilepsy [9]. Although still complex to implement and not yet in use with human subjects, optogenetics has allowed for a variety of new applications of neuroscience: more effective restoration of vision, treatment of post-traumatic stress disorder, movement control, and triggering the recall of thoughts [2,11].

In the world of computer networking, a device referred to as an Intrusion Prevention System (IPS) is used to keep unwanted traffic out of private computer networks. This device is positioned at the edge of the network and filters all traffic to internal devices. If the traffic appears to be dangerous to the machines residing on the network, the IPS rejects the traffic. This is done by examining the traffic and comparing it to a set of static rules regarding the types of traffic allowed or disallowed [15]. The IPS examines the traffic's origin, its destination, and what type of service it is requesting. Intrusion Prevention Systems are far from perfect; computer networks are compromised daily around the world, costing companies and governments billions of dollars each year [1]. When a computer network is compromised, sensitive or valuable data is often lost. Contrast this with the effects of a compromised BCI-enabled device, given its ability to affect a person's brain. The outcome of a successful attack could be much worse and potentially result in the loss of human life [4].

There are other methods employed to keep computer networks safe in addition to an IPS. Antivirus programs typically reside on a user's personal computer and watch for abnormal or malicious looking program activity. Because the programs an antivirus system examines are rarely identical, it must take a more dynamic approach than the methods used by an IPS in how it defends the computer. To achieve this, it maintains a list of what dangerous program activity looks like, referred to as signatures. If it sees one of these signatures appear within a program's code, it will prevent the program from executing. Antivirus software also watches for programs that were created by individuals known to produce malicious software. This approach has facets that could be implemented in a neurosecurity system.

A neurosecurity system would require certain functionality that would ensure its effectiveness with dynamic input. First, it must be resilient to attacks at the network layer. If the system relies on a TCP/IP network, the proper steps must be taken to ensure that traffic routed to the device travels through secure channels. Common network security methods such as encryption would do well in this situation, as would certificate authentication. Furthermore, the neurosecurity application itself must be developed in a manner that protects the program code from exploitation. The hardware used by any BCI-enabled device must also be resilient to attack. These concepts are not new, but it is crucial to make sure that the manner in which a neurosecurity system is implemented is effective in preventing intrusion.

There are several actions malicious entities could perform after a successful attack against a BCI-enabled device, whether it is a device affecting the state of the brain or an external device such as a prosthetic limb. If an attacker were able to access the BCI, they could potentially release harmful or deadly combinations of neurotransmitters into the brain, capture the user's thoughts, or modify the user's neurological processes [4]. An attack on a BCI-enabled device that does not interface directly with the nervous system (e.g. a prosthetic limb) may not have direct physical effects on the user, however it could disable a device the user requires to sustain an important part of their life. Considering that BCI-enabled devices may one day permeate educational, government, military, and private settings, devices in need of protection could be as prevalent as personal computers are today.

2 Signal Processing and Neural Networks

Several different methods would be necessary to develop a security system to protect a brain or BCI-enabled device. In the field of neuroscience, there are methods by which a brain wave captured using a device such as an EEG headset can be characterized and classified [16,17]. So far, these methods have been used to classify whether a particular brain wave falls on the spectrum of a specific disorder such as epilepsy [16]. This requires a brain wave to first be converted from an analog signal into a digital format for a computer program to process. There are several methods use by researchers to convert the analog signal, the most popular currently being the Discrete Wavelet Transform (DWT) algorithm which takes raw brain waves as input and produces a matrix of numbers [7,17]. Wavelet transforms are also extremely adjustable in the depth of granularity with which they process a given signal, a useful feature that a neurosecurity system could employ. Examining a brain wave too closely results in unnecessary processing and increased storage requirements, whereas not examining it in enough detail would generate outputs that are not accurate enough to be useful.

Because no two brain waves are identical, a set of hardcoded rules would limit the usefulness of filtering signals in a BCI-enabled device. An artificial neural network (ANN) is modeled after a simple brain and consists of a directed graph with weighted edges between the vertices [16]. An ANN is trained by adding weight to particular edges to represent the strength of that edge and direct the flow of data within the ANN, and are efficient at solving nonlinear problems that share varying degrees of similarity.

One of the properties ANNs share with biological brains is the ability to learn. This can be done in the form of "training", whereby an ANN is fed data in a controlled manner with the outcomes known, and is rewarded for correctly classifying or otherwise outputting the expected result. This property also allows ANNs to learn from experience, which make them strong candidates for keeping pace with evolving intrusion techniques in the paramount task of guarding the brain. As such, ANNs are an ideal technology for working with brain waves [16]. After brain waves have been converted into a digital format using a DWT, they will be used in conjunction with a predetermined classification enumerating the danger of each input to train an ANN. The ANN then learns the patterns between the input and the classification, and after enough training, will develop signatures similar to those used by antivirus programs. Once these signatures have been developed, just the digitized brain waves can be input, and the ANN will return the danger classification that best matches that input. This process will result in an ANN that can examine input to BCI-enabled devices for dangerous patterns, much like an antivirus examines program code for malicious functionality.

3   Security System Architecture and Interface

Currently, most BCI-enabled devices can only read activity in the brain for the purpose of interpreting the intentions of the user. The applications that directly stimulate specific parts of the central nervous system to produce some useful effect (e.g. cochlear) are generally ineffective because of the electrical stimuli used. This method of neurological modification will trigger or even harm surrounding parts of the brain. However, through the development of more precise technologies like optogenetics, seemingly futuristic methods become realistic [10]. The aforementioned functions merely scratch the surface; it has already been shown that the bodies of mammals–rats and monkeys–can be controlled through the use of optogenetic BCIs [6]. Future applications will likely go beyond medical applications of neuroscience, and will be used in everyday life to teach and enable humanity. Because of this widespread deployment, neuroscience and BCI-enabled technologies could be more damaging than any disease outbreak in history [5].

To enable technology developers to include a neurosecurity system with their device without unnecessary effort, the security system must include what is referred to as an Application Programming Interface (API). An API is used to tie a program to another one without requiring existing code to be rewritten. Rather, the functions that are required to allow the new program to interact with the existing program are made accessible to the developer. The availability of an API will help to ensure widespread deployment of the neurosecurity system.

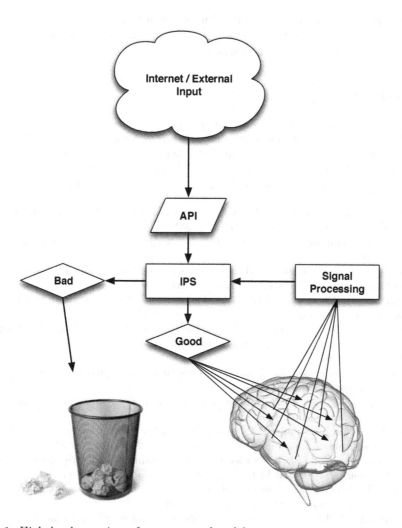

Fig. 1. High level overview of process employed by neurosecurity system providing security analysis on input to a brain-computer interface

4 Conclusion and Future Directions

Employing an artificial neural network security system alongside BCI-enabled technologies will be essential to protecting the user's brain and BCI-enabled devices from malicious activity that affect the state of the brain. As we continue to merge technology and our biology, the need for a secure communication channel becomes a serious concern. Prosthetic limbs, medication dispensers, memory boosters, secondary processing units and even implanted communication devices may soon be used to enhance the user's life, we cannot afford to leave the security of BCI technology as an afterthought. Doing so could result in widespread negative impacts on humanity. By developing a neurosecurity system before it is required, these vulnerabilities can be mitigated in a manner that protects both the BCI-enabled devices and the users.

References

1. Norton study calculates cost of global cybercrime (September 2011)
2. Allen, B.D.: Targeted read-out, analysis, and control to elucidate dynamic-emotional processing. Massachusetts Institute of Technology (2010)
3. Arenkiel, B.R., Peca, J., Davison, I.G., et al.: In vivo light-induced activation of neural circuitry in transgenic mice expressing channelrhodopsin-2. Neuron 54(2), 205–218 (2007)
4. Denning, T., Matsuoka, Y., Kohno, T.: Neurosecurity: security and privacy for neural devices. Neurosurg Focus 27 (July 2009)
5. Essers, L.: Computer viruses could cross frontier into biological realm. PC World (March 2012)
6. Gerits, A., Farivar, R., Rosen, B.R., et al.: Optogenetically induced behavioral and functional network changes in primates. Current Biology (July 2012)
7. Hazarika, N., Chen, J.Z., Tsoi, A.C., Sergejew, A.: Classification of eeg signals using the wavelet transform. Signal Processing 59(1), 61–72 (1997)
8. Knöpfel, T., Lin, M.Z., Levskaya, A., Tian, L., Lin, J.Y., Boyden, E.S.: Toward the second generation of optogenetic tools. The Journal of Neuroscience 30(45), 14998–15004 (2010)
9. Kokaia, M., Andersson, M., Ledri, M.: An optogenetic approach in epilepsy. Neuropharmacology (January 2012)
10. Lebedev, M.A., Tate, A.J., Hanson, T.L.: Future developments in brain-machine interface research. Clinics 66(1) (2011)
11. Liu, X., Ramirez, S., Pang, P.T., et al.: Optogenetic stimulation of a hippocampal engram activates fear memory recall. Nature 484(7394) (April 2012)
12. Niedermeyer, E., da Silva, F: Electroencephalography: Basic Principles, Clinical Applications, and Related Fields. Lippincot Williams & Wilkins (2004)
13. Peron, S., Svoboda, K.: From cudgel to scalpel: toward precise neural control with optogenetics. Nature Methods 8(1), 30–34 (2010)
14. Postelnicu, C., Talaba, D., Toma, M.: Brain computer interfaces for medical applications. Bulletin of the Transilvania University of Braşov 3(52) (2010)
15. Scarfone, K., Mell, P.: Guide to intrusion detection and prevention systems. Recommendations of the National Institute of Standards and Technology (Febuary 2007)
16. Subasi, A., Ercelebi, E.: Classication of eeg signals using neural network and logistic regression. Computer Methods and Programs in Biomedicine, 87–99 (2005)
17. Zhanga, Z., Kawabatab, H., Liuc, Z.Q.: Electroencephalogram analysis using fast wavelet transform. Computers in Biology and Medicine, 429–440 (2001)

Inconspicuous Personal Computer Protection with Touch-Mouse

Ming-Chun Huang[1], Wenyao Xu[2], Jason J. Liu[1],
Yi Su[1], Lei He[2], and Majid Sarrafzadeh[1]

[1] Computer Science Department, University of California, Los Angeles
[2] Electrical Engineering Department, University of California, Los Angeles

Abstract. We present a hassle-free personal information protection design that continuously monitors user identity with a Microsoft touch-mouse [1] under a windows-based computer environment. This is the first design which investigates the relationship between time-indexed pressure map trajectories extracted from a touch-mouse and user behavior patterns categorized by common mouse action primitives. This design serves as an assistive method to enhance existing password and biometric based security mechanisms, enabling continuous and unobtrusive personal identity monitoring. Commercialized windows-based systems can be seamlessly integrated with the proposed system and this design can offer a convenient and lightweight solution for physical computer intrusion detection.

1 Introduction

Personal computer (PC) safety and security issues have received increasing public attention in recent years because more and more private information, ranging from work-related documents, emails to life-related family photos, social networking and chatting history, are stored electronically. The increased reliance on computers for daily personal activities makes the cost of losing computer information expensive and unacceptable. In order to enhance personal information safety, modern personal computers optionally enable built-in password managers, fingerprint scanners, voice recorders, and even vision pattern trackers shown in Fig. 1 to assist PC owners to be more aware about preserving their private information [2,3]. In general, the methods to maintain safety and security are categorized into three types. Biometrics is a commonly used solution for user identity verification, such as voice recognition [4], fingerprint recognition [5], iris recognition [6], and face recognition [7]. Biometrics-based identification methods are reliable and unique for individual users. However, hardware and dedicated biometric sensor setup is usually mandatory in order to sample special biometric features. Moreover, biometric identification process is often complicated and time consuming. Voice and fingerprint recognitions takes 10-30 seconds. Reliable iris and face recognitions takes a couple of minutes. Therefore, biometric checking is only requested at the login stage. On the other hand, for password-based protection, no extra hardware is required but a password-based system security

L. Marinos and I. Askoxylakis (Eds.): HAS/HCII 2013, LNCS 8030, pp. 29–38, 2013.

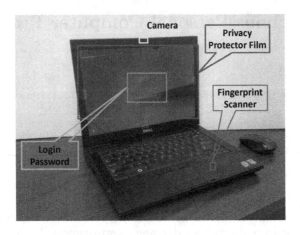

Fig. 1. Commonly used user identity verification tools

is highly-related to the complexity of the password. For example, whenever a user creates his/her own password, it is recommended to include a combination of numbers, letters and special characters such as *, !, @ with sufficiently long password length. Both biometric or password-oriented designs are usually exploited as one-time user identity verification methods only at the login stage, rather than serving as a continuous user identity monitoring method. These designs inherently interfere with user activities and require users' attention to complete the verification processes. Therefore, if a user forgets to logout his/her own PC, all these safety mechanisms fail to protect user information. To compensate this obvious drawback for both biometric and password based system, behavior pattern based methods, enabling the concept of continuously analyzing user inputs and correlating with user identities, have been proposed. Because these new methods do not require any user attention while monitoring, they are preferable to serve as a continuously monitoring system and are used to provide user identity re-authentication for reducing the risk of unauthorized PC abuse. Researchers have developed systems to analyze behavior patterns collected from keyboard, mouse, and memory usage to continuously monitor and detect abnormal PC access patterns. F. Monrose and A. Rubin [8] proposed an authorization method via keystroke dynamics. M. Rusara and C. Brodley [9] used mouse movement and flicks to re-authenticate the user identity on the fly. Furthermore, there were methods detecting indirect user behaviors such as audit logs [10], call-stack [11] and call-trace [12], to verify user identity. While these systems offered continuous re-authentication for intruders defense, the applicability of these systems was limited due to the fact that users tended to adjust their behaviors while using a variety of computer applications. To tackle this issue, instead of using behavior features which were application dependent, we found that the relationship between touch-mouse pressure maps and mouse events rarely changed under a variety of applications. By using these application independent features, our novel security add-on with a touch-mouse is capable of robust, continuous, and inconspicuous monitoring of user identity across a variety of applications.

2   Background

2.1   Microsoft Touch-Mouse

Our system adopts a novel re-authentication method by extracting user behavior patterns from a Microsoft touch-mouse. A photograph of the Microsoft touch-mouse and its pressure map is shown in Fig. 2. In addition to providing the same mouse event information as a traditional mouse (mouse displacement, flicking interval and frequency), the touch-mouse is equipped with a highly reliable and calibrated surface capacitive sensor array. Each Microsoft touch-mouse has 195 capacitive sensors in total (13×15) covering the mouse surface. Quantified capacitance values can be utilized to estimate finger pressure values via computing a function of contact area and the width of the interval between two sides of a capacitor. Pressure distributions on a palm and fingers can be easily sampled and recorded by the touch-mouse. Our testing results revealed that the harder a finger presses on the mouse surface, the higher the capacitance value returned. Different users generate different pressure maps shown in Fig. 2, because each user has his/her own habit of holding a PC mouse.

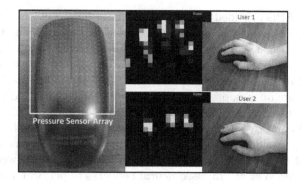

Fig. 2. Microsoft touch-mouse and user pressure map samples

2.2   Related Work

Under Graphical User Interface (GUI) environments, the most common mouse activities are moving and button flicking. The combinations of a sequence of moving and flicking generates plenty of compound mouse events, such as drag and drop, and batch selection. To better support navigation functionality in GUI environment, a mouse wheel was introduced for scrolling web pages and documents directly. Later, the touch-mouse was further enhanced to improve the user experience. The concept of mouse gestures, along with the invention of touch-mouses, are designed to provide users more power in controlling their computers, such as zoom in/out the current window and rotate a photo. In Fig. 3, commonly used mouse gestures provided by Microsoft touch-mouse are shown and these gestures can be viewed as features which are exploited in this design to model user behaviors for user identity verification.

Fig. 3. Microsoft touch-mouse events categories

By using the APIs provided by Microsoft, time stamps, button flicking events, and mouse displacements can be easily extracted and by grouping these simple mouse events together, compound features can be created accordingly. In the prior literature of mouse behavior pattern monitoring, only simple mouse events were extracted to perform user behavior identification. With the lack of palm and finger pressure images, previous experiments primarily utilized time stamps, relative mouse displacement information, and mouse button flicking events as features to train and test a variety of classifiers. Pusara and Brodley [9] showed a decision tree classifier which could discriminate multiple users with a false positive rate of 0.43% and a false negative rate of 1.75% in a well-controlled environment. Ahmed et al. [13] used neural networks to perform a series of classification experiments which resulted in low recognition error rate with limited and known actions among a small group of users. Although their experimental results looked very promising, they pointed out that analyzing mouse movements alone was still not sufficient for user re-authentication. This was because user behaviors in using a mouse could vary dramatically across different applications. Mouse event patterns collected from an exciting game can be far away from the patterns extracted by using a photo editing application. Therefore, a trained classifier by recognizing a user identity from one application might not be able to be applied to other applications. In reality, the range of the applications that a user might use may be unlimited.

3   Behavioral Model of Touch-Mouse

Our idea originates from the observation that mouse events are correlated with their corresponding pressure map sequences and their relationship does not significantly vary under different application scenarios. Instead of analyzing mouse

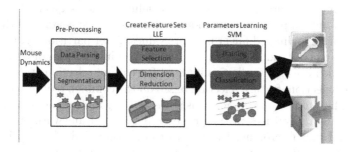

Fig. 4. Framework of behavior recognition

events and pressure map sequences separately, we propose to synchronize mouse events with the corresponding pressure map sequences via time stamps as indices and analyze both information together. This observation provides a fundamentally different basis from those existing mouse-based user behavior analysis methods. By creating a novel mapping between mouse events and a sequence of pressure maps, the dependence between the proposed re-authentication algorithm and the type of applications can be greatly reduced. Therefore, user behavior patterns are not unlimited anymore, but depend on the number of the action primitives supported by Microsoft touch-mouse. In addition, different users are likely to have distinct habits in using their touch-mouse, such as flicking different locations of a touch-mouse surface or scrolling with different forces; therefore, this method is able to effectively identify the inter-class differences and tolerate minor intra-class variations. In this paper, targeted action primitives are categorized by static holding, dynamic clicking/moving, and scrolling, which are commonly used in PC applications.

4 Algorithm for User Re-authentication

The user identification problem can be formulated into a standard learning and testing procedure as shown in Fig. 4. The key idea in this paper is to pair pressure map sequences with the available mouse action primitives and generate low dimension trajectories of the pressure maps as training and classification features. Our program starts when a target PC is powered on. It stays in memory and runs as a background process. Mouse pressure maps are provided by calling Microsoft touch-mouse APIs and mouse events are recorded via a regular mouse event library supported in C#.

Basic algorithm flow was described as follows:

1. Data Parsing: parse collected pressure maps and mouse event logs; After data parsing, a sequence of time-indexed pressure maps which contain 13*15 pixels and a sequence of time-indexed mouse event logs is generated.
2. Segmentation: data segmentation based on the mouse event logs; This stage tries to group a sequence of pressure maps and mouse events to generate

meaningful segmentations. The primary delimiters for segmentation are the timing of button press/release, mouse relative displacements, and the center of mass of the palm and finger pressure values. After partitioning, a sequence of pressure maps and mouse events are grouped into a series of time-indexed units, which are the smallest units used for feature selection stage.

3. Feature Selection: feature selection based on the common mouse action primitives; The simplest mouse action is static holding and the most complicated mouse action primitives in the proposed detection framework are drag and drop, and finger scrolling. Drag and drop is composed of an initial mouse button press, hold, mouse move, and ends with the mouse button release. Scrolling is composed of a similar process but instead of detecting mouse displacements, it exploits the center of mass of the palm and finger pressure to determine dragging. In total, eleven features are selected.

4. Dimension Reduction: Extracted features from the procedure above include a sequence of pressure maps and mouse action primitives; Locally Linear Embedded (LLE) dimension reduction algorithm [14] transforms pressure map information into dimension-reduced 2-D trajectories. These generated mouse trajectories and action primitives become the inputs for the cluster training and input classification.

5. Training and Classification: trajectory samples are trained and classified by the Supported Vector Machine (SVM) program; Basic binary training and classification procedures are applied on the trajectory and action primitive sample pairs from both training and testing data sets [15, 16].

The proposed framework provides continuous re-authentication based on the classification results. We utilize the built-in password function in PC to verify user identity if a re-authentication signal is triggered. Nevertheless, we did not limit the possibility of using other identity verification methods. With appropriate programming integrations, this framework should be able to seamlessly combine with most existing biometric or password-oriented verification mechanisms.

5   Evaluation

In this section, we discuss a series of experiments to evaluate the proposed re-authentication method. The first experiment tested the repeatability of our algorithm. The second one investigated the validity of our assumption: mouse events are highly correlated with their corresponding pressure map sequences and this relationship does not significantly vary under different application scenarios. The third experiment investigated the evaluation of defense against intruders. We would like to investigate how likely intruders could bypass our re-authentication system. We specially compared the performance of static mouse action primitives with the compound/dynamic action primitives to investigate if pressure maps could effectively assist the system to defend against intruders under a variety of applications.

5.1   Evaluation of Mouse Action Primitives Repeatability Off-Line Testing

This experiment primarily investigated the repeatability of the proposed design support in a well-controlled environment. Both training and testing processes were conducted off-line.

Experimental Setup and Description. 15 subjects participated in data collection, in which a total of 11 mouse action primitives were included. In each mouse action primitive, each subject was asked to repeat the experiment 100 times. In the experimental processes, we noticed that the user behaviors tended to be biased. For instance, if a tester had limited or no experience with a Microsoft touch-mouse, his/her behavioral patterns on touch-mouse was not significant. Sometimes he/she may even accidentally perform incorrect actions, such as doing scrolling when a zoom in action was expected. Therefore, an off-line training for each subject was given. Every subject was given specific instructions on how to use touch-mouse and they were given time to get used to the mouse before starting data collection processes. To minimize unnecessary interrupts, a background software was programmed to record the mouse actions without interrupting the experiment progress.

Evaluation Result Analysis. In the evaluation phase, the collected data set was divided into two categories. Half of them were used for training, and the remaining data was used for testing. On average, in more than 80% of the testing cases, our training data set could correctly recognize user identities. The highest accuracy was in the static hold primitive and the lowest accuracy was in three-finger scrolling primitive. Our result revealed that with more mouse dynamics came more variations in the data set. This result suggested using static mouse features over dynamic features in user identity monitoring under a fixed and controlled data collection environment.

5.2   Evaluation of Mouse Action Primitives Repeatability Testing Under Distinct Applications

This experiment was designed to test if the proposed system could survive under distinct applications. In other words, even though the behavior of a subject using a touch-mouse was different in distinct applications, the relationship between pressure maps and mouse action primitives should not significantly vary across distinct applications.

Experimental Setup and Description. The experimental setup was very similar to the first experiment. However, all data set gathered from the previous experiments were reused as a training data set only. Testing data was collected on-line for 10 minutes. In the 10 minutes, subjects were requested to play computer games, surf web, and editing photos randomly. These three totally different applications were selected in order to verify if the proposed features had any dependence on the type of applications. During testing, the frequency of a re-authentication warning was recorded.

Evaluation Result Analysis. A promising result revealed in Fig. 5 that, compared with the first experiment, the accuracy was similar across different types of applications. The selected features apparently had little dependence on application types. Since three finger scrolling was not used in gaming, it was not recorded and compared in this experiment. Nevertheless, static mouse actions still on average had higher accuracy than compound/dynamic mouse action primitives.

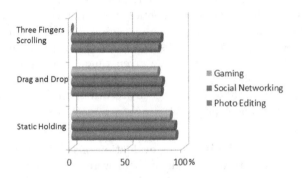

Fig. 5. Our design provides consistent accuracy under distinct applications. Three-finger scroll function is not used in gaming application.

5.3   Evaluation on Defense against Intruders

From the previous two experiments, static mouse action tended to result in a better accuracy. The following experiment attempted to understand if static mouse action primitives could effectively prevent unauthorized intruders as well.

Experimental Setup and Description. In this experiment, we investigated if the proposed algorithm could defend against intruders with unauthorized PC access by using static, dynamic action primitives, and pressure map trajectories. Different subjects have different behaviors in using their touch-mouse and the manifold trajectories were different for distinct action primitives as shown in Fig. 6. Three subjects were randomly picked as PC account owners. The data set of the selected subjects were trained and loaded separately in different user accounts, and then the remaining 12 people were asked to attack the trained system. To increase the success of attack, these three selected subjects showed how they used their touch-mouse to other participants.

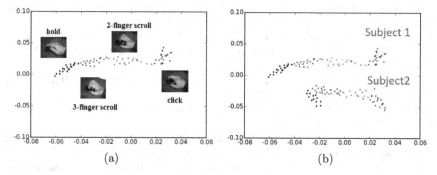

(a)   (b)

Fig. 6. Visualization of dimension reduced trajectories and hand postures. Visualization of two dimension reduced trajectories from two selected subjects.

Evaluation Result Analysis From the experimental result, static movement, 36% intrusion rate, could not effectively prevent intruders attack, because after few trial-and-errors, static mouse action primitives could be mimicked eventually. Nevertheless, we did not observe any complex dynamic mouse action primitives and pressure map trajectories pairs, such as drag and drop, or scrolling, that could be mimicked by any attacker. This observation provided a design trade-off between user-friendliness and security level. If a computer contained highly confidential information, it should utilize all mouse action primitives and pressure maps to increase data safety. Inevitably, false-alarms might happen more frequently and take more user attention to respond to the re-authentication requests.

6   Conclusion and Future Work

Our design can effectively integrate with existing security mechanisms to provide continuous and hassle-free re-authentication by using a commercially available product - Microsoft touch-mouse. This system can serve as a robust abnormal pattern detector, which delegates final verification tasks to the existing password or biometric-based verifiers. To demonstrate the validity of this system, we performed experiments with 15 subjects under three type of application scenarios: web page-browsing, gaming, and photo editing. The experimental results demonstrated the possibility of preventing physical computer intrusion with a touch-mouse based user identity monitoring system.

References

1. Microsoft touch-mouse - Microsoft hardware,
   http://www.microsoft.com/hardware/en-us/products/
   touch-mouse/microsite/
2. Liu, S., Silverman, M.: A practical guide to biometric security technology. IT Professional 3(1), 27–32 (2001)

3. Prabhakar, S., Pankanti, S., Jain, A.K.: Biometric recognition: Security and privacy concerns. IEEE Security Privacy Mag. 1(2), 33–42 (2003)
4. Gish, H., Siu, M.H., Rohlicek, R.: Segregation of Speakers for Speech Recognition and Speaker Identification. In: Proc. of Conference on Acoustics, Speech, and Signal Processing, pp. 14–17. ACM Press (1991)
5. Isenor, D.K., Zakey, S.G.: Fingerprint identification using graph matching. Pattern Recognition 19(19), 113–122 (1986)
6. Wildes, R.P.: Iris recognition: an emerging biometric technology. Proc. of the IEEE 85(18), 1348–1363 (1997)
7. Lanitis, A., Tayler, C.J., Cootes, T.F.: Automatic face identification system using flexible appearance models. Image and Vision Computing 13(13), 393–401 (1997)
8. Monrose, F., Rubin, A.: Authentication via Keystroke Dynamics. In: Proc. of Conference on Computer and Communications Security, pp. 48–56. ACM Press (1997)
9. Rusara, M., Brodley, C.: User Re-Authentication via Mouse Movements. In: Proc. of VizSEC/DMSEC, pp. 48–56. ACM Press (2004)
10. Igun, K., Kemmerer, R.A., Porras, P.A.: State Transition Analysis: A Rule-Based Instrusion Detection Approach. In: Proc. of Software Engineering, pp. 181–199. ACM Press (1995)
11. Feng, H.H., Kolesnikov, O.M., Fogla, P., Lee, W., Gong, W.: Anomaly detection using call stack information. In: Proc. of IEEE Symposium on Security and Privacy, pp. 62–78. IEEE Press (1998)
12. Denning, D.E.: Forgot username/password? Software Engineering 2(13), 222–232 (1987)
13. Ahmed, A.A., Traore, I.: A new biometric technology based on mouse dynamics. IEEE Transaction on Dependable and Secure Computing 4(3), 165–179 (2007)
14. Saul, L.K., Roweis, S.T.: Think globally, fit locally: unsupervised learning of low dimensional manifolds. Journal of Machine Learning Research 4, 119–155 (2003)
15. Liu, J.J., Xu, W., Huang, M.C., Alshurafa, N., Sarrafzadeh, M.: A dense pressure sensitive bedsheet design for unobtrusive sleep posture monitoring. In: IEEE International Conference on Pervasive Computing and Communications, IEEE (2013)
16. Kouropteva, O., Okun, O., Pietikainen, M.: Classification of handwritten digits using supervised locally linear embedding algorithm and support vector machine. In: Proc. of European Symposium on Artificial Neural Networks, pp. 229–234. ESANN (2003)

Gamified CAPTCHA

Junya Kani[1] and Masakatsu Nishigaki[2]

[1] Graduate School of Informatics, Shizuoka University, Japan
gs12012@s.inf.shizuoka.ac.jp
[2] Graduate School of Science and Technology, Shizuoka University, Japan
nisigaki@inf.shizuoka.ac.jp

Abstract. The Completely Automated Public Turing test to tell Computers and Humans Apart (CAPTCHA) has been widely used as a technique that will allow a machine to distinguish between input from a human and that of another machine. The security of current CAPTCHA methods is not sufficient to protect against advanced modern malware. This paper focuses on applying gamification, the use of game elements in non-game human interaction systems, in order to improve the security and usability of CAPTCHA systems. We propose to use movie-based quizzes to achieve a Gamified CAPTCHA system that employs the human capability to recognize the strangeness of a short movie story.

Keywords: CAPTCHA, Entertainment, strangeness, quiz.

1   Introduction

With the expansion of Web services, denial of service (DoS) attacks by malicious automated programs (e.g., bots) are becoming a serious problem as masses of Web service accounts are being illicitly obtained, bulk spam e-mails are being sent, and mass spam blog posts are being created. Thus, the Turing test is becoming a necessary technique to discriminate humans from malicious automated programs and the CAPTCHA [1] system developed by Carnegie Mellon University has been widely used. The simplest CAPTCHA presents distorted or noise added text (Fig.1) to users who visit Web sites and want to use their services. We refer to this simple CAPTCHA as text recognition based-CAPTCHA. If they can read the given text, they are certified as human. If they cannot read the text, they are certified to be malicious automated programs (bots).

However, many researchers have recently pointed out that automated programs with optical character reader (OCR) and/or machine learning can answer those conventional text recognition based-CAPTCHA [2]. Indeed, these sophisticated malwares have been spreading and they have cracked the text recognition based-CAPTCHA [3 ,4].

It can be made more difficult for automated programs to pass tests (i.e. read texts) by increasing the distortion or noise. However, it also becomes more difficult for humans to read such texts. We therefore need to adopt even more advanced human cognitive processing capabilities to enhance CAPTCHA to overcome this problem.

L. Marinos and I. Askoxylakis (Eds.): HAS/HCII 2013, LNCS 8030, pp. 39–48, 2013.

Image recognition-based CAPTCHA such as Asirra [6] (Fig.2) is known as one of the effective solutions for enhancing CAPTCHA, because image recognition is a much more difficult problem for a machine than character recognition [5]. Labeled images are used in image recognition based-CAPTCHA to confirm that a user can recognize the meaning of the image. In Asirra, several photos of animals (i.e. images of cats and dogs with diverse backdrops, angles, poses, and lighting) are presented to a user, and the user is then asked to select a specific animal in a test. For example, suppose that the user is asked to select a "cat"; if he or she can select all photos labeled as cat in the test, then he or she is certified to be human. If not, he or she is certified to be an automated program.

However, a technique that has effectively been used to breach image recognition-based CAPTCHA has been reported and shocked researchers [7, 8]. Advancements made to cracking capabilities (CAPTCHA cracking algorithms and CPU processing speeds) will continue indefinitely. No matter how advanced malicious automated programs are, a CAPTCHA that will not pass automated programs is required. Hence, we have to find another human cognitive processing capability to tackle this challenge.

While we desire to enhance CAPTCHA safety, we of course must be conscious of the trade-off between safety and usability. Even supposing we have a CAPTCHA system that has high resistance to malware, but if it is difficult to read for humans, then the CAPTCHA cannot be used. Furthermore, proving that one is human can be an annoyance for users. Therefore, CAPTCHA systems should also be designed to be user-friendly.

To endeavor overcoming this challenge, we had previously focused on the human capability to "understand humor", by proposing the "four-panel cartoon CAPTCHA" [9]. This four-panel cartoon CAPTCHA is presented with the four rearranged randomly panels, and users that are able to sort in the correct order are then identified as human. Even if the panels of a four-panel cartoon are rearranged randomly, a human can understand the meaning of the pictures and utterances in each panel, and thereby sort the order in which the panels must be rearranged in order to create a funny story. For a malware, however, even if image processing and natural language processing abilities developed to the level where the computer could recognize the meaning of the pictures and utterances, it would be still difficult for the computer to arrange the four panels in the correct order unless it also was able to understand humor. Furthermore, because reading cartoons is fun and entertaining for humans, a four-panel cartoon CAPTCHA will most likely be seen as an agreeable and enjoyable Turing Test that does not adversely affect the convenience for users.

We believe that entertainment is one of the good driving-forces for enhancement of usability of security technologies, and this motivates us to explore how to improve the entertainment value. This paper is now focusing on the human capability of solving a "quiz". When a human challenges a difficult quiz, he or she feels engaged and eager to solve the problem. People may often want to do it again when they fail to get the correct answer. We try to use such human characteristics to develop even safer and more enjoyable CAPTCHA system. This is essentially the application of gamification, or the use of game elements in non-game scenarios, to engage users when solving CAPTCHA challenges. This is why we entitled it "Gamified CAPTCHA". It should be noted that the four-panel cartoon CAPTCHA makes use of the fun activity in a "passive" manner; the user reads cartoon and will just be satisfied. On the other hand, the Gamifird CAPTCHA makes use of the fun activity in an "active" manner; the user tries the quiz and will want one more try.

This paper will discuss Gamified CAPTCHA with quiz solving. In particular, we play a movie, in which the scenes were altered, for the user. The human will be able to pick out the altered scenes by recognizing the strangeness in the movie. Furthermore, even if the user cannot pick out the altered scenes, the user will want to do it again. By contrast, it will be difficult for malware to solve Gamified CAPTCHA unless the malware can recognize the strangeness of a story with altered scenes. In this paper, we implement Gamified CAPTCHA for swapped scenes, deleted scene, and reversed scene, and we evaluate the effectiveness of this proposal through experimentation. Fig.3 shows a concept image.

Fig. 1. CAPTCHA used by Google

Fig. 2. Asirra

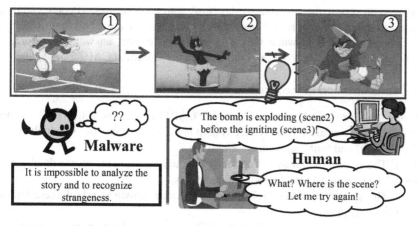

Fig. 3. Concept Image (Referenced by "Tennis Chumps", Tom and Jerry DVD VOL.7, Warnerbros.)

2   Gamified CAPTCHA

2.1   Quiz Use to Leverage Entertainment Value

For the enhancement of CAPTCHA, we need to think of both safety and usability. For safety enhancement, there is a need to use more advanced human cognitive processing capability. For usability of CAPTCHA, there is a need to make CAPTCHA fun. Therefore, using the four-panel cartoon CAPTCHA with the capability to understand humor can be an effective direction. This paper tries to even leverage for the "entertainment value"of CAPTCHA by using a "quiz", in order to engage the user and make the activity more enjoyable. In this paper, we refer to it as "Gamified CAPTCHA".

In particular, we will play a movie, where the scenes in it are altered (i.e., swapped, deleted or reversed), to a user. It is expected that a human can correctly understand the story of the movie and recognize the strangeness of the altered scenes, even when he or she watches the altered version of the movie. For malware, on the other hand, even if technologies such as image processing capabilities are developed, it would continue to be difficult for the malware to correctly pick out the swapped, deleted, or reversed scenes, unless the malware recognizes the strangeness of the story with altered scene(s).

The four-panel cartoon CAPTCHA has its merit that users can solve the CAPTCHA while having fun because reading a cartoon is fun and entertaining for humans. Therefore, in this work the Gamified CAPTCHA uses a funny movie for the quiz. As an example, we used the animated movies "Tom and Jerry". The movie was played without sound in order to avoid making a jumping sound which may clue the malware into the skipping scene.

Existing CAPTCHA systems are often a burden for users. Failure to answer the CAPTCHA test correctly is directly linked to a decrease in usability, resulting in frustration for the user. For the Gamified CAPTCHA, on the other hand, even if the user cannot correctly answer, it would be expected that the user would feel encouraged to repeat the test due to the 'fun' nature of the quiz. People often say "Please let me have one more try!" when they challenge the quiz, and these words are more likely to be uttered when they fail to get the correct answer. Therefore, we would expect that the user would not mind doing the Gamified CAPTCHA again.

2.2   Authentication Procedure

Authentication procedure of the Gamified CAPTCHA is as follows. It is here assumed that the Gamified CAPTCHA system has a movie database, in which enough number of short and funny movies are archived.

Step1. The system randomly selects one of the movies from the movie database.
Step2. The system divides the movie into scenes.
Step3. The system randomly selects scene(s) in the movie to which the alteration process is applied.
Step4. The system randomly selects the scene swapping, deletion, or reversion.
Step5. The system performs the scene alteration.

(i)   If swapping is chosen: The system randomly selects two scenes (Scene A, Scene B), and then swaps these scenes. See fig.4 for an example. The order of the swapped scenes will no longer make sense to the human, which will bring a feeling of strangeness to the viewers.

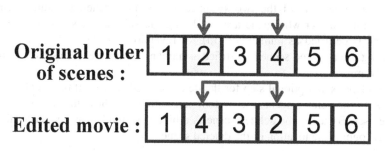

Original order of scenes :

Edited movie :

Fig. 4. Swapping CAPTCHA

(ii)   If deletion is chosen: The system randomly selects one scene, and then deletes the scene. See fig.5 for an example. The movie will skip playing the scene, which will bring a feeling of strangeness to the viewers.

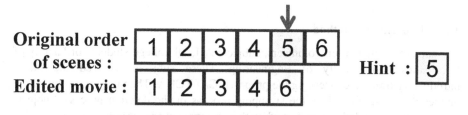

Original order of scenes :

Edited movie :

Hint : 5

Fig. 5. Deletion CAPTCHA

(iii)   If reversion is chosen: The system randomly selects one scene, and then reverses the scene. That is, the scene will be played with reverse playback, which will bring a feeling of strangeness to the viewers. See figure 6 for an example.

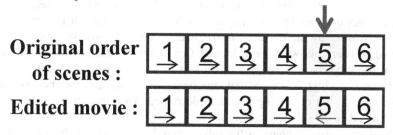

Original order of scenes :

Edited movie :

Fig. 6. Reversion CAPTCHA

Step6. The system plays the altered movie to the user.

Step7. The user clicks on the screen as soon as the user feels strangeness in watching the movie.

Step8. If the user clicked the altered scene correctly, the system certifies the user as human. To be more precise, (i) for swapping, the user who made a click during either one of the two swapped scenes is certified as human, (ii) for deletion, the user who made a click during the subsequent scene of the deleted scene is certified as human, or (iii) for reversion, the user who made a click during the reversed scene is certified as human. Otherwise, the user is certified as malware.

Step9. (This is an optional step for the deletion CAPTCHA.) If the user has trouble finding the deleted scene, the system can optionally show the deleted scene to the user. By using the deleted scene as a hint, it would become easier for the user to recognize the location of the deleted scene.

3   Verification Experiment

We conducted basic experiments to evaluate the authentication rate and the entertainment value of the proposed method. Due to time constraints, the experiment was not yet performed on the reversion CAPTCHA.

3.1   Experiment Method

The subjects included ten volunteers, subjects A-J, all college students of Faculty of Informatics and Faculty of Engineering. These subjects received the initial introductory training concerning the proposed CAPTCHA. Then they were shown the movies that were altered by the swapping process or the deletion process. Subjects were instructed to click the mouse when they recognized any strangeness.

As mentioned in Section 3.1, the movies should be fun to watch and easy for understanding the story without voice. To meet these conditions, we adopted the "Tom and Jerry" cartoon movies in this experiment. We prepared four "Tom and Jerry" movies, each of approximately 30 seconds in length. Two of them were used for the swapping CAPTCHA and the remainder used for the deletion CAPTCHA. Here, the length of the scenes that had been swapped was about five seconds (the total time of two scenes), and the length of the scenes that had been deleted was one to two seconds.

The number of times for watching the movie was unlimited. That is, we allowed the subjects to replay the movie as many times as desired. However, the number of submitted answers allowable was limited (up to three times). In the case of the deletion, the subjects were optionally allowed to see an image of one frame of the deleted scene as a hint. It is noted that after seeing a hint, the quiz then becomes easier to solve and the fun of solving it is then decreased. Therefore, the hint image was shown only when the subject asked to see it.

In the case of the swapping, if the subject could click during either of the scenes that were swapped, the answer was correct. In the case of the deletion, if the subjects could click before or after the scene that was deleted (within approximately one second), the answer was correct. The "clicking before the deleted scene" is available to account for the case where the user has watched the movie once and has replayed it. In that case, the user may anticipate the scene and try to click just before the scene.

As a comparison experiment, we also tested a text recognition-based CAPTCHA. Intrinsically, we should create a variety of tests with respect to different texts/movies. Also, we should randomize the order of tests to take into account the effect of the experimental sequence. However, as this was a basic experiment, all of the subjects took the same tests in the following order: two questions of text recognition-based CAPTCHA, two questions of the swapping CAPTCHA, and finally two questions of the deletion CAPTCHA.

After completing all CAPTCHA tests, we had the subjects respond to the following questionnaire.

- Did you enjoy solving the CAPTCHA? (Enjoyed) : Yes (5) – No (1)
- Was it user-friendly? (User-friendly) : Yes (5) – No (1)
- Was it easy solving the CAPTCHA? (Easy) : Yes (5) – No (1)
- Are you happy when you are correct? (Happy) : Yes (5) – No (1)
- Did you want to do it again? (One-more-time) : Yes (5) – No (1)
- Overall points: Good (5) – Bad (1)

3.2 Experiment Result

The experimental results are shown in Tables 1-4. Table 1 summarizes the average rate of correct answers for the swapping CAPTCHA and the deletion CAPTCHA. Tables 2-4 show the points from the questionnaire responses regarding the text recognition-based CAPTCHA, the swapping CAPTCHA, and the deletion CAPTCHA, respectively.

Table 1. Authentication rate for Gamified CAPTCHA

CAPTCHA	Percentage
Swapping CAPTCHA(1 question)	90%
Swapping CAPTCHA(2 question)	100%
Deletion CAPTCHA(1 question)	100%
Deletion CAPTCHA(2 question)	100%

Table 2. Text recognition based-CAPTCHA result of questionnaire

Ques. \ Subject	A	B	C	D	E	F	G	H	I	J	Ave.
Enjoyed	1	1	1	1	1	1	2	5	3	3	1.9
User-friendly	1	1	3	4	5	3	3	2	2	3	2.7
Easy	3	2	1	5	5	4	4	2	2	3	3.1
Happy	1	1	3	1	1	1	3	2	3	2	1.8
One-more-time	1	1	1	1	1	1	2	1	2	1	1.2
Overall	1	1	2	5	1	4	3	1	2	2	2.2

Table 3. Swapping CAPTCHA result of questionnaire

Ques.＼Subject	A	B	C	D	E	F	G	H	I	J	Ave.
Enjoyed	5	5	4	4	5	4	3	5	4	4	4.3
User-friendly	2	1	5	1	4	1	3	5	3	2	2.7
Easy	2	5	4	3	4	2	3	3	3	2	3.1
Happy	5	4	4	4	5	4	5	5	4	4	4.4
One-more-time	5	5	4	4	5	2	5	5	4	4	4.3
Overall	3	4	4	2	5	3	4	4	4	3	3.6

Table 4. Deletion CAPTCHA result of questionnaire

Ques.＼Subject	A	B	C	D	E	F	G	H	I	J	Ave.
Enjoyed	4	5	5	5	5	2	4	5	5	4	4.4
User-friendly	2	1	5	1	1	1	4	4	2	4	2.5
Easy	1	3	3	1	1	1	2	4	1	3	2
Happy	5	4	4	3	5	5	5	5	5	4	4.5
One-more-time	5	5	4	4	5	2	5	5	4	5	4.4
Overall	3	5	4	1	5	2	5	5	4	4	3.8

Let us begin by taking a look at Tables 2-4. For the questions of "Enjoyed", "Happy", and "One-more-time", these averages were four or more points for the Gamified CAPTCHA (Tables 3 and 4), while these were two or fewer points for the text recognition–based CAPTCHA (Table 2). For the question of "User-friendly", the average is about three points for Gamified CAPTCHA (Tables 3 and 4) as well as the text recognition-based CAPTCHA (Table 2). Therefore, we can confirm that the Gamified CAPTCHA has higher entertainment value compared to the text recognition-based CAPTCHA. However, it must be noted that we have not yet studied how much the entertainment value would be leveraged by using quizzes, instead of four-panel cartoons. We should carry out further investigations to compare the Gamified CAPTCHA with the four-panel cartoon CAPTCHA.

As for the question of "Easy" in Tables 2-4, we found the difficulty for the swapping CAPTCHA and the text recognition-based CAPTCHA to be the same, while the deletion CAPTCHA was more difficult. However, in the experiment for the deletion CAPTCHA, many of the subjects were able to answer correctly without a hint image. Presenting the hint image will reduce the difficulty of the deletion CAPTCHA. From these results, we can see that the Gamified CAPTCHA presents a moderate level of difficulty for a human. This observation is also supported by Table 1. As per the "Average rate for all subjects" in Table 1, it was shown that the authentication rate is sufficiently good for the swapping CAPTCHA (about 90%) and the deletion CAPTCHA (100%). This result would confirm the recognizableness of the Gamified CAPTCHA.

4   Discussion

4.1   Operation

A large volume of movie data would be required to put a Gamified CAPTCHA system into actual operation on the Internet. From the point of view of the movie fees, it is considered to be an effective way to take advantage of movie sites such as "You Tube". However, the movies posted on such movie sites are a mixture of good and bad. Not all movies necessarily have a story that is easy to understand by everyone. The clarity of the story is considered to be directly linked to the rate of correct answers of the Gamified CAPTCHA. Therefore, the question of how to collect the movies that are easy to understand in large quantities and at low cost is an important issue. In the case of using copyrighted movies, the question would become even more complex. That would be because we must obtain not only merely licensing, but also the approval for the movie to be altered.

4.2   Time-Consumption

In the current stage, the Gamified CAPTCHA uses a movie of about 30 seconds in length. Therefore, the Gamified CAPTCHA test is considered to be very time-consuming, compared to the text recognition-based CAPTCHA. Even though the entertainment value leveraged by quizzes may increase the convenience and actual usability, 30 seconds is still long enough. Therefore the reduction of the time required for answering is another important issue in the Gamified CAPTCHA.

4.3   Security

It is expected that it would be difficult for malwares to recognize the strangeness in the altered movie and defeat the Gamified CAPTCHA. Therefore, we now focus on brute force attack. In the next stage of this study, we will of course have to cope with not only brute force attack but also a variety kind of attacks.

In the case of the swapping CAPTCHA, if a malware can make a click at the place when the scenes were swapped, the malware is authenticated as a human. Supposed that the movie is about 30 seconds in length and the swapped scenes are about 5 seconds in total, and then this means that even malware could respond with a correct answer at a rate of one out of every six tries. In the case of the deletion CAPTCHA, if a malware can make a click at the place before or after the scenes were deleted, the malware is authenticated as a human. Supposed that the movie is about 30 seconds in length and the tolerance time is 2 seconds (before or after the extracted scene by approximately one second), this then means that even malware could respond with a correct answer at a rate of one out of every fifteen tries. In the case of the reversion CAPTCHA, if a malware can make a click at the place when the scenes were played with reverse playback, the malware is authenticated as a human. Supposed that the movie is about 30 seconds in length and the reversed scenes are about 2.5 seconds in total, and then this means that even malware could respond with a correct answer at a rate of one out of every twelve tries. Ensuring safety against brute force attack is one of the very important issues of the Gamified CAPTCHA.

5   Conclusion and Future Work

In this study, we focused on "quiz" to enhance the usability and security in the CAPTCHA system, and proposed the Gamified CAPTCHA. The fun nature of the quiz will leverage the entertainment value of the CAPTCHA tests, and therefore, the users will feel encouraged to repeat it. At present, there continues to be room for improvement in terms of both security and usability. We are planning to upgrade the Gamified CAPTCHA based on the knowledge obtained through the experimental results.

References

1. The Official CAPTCHA Site, http://www.captcha.net
2. PWNtcha-Captcha Decoder, http://caca.zoy.org/wiki/PWNtcha
3. Yan, J., Ahmad, A.S.E.: Breaking Visual CAPTCHAs with Naïve Pattern Recognition Algorithms. In: 2007 Computer Security Applications Conference, pp. 279–291 (2007)
4. Elson, J., Douceur, J., Howela, J., Saul, J.: Asirra: a CAPTCHA that exploit interest-aligned manual image categorization. In: 2007 ACM CSS, pp. 366–374 (2007)
5. Chellapilla, K., Larson, K., Simard, P., Czerwinski, M.: Computers beat humans at single character recognition in reading-based Human Interaction Proofs (HIPs). In: 2nd Conference on Email and Anti-Spam (CEAS) (2005)
6. MSR Asirra Project, http://research.microsoft.com/asirra/
7. Golle, P.: Machine Learning Attacks Against the ASIRRA CAPTCHA. In: 2008 ACM CSS, pp. 535–542 (2008)
8. Vaughan-Nichols, S.J.: How CAPTCHA got trashed, Computerworld (July 15, 2008), http://www.computerworld.com.au/article/253015/how_captcha_got_trashed/
9. Yamamoto, T., Suzuki, T., Nishigaki, M.: A Proposal of Four-panel cartoon CAPTCHA. In: Proceedings of IEEE International Conference on Advanced Information Networking and Applications 2011, pp. 159–166 (2011)

Recognition of Human Identity
by Detection of User Activity

Giuseppe Scardino, Ignazio Infantino, and Filippo Vella

ICAR - CNR, Viale delle Scienze, Ed 11 - 90128 Palermo, Italy
{scardino,infantino,filippo.vella}@pa.icar.cnr.it

Abstract. The paper describes a system able to recognize the users identity according how she/he looks at the monitor while using a given interface. The system does not need invasive measurements that could limit the naturalness of her/his actions. The proposed approach clusters the sequences of observed points on the screen and characterizes the user identity according the relevant detected patterns. Moreover, the system is able to identify patterns in order to have a more accurate recognition and to create prototypes of natural facial dynamics in user expressions. The possibility to characterize people through facial movements introduces a new perspective on human-machine interaction. For example, a user can obtain different contents according her/his mood or a software interface can modify itself to keep a higher attention from a bored user. The success rate of the classification using only 7 parameters is around 68%. The approach is based on k-means that is tuned to maximize an index involving the number of true-positive detections and conditional probabilities. A different evaluation of this parameter allows to focus on the identification of a single user or to spot a general movement for a wide range of people The experiments show that the performance can reach the 90% of correct recognition.

1 Introduction

Over the last few years the approach followed in the field of human-computer interfaces (HCI) has sensibly changed. The focus has been shifted on the so-called human-centered design, namely the creation of interaction systems made for humans and based on models of human behaviour [1] and cognitive capabilities [2]. This type of design requires a thorough analysis and proper processing of the information flowing in man-machine communication: linguistic messages, the non-linguistic vocalizations, emotions, attitudes, facial expressions, head movements and hand movements, body posture, and, finally the context in which they are transmitted [3]. In general, the modelling of human behaviour is a challenging task and is based on various behavioural signals: behavioural and affective states (e.g. fear, joy, inattention, stress), the manipulative behaviour (actions used to act on environment objects or self-manipulative actions such as lip biting), the specific signs of culture (conventional signs, such as a head nod or a thumbs-up). The behaviour detected by the actions should also be associated

L. Marinos and I. Askoxylakis (Eds.): HAS/HCII 2013, LNCS 8030, pp. 49–58, 2013.
© Springer-Verlag Berlin Heidelberg 2013

to a model of human intentions [4] able to take into account the context and be consistent with a cognitive model of the user [5]. Such models could then be integrated into a cognitive architecture with the aim of representing not only the user's mental model [6] but also the main mechanisms of human reasoning such as perception, memory, decision, planning, emotional and affective states, motivation, sociability, and so on (see for example [7], [2]).

A full understanding of human behaviour [1] hinges on the perception of complex signals such as facial expressions, posture and body movements and on the modelling of the context through the identification of objects, and interactions with other components the real environment. The modern techniques of computer vision, and sophisticated machine learning methods allow us to collect and process such data in a more accurate and robust way [8]. If an automated system captures the temporal extension of these signals, it is possible make predictions and create expectations about their possible evolution. It is also possible to detect human intentions, in a simplified way, classifying the elementary actions of a human agent and identifying the usual task associated to the action[4]. The particular way to execute a given task is the basis of a biometric recognition.

For example in [9] the identity is guessed from footsteps, a multimodal system in [10] uses face and speech information, dynamic keystroke analysis are used in [11], and so on.

1.1   Aims and Motivation of the Presented Work

On the basis of the above considerations, the paper proposes a system to model user behaviour and identity recognition in a common real situation: when a user is in front of a computer screen her/his actions are bound to what she/he is viewing at and the way she/he can interact with the application. A way to characterise the user behaviour is to consider head/eyes movements, facial expressions and which region of the monitor scene is observed. The aim of this work is to capture the user behaviour when she/he is browsing an internet page or is using a software interface. This application allows to classify the user reactions in front of a computer and to distinguish different users by its personal movement when interacts with the computer.

2   User Activity Detection

The combination of computer vision [12] and models of human actions [13] make possible to design sophisticated user interfaces and user modelling systems. The proposed system uses the Microsoft Kinect camera to track the point of the screen where the user is looking at. The Kinect system allows to obtain information on skeleton and face movements, using an infrared sensor and a VGA camera (640 x 480 pixel). Using the Microsoft SDK 1.5, the Kinect camera is able to provide information about the user position and to segment the user head. The head position and orientation are characterised with angles along three axes for all the possible orientations, according the movements of yaw, pitch and roll.

The values of the angles provide information about where the user is looking. Given the orientation of the head, a line orthogonal to the eyes line and parallel to the desk is considered. The point where this line meets the screen plane is the point where the user is looking at. The user activity is described through: gaze tracking, facial expression, face coefficients.

2.1   Gaze Tracking

To exactly estimate the point where the user is looking, it is necessary to know where the monitor and the user are positioned in the space. This information is obtained though a calibration step, where it is possible to know the monitor position and the user position in 3D space. The procedure requires that the user, positioned in front of the monitor, looks for few seconds at each monitor corners remaining in a fixed position. In this phase, the angles of the head are saved and provide a reference for all the head movements.

The position where the user is looking on the screen is calculated comparing the angles of the head at a given moment with the values stored in the calibration phase. In order to make the algorithm more robust, the values of all four corners are stored although three points would be enough to perform the calibration. If a value is not detected or it is affected by a large error it is possible to estimate the correct parameters trusting on three of the four values.

After the calibration session, the user can use normally the computer. During the work session, the system stores the information about the point where the user is looking at. The calibration values are valid for different sessions until the monitor, or the kinect camera or the user position are moved. This feature allows to make an unique calibration per user and use the system parameters for multiple captures without making any others calibrations.

Tracking Precision. The chosen method is quite simple, but it provides promising results and it is not constrained to a fixed user position. The user can move in a circle with radius of $35/40$ cm from the initial calibration position with a slight error in gaze estimation. This case covers the standard scenario where the user is sat at the desk and can move its chair in a limited space. Considering the case shown in figure 1, the user is in front of the monitor. The calibration estimates the values of position and angles of user head when she/he looks at the points A and B. The C point is calculated as follows:

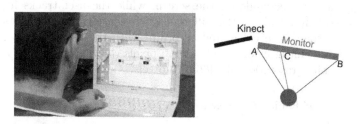

Fig. 1. User position in front of the monitor and Kinect sensor

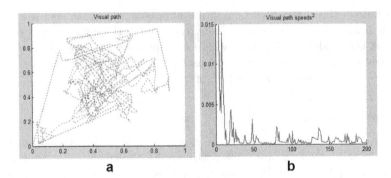

Fig. 2. Tracking activity of human working on his laptop. On the left (a) is represented the diagram of estimated points observed on the monitor and on the right (b) the velocity of movements.

1. roto-translate the values to obtain the center of the axis on the user position;
2. calculate the max value between the saved angle on the top right and bottom right monitor corners in ZX plan;
3. calculate the min value between the saved angle on the top left and bottom left monitor corners in ZX plan;
4. calculate the difference between max and min value calculated at point 2 and 3: $deltaAngleZX = maxValue - minValue$;
5. the mouse position on x screen cordinates are obtained by this formula:

$$xPosition = \frac{actualPosition.ZXangle - maxValue}{deltaAngleZX} * xScreenResolution$$

The same procedure is used to obtain the screen position on y axis using the angles on ZY plan. The obtained values have ripples and the evaluation is affected from noise given by Kinect sensor. To make the estimation more stable has been employed a Kalman filter [14] that allows to have a robust estimation also when noise is present. The Kalman filter is a recursive estimator which evaluates the state of a dynamic system from a series of measurements. This filter has the drawback of being not sufficiently responsive when there are small variations in the input data. An example of acquired data during a tracking session are shown in figure 2.

To measure the accuracy of the tracking system we developed a routine that shows a small moving rectangle on the screen, while the user tracks it with the gaze. The system calculates the difference between the rectangle position and the value on the screen calculated according with the user gaze position. Experiments show a mean errors of about 9.0 pixels (both along x axis and y axis), using a monitor resolution of 1366x778 pixels.

2.2   Extraction of Facial Expression

To detect the facial expression we used some information about the user and which screen region she/he is viewing. The gathered information are: x, y screen coordinates, the six coefficients of Animation Units characterizing the human face. These six coefficients, called Animation Units (AU)[15], are a subset coefficients defined in the Candide3 model [16] that uses 87 2D points on the face to track the user head. From these six values it is possible to classify the facial expression considering seven basic expressions: neutral face, upper lip raised, jaw lowered, lip stretched, brow lowered, lip corner depressed and outer brow raised.

The range of these coefficients is between -1.0 and 1.0. The first coefficient indicate the lips movement, the value +1 indicates the lips completely opened and -1 completely closed. The second is referred to the lower jaw movement, so +1 indicates completely opened and -1 closed. The third coefficient, indicates how the lips are stretched, the value is defined as follow: 0 is neutral, +1 is fully stretched (joker smile), -0.5 rounded (pout) and -1 is fully rounded (kissing mouth). The fourth coefficient is an index referred to the brow, -1 is for brow raised and +1 for fully lowered. The fifth, the lip corner depressor, indicates -1 for a very happy smile and +1 for a very sad frown. The last coefficient is an index of the outer brow, -1 indicates fully lowered (a very sad face) and +1 raised (deep surprise).

The afore-mentioned six coefficients are related to the configuration of facial features and can be used to classify the emotional state of the user. Through a series of IF-THEN rules and a set of threshold values basic facial expressions are detected (neutral, smiling, angry, sad, surprised, fearful). The rules and thresholds, as used in Microsoft original source code, allow to obtain the facial expression from the six Animation Units as described here:

if (AU[3] > 0.1 and AU[5] > 0.05) the eyebrows are lowered, so set an angry configuration.

else if (AU[3] < -0.1 and AU[2] > and AU[4] > 0.1) eyebrow up and mouth stretched, fearful configuration.

else if (AU[1] > 0.1 and AU[3] < -0.1) eyebrow up and mouth open, surprised configuration.

else if ((AU[2] - AU[4]) > 0.1 and AU[4] < 0) lips are stretched, assume smiling configuration.

else if ((AU[2] - AU[4]) < 0 and AU[5] < -0.3) lips low and eyebrow slanted up, sad configuration.

else by default, set a neutral configuration.

2.3   Activity by Temporal Sequences

We take into account a dynamic evolution of the users activity by sequence of facial action units. Moreover an important parameter that can be extracted is the movement speed of her/his observed point on the screen. We consider that this speed is an own characteristic of the user and different users have different statistics in the fruition of a content on the computer screen. For each couple of frames we calculate the difference, in absolute value, between the position in the current frame and the position in the previous frame estimating the speed at a given moment. We form in this way a vector containing the values of the six animation units at a given time t and the speed at the same time.

$$\mathbf{V_t} = [p_1, p_2, p_3, p_4, p_5, p_6, s]$$

The value of $\mathbf{V_t}$ are saved every 0.3 second in order to store the face parameters and to follow the head movement. To consider a temporal evolution of these parameters, a temporal window of 10 samples is considered. The temporal window is then moved considering the newest values and discarding the oldest one. Our hypothesis is that every user has a different behaviour in front of a computer and this is tightly correlated with her/his personality. The behaviour can be extracted detecting characteristic dynamic facial configuration and classifying new detections according their classes. The next step is the clustering of captured data ($\mathbf{V_t}$) and aggregate them in homogeneous sets. Each cluster can be annotated counting how many samples of a given user are mapped on the cluster itself. The presence of a single or more labels (identifying multiple users) is considered as a measure indicating how trustable the labels are. If a clusters is composed by values of a single user, the values that are in that cluster are very discriminating and identify with good accuracy the user. On the other side, if a cluster is annotated with labels coming from multiple users the values aggregated in this cluster are bound to multiple users and its values are not very discriminating. These values are not peculiar of a single user and have a reduced identification capability. We adopted the well known k-means to cluster the $\mathbf{V_t}$ vectors with different numbers of target clusters.

2.4 Experiment Setup

In order to test our system with first experiments, we asked four volunteers to use an internet browser in front of a screen, free to take their usual position during a work session with a laptop. The session included the navigation on the internet from the same web page of a popular news site. The dataset is being extended with the capture of user behaviour in relation to different types of sites (e-commerce portals, social networks, web search portals, and so on).

The kinect camera was placed in front of them and close to the monitor. It was asked to the users to act and browse normally according their usual behaviour. The captured values have been elaborated in real time to extract the face parameters and to evaluate the speed of the gaze movement at a given instant.

2.5 K-Means Based Clustering

The users have been using the browser without constraints for approximately 2400 seconds, recording the location of the observed points, the six coefficients of facial expression, and a thumbnail image of the observed regions. The dataset is composed of 6659 acquisitions of the parameters of interest. For this experiment setup, only the six coefficients and the module of velocity of observed location are used to identify the user. Ten sequential instants of these parameters are grouped to create input vector of size of 70 to perform k-means clustering [17].

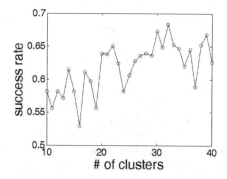

Fig. 3. This figure shows the accuracy rate to vary the cluster numbers

For the training phase sequences of 600 consecutive elements for each user have been extracted (i.e. 2400 acquisitions of 6659) and were created the 2400 sequences considering a temporal window of ten samples.

After fixing the number of clusters, we have performed the standard k-means with a repetition of 10 for the random assignments of initial seeds. The clusters obtained were then labeled with the name of the user with the greatest number of occurrences of the recordings. The optimal number of clusters was obtained by analyzing the trend of the rate of success in the classification see figure 3, and is equal to 32 (corresponding to a success rates of 0.68). It is observed that with a cluster number greater than 10, there are many clusters that collect the data of a single user, while the remaining portion is often related to only 2 users, but with a clear predominance of a user relative to each other.

Always with the time window of 10 successive instants, test data have been associated with closest clusters according to the Euclidean distance. The users label associated with the nearest cluster is the one that is attributed to the test input, and can be compared with the correct label.

2.6 Results Evaluation

The success rate of classification obtained using 7 parameters recorded is around 68%, which is an encouraging result that warrants further in-depth testing.

Having chosen an approach based on a supervised k-means, allows us to search among the resulting clusters those that best identify a particular user. In this way we have typical behavioural patterns that may be the target of research to identify a user, or a class of users in case of wide-ranging trials. The identified pattern presents correct recognition rates that can reach over 90% in our experiments.

To determine the ore representative pattern (center cluster), we have created an index R that takes into account not only the true-positive rate, but also the probabilities P1 and P2. R is the index of representative of the cluster in relation to the user

$$R_u = P1_i * P2_i * (TP_i/N2_i) * 10^4 \tag{1}$$

where

$$P2_i = \frac{N2_i}{\sum\limits_{i=1}^{32}(N2_i)} \tag{2}$$

with $i = 1, ..., 32$ and $u = 1, ..., 4$

Table 1 shows the calculated values of the 32 clusters obtained in the trials. The first column shows the cluster id. The second one is relative to the label of the user who is present in greater numbers in that cluster. The third column shows L1, i.e. the percentage of that label with respect to all the labels in the cluster. The fourth column shows the percentage P1 of samples of the training set that belong to the cluster. N2 is the number of elements in the data set of tests that were considered to belong to the cluster. TP is the number of true positives detected. R is the index of representative of the cluster in relation to the user.

Table 1. Cluster Stats. The table is divided in two columns, on the left are shown clusters from 1 to 16 and on the right are shown clusters from 17 to 32. The 15th and 16th clusters are not calculable because no data from test set is present in the clusters.

Cluster	User	L1	P1	N2	TP	R	Cluster	User	L1	P1	N2	TP	R
1	1	0.87	0.124	103	0	0.00	17	3	0.64	0.061	67	10	1.43
2	1	1.00	0.016	4	0	0.00	18	3	1.0	0.011	145	130	3.44
3	1	0.67	0.052	13	0	0.00	19	3	1.0	0.063	51	15	2.22
4	1	0.94	0.028	131	131	**8.74**	20	3	0.95	0.049	410	231	**26.51**
5	1	1.00	0.033	53	52	4.03	21	3	0.54	0.040	193	183	17.05
6	2	1.00	0.015	159	42	1.52	22	3	0.72	0.018	76	0	0.00
7	2	0.96	0.021	120	29	1.42	23	3	0.84	0.025	124	0	0.00
8	2	1.00	0.011	197	126	3.34	24	4	0.88	0.014	39	35	1.17
9	2	1.00	0.009	232	208	4.28	25	4	0.92	0.016	655	622	**23.18**
10	2	0.71	0.026	81	27	1.64	26	4	0.74	0.022	234	161	8.37
11	2	0.73	0.020	84	50	2.40	27	4	1.00	0.035	32	18	1.50
12	2	1.00	0.026	63	41	2.49	28	4	1.00	0.024	283	253	14.14
13	2	1.00	0.028	105	79	5.19	29	4	0.85	0.038	134	88	7.94
14	2	1.00	0.044	229	194	**20.17**	30	4	1.00	0.060	150	137	19.35
15	2	1.00	0.043	0	0	-	31	4	0.62	0.005	7	7	0.09
16	2	1.00	0.004	0	0	-	32	4	0.91	0.014	74	34	1.10

2.7 User Distinctive Basic Dynamic Facial Expressions

In figure 1 are listed for each user clusters most representative according to the index R. The center cluster corresponding to it shows us the values of the related face configuration coefficients in the 10 consecutive instants. Starting from the element of the entire dataset that is more close to it, it is possible to recover the 3D configuration of the 87 points of the face and their temporal evolution. This set of values constitutes a kind of dynamic basic distinctive facial configuration of the user.

3   Conclusion and Future Works

The presented work demonstrates the potential of the detection of facial expressions with rgbd sensors available on the market today. In particular, in the context of user modelling we have demonstrated that it is possible to recognize the user's identity from his facial expressions and from what she/he observes on a monitor, without invasive measurements that limit the naturalness of her/his actions. The proposed approach uses k-means clustering, and a phase of the training on consecutive users movements, allow us to characterize the identity of user with near 90% of success rate. It is possible to identify patterns in order to have more accurate recognition, and to create prototypes of natural dynamics facial expressions of the user.

The possibility to characterize people through facial movement introduces new view on human-machine interaction, in fact, a user can obtain different contents according your mood, or a software interface can modify itself to keep more attention from a bored user.

The ongoing experimentation involves more extensive testing on a larger number of users, different types of software with which they interact, the possibility to integrate visual memory and the integration of the whole system in a defined cognitive architecture.

Acknowledge. Financial support of the research is partially given by "Ministero dello Sviluppo Economico e Innovazione (MISE), bando MADE IN ITALY", project MI01_00424.

References

1. Pantic, M., Patras, I.: Dynamics of Facial Expression: Recognition of Faci-al Actions and Their Temporal Segments Form Face Profile Image Sequences. IEEE Trans. Systems, Man, and Cybernetics Part B 36(2), 443–449 (2006)
2. Gaglio, S., Infantino, I., Pilato, G., Rizzo, R., Vella, F.: Vision and emotional flow in a cognitive architecture for human-machine interaction. Frontiers in Artificial Intelligence and Applications 233, 112–117 (2011); cited By (since 1996) 1
3. Infantino, I., Rizzo, R., Gaglio, S.: A framework for sign language sentence recognition by commonsense context. IEEE Transactions on Systems, Man and Cybernetics Part C: Applications and Reviews 37(5), 1034–1039 (2007); cited By (since 1996) 5.
4. Kelley, R., Tavakkoli, A., King, C., Nicolescu, M., Nicolescu, M., Bebis, G.: Understanding human intentions via hidden markov models in autonomous mobile robots. In: Proceedings of the 3rd ACM/IEEE International Conference on Human Robot Interaction (HRI 2008) (2008)
5. Infantino, I., Lodato, C., Lopes, S., Vella, F.: Implementation of a Intentional Vision System to support Cognitive Architectures. In: Proc. of 3rd International Conference on Computer Vision Theory and Applications VISAPP 2008, International Workshop on Robotic Perception (VISAPP-RoboPerc 2008) (2008)

6. Carroll, J.M., Olson, J.: Mental Models In Human-Computer Interaction. In: Helander, M. (ed.) Handbook of Human-Computer Interaction, pp. 135–158. Elsevier Ltd., Amsterdam (1990)
7. Infantino, I., Pilato, G., Rizzo, R., Vella, F.: I feel blue: Robots and humans sharing color representation for emotional cognitive interaction. In: Chella, A., Pirrone, R., Sorbello, R., Jóhannsdóttir, K.R. (eds.) Biologically Inspired Cognitive Architectures 2012. AISC, vol. 196, pp. 161–166. Springer, Heidelberg (2013)
8. Kelley, R., Tavakkoli, A., King, C., Nicolescu, M., Nicolescu, M.: Understanding Activities and Intentions for Human-Robot Interaction. In: Human-Robot Interaction. InTech (2010)
9. Orr, R., Abowd, G.: The smart floor: a mechanism for natural user identification and tracking. In: CHI 2000 Extended Abstracts on Human Factors in Computing Systems, pp. 275–276. ACM (2000)
10. Ben-Yacoub, S., Abdeljaoued, Y., Mayoraz, E.: Fusion of face and speech data for person identity verification. IEEE Transactions on Neural Networks 10(5), 1065–1074 (1999)
11. Bergadano, F., Gunetti, D., Picardi, C.: Identity verification through dynamic keystroke analysis. Intelligent Data Analysis 7(5), 469–496 (2003)
12. Turk, M.: Computer vision in the interface. Communications of the ACM 47(1), 60–67 (2004)
13. Aggarwal, J., Park, S.: Human motion: Modeling and recognition of actions and interactions. In: Proceedings. 2nd International Symposium on 3D Data Processing, Visualization and Transmission, 3DPVT 2004, pp. 640–647. IEEE (2004)
14. Kalman, R.E.: A New Approach to Linear Filtering and Prediction Problems. Transactions of the ASME–Journal of Basic Engineering 82(Series D), 35–45 (1960)
15. Microsoft: Face tracking,
http://msdn.microsoft.com/en-us/library/jj130970.aspx
16. Ahlberg, J.: TCANDIDE-3 – an updated parameterized face. Technical report, Dept. of Electrical Engineering, Linkping University, Sweden (2001),
http://www.icg.isy.liu.se/candide/
17. Basu, S., Bilenko, M., Mooney, R.: A probabilistic framework for semi-supervised clustering. In: Proceedings of the tenth ACM SIGKDD International Conference on Knowledge Discovery and Data Mining, pp. 59–68. ACM (2004)

Learning a Policy for Gesture-Based Active Multi-touch Authentication

Raquel Torres Peralta, Anton Rebguns, Ian R. Fasel, and Kobus Barnard

Universidad de Sonora, Departamento de Ingenieria Industrial,
The University of Arizona, Department of Computer Science,
Tucson, AZ 85721-0077
{rtorres,anton,kobus}@cs.arizona.edu,
ianfasel@gmail.com

Abstract. Multi-touch tablets can offer a large, collaborative space where several users can work on a task at the same time. However, the lack of privacy in these situations makes standard password-based authentication easily compromised. This work presents a new gesture-based authentication system based on users' unique signature of touch motion when drawing a combination of one-stroke gestures following two different policies, one fixed for all users and the other selected by a model of control to maximize the expected long-term information gain. The system is able to achieve high user recognition accuracy with relatively few gestures, demonstrating that human touch patterns have a distinctive "signature" that can be used as a powerful biometric measure for user recognition and personalization.

1 Introduction

Tabletop devices allow the interaction by touch using a comfortable interface highly visible to those individuals close to the display. This particular characteristic has made the authentication of a user a challenging task.

Currently, one solution is to use a password. However, a relevant issue with touch devices is the lack of privacy while typing characters. The same problem applies to a gesture-based authentication systems. The alternative then is to use special "signature" a user leaves unconsciously on the touch of the surface and within the gesture itself. But, does this special signature exists? To answer this question, we examined basic one-stroke gestures of 8 different users using different representations based on speed and shape with the goal of finding the features that differentiate one user from the rest when drawing a set of gestures.In this paper, we propose a new gesture-based authentication system for touch devices, which does not consist on a secret combination, but rather in the shape and speed when drawing a particular gesture. The authentication can be made after a series of gestures requested systematically and strategically by the system with no need of privacy. Although no high-precision equipment was used, it was possible to achieve high recognition rates after a few gestures.

L. Marinos and I. Askoxylakis (Eds.): HAS/HCII 2013, LNCS 8030, pp. 59–68, 2013.

2 The Experiment

The samples were collected at a business office, using a 36in x 22in multi-touch tablet in horizontal position (as a table). Gestures were restricted to an area of 20 x 20 inches on the surface. Within that constraint, participants freely performed the gesture the size they preferred using either hand. The data was captured using the Touchlib library. Eight participants had three sessions scheduled at different days and times (one participant at a time).

2.1 Procedure

The participants were between 24 and 33 years old. Four were male and four were female. They were asked to reproduce eight different gestures (Figure 1) over the tablet, including breaks to avoid fatigue. The samples were asked to be provided sequentially (The participant performed the same gesture a number of times before passing to the next one) and randomly (The gestures were performed in an unordered sequence).

G1	G2	G3	G4	G5	G6	G7	G8

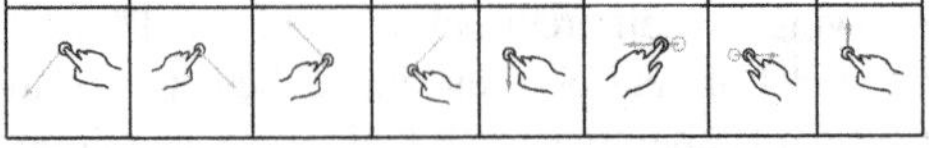

Fig. 1. Vocabulary of gestures. The gestures were selected considering the possibility of using them in different devices of different size.

The samples were collected using a multi-touch tablet using a frustrated total internal reflection (FTIR) technology, which is very sensitive to light pollution such as reflections from shiny clothes. Given the characteristics of the device, the trajectories captured are more susceptible to noise than other non-optical devices, exhibiting more detection of false-blobs not part of the gesture. In some cases the number of false blobs detected as part of the trajectory provided a noisy sample even after the noise reduction process. In general, we did not attempt to exclude such cases from the dataset, since the intention was to test the approach using the data as obtained from a real setting.

3 Data Representation

In this study, a gesture is a series of touches belonging to the same trajectory. Trajectories with less than 3 blobs are considered "orphan blobs" and were removed from our data to reduce noise. All samples were then resized to 30 points long using interpolation and smoothed with local regression using weighted linear least squares and a 2nd degree polynomial model. The smoothing was done using the rloess function in Matlab.

Our vocabulary of gestures consists of simple one-stroke gestures to identify the characteristics of basic movements. In order to extend the potential application of this study beyond FTIR multi-touch tablets, we worked only with x and y coordinates which represent 2D trajectories. We worked with two basic representations based on shape and speed.

1. Angle Representation. The trajectories were converted to a vector of 29 points, each one representing the angle between successive points. Giving a pair of points (x_1, y_1), (x_2, y_2):

$$Angle = \frac{arctan(y_2 - y_1, x_2 - x_1) \times 180}{\pi} \tag{1}$$

2. Speed. Since the system captures the data of the touch in equal time intervals, the speed at each time is represented as the distance between consecutive points along the trajectory.

A total of 34 samples per user per gesture were collected from the sequential and random sets. The trajectories included in this work were all restricted to five points long, leaving 25 to 29 samples per user per gesture after filtering. For training, 768 samples were randomly selected (12 per user-gesture), leaving the rest for the testing set, having a total of 1000 samples (13 to 17 per user-gesture). The results and procedures presented in this paper assume the accurate recognition of the corresponding gesture for every sample.

4 User Recognition Using One Gesture

We trained a multi-class SVM for each gesture (eight classes, one per user). The models were trained using LIBSVM [2], with RBF kernels with soft margins, with the kernel degree and margin slack variables determined empirically through 5-fold cross validation using a grid search, independently for each model. The model prediction is the Platt's probability output [8] of the sample belonging to each user. The predictions were 30% accurate for the angle representation, while speed achieved 34.3%. Assuming independence, the angle and speed probability distributions were multiplied to create the third representation of angle and speed combined, increasing the accuracy to 38%, which was still not acceptable.

Table 1. User recognition average results using speed representation for user 1 performing gesture 1. This user is predicted 70.5% as user 1, 17.6% as user 4, 5.8% as user 2 and 5.8% as user 7.

	User 1	User 2	User 3	User 4	User 5	User 6	User 7	User 8
User 1	70.6%	5.9%	0.0%	17.7%	0.0%	0.0%	5.9%	0.0%

The results suggest that some users share certain similarities in the way they draw the gestures. In Table 1, the results for user recognition using the speed representation for gesture 1 shows that user 1 is correctly predicted 70.5% of the time, but also is predicted as user 4 (17.6%), user 2 (5.8%), user 7 (5.8%), but never as user 3, user 4, user 5 or user 8.

5 Combining Gestures for Authentication

The results above suggest that user authentication can not be accurately achieved using just one sample of one-stroke gestures. Thus, we investigate a strategy of combining several gestures to reduce uncertainty over the user's identity. We observed that most users tend to be predicted as one or two specific users, and some gestures are more informative than others depending on the individual, which makes the order they are obtained an important factor to reduce the number of samples needed for authentication.

6 Multi-action Category Model

The SVM model outputs a probability distribution[1] over all classes (8 different users) for a gesture drawn by a user (similar to the sample provided by Table table:SpeedG1). When combining gestures, the probabilities could be multiplied to provide a result assuming independence. However, the independence assumption may be too strong. For instance, if a gesture is repeated by a user, then taking products of the SVM Platt's probability estimates would usually result in an overly high confidence for one user even if that user only gets slightly higher probability on each individual trial. These problems suggest an intermediate representation to deal with the lack of independence that allow the combination of several samples to increase accuracy in the authentication process.

A similar problem is presented by Regbuns et al [9], where an InfoMax controller has been implemented on a robot to identify objects.The acoustic similarities are represented by a Dirichlet distribution using a Latent Dirichlet Allocation (LDA) model [1]. This approach is implemented in the authentication problem to reduce the number of gestures needed during the process.

6.1 Semi-latent Dirichlet Allocation for an Intermediate Representation

In the user recognition problem, the similarities in the way users draw a gesture was the main reason of a low accuracy rate (users were predicted as one or two users who used to draw the gesture in a very similar way). Thus, it is important to explicitly model the fact that some users look somewhat like others under certain actions/gestures.In our framework we use the Platt's probability outputs obtained by the SVM multiclass model for user recognition to represent the correlations between one user and the rest when drawing a specific gesture. Then, a LDA samples a Dirichlet distribution of shape-speed correlations that can be used by an Infomax controller to learn the best policy per user. The Dirichlet distribution describes how latent clusters mixing proportions ϕ vary among a collection of samples. Originally, the number of underlying latent clusters is unknown and determined in the training phase according to the observations. If the number of clusters is known in advance, that can be used to an advantage, as done, for example, by Wang et al. [12]. The same approach is used in this work to train the model using the already known number of classes, specifically, the number of users.

---

[1] The multiclass model was trained and tested using the LIBSVM library which provides the Platt's probabilistic outputs [8], following the improved version provided by Lin et al [5].

In this model, ϕ represents the Platt's probability distribution of a sample from a specific gesture belonging to the different users.

The model parameters were obtained using the set of outputs of the user recognition model for the training set, with the angle-speed combined representation (section 4). The probability of generating probabilities ϕ by drawing gesture a by user i is

$$p(\phi|a, i) = \frac{\Gamma(\sum_{j=1}^{N} \alpha_{aij})}{\prod_j \Gamma(\alpha_{aij})} \prod_{k=1}^{N} \phi_k^{\alpha_{aik} - 1} \tag{2}$$

where $\alpha_{ai} = (\alpha_{ai1}, ..., \alpha_{aiN})$ are the Dirichlet distribution parameters over probabilities for user i under gesture a, and N is the number of classes, in this case, the number of users.

6.2 Handcoded and Learned Policies

A policy describes a particular order the gestures must be obtained during the authentication process. For this study, we define a handcoded policy where the samples are requested each of the eight gestures in turn, cycling if needed (G1, G2,...G8, G1, G2...). Also, we used a model of control to find the best policy to reduce the number of gestures required to authenticate each user on section 7. The LDA representation then was used for each gesture and the policies were tested separately on section 8.

7   InfoMax for Optimal Policy Learning

A handcoded policy could work well for some users, but not for all. One way to reduce the number of gestures needed to increase accuracy is to ask for the most informative gestures per individual. For this purpose we used Infomax, a model of control that maximizes the information gained about events of interest, used to model behaviors in agents [6]. In this work, Infomax is used to learn the best policy for each user. Following the approach proposed by Regbuns et al [9], an optimal policy for gesture selection can be found using the *Policy Gradients with Parameter Exploration* (PGPE) algorithm [11].

Let q_t be a d-dimensional vector combining the system's current beliefs about the user and its known internal state. Define the set of possible gestures $A = \{gesture\ 1,$ *gesture 2, gesture 3, gesture 4, gesture 5, gesture 6, gesture 7, gesture 8*$\}$. Then let the function $F_\theta : Q \rightarrow A$ be a deterministic controller with k-dimensional parameter θ which at each time t takes as input a state-variable q_t and outputs an action (gesture to perform) a_t. Then, q_t is the representation, constructed by $(p', c', \psi(t))$s where p' a vector of 8 elements representing the current beliefs of the system for each user, c' is a vector of counters for each gesture provided by the user ignoring order and $\psi(t) = (\psi_1(t), \psi_2(t), \psi_3(t))$ is a vector of Radial Basis Functions (RBFs) of the time t. The center of the RBFs are equally distributed over the specified number of steps (gestures provided for episode) and the learned policy relies on the completition of all steps. Let a history $h = (q_1, a_1, ..., q_T, a_T)$ be a sequence of T state-gesture pairs induced by using a controller with parameters θ. The reward at time t of history h is the scaled negative Shannon entropy of the belief distribution.

$$\mathcal{R}(q_t|h) = \left(\sum_i p_i^{(t)} \log p_i^{(t)} \right) \tag{3}$$

where $p_i^{(t)}$ is the system's belief of the current user being user i at time t.

7.1 Policy Learning

To find the parameters θ that maximizes the total reward over training histories, of length L,

$$\Phi(\theta) = argmax(Hmax - (E_h[\sum_{t=1}^{L} \mathcal{R}(q_t|h)p(h|\theta)])/Hmax) \tag{4}$$

Where E_h is the expected total reward over histories and Hmax is the maximum possible entropy, the *Policy Gradients with Parameter Exploration* (PGPE) algorithm [11] is used.

InfoMax policies were trained for 500 episodes of PGPE using the gesture-user specific Dirichlet distributions. The experiments were performed in simulation by sampling sequences called for by the controller. For each episode, a set of samples from all users were sampled, and the system's beliefs about the users were initialized to uniform. At each time step, provided the state vector q_t, an action is selected using the current policy. Each full learning trial of PGPE was repeated 20 times. The results show averages across 150 experiments. The software used for these experiments is based on the library developed by the Arizona Robot Lab, available online.[2]

8   Results

We compared the accuracy of the learned policies against the handcoded policy.and ran separate experiments for the two most accurate representations for user recognition, speed and speed combined with angle, to measure the improvement for each (see Figure 2). In what follows, the number of steps represent the number of gestures required during the authentication process.

8.1   Speed

The speed representation achieved 34% (average overall gestures) for user recognition. Using this representation, the handcoded policy reaches a 50% of accuracy after the first gesture (G1) while the learned policy has 64%. After 9 gestures, the Handcoded policy has 77% of accuracy and the learned policy gets 88% (Figure 2).

---

[2] The package can be found at http://code.google.com/p/ua-ros-pkg/. For the package documentation check http://ros.informatik.uni-freiburg.de/ roswiki/doc/api/ua_audio_infomax/html/index.html. The number of objects in the modified version is set to 1 and the entropy computation is modified as specified in this paper.

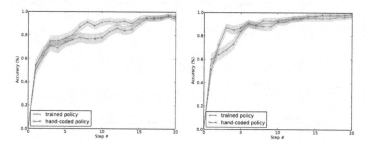

Fig. 2. Accuracy per step, hand-coded(red) vs learned policy(green) for both representations. The accuracy is averaged overall users.

Table 2. Classification Accuracy per Step for Speed Representation. The Number of Steps indicate the number of gestures provided by the user. The accuracy is expressed as an average percentage overall 8 users at the corresponding number of steps.

Number of Steps	1	4	7	9	11	13	15
Accuracy for Learned Policy	50%	75%	87%	88%	92%	92%	94%
Accuracy for Handcoded Policy	54%	69%	78%	77%	83%	84%	90%

8.2 Angle and Speed Combined

Recall that this representation had only 38% success in recognizing the user from a single gesture. In Table 3, the learned policy has 60% of accuracy while the handcoded has 50%. The diferences between both policies may not be large, but the learned policy shows a constant increment at each step.

Table 3. Classification accuracy per step for angle and speed representation. The number of steps indicate the number of gestures provided by the user. The accuracy is expressed as an average percentage overall samples from 8 users at the corresponding number of steps.

Step Number	1	4	7	9	11	13	15
Accuracy for Learned Policy	60%	73%	89%	93%	94%	95%	95%
Accuracy for Handcoded Policy	51%	85%	89%	88%	92%	95%	97%

User 3 has a high recognition rate. It is the one with a higher probability from the first gesture by the handcoded and the learned policy (see Figure 3). However, the latter has a higher rate from the first gesture following the best policy.

Contrary to the predictability of user 3, user 8 is not easy to recognize. The joint distribution following the handcoded policy favors user 8 after 11 gestures. With the learned policy, user 8 gets the higher value after only 3 gestures (G6, G1, G3) as shows Figure 4. The learned policy outperforms or ties the handcoded policy in almost every case.

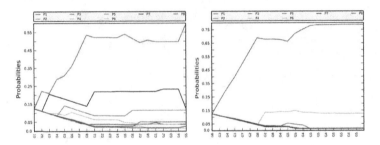

Fig. 3. Probabilities for the Handcoded policy using the Angle and Speed Combined Representation with samples provided by User 3. The X axis shows which gesture is provided while the Y axis shows the probability. The probability distribution shows User 3 as the highest after the first gesture.

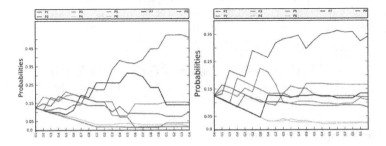

Fig. 4. Probabilities per step with the handcoded policy using the angle and speed combined representation with samples provided by user 8. The X axis shows which gesture is provided while the Y axis shows the probability. The handcoded policy (left) recognizes user 8 after 11 gestures while the learned policy (right) recognizes user 8 on the 3rd gesture.

9   Related Work

In the past, there has been interest in recognizing Tabletop devices' users. Some projects, such as the DiamondTouch table [4] and the IR Ring [10] have made use of extra devices to detect the origin (user) of the touch.

These approaches yield the problem that identifying a device is not the same as identifying a user, thus, anyone holding the device can be authorized.

Microsoft has implemented a gesture-based login for their TabletPC [3]. A user chooses a photo, and performs a sequence of secret getures which must be performed in the right order. Even when involving different levels of secrecy, the approach does not solve the shoulder surfing problem.

Because conventional approaches to user authentication have limited value when applied to collaborative multi-touch devices, there is a clear need to explore alternative methods. One recently introduced method [7] has been to include biometric data.

---

[3] Building Windows 8 - An inside look from the Windows engineering team. Signing in with a picture password. http://blogs.msdn.com/b/b8/archive/2011/12/16/signing-in-with-a-picture-password.aspx

The user places five fingers in the surface of the device and makes a rotation gesture. This approach is more than 90% accurate recognizing the user, and it confirms the existence of a singular signature in gestures that could make individuals differentiable, but the approach is not useful for small surfaces. A similar study using simple stroke gestures [3] showed that some users are harder to identify than others, as found in this work.

10   Advantages and Limitations

This method deals with the issue of similarities between some users on some of the gestures and the resulting lack of independence. The method also reduces the number of gestures needed based on the user. More generally, it provides a framework for this kind of problem that can be used with a number of alternatives for its components. For example, the angle and speed representations can be replaced by others. Also, the model's features could be different from outputs of an SVM as used here. Finally, other approaches to learning a good policy could be used instead of the one we chose.

One disadvantage of this method is that in some cases it could take a lot of samples to reach an acceptable probability about a user's identity (some users are harder to identify than others). One weakness is the limited number of participants, but the data is realistic, and notably samples for each user are hard to distinguish from the others. Since the number of users that share these devices is usually small, our experiments are informative for many applications. However, for deployment, data from a larger set if people is called for. In a future work, new representations must be tested and a different device, as a smart phone or a tablet, should be used to obtain cleaner data.

11   Conclusions

Authentication for Tabletop devices' passwords should not depend on a secret combination of characters or gestures, but on a private signature not subject for duplication. Our experiments suggest that authentication with a single one-stroke sample using shape, speed or both features is not enough, since some users tend to look alike from system's point of view. However, the combination of several samples can make possible the authentication of a user without the need of secret combinations. Having a Dirichlet distribution as an intermediate representation is a way to deal with the correlations between users. Also, an Infomax controller can learn the best policy to reduce the number of gestures required to obtain high recognition accuracy. The results showed that user authentication based on 2D gestures is a challenging task that might require more multidisciplinary studies (involving for instance, usability, psychology and even anatomy) to improve the results here presented.

Acknowledgements. We thank Federico Cirett and the Teknol company for their support during the data recollection process. This work was funded by ONR contract N00014-09-1-0658 and DARPA contract N10AP20008. Co-Author R.T.-P. was funded by a Conacyt Fellowship during this study.

References

1. Blei, D.M., Ng, A.Y., Jordan, M.I., Lafferty, J.: Latent dirichlet allocation. Journal of Machine Learning Research 3(2003) (2003)
2. Chang, C.-C., Lin, C.-J.: LIBSVM: A library for support vector machines. ACM Transactions on Intelligent Systems and Technology 2, 27:1–27:27 (2011), Software available at http://www.csie.ntu.edu.tw/~cjlin/libsvm
3. De Luca, A., Hang, A., Brudy, F., Lindner, C., Hussmann, H.: Touch me once and i know it's you!: implicit authentication based on touch screen patterns. In: Proceedings of the 2012 ACM Annual Conference on Human Factors in Computing Systems, CHI 2012, pp. 987–996. ACM, New York (2012)
4. Dietz, P., Leigh, D.: Diamondtouch: A multi-user touch technology. In: ACM Symposium on User Interface Software and Technology (UIST), pp. 219–226. ACM Press (2001)
5. Lin, H.-T., Lin, C.-J., Weng, R.C.: A note on platt's probabilistic outputs for support vector machines. Mach. Learn. 68, 267–276 (2007)
6. Movellan, J.: An infomax controller for real time detection of social contingency. In: Proceedings of the 4th International Conference on Development and Learning, pp. 19–24 (July 2005)
7. Sae-Bae, N., Ahmed, K., Isbister, K., Memon, N.: Biometric-rich gestures. a novel approach to authentication on multi-touch devices. In: Proceedings of the 2012 ACM Annual Conference on Human Factors in Computing Systems, CHI 2012, pp. 977–986 (2012)
8. Platt, J.C.: Probabilistic outputs for support vector machines and comparisons to regularized likelihood methods. In: Advances in Large Margin Classifiers, pp. 61–74. MIT Press (1999)
9. Rebguns, A., Ford, D., Fasel, I.: Infomax control for acoustic exploration of objects by a mobile robot. In: AAAI Workshop on Lifelong Learning. AAAI (2011)
10. Roth, V., Schmidt, P., G'uldenring, B.: The ir ring: authenticating users' touches on a multitouch display. In: Proceedings of the 23nd Annual ACM Symposium on User Interface Software and Technology, UIST 2010. ACM (2010)
11. Sehnke, F., Osendorfer, C., Rucksties, T., Graves, A., Peters, J., Schmidhuber, J.: Parameter-exploring policy gradients. In: Neural Networks, pp. 551–559 (2009)
12. Wang, Y., Sabzmeydani, P., Mori, G.: Semi-latent dirichlet allocation: A hierarchical model for human action recognition. In: 2nd Workshop on Human Motion Understanding, Modeling, Capture and Animation (2007)

Part II
Human Factors in Security

Studying the Effect of Human Cognition on Text and Image Recognition CAPTCHA Mechanisms

Marios Belk[1], Panagiotis Germanakos[1], Christos Fidas[1], George Spanoudis[2], and George Samaras[1]

[1] Department of Computer Science, University of Cyprus, CY-1678 Nicosia, Cyprus
{belk,pgerman,christos.fidas,cssamara}@cs.ucy.ac.cy
[2] Department of Psychology, University of Cyprus, CY-1678 Nicosia, Cyprus
spanoud@ucy.ac.cy

Abstract. This paper investigates the effect of individual differences in human cognition on user performance in CAPTCHA tasks. In particular, a three-month ecological valid user study was conducted with a total of 107 participants who interacted with a text-recognition and an image-recognition CAPTCHA mechanism. The study included a series of psychometric tests for eliciting users' speed of processing, controlled attention and working memory capacity, with the aim to examine the effect of these cognitive processes on the efficiency and effectiveness of user interactions in CAPTCHA tasks. Preliminary results provide interesting insights for the design and deployment of adaptive CAPTCHA mechanisms based on individual differences in cognitive processing since it has been initially shown that specific cognitive processing abilities of individuals could be a determinant factor on the personalization of CAPTCHA mechanisms.

Keywords: Individual Differences, Cognitive Processing Abilities, CAPTCHA, Efficiency, Effectiveness, User Study.

1 Introduction

A CAPTCHA (Completely Automated Public Turing test to tell Computers and Humans Apart) [1] is a computer program widely used today for protecting Web applications against automated software agents whose purpose is to degrade the quality of a provided service, whether due to misuse or resource expenditure. A typical example of a text-based CAPTCHA challenge (Figure 1) verifies that the entity interacting with a remote service is a human being, and not a machine, by requiring from a legitimate user to type letters or digits based on a distorted image that appears on the screen. Such a challenge is based on the assumption that a distorted text-based image can be easily recognized by the human brain but present significant difficulty for optical character or image recognition systems.

Research on CAPTCHA mechanisms has received significant attention lately with the aim to improve their usability and at the same time prevent adversarial attacks by malicious software. Researchers promote various CAPTCHA designs based on

L. Marinos and I. Askoxylakis (Eds.): HAS/HCII 2013, LNCS 8030, pp. 71–79, 2013.
© Springer-Verlag Berlin Heidelberg 2013

text- and speech-recognition challenges, and image puzzle problems [2, 3, 4]. Nevertheless, a variety of studies have been reported that underpin the necessity for improving the usability of CAPTCHA mechanisms [5, 6, 7, 8]. Results from a recent study, which investigated users' perceptions towards CAPTCHA challenges, claim that current implementations do not provide an acceptable trade off solution with regards to CAPTCHA usability [5]. Another large-scale study which evaluated CAPTCHAs on the Internet's biggest Web-sites revealed that CAPTCHAs are difficult for humans to solve [6].

LIFE

Fig. 1. Example of a text-recognition CAPTCHA

Taking into consideration that human computer interactions with regard to CAPTCHA mechanisms are in principal cognitive tasks that embrace to recognize and process information, we suggest that these interactions should be analyzed in more detail under the light of cognitive theories. Theories of individual differences in human cognition aim to describe and explain how and why individuals differ in cognitive abilities [9, 10]. In this respect, various researchers attempted to explain the functioning of the human mind in terms of more basic processes, such as speed of processing, controlled attention and working memory capacity [11]. *Speed of processing* refers to the maximum speed at which a given mental act may be efficiently executed [12, 13]. *Controlled attention* refers to cognitive processes that can identify and concentrate on goal-relevant information and inhibit attention to irrelevant stimuli [12, 14]. *Working memory capacity* is defined as the maximum amount of information that the mind can efficiently activate during information processing as an empirical model of cognitive functions used for temporarily storing and manipulating information [15, 16].

To this end, given that the aforementioned cognitive factors have a main effect on mental tasks, such as information processing, comprehension, learning, and problem solving [9, 15], we suggest that such characteristics should be utilized as part of an adaptive interactive system specialized in personalizing CAPTCHA tasks to the cognitive processing abilities of each user. In this respect we further describe the results and findings of a user study that aimed to investigate whether there is a main effect of users' cognitive processing abilities, targeting on speed of processing, controlled attention and working memory capacity, on the efficiency and effectiveness of different types of CAPTCHA mechanisms. In particular, a text- and an image-recognition CAPTCHA mechanism were deployed in the frame of an ecological valid experimental design, to investigate the effect of cognitive processing abilities of individuals towards efficiency and effectiveness with regard to CAPTCHA tasks.

The paper is structured as follows: next we describe the context of the empirical study and its methodology. Thereafter, we analyze and discuss the findings of the study. Finally, we summarize our findings and outline the implications of the reported research.

2   Method of Study

2.1   Procedure

A Web-based environment was developed within the frame of various university courses which was used by the students throughout the semester as an online blog for posting comments related to the course, as well as for accessing the courses' material (i.e., course slides, homework, etc.) and for viewing their grades. The participants were required to solve CAPTCHA challenges throughout the semester primarily before posting comments on the online blog. In particular, participants were randomly provided with different variations of CAPTCHA mechanisms (i.e., text-recognition or image-recognition). For example, in case a user solved a text-recognition CAPTCHA at time 0, the system would provide the same user to solve an image-recognition CAPTCHA at time 1 in the future with the aim to engage the whole sample with different types of CAPTCHA.

The text-recognition mechanism was developed using available open-source software that produced distorted images of random characters[1]. Furthermore, we have utilized Microsoft ASIRRA (Animal Species Image Recognition for Restricting Access) [3] as the image-recognition CAPTCHA mechanism that produced pictures and asked the participants to select the appropriate pictures belonging to a specific group (i.e., select pictures that illustrate cats among dogs). Figure 2 and Figure 3 respectively illustrate the text- and image-recognition CAPTCHA mechanisms utilized in the study.

Fig. 2. Text-recognition CAPTCHA used in the study

Both client-side and server-side scripts were developed to monitor the users' behavior during interaction with the CAPTCHA mechanism. In particular, the total time (efficiency) and the total number of attempts (effectiveness) required for successfully solving the CAPTCHA challenge were monitored on the client-side utilizing a browser-based logging facility that started recording time as soon the CAPTCHA challenge was presented to the users until they successfully completed the CAPTCHA task. For user identification, the Web-site further utilized the participants' username since the course's Web-site required user authentication for accessing the course's material.

---

[1] Securimage v. 3.0, http://www.phpcaptcha.org.

Fig. 3. Image-recognition CAPTCHA used in the study

Controlled laboratory sessions were also conducted throughout the period of the study to elicit the users' cognitive factors (speed of processing, controlled attention and working memory capacity) through a series of psychometric tests [9, 15, 16]. With the aim to apply the psychometric tests in a scientific right manner, we conducted several sessions with a maximum of 5 participants by following the protocol suggested by the inventors of the psychometric tests. The psychometric tests utilized in the study are described next.

Users' Speed of Processing Elicitation Test. A Stroop-like task was devised to measure simple choice reaction time to address speed of processing. Participants were instructed to read a number of words denoting a color written in the same or different ink color (e.g., the word "red" written in red ink color). A total of 18 words were illustrated to the participants illustrating the words "red", "green" or "blue" either written in red, green or blue ink color. The participants were instructed to press the R key of the keyboard for the word "red", the G key for the word "green" and the B key for the word "blue". The reaction times between 18 stimuli and responses onset were recorded and their mean and median were automatically calculated.

Users' Controlled Attention Elicitation Test. Similar to the speed of processing elicitation test, a Stroop-like task was devised, but instead of denoting the word itself, participants were asked to recognize the ink color of words denoting a color different than the ink (e.g., the word "green" written in blue ink). A total of 18 words were illustrated to the participants illustrating the words "red", "green" or "blue" either written in red, green or blue ink color. The participants were instructed to press the R key of the keyboard for the word written in red ink color, the G key for the word written in green ink color and the B key for the word written in blue ink color. The reaction times between 18 stimuli and responses onset were recorded and their mean and median were automatically calculated.

Users' Working Memory Capacity Elicitation Test. A visual test addressed storage capacity in short-term memory [15, 16]. In particular, the psychometric test illustrated a geometric figure on the screen and the participant was required to memorize the figure. Thereafter, the figure disappeared and 5 similar figures were illustrated on the screen, numbered from 1 to 5. The participant was required to provide the number (utilizing the keyboard) of the corresponding figure that was the same as the initial figure. The test consisted of 21 figures (seven levels of three trials each). As the participant correctly identified the figures of each trial, the test provided more complex figures as the levels increased indicating an enhanced working memory capacity.

2.2   Participants

The study was conducted between September and November 2012 with a total of 107 participants (52 male, 55 female, age 17-26, mean 22). Participants were undergraduate students of Computer Science, Electrical Engineering, Psychology and Social Science departments.

2.3   Analysis of Results

Overarching aim of the study was to investigate whether there is a significant difference with regard to time (efficiency) and total number of attempts (effectiveness) needed to solve a text- and image-recognition CAPTCHA mechanism among users with different cognitive processing abilities. For our analysis, we separated participants into different groups based on their cognitive processing abilities (limited, intermediate, enhanced) of each cognitive factor (speed of processing, controlled attention, working memory capacity).

CAPTCHA Solving Efficiency. A series of three by two way factorial analyses of variance (ANOVA) were conducted aiming to examine main effects of users' cognitive processing differences (i.e., limited, intermediate, enhanced) and CAPTCHA type (i.e., text- and image-recognition) on the time needed to accomplish the CAPTCHA task. Figure 4 illustrates the means of performance per cognitive factor group in regard with the speed of processing (SP), controlled attention (CA) and working memory capacity (WMC) dimension, and CAPTCHA type.

Results revealed that there is a main effect of the speed of processing and controlled attention dimensions on the time needed to solve a CAPTCHA challenge (SP: $F(1,424)=3.819$, $p=0.023$; CA: $F(1,424)=28.889$, $p=0.029$). On the other hand, no safe conclusions can be drawn at this point in time whether there is a main effect of working memory capacity of users on the time needed to solve a CAPTCHA challenge (WMC: $F(1,424)=1.172$, $p=0.311$) since users across all three groups did not perform significantly different in both types of CAPTCHA challenges. Accordingly, these findings suggest that speed of processing and controlled attention abilities primarily affect the users' interactions with CAPTCHA challenges, whereas in the case of working memory, results indicate that different capacities of working memory may affect performance, however not significantly. Such a result might be based on the fact that enhanced speed of processing and controlled attention is needed to efficiently focus a person's attention on the distorted characters among the added noise of current text-recognition CAPTCHAs, as well as the recognition of particular objects in image-recognition CAPTCHAs.

A further comparison between CAPTCHA types (text- vs. image-recognition) for each cognitive processing dimension revealed that users with enhanced cognitive processing abilities performed significantly faster in text-recognition CAPTCHAs than image-recognition CAPTCHAs (SP: $F(1,151)=12.155$, $p=0.001$; CA: $F(1,160)=13.751$, $p<0.001$; WMC: $F(1,142)=13.375$, $p<0.001$). On the other hand, users with intermediate and limited speed of processing and controlled attention, no significant differences were observed between solving efficiency in text- and image-recognition CAPTCHAs. In this respect, from a user-adaptation point of view, an adaptive CAPTCHA mechanism could recommend users with intermediate and limited speed of processing and controlled attention abilities an image-recognition CAPTCHA as an alternative security solution to the currently dominant text-recognition CAPTCHAs, with the aim to provide an improved user experience. In the same context, in the case of users with enhanced speed of processing and controlled attention, the adaptive CAPTCHA mechanism could recommend a text-recognition CAPTCHA given that users with enhanced cognitive processing abilities performed significantly faster in text- than in image-recognition CAPTCHAs.

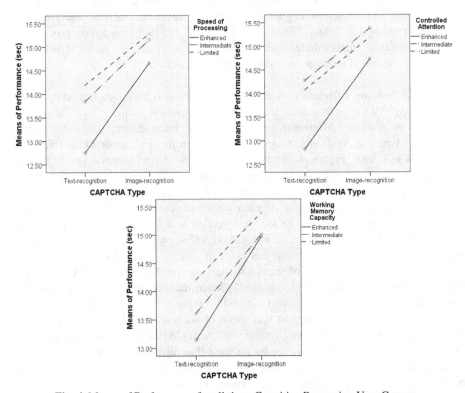

Fig. 4. Means of Performance for all three Cognitive Processing User Groups

Regarding the working memory capacity dimension, it is yet not clear whether it could be used as a personalization factor since results did not reveal significant differences between user groups for both types of CAPTCHA. In this respect, an adaptive CAPTCHA mechanism that would decide on a CAPTCHA type according to this user characteristic would not be able to clearly distinguish performance differences among groups of users.

CAPTCHA Solving Effectiveness. For each user session the total number of attempts made for successfully solving the CAPTCHA challenge was recorded. Table 1 and Table 2 respectively summarize the means of attempts per cognitive processing group (i.e., SP, CA, WMC groups) for each CAPTCHA type (i.e., text- and image-recognition). Shapiro-Wilk tests revealed that these distributions do not follow the normal distribution. In the case of text-recognition CAPTCHAs, on average, users with limited CA and limited WMC needed more attempts to solve the CAPTCHA challenges than the other two groups (intermediate and enhanced groups). The Kruskal-Wallis test revealed that the differences between controlled attention users was statistically significant (H(2)=9.167, p=0.001), as well as in the case of working memory capacity users (H(2)=6.464, p=0.039). In the case of the speed of processing user group, no significant differences have been observed between number of attempts of each user group, as the Kruskal-Wallis test revealed (H(2)=3.744, p=0.154), suggesting that this cognitive dimension might not significantly affect the effectiveness of CAPTCHA.

Table 1. Means of Attempts per User Group for Text-recognition CAPTCHA

	Speed of Processing		Controlled Attention		Working Memory Capacity	
	Mean	Std. Dev.	Mean	Std. Dev.	Mean	Std. Dev.
Enhanced	2	1.37	1.71	1.07	1.82	1.06
Intermediate	1.71	1.1	1.38	0.81	1.51	0.98
Limited	1.6	1.05	2.1	1.42	2.21	1.66

In the case of image-recognition CAPTCHAs, no significant differences in solving effectiveness have been observed between the user groups since the majority of image-recognition CAPTCHAs were solved at first attempt across all user groups, indicating that cognitive processing abilities might not primarily affect user effectiveness in image-recognition CAPTCHA tasks.

Table 2. Means of Attempts per User Group for Image-recognition CAPTCHA

	Speed of Processing		Controlled Attention		Working Memory Capacity	
	Mean	Std. Dev.	Mean	Std. Dev.	Mean	Std. Dev.
Enhanced	1.5	0.59	1.17	0.57	1.26	0.45
Intermediate	1.13	0.35	1.21	0.41	1.35	0.56
Limited	1.17	0.38	1.46	0.5	1.3	0.48

To this end, initial findings indicate that differences in controlled attention and working memory capacity might affect the effectiveness of text-recognition CAPTCHA challenges since users of the intermediate and enhanced user groups needed less attempts than the ones of the limited user groups. On the other hand, no safe conclusions can be drawn whether there is a main effect of users' cognitive processing abilities on the solving effectiveness of image-recognition CAPTCHAs since no clear differences have been recorded between solving attempts among user groups.

3   Conclusions

This paper reported the results of a three-month ecological valid user study that entailed credible psychometric-based tests for eliciting users' cognitive characteristics and two variations of CAPTCHA mechanisms (text- and image-recognition), with the aim to investigate whether individuals with different cognitive processing abilities perform differently in terms of efficiency and effectiveness in CAPTCHA tasks.

Initial results demonstrate a main effect of cognitive processing abilities primarily in solving efficiency of text-recognition CAPTCHA mechanisms. In particular, results revealed that users with enhanced controlled attention and speed of processing performed significantly faster than users with limited processing abilities in text-recognition CAPTCHAs. A comparison between text- and image-recognition CAPTCHAs revealed that users with enhanced cognitive processing abilities performed significantly faster in the text-recognition CAPTCHAs, however, users with intermediate and limited speed of processing and controlled attention did not significantly perform differently in text- than image-recognition CAPTCHAs. Given that no significant differences were observed in this case, users with limited and intermediate cognitive processing abilities could benefit with an image-recognition CAPTCHA than text-recognition. Regarding effectiveness (total number of attempts), initial findings indicate that differences in controlled attention and working memory capacity might affect the effectiveness of text-recognition CAPTCHA challenges since users with limited cognitive processing abilities needed significantly more attempts than the other two user groups. On the other hand, speed of processing has not affected the effectiveness of solving CAPTCHA since the differences among user groups were not significant. Furthermore, in the case of image-recognition CAPTCHAs, given that the majority of user interactions solved the challenge at first attempt, results suggest that cognitive processing abilities do not strongly affect image-recognition in these particular CAPTCHA tasks.

The limitations of the reported study are related to the fact that participants were only university students with an age between 17 to 26 years. In this respect, further studies need to be conducted with a greater sample of varying profiles and ages in order to reach to more concrete conclusions about the effect of individuals' cognitive processing abilities on their performance in CAPTCHA challenges. On the other hand, there has been an effort to increase ecological and internal validity of the research since the CAPTCHA tasks were integrated in a real Web-based system and the participants were involved at their own physical environments without the intervention of any experimental equipment or person.

The majority of CAPTCHAs utilized today on the Internet are primarily based on text-recognition challenges [17]. The results of this study suggest enhancing current CAPTCHA mechanisms to embrace both text- and image-recognition CAPTCHA challenges. Such an endeavor would have many positive implications on the usability and user experience of security-related interactions since adapting CAPTCHA challenges based on individual differences in cognitive processing could improve the effectiveness and efficiency of such tasks, minimize the users' added cognitive loads and learning efforts, as well as minimize erroneous interactions in CAPTCHA tasks.

Acknowledgements. The work is co-funded by the PersonaWeb project under the Cyprus Research Promotion Foundation (ΤΠΕ/ΠΛΗΡΟ/0311(ΒΙΕ)/10), and the EU projects Co-LIVING (60-61700-98-009) and SocialRobot (285870).

References

1. von Ahn, L., Blum, M., Langford, J.: Telling Humans and Computers Apart Automatically. Communications of the ACM 47, 56–60 (2004)
2. von Ahn, L., Maurer, B., McMillen, C., Abraham, D., Blum, M.: reCAPTCHA: Human-Based Character Recognition via Web Security Measures. Science 321(5895), 1465–1468 (2008)
3. Elson, J., Douceur, J., Howell, J., Saul, J.: Asirra: A CAPTCHA that Exploits Interest-Aligned Manual Image Categorization. In: 14th ACM Conference on Computer and Communications Security, pp. 366–374. ACM Press, New York (2007)
4. Vikram, S., Fan, Y., Gu, G.: SEMAGE: a New Image-based Two-factor CAPTCHA. In: 27th ACM Conference on Computer Security Applications, pp. 237–246. ACM Press, New York (2011)
5. Fidas, C., Voyiatzis, A., Avouris, N.: On the Necessity of User-friendly CAPTCHA. In: 29th ACM Conference on Human Factors in Computing Systems, pp. 2623–2626. ACM Press, New York (2011)
6. Bursztein, E., Bethard, S., Fabry, C., Mitchell, J.C., Jurafsky, D.: How Good are Humans at Solving CAPTCHAs? A Large Scale Evaluation. In: IEEE International Symposium on Security and Privacy, pp. 399–413. IEEE Press, Washington (2010)
7. Yan, J., El Ahmad, A.S.: Usability of CAPTCHAs or Usability Issues in CAPTCHA Design. In: 4th ACM Symposium on Usable Privacy and Security, pp. 44–52. ACM Press, New York (2008)
8. Hernandez-Castro, C., Ribagorda, A.: Pitfalls in CAPTCHA Design and Implementation: The Math CAPTCHA, A Case Study. J. Computers and Security 29, 141–157 (2010)
9. Demetriou, A., Spanoudis, G., Shayer, S., Mouyi, A., Kazi, S., Platsidou, M.: Cycles in Speed-Working Memory-G Relations: Towards a Developmental-Differential Theory of the Mind. J. Intelligence 41, 34–50 (2013)
10. Hunt, E.B.: Human Intelligence. Cambridge University Press, New York (2011)
11. Demetriou, A., Spanoudis, G., Mouyi, A.: Educating the Developing Mind: Towards an Overarching Paradigm. J. Educational Psychology Review 23(4), 601–663 (2011)
12. MacLeod, C.M.: Half a Century of Research on the Stroop Effect: An Integrative review. J. Psychological Bulletin 109, 163–203 (1991)
13. Posner, M.I., Raicle, M.E.: Images of Mind. Scientific American Library, New York (1997)
14. Stroop, J.R.: Studies of Interference in Serial Verbal Reactions. J. Experimental Psychology 18, 643–662 (1935)
15. Baddeley, A.: Working Memory: Theories, Models and Controversies. Annual Review of Psychology 63, 1–29 (2012)
16. Baddeley, A.: Working Memory. J. Science 255(5044), 556–559 (1992)
17. Bursztein, E., Martin, M., Mitchell, J.: Text-based CAPTCHA Strengths and Weaknesses. In: 18th ACM International Conference on Computer and Communications Security, pp. 125–138. ACM Press, New York (2011)

Relationships between Password Choices, Perceptions of Risk and Security Expertise

Sadie Creese[1], Duncan Hodges[1], Sue Jamison-Powell[2], and Monica Whitty[2]

[1] Cyber Security Centre, Department of Computer Science, University of Oxford, UK
{sadie.creese,duncan.hodges}@cs.ox.ac.uk
[2] Department of Media and Communications, University of Leicester, UK
sjp66@leicester.ac.uk, mw229@le.ac.uk

Abstract. *'Despite technological advances, humans remain the weakest link in Internet security'* [1], this weakness is typically characterised in one of two domains. First, systems may not enable humans to interface securely, or the security mechanisms themselves are unusable or difficult to use effectively. Second, there may be something fundamental about the behaviour of some people which leads them to become vulnerable.

This paper examines the links between perceptions of risk associated with online tasks and password choice. We also explore the degrees to which the said perceptions of risk differ according to whether the password user is a security expert or not, and whether they have experienced some form of attack.

1 Introduction

The security industry continues to evolve new solutions providing enhanced security. However, these solutions are often not fully exploited and increased security is often not realised. There is a widely held view that one reason for this is that the technology and/or processes are simply too difficult for humans to interact with effectively. Whether this is correct or not it is clear that understanding how humans interact with security systems is key to improving the use of security systems. In this study we consider the use of passwords, and how it might relate to perceptions of risk.

As society continues to exploit the opportunities provided by technology there is significant increase in services made available remotely (whether commercial, financial or government services). Within the corporate environment there is huge demand for the provision of enterprise services (e.g. business emails) remotely, enabling both remote working and access via mobile devices. These outward-facing services are typically secured via a username and password, hence usernames and passwords represent the *keys to your digital life* [2]. Human factors are key to understanding the choice of passwords [3]; despite the publicity and advice surrounding the choice of passwords, choosing **memorable**, long and strong passwords is difficult and unintuitive to humans [4]. For many there is a temptation to choose a single very strong password and reuse this across many services; Brown et al. [5] found that around 7% of people use a unique password

L. Marinos and I. Askoxylakis (Eds.): HAS/HCII 2013, LNCS 8030, pp. 80–89, 2013.

for every service and 60% of passwords are used for another service. For these reasons, passwords are demonstrably not fit for the purpose of securing the large number of online personas we all sustain. However, passwords continue to be pivotal in securing not just our digital life but, in this connected-age our natural life too.

Enterprise portals continue to be secured with simple usernames and passwords, relying on the ability of the users to provide significant levels of protection to the enterprise (whether reputational, intellectual-property, or tangible fiscal assets). Whenever an enterprise engages in an activity, whether online or in the natural-world, they perform a risk assessment. From this risk assessment it is possible to analyse the best way to mitigate this risk [6]. Indeed, passwords are almost always used as an essential element of access control, which is fundamental to any form of information or network security. We subconsciously engage in these risk assessments throughout our daily lives, (e.g. deciding whether to fight or flee or choosing a place to cross the road) [7]. If an incorrect risk assessment is performed then the process employed to mitigate this risk (in most cases one or more security processes) will often be inappropriate for the given situation [8]. In the findings reported here we examine the non-expert's ability to perform risk assessments in different environments and whether there might be links between risk perception and password choice.

In this study we explored four main research hypotheses:

1. There is no significant difference between the opinion of security experts and non-experts in levels of risk associated with offline activities (e.g. leaving a car unlocked in a city centre car park).
2. There is a significant difference between opinion of security experts and non-experts in levels of risk associated with online activities.
3. Non-experts who have had their security compromised consider the likelihood and impact of the event occurring to be higher.
4. Those non-experts whose risk assessments differed from experts choose passwords that are of a lower quality, since in general they are likely to undervalue password choice as a risk mitigation strategy.

It is inappropriate to argue an individual's risk assessment is 'right' or 'wrong'. However, we can compare the risk assessments performed by a group recruited from the general public to that of a cohort of experts who work in cyber security to see if we can explain weak password choice in non-experts as resulting from a different perception of risk to the experts who would normally recommend strong password choice.

2   Method

Data collection for the study was conducted using an online portal in which users were asked a number of questions. The questions dealing with risk and attack scenarios are described below. The users were also asked to create a password to allow them to continue the study later, and it was the quality of this password that was measured. These passwords were automatically assessed (following the protocol described below in section 2.3) before being salted, hashed and stored; this allowed the passwords to be metricised and yet stored as securely as possible. Respondents also participated in a further study surrounding password variability across different scenarios, allowing us to verify the password used for this study was representative of their normal choices (which we can confirm in accordance with the earlier findings of Brown et al. [5]). Given that we required data from non-experts and known security experts we recruited participants via two different routes. Fifty security experts were recruited via personal contacts including practitioners in industry, government and academia and fifty non-experts participants were staff and students of The University of Leicester recruited via an advert placed upon the University's weekly information email.

Below we describe the particular methods used to, a. compare perceptions of risk between experts and non-experts through common activities and threat scenarios and b. measure the strength of password choices.

2.1   Risk Assessments

In order to measure the risk assessments made by the participants they were asked to rate the level of risk they would normally face when engaging in of a number of activities, the risks were assessed on a scale of 1 to 5 (negligible, little, some, high and very-high risk). The following 20 activities were chosen as representing a good cross-section from cyberspace and the natural world. All participants were required to answer all the questions:

1. Online banking
2. Using Amazon to purchase items using a credit-card
3. Sending credit card details over email
4. Using eBay to purchase items using Paypal
5. Using unsecured WiFi in a coffee shop
6. Downloading and using pirated or cracked versions of software
7. Leaving your car unlocked in city centre multi-story car park
8. Using social networking sites (e.g. Facebook, LinkedIn) with open privacy settings
9. Using social networking sites (e.g. Facebook, LinkedIn) with closed privacy settings
10. Using photo sharing sites (e.g. Flickr, Instagram)
11. Geotagging content in Twitter or 'Checking-in' to a location on Facebook / Foursquare
12. Opening an email from an unknown sender
13. Leaving a credit card behind a bar to guarantee a tab
14. Clicking on a link in an email from an unknown sender
15. Using online dating services
16. Flying from the UK to the US
17. Using a cybercafe
18. Not updating your operating system (e.g. Windows, Mac OS X)
19. Not updating your web-browser (e.g. Internet Explorer, Firefox, Google Chrome)
20. Not updating other applications (e.g. Adobe PDF reader, Microsoft Office / Word, iTunes)

2.2   Threat Scenarios

All participants were asked to assess how likely they felt they were to face the following 13 scenarios (rated on a scale of 1 to 5 from very unlikely, unlikely, possible, likely, very likely), experts were asked to consider how likely the general public were to face the scenario.

1. Your computer, email account or data is hacked into and your identity is stolen
2. Your computer, email account or data is hacked into and money is stolen
3. Your computer or software is damaged and you lose work, pictures, music or data
4. Your computer is hacked into and used to either attack other organisations or to send spam
5. You are conned into going to a fake website and handing over personal information
6. You and your family's privacy is intruded upon or you are bullied
7. The government 'snoops' on your communication
8. Your employer 'snoops' on your communication
9. A neighbour 'hacks' into your WiFi to use your broadband
10. Your laptop or phone is lost or stolen
11. Your personal data is used to provide strongly targeted adverts
12. A web-based service holding your personal data is broken into by hackers and your personal data is released
13. Your email or social networking account is hacked and used to send phishing messages to your friends

The non-expert cohort were also asked to rate the impact of the given scenario (inconvenient, noticeable, severe) and whether they believed the scenario had happened to them before.

2.3   Password Metrication

In order to metricise the quality of passwords we focused on assessing the quality of the password in the context of a particular threat environment. Specifically, threats conducted using two types of attacks to which most members of the public are likely to be subjected to on a regular basis, these are brute-force attacks and dictionary attacks.

There are other attacks which we do not consider: those associated with compromised clients where static credentials are stolen (e.g. via keylogging malware) or those attacks associated with very capable attackers such as state-sponsored actors or highly-resourced Advanced Persistent Threats (APTs). The quality of the password is unlikely to have an effect on the users vulnerability to these attacks.

The most common attack on encrypted passwords are Time-Memory Trade Off (TMTO) attacks [9] such as rainbow tables. In order to metricise the 'cost' of cracking a particular password we can assess the size of the keyspace that needs to be explored in order to encapsulate the password. This keyspace can be trivially calculated from the alphabet required to encapsulate the password and the length of the password, and has a direct relation to the cost to the attacker. The larger the keyspace the more expensive (in terms of time) it is to create, index, and lookup using a rainbow table, and the more costly it is to efficiently store. Whilst some of these are one-time, initial costs the attacker will always have to make a cost-benefit analysis balancing the 'cost' of the keyspace against the success-rates (and ultimately benefit).

TMTO attacks assume users create passwords by randomly selecting characters from a characterset. In general, attacks will attempt to leverage some knowledge of the fact that the password was created by a human (so likely to have the weaknesses mentioned in the introduction), for example the password Password requires a keyspace of 54 trillion but it is an obvious and so easily guessable choice.

In order to measure relative strength of passwords we identify a password's resilience to these dictionary attacks. We score the password through comparison with a number of dictionaries. Many open-source hacking/cracking tools are distributed with dictionaries which can be used to crack hashes and compromise systems, these dictionaries provide a good indication of the capability of very low-skilled attackers. We employ dictionaries from two tools, those distributed with Cain and Abel and John the Ripper. We also use password lists released following data-breaches: the RockYou, PHPbb and Yahoo-Voice breaches. If a password appears on any of these lists or in either of the dictionaries it can generally be regarded as a very weak password and extremely vulnerable to many forms of attack.

3 Results and Discussion

3.1 Expert versus Novice Risk

In order to compare the two cohorts' perceptions of risk the kernel density function of the risk assessments for the expert and non-expert groups was considered for each question. Two examples are given in figure 1(a) and figure 1(b) below showing two activities where experts and non-experts agree and disagree respectively.

In order to evaluate the risk assessments associated with each question the two cohorts can be compared using a t-test in order to compare the distributions. Table 1 shows the comparisons between the two cohorts for every activity question, in addition to the p-value arising from the t-test. The p-value is the probability that the two samples are sourced from the same distribution, meaning that the two cohorts share the same perception of risk (for this question). Risk assessments of natural-world activities are shaded, a star in the p-value column denotes a significance of < 0.01, i.e. the cohorts are very unlikely to share the same perception of risk levels.

From table 1 it is clear that the risk assessments of our non-expert cohort were similar to that of our experts for 14 of 20 everyday activities. Of the six activities significant differences between the two cohorts 5 were associated with cyberspace and one with the natural world, the natural world activity being flying from the UK to the US (this particular difference is opinion is likely to be explained because the expert cohort are used to assessing risk in an objective, evidence-based manner rather than on an emotive or 'hype-driven' level [7]).

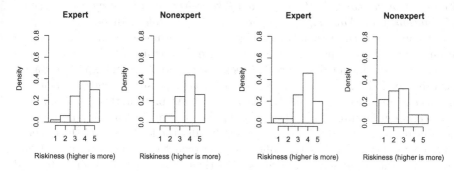

(a) Using unsecured WiFi in a coffee shop   (b) Not updating other applications

Fig. 1. Example distributions of respondents for two example questions

Table 1. Average risk assessments for each cohort

Question	Expert	Non-expert	p-value
Online banking	3.00	3.20	0.3295
Using Amazon	2.90	2.88	0.9031
Emailing credit card details	4.12	4.62	0.0033*
Using eBay to purchase items using Paypal	2.92	2.78	0.3662
Using unsecured WiFi in a coffee shop	3.88	3.90	0.9140
Downloading and using pirated software	4.40	4.38	0.9059
Leaving your car unlocked	4.12	4.46	0.0318
Using social networking sites with open settings	3.72	3.88	0.3762
Using social networking sites with closed settings	2.76	2.34	0.0050*
Using photo sharing sites	3.00	2.92	0.6262
Geotagging content or checking-in to a location	3.38	3.38	1.0000
Opening an email from an unknown sender	3.38	3.86	0.0310
Leaving a credit card behind a bar to guarantee a tab	3.32	3.82	0.0124
Clicking on a link in an email from an unknown sender	4.24	4.48	0.1398
Using online dating services	3.20	3.48	0.0875
Flying from the UK to the US	1.86	2.36	0.0080*
Using a cybercafe	3.06	2.94	0.4905
Not updating your operating system	3.96	2.90	1.1380e-06*
Not updating your web-browser	3.96	2.94	1.6333e-06*
Not updating other applications	3.74	2.50	8.8584e-08*

The experts and non-experts agree on a number of online risky activities, such as clicking on a link in an email from an unknown sender. We believe this indicates that the non-expert cohort has been educated in basic security practices. The three activities where the two cohorts differ the most are surrounding patching and updating software, particularly applications other than the operating system and web browser (the examples in the survey were Adobe PDF reader and Microsoft Office). This suggests that there is still more education required to highlight the risks associated with these types of activities.

3.2 Effect of Past Experiences

Considering the likelihood of the scenarios shown in section 2.2 we note that there were a relatively small number of scenarios which engendered a significantly different response from the expert and non-expert cohorts. Two scenarios were of note: *'You are conned into going to a fake website and handing over personal information'* and *'Your laptop or phone is lost or stolen'*. In both, the expert cohort considered the scenario more likely than the non-experts. This may be because experts are exposed to more incidences by virtue of their career.

The most significant difference between the expert and non-expert scenarios was the question *'A web-based service holding your personal data is broken into by hackers and your personal data is released'*. At present this is becoming a more common feature of the threat landscape [10], again this may be because the education of the public may be lagging behind the knowledge of the experts.

Of particular interest is the difference between the scenario likelihood and impact for those participants who believe themselves to have been subjected to that attack versus those who do not. We consider the four scenarios which had the most self-reported non-expert victims: *Your computer or software is damaged and you lose work, pictures, music or data* (42% of respondents), *Your laptop or phone is lost or stolen* (24% of respondents), *Your computer is hacked into and used to either attack other organisations or to send spam* (22% of respondents) and *Your email or social networking account is hacked and used to send phishing messages to your friends* (20% of respondents). There was no significant difference between the perceived impact of the attack scenarios between the two groups. This could imply that the cohort correctly measure the potential impact of a scenario before it occurs (although more research is required to validate such a claim). However, there were two scenarios where those who have not been victims believe the scenario is significantly less likely, shown in figures 2(a) and 2(b).

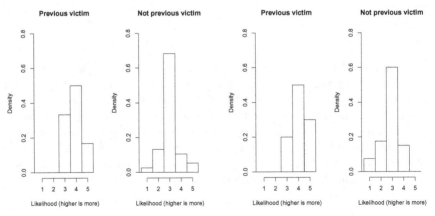

(a) Your laptop or phone is lost or stolen (b) Your email or social networking account is hacked and used to send phishing messages to your friends

Fig. 2. Effects of past experience when evaluating the likelihood of two scenarios

The first (having a laptop stolen) is likely to be related to optimism bias [11] which causes people to incorrectly assess the likelihood of some scenarios, particularly surrounding some crimes. The second may be due to it being a relatively new attack which is unlikely to be salient for those to whom it has not occurred.

3.3   Risk Perception and Password Strength

In order to explore the affect of risk awareness on password complexity we considered the questions which demonstrated a statistical significance between the expert and non-expert cohort, i.e. the six starred questions from table 1.

A vector of the average expert score in each of these questions was calculated to provide an average set of answers for the expert cohort. We then used the root mean square (RMS) error between this vector and the answers provided by any participant to calculate the 'distance' an individual respondent is from the average score of the experts. The kernel density of the errors from the two cohorts are shown in figure 3(a). As can be seen there is a clear difference between the two populations. The non-expert group shows a bimodal distribution with one mode showing an RMS error consistent with the expert group and one showing a higher error. We hypothesise that the mode with a lower error is related to a technically aware group within the non-expert cohort. There also appears to be one of the expert cohort who displays a higher error which would be more consistent with the non-expert cohort. From figure 3(a) it can be seen that the experts do not completely agree with each other; since the expert cohort is made up of experts from different fields it is not surprising they have slightly different views. However, 96% of the expert respondents had an RMS error of less than 0.5, hence, non-experts with an error greater than 0.5 can be considered to assess risk in a very different manner to the expert cohort.

When considering a security question, if two entities assess risk differently then we should expect them to attempt to mitigate those risks in a different way. Within the context of this study we can analyse the quality of the mitigation (measured by the password keyspace) associated with the non-experts, this is shown in figure 3(b). As can be seen there is a decreasing trend with a large spread, i.e. those non-experts whose risk assessments differ greatly from the expert risk assessment use passwords that have a smaller keyspace (are technically weaker). Hence, considering the password keyspace we can suggest that our final research hypothesis appears to be supported.

Of further note, we considered the non-experts whose passwords were present in the dictionaries described in section 2.3 we see no significant difference between the distributions of their RMS error (i.e. there was no correlation between the password being a word in a hacking dictionary and how the respondent assessed risk). This can be explained by a number of respondents who had very 'expert-like' risk assessments whose passwords, whilst demonstrating a large keyspace, were in the hacking dictionaries used. Choosing strong, high-entropy, memorable passwords is hard and hence people may gravitate towards common combinations of substrings.

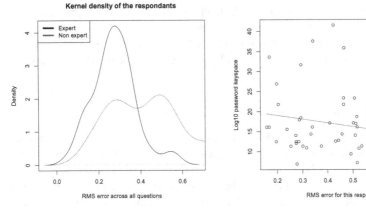

(a) KDE of the RMS errors   (b) Password keyspace versus the RMS error

Fig. 3. Effects of the RMS error surrounding the risk assessments

4 Conclusions

Considering our first hypothesis which stated that experts and non-experts would provide similar assessments of offline risks. We found that, in fact, they provided subtly different risk assessments. The shaded rows in table 1 show the offline risk assessments where the most significant difference was associated with flying from the UK to the US. We conclude that the expert cohort, due to their employment are used to assessing risk in an evidence-based manner rather than an emotive, hype-influenced manner, this allows them to make a more rational decision surrounding the risks associated with flying [7].

Our second hypothesis stated that experts and non-experts would show some difference between their assessments of online risk. In general, considering table 1 we found that the non-expert cohort provided similar risk assessments to our expert cohort. We conclude that the non-expert cohort have been educated in basic online security practices (indeed 94% claim to have an AV product which is kept up-to-date and 94% claim to be good at identifying phishing). However, it should be noted that we found significantly different appreciations of the risk associated with updating and patching software indicating more education is needed on the vulnerability and attacks associated with client applications like Office and PDF readers.

Our third hypothesis stated non-experts who have had their security compromised consider the likelihood of the event occurring to be higher, and consider the impact of the event as greater. We found no significant difference surrounding the impact - indicating that the non-experts were good at assessing the potential impact of a variety of security incidents (since they do not change their view after becoming a victim). We found two examples of difference surrounding the likelihood of the scenarios. The first being a natural-world incident (loss (or theft) of a laptop) which we can explain due to unrealistic-optimism or optimism-bias, where others are expected to be victims of misfortune [11]. The second concerns a relatively un-publicised form of breach, which the non-experts who had considered relatively rare - yet those who had been victims considered it significantly more likely, which may be related to the public embarrassment associated with this form of breach making the incident very memorable.

The final hypothesis focussed upon whether there was a correlation between the risk perceived and the quality of the passwords used. We analysed the non-expert participants and found a negative correlation between the similarity of the risk perceived by the average expert and the quality of the password, this goes some way to confirming the hypothesis. However, it should be noted that whilst there is a correlation there are some outliers and we cannot conclude that participants are making risk-based decisions when they choose passwords. Further work will explore the decision-making process and links between password choices and psychology.

References

1. Tam, L., Glassman, M., Vandenwauver, M.: The psychology of password management: a tradeoff between security and convenience. Behaviour & Information Technology 29(3), 233–244 (2010)
2. Get Safe Online (2010), Use strong passwords,
   http://www.getsafeonline.org/nqcontent.cfm?a_id=1127
3. Gehringer, E.F.: Choosing passwords: security and human factors. In: 2002 International Symposium on Technology and Society, pp. 369–373 (2002)
4. Herley, C., van Oorschot, P.C., Patrick, A.S.: Passwords: If Were So Smart, Why Are We Still Using Them? In: Dingledine, R., Golle, P. (eds.) FC 2009. LNCS, vol. 5628, pp. 230–237. Springer, Heidelberg (2009)
5. Brown, A.S., Bracken, E., Zoccoli, S., Douglas, K.: Generating and remembering passwords. Applied Cognitive Psychology 18(6), 641–651 (2004)
6. National Institute of Standards and Technology, Guide for conducting risk assessments. NIST special publication, 800-30 (2012)
7. Schneier, B.: Beyond Fear: Thinking sensibly about security in an uncertain world. Springer (2003)
8. Siegel, C.A., Sagalow, T.R., Serritella, P.: Cyber-risk management: technical and insurance controls for enterprise-level security. Information Systems Security 11(4), 33–49 (2002)
9. Hellman, M.: A cryptanalytic time-memory trade-off. IEEE Transactions on Information Theory 26(4), 401–406 (1980)
10. Trend Micro, TrendLabs Annual Security Roundup, a look back at 2011: Information is currency (2012)
11. Weinstein, N.D.: Unrealistic optimism about future life events. Journal of Personality and Social Psychology 39(5), 806 (1980)

Influence of Trust Assurances in Mobile Commerce Applications on the Formation of Online Trust

Martin Hesseler[1], Gerhard Hartmann[2], and Stefan Karsch[2]

[1] Centigrade GmbH
[2] Institute of Informatics, Faculty of Informatics and Engineering Science, Cologne University of Applied Sciences

Abstract. In this paper we investigate the influence of Trust Assurances in Mobile Commerce Applications on the formation of Online Trust. In comparison to existing measuring approaches we therefore developed a more detailed approach of capturing Online Trust. We carried out a study in which Online Trust was captured after an initial interaction with an unknown business partner in form of a fictional Mobile Commerce Application. The generated quantitative and qualitative data allowed for conclusions concerning the formation of Online Trust as well as the influence of Trust Assurances.

1 Introduction

In [1] Online Trust is defined as *an attitude of confident expectation in an online situation of risk that ones vulnerabilities will not be exploited.* According to [2] trust in online-environments is considered to be relevant to business success especially in the context of business-to-customer (B2C) relations. Beyond that we strongly agree with Riegelsberger et al. [3], that beside refocusing from the objective to *increase user's trust* **perceptions** to *enable correct trust* **decisions**, designing systems in order to allow for sound trust decisions could enhance an organization's socio-technical systems for more productivity and adaptability (cf. [4]). We consider Trust Assurances as potentially being able to contribute to such sound trust decisions.

Trust Assurances, issued by trustworthy entities, are controversially discussed in literature as possible key factors for the formation of online trust. Results found in literature span from a *higher online transaction expectations and stronger intent to purchase online* [5], to no *relationships between assurance seals and trust in e-retailers* [6].

The current prevalence of Smartphones and their ever increasing capabilities lead to a general movement of online activity towards mobile scenarios. In particular, this compromises commercial online activity, usually described as Mobile Commerce. Formation of Online Trust and usage of Trust Assurances in mobile commerce applications is complicated by additional parameters like volatile usage environments and the limited display capabilities of mobile devices.

L. Marinos and I. Askoxylakis (Eds.): HAS/HCII 2013, LNCS 8030, pp. 90–99, 2013.

This paper is organized as follows: we introduce a new conceptualization of capturing Online Trust, then report on a preliminary study we carried out, applying our approach of capturing Online Trust to given web-based systems. Subsequently we introduce the study environment and process we used for exploring the effect of Trust Assurances in Mobile Commerce Applications on the formation of Online Trust. Finally, we discuss the results and draw some conclusions.

2 Related Work

In [1] a high-level model of Online Trust is introduced. It distinguishes between external and internal factors contributing to Trust (as an attitude). External factors are *characteristics of the trustor*, the *object of trust* (more detailed: it's *navigational architecture, interface design elements, information content accuracy, seals of approval from organizations*) and the *situation* (including e.g. *the level of risk*). Internal factors within this model are: perceived *credibility*, perceived *ease of use* and perceived *risk*.

In [7] a measuring approach of Online Trust based on the three internal factors: *perceived Credibility, Perceived Ease of Use, and Risk* was developed.

[8] presented an extensive literature review on antecedents of trust in online transactions and services. They described three clusters of antecedents: customer/client-based, website-based, and company/organization-based antecedents. Customer/client-based antecedents contain propensity to trust, experience and proficiency in internet usage.

Zhang & Zhang [9] described a similar but more comprehensive approach by introducing Trust stages with Trust factors associated with each stage. They categorized the *antecedents* into: Trustor Factors, Trustee Factors, Trustee Website Factors, System Trust (subdivided into Situational Normality, Structural Assurance and Facilitating Conditions), Interaction and External Environmental Factors. In addition they integrated the *belief-attitude-intention-behavior* logic of the theory of planned behavior (TPB) [10]. The resulting Integrated Model allows for dynamic development of trust by being iterative. The final two-stage based factor explanation is composed of the above mentioned *antecedents* and the *belief, attitude, intention and behavior* logic. Additionally, the Model distinguishes between two stages (*initial trust stage* and *committed trust stage*) to show the influences of the factors in different stages of trust formation (see https://dl.dropbox.com/u/2653880/HCII2013/InfluencingFactorsTable.pdf).

Vermeeren et al. described a multi-year effort of collecting user experience evaluation methods [11] resulting in a list of 96 evaluation methods, which were categorized regarding scientific quality, scoping, practicability, utility and specificity. We analyzed the list with respect to our approach to capture online Trust.

In this paper we consider Online Trust as a subset of user experience, defined as *a person's perceptions and responses that result from the use or anticipated use of a product, system or service* [12]. The followings steps address the antecedents that form and influence online trust (as an experience) and that result from the use and anticipated use.

3   Methodology

In this paper we investigate the influence of Trust Assurances in Mobile Commerce Applications on the formation of Online Trust. Existing trust models for eCommerce focus on Online Trust in general. Therefore, we decided to develop a more detailed approach for capturing Online Trust in Mobile commerce Applications. Our approach utilizes the Integrative Online-Trust Model by Zhang & Zhang (see [9]) by applying User Experience capturing methods from [11] to the model's stages and factors, contributing to a resulting Trust Experience of humans while interacting with web-based systems. Based on this we designed an exploratory, descriptive study in order to investigate the influence of Trust Assurances in Mobile Commerce Applications on the formation of Online Trust (see 1).

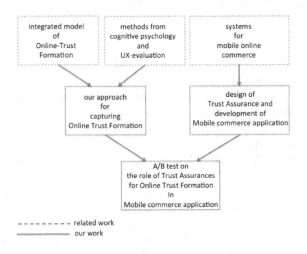

Fig. 1. Overview of our empirical study on the influence of Trust Assurances in mobile commerce applications on the formation of Online Trust

In our setup, Online Trust was captured after an initial interaction with an unknown business partner in form of a fictional Mobile Commerce Application based on the methodology described above. We expect that the resulting quantitative and qualitative data will allow for conclusions concerning the formation of Online Trust as well as the influence on Trust Assurances. In the first step we carried out a preliminary study (see 3.2) and then applied the resulting approach to a mobile eCommerce-system in order to investigate the role of Trust Assurances in terms of Online Trust formation (see 4).

3.1 Conceptualization

Our selected approach from [9] allows us to consider:

- which factors contribute to Online-Trust formation,
- how the Online-Trust formation process is related to a complete interaction cycle and
- what happens to Online-Trust when reusing an online-system.

We operationalized the *factors* of the Trust model [9] according to the semiotic approach of [13] to allow for the capturing of data related to Trust.

For the operationalization of the mentioned Online-Trust *factors* we used definitions of these factors from either [9] itself or related work. In the rare cases where no definition was found we performed a semantic analysis. Additionally we incorporated the stages from [9] according to [11] by dividing the questionnaire into three parts: questionnaire 1 - general information independent of the stages, questionnaire 2 - after an initial trust formation process, questionnaire 3 - after the overall service. The particular factors captured by each part are shown in figure 2.

Questionnaire 1 is captured independently of user interaction with the technical system, as the factors considered are independent of the usage of a product, system or service and thus independent of the stages. They are also considered to be quite stable concerning the formation of online trust and the two stages.

Questionnaire 2 needs to be captured directly after the initial trust formation process and before a first purchase. The data assessed here correlates to the initial trust formation phase. Questionnaire 3 needs to be captured after the whole service is completed. It correlates to the committed trust stage. A detailed view of the resulting conceptualization is available via https://dl.dropbox.com/u/2653880/HCII2013/Conceptualisation.pdf.

We revised the design of the capturing procedures in terms of completeness, construct validity and reliability. Since the majority of the capturing procedure delivers qualitative data, we decided to enrich the capturing process by video-audio logging and eye-tracking. Additionally, the laddering technique for a summative interview at the end of the human-system interaction process was applied. In our opinion these data potentially allow for the deduction of a cause-effect relationship in terms of a given User Experience.

Figure 2 illustrates the assignment of capturing procedures to the integrated model of online trust formation. The capturing process starts with questionnaire 1. Subsequently the participants perform predefined tasks using the interactive system, followed by questionnaire 2. Questionnaire 3 is used after experiencing the complete service (e.g. purchased product has arrived at the customer and payment has been completed).

3.2 Preliminary Study

We conducted a preliminary study in order to assess the practicability of our approach. We invited 26 subjects covering a selected sociodemographical range

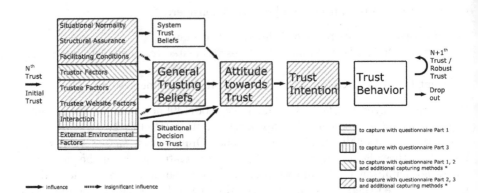

Fig. 2. Assignment of capturing procedures to the integrated model of online trust formation

between the ages of 18 to 62 and with different levels of computer literacy and online-purchase experience levels. The preliminary study was carried out as an in-vitro study using the usability-laboratory of our institute. We instructed the subjects on the background and process of our study and used fictional scenarios and existing real-world web sites. In order to ensure that the subjects had substantial interaction with the interactive systems before they where confronted with questionnaire 2, the subjects were asked to carry out certain tasks. The tasks were designed to capture the factors described in the initial trust stage and concluded with a purchase process. Questionnaire 2 was started right before the subjects were about to finalize their order (pushing the submit button), to capture the subject's attitude towards trust factors and not their resulting behavior. The preliminary study did not contain questionnaire 3 owing to the fact that the whole service needed to be experienced to answer the questions. Note that the preliminary study was conducted with german participants with the questionnaire in german language.

3.3   Results of the Preliminary Study

The results of this preliminary study showed that significant insight on the formation of Online Trust could be gained from the data resulting from the capturing procedure in order to better understand why users trust or don't trust interactive systems. It turned out that single *factors* could affect the resulting Trust evidently. To give an example: in one of the websites in use (Online Wine-Shop) an inconsistency in vintage between the textual and the visual label informations had a significant impact on the model-factor Perceived Information Quality. This significantly effected the resulting Trust formation negatively (distrust) for almost all subjects.

Overall: since we could draw on well established definitions for the majority of the *factors* (and the definitions often included indicators themselves) we rate the validity to be high. The questionnaires were found to be practicable, feasible in due time, the wording was understood by the subjects and qualitative and quantitative data from the capturing procedure (e.g. fixations from eye-tracking to verbal statements or comments within the questionnaire or the laddering technique) amounted to a reasonably consistent overall picture.

The captured data allowed for exploring causes and effects on the formation of Online Trust based on the features of the web-based system, the individual characteristics of the users (more precisely: their perception of the system's features) and the context of interaction (stages as well as iterated usage).

4 Approach to Integrate Trust Assurances in a Mobile Commerce Applications

We decided to use a third-party assurance because the intended app represents an unknown and unfamiliar vendor. [14] states that a "third-party assurance is unnecessary for vendors with a high reputation, while unknown vendors can enhance consumers' purchasing likelihood by obtaining EC third party assurance".

In [15] Moores writes "However, in order for privacy seals to be effective, B2C Web sites must display them more prominently so that online consumers can begin to recognize these graphic images and understand their function". Kim and Benbasat describe different *assurance delivery modes* in which a Trust Assurance can be presented [16]. They suggest the mode *easy access and easy return*, where a hyperlink is provided to access the Trust Assurance. The hyperlink opens a pop-up window. Minimal cognitive effort (such as one click) is required.

The Trust Assurance was integrated as can be seen under (see https://dl.dropbox.com/u/2653880/HCII2013/MobileCommerceApp-TrustAssurance.jpg). Based on the conventions of Android and similar mobile user interfaces this integration displays the possibility to access additional information on the Trust Assurance through direct manipulation. The visual representation of the seal was designed using the following steps:

– we analyzed existing and established Seals in order to develop design dimensions (i.e. rows of the morphological matrix) of a morphological matrix,
– we then created sketches for each separate design dimension and based on this, synthesized a final resulting design solution.

The final design of the Seal is shown in Figure 4. The color was used to implement a visual traffic light metaphor.

4.1 Execution of the Main Study

The questionnaires developed for Part 1 and Part 2 (see 3.1) were applied via structured interviews. The study was carried out with a group of 24 subjects.

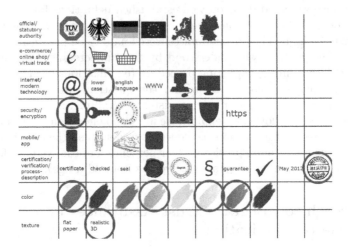

Fig. 3. Morphological Matrix of the Design Suggestion of a Trust Assurance Seal (translated in english)

Fig. 4. Seal of the Trust Assurance

Half of the subjects used the app without the Trust Assurance. Regarding the internet and online purchase experiences and the usage of a smartphone the group showed a high heterogeneity. Detailed data are presented in https://dl. dropbox.com/u/2653880/HCII2013/QuantitativeResultsTable.pdf.

The app as an interaction tool ran within an emulator of the Android operating system to allow the usage of a stationary eye-tracking system of the lab. The process was structured as follows: At first the task and further information were given to the subjects by the conductor of the study. The subjects received the following informations: 1) information about the task: completing the purchase of a magazine and getting an impression of the business partner; 2) financial information: the app is fictional, the subjects will not be required to pay real money and personal data is not stored; 3) information on usage of the IT environment, e.g. on touch gestures: touch gestures, navigational elements to use, input options to use, 4) information on available time: note that there is no time limit. We started with Part 1 (general information). After completing the purchase process the interview started with Part 2, with the questions referring to initial trust formation during interaction. Part 3 was not used in this study as this part is related to a summative assessment of the Trust attitude, *after the whole service is experienced* (i.e. purchased product arrived with the customer).

5 Results and Discussion

We gathered quantitative and qualitative data using different capturing procedures (questionnaires, laddering technique, eye-tracking). A detailed table of the results is accessible via https://dl.dropbox.com/u/2653880/HCII2013/ResultsMainStudy.pdf

The qualitative data proved to be crucial for an understanding of the formation of Online Trust, because they contain background informations and thoughts behind the ratings of the subjects.

The Table QuantitativeResultsTable.pdf (under the same URL-prefix as above) shows predominantly quantitative data. It distinguishes between the group of subjects which used the app version including the Trust Assurance ("results with TA", group 1) and the group which used the app version without the Trust Assurance ("results without TA", group 2).

The results from the questionnaire Part 1 show that we succeeded in dividing the subjects into equal groups concerning the attributes. T-tests showed that there is no significant difference for each *factor* at a level of significance of $\alpha = 0.05$. The demographic factors, the experiences of purchasing online, the knowledge of the internet, the technical environment and the general attitude towards trust and risk are quite similar in both groups.

The results concerning the interaction (questionnaire Part 2) show clearer differences. The following *factors* were higher rated by group 1 (with TA) than by group 2 (without TA). T-tests showed a significance for the *factor* **Perceived Security** at a level of significance of $\alpha = 0.05$. There was no significance for other *factors*. Concerning the Trustworthiness of the Business Partner (**Belief - Trustee is benevolent, of Integrity and Capable**) 16.7% of the subjects of group 2 (without TA) said that their business partner is not trustworthy. In contrast, 100% of the subjects of group 1 (with TA) said that their business partner is trustworthy. In addition, the *factor* **Attitude - The Trustee is Exchangeable** was 0.5 lower rated by group 1 (Business Partner is less Exchangeable). However, the result of the resulting intention to purchase showed that group 2 had a higher intention (difference: 0.17). Additionally, the subjects of group 1 rated the *factor* **Time Pressure** 0.25 points higher.

Due the inherent complexity of the term Trust, the quantitative data should not be interpreted without the consideration of the qualitative data. This is particularly true for *intention to purchase* which is influenced by subjective perceptions of all prior factors and thus represents a summative assessment. Qualitative data (subjects statements) reveal that factors may have some impact on other factors as well. The following link shows different reasons mentioned by the subjects for the specific extent of the formation of Online Trust: `https://dl.dropbox.com/u/2653880/HCII2013/QualitativeResultsTable.pdf`. A detailed description of the individual reasons is accessible via `https://dl.dropbox.com/u/2653880/HCII2013/ResultsMainStudy.pdf`.

The results show that the individual perceptions and individual assessments of the subjects are crucial for the extent of formation of Online Trust.

6 Conclusion and Future Directions

In this paper we introduced an Online Trust capturing approach offering a high level of detail. This approach (questionnaires related to the model's *stages* and *factors*, laddering technique, eye-tracking) allows for model-consistent interpretation of a resulting Online Trust attitude in terms of causes and effects. Based on the results of our study and in contrast to other publications, we prefer to use the term capturing instead of measuring. The term measuring in our opinion indicates a degree of precision, which is impossible to achieve when dealing with an attitude (Trust).

An approach to integrate Trust Assurances in Mobile Commerce Applications was developed. The Seal was integrated as an entry of the tab menu presented within a subarea of the app. On this basis we investigated the influence of Trust Assurances in Mobile Commerce Applications on Online Trust. The resulting quantitative and qualitative data allowed for conclusions concerning the formation of Online Trust as well as the influence of Trust Assurances.

The usage of the app in the study showed that 83.3% of the subjects who were given the option of using the Trust Assurance Tab did so. In addition, qualitative data showed that the presentation of the Trust Assurance was recognized positively by some subjects.

Findings regarding the perception of the Trust Assurance during an interaction with a Mobile Commerce Applications were based on data generated by the use of an eye-tracking system during the interaction of the subjects with the app. The analysis of the data showed that all subjects in group 1 (with TA) looked at the tab of the Trust Assurance at least once. Furthermore, the analysis showed that 16.7% of the subjects neither used the tab of the Trust Assurance nor the information tab (imprint, general terms and conditions, privacy statement). Detailed informations are available via the links mentioned above.

Results show that the influence of Trust Assurances can be explicit and/or implicit. The quantitative data indicates that there is a tendency of an implicit influence. Especially the *factor* Perceived Security, which showed a significant difference in the ratings of the subjects supports this interpretation. However, the individual experiences and attitudes as well as the individual aspects that are considered important by the subjects which are conscious and were explicitly mentioned during the interview, are crucial for the formation of Online Trust. We interpret the results according to this more or less obvious statement: The greater the importance the subject ascribes to Trust Assurance in general, the greater the impact of its presence or in fact absence on the formation of Online Trust.

In future, implicit (and subconscious) influences on the formation of Online Trust should be investigated, based on a larger sample size. We will also focus on *in-vivo* contexts of a mobile application by using eye-tracking glasses.

References

1. Corritore, C.L., Kracher, B., Wiedenbeck, S.: On-line trust: concepts, evolving themes, a model. Int. J. Hum.-Comput. Stud. 58(6), 737–758 (2003)
2. Joseph-Vaidyan, K.V.: Factors that enhance customer trust in e-commerce Web sites: An examination of e-commerce success metrics using Internet audience rating. ProQuest / UMI (2011)
3. Riegelsberger, J., Sasse, M.A., McCarthy, J.D.: The mechanics of trust: a framework for research and design. Int. J. Hum.-Comput. Stud. 62(3), 381–422 (2005)
4. Uslaner, E.: The Moral Foundations of Trust. Cambridge University Press, Cambridge (2002)
5. Kovar, S., Burke, K., Kovar, B.: Consumer responses to the cpa webtrust assurance. Journal of Information Systems 14(1), 17–35 (2000)
6. Kimery, K., McCord, M.: Third party assurances: the road to trust in online retailing. In: Proceedings of the 35th Hawaii International Conference on System Sciences (2002)
7. Corritore, C.L., Marble, R.P., Wiedenbeck, S., Kracher, B., Chandran, A.: Measuring online trust of websites: Credibility, perceived ease of use, and risk. In: AMCIS 2005, pp. 370–370 (2005)
8. Beldad, A., de Jong, M., Steehouder, M.: How shall i trust the faceless and the intangible? a literature review on the antecedents of online trust. Computers in Human Behavior 26, 857–869 (2010)
9. Zhang, X., Zhang, Q.: Online trust forming mechanism: approaches and an integrated model. In: Proceedings of the 7th International Conference on Electronic Commerce, ICEC 2005, pp. 201–209. ACM, New York (2005)
10. Ajzen, I.: From intentions to actions: A theory of planned behavior. In: Action Control: From Cognition to Behavior, pp. 11–39. Springer (1985)
11. Vermeeren, A.P.O.S., Law, E.L.C., Roto, V., Obrist, M., Hoonhout, J., Väänänen-Vainio-Mattila, K.: User experience evaluation methods: current state and development needs. In: Proceedings of the 6th Nordic Conference on Human-Computer Interaction: Extending Boundaries, NordiCHI 2010, pp. 521–530. ACM, New York (2010)
12. ISO: Ergonomics of human-system interaction - part 210: Human-centered design for interactive systems (iso 9241-210:2010) (2010)
13. Kromrey, H.: Empirische Sozialforschung: Modelle und Methoden der Datenerhebung und Datenauswertung. Uni-Taschenbücher M. Leske + Budrich (1994)
14. Noteberg, A., Christiaanse, E., Wallage, P.: Consumer trust in electronic channels: the impact of electronic commerce assurance on consumers' purchasing likelihood and risk perceptions. e-Service Journal 2(2), 46–67 (2003)
15. Moores, T.: Do consumers understand the role of privacy seals in e-commerce? Commun. ACM 48(3), 86–91 (2005)
16. Kim, D., Benbasat, I.: Designs for effective implementation of trust assurances in internet stores. Commun. ACM 53(2), 121–126 (2010)

A Comparison of American and German Folk Models
of Home Computer Security

Michaela Kauer, Sebastian Günther, Daniel Storck, and Melanie Volkamer

Technische Universität Darmstadt, Institute of Ergonomics, Germany
kauer@iad.tu-darmstadt.de

Abstract. Although many security solutions exist, home computer systems are vulnerable against different type of attacks. The main reason is that users are either not motivated to use these solutions or not able to correctly use them. In order to make security software more usable and hence computers more secure, we re-ran the study by Wash about "Folk Models of Home Computer Security" in Germany. We classified the different mental models in eleven folk models. Eight of the identified folk models are similar to the models Wash presented. We describe each folk model and illustrate how users think about computer security.

Keywords: (ACM classification)H.5.2 Information Interfaces and Presentation: User Interfaces evaluation/methodology, user-centered design; H.5.3 Information Interfaces and Presentation: Group and Organization Interfaces, collaborative computing.

1   Introduction

In the beginning of the computer era, computers were used by experts only and they were not connected to a worldwide network. Those experts were familiar with the use of the systems, knew the pitfalls, and knew how to protect their computers. Nowadays, computers and other devices, such as smartphones, are widely spread in Germany and nearly each and every household has a home computer. In contrast to the beginning, most users are not trained with the systems and have an incomplete mental model and knowledge of computer and Internet security many studies like [5, 6, 7, 8] show in different contexts. Correspondingly home computers are vulnerable against many different attacks with many different consequences, often although security software is used. Typical attacks against home computers are: malware infections while the consequence can be that users cannot access their data anymore or the computer is used as bot node in a botnet. The problem with security solutions is that they are often not usable and thus not able to protect users effectively e.g. because users configure the security solution in insecure way [2]. In addition, there is often a small timeframe after a new attack has been deployed and the security solution being updated. Such attacks can only be detected and fraud can only be prevented if users become more aware, too. This awareness can either be communicated by the

L. Marinos and I. Askoxylakis (Eds.): HAS/HCII 2013, LNCS 8030, pp. 100–109, 2013.

security solution or by independent trainings or information, e.g. on TV. However, both the more usable security solution as well as the awareness communication can only be successful if it takes the user's mental model and knowledge into account. Therefore, it is essential to understand users' mental models and group them in so called folk models, while folk models are mental models that are shared among several members of a culture [8].

In a first study Rick Wash investigated in a qualitative study the folk models on home computer security of North American home computer users living on the west coast. It can be expected that those model differ between cultures and therefore, this paper shows a re-run of the study in Germany and a comparison of the results. First, a short introduction to mental models in the context of Internet and Computer security is provided (section 2), followed by the description of the study methodology (section 3). In section 4 the results of our study are presented and compared to the results of the original study. The paper closes in section 5 with a discussion of the results.

2   Mental Models in Security

The idea to use folk models or mental models for a better understanding of user behavior in the security area is not new. Asgharpour and colleagues [1] used a closed card sorting to correlate security risks with mental models. For their approach they chose five existing mental models (e.g. physical safety, criminal behavior; cf. [3]) and instructed experts and non-experts to sort the security risks to the fitting mental model. The main finding of their work was the fact that experts and non-experts differ significantly in terms of their mental models. Therefore, the authors concluded that security advice should be adapted to the mental models of non-experts. Within their study they used predefined models, so that between 30% (non-experts) and 40% (experts) of the security terms were not categorized into the existing mental models. This is a clear hint that users do have additional/different mental models, which have to be identified.

One step towards the identification of occurring mental models for security was done by Rick Wash [8]. In his study about home computer security Wash [8] talks about folk models. In this context folk models are "[..]mental models that are not necessarily accurate in the real world, thus leading to erroneous decision making, but are shared among similar members of a culture"[8]. So it can be expected that if security software were designed to fit to folk models about possible threats, this software may have a decreased rate of unexpected behaviors for users. The study of Wash was conducted in America with 33 participants from a mixed citizenship. Overall, he indentified eight folk models that exist within the context of home computer security. Until now, no intercultural comparison was conducted to see if those folk models identified by Wash may be generalized. Within this paper the study of Wash was re-run in Germany and the results of both studies are compared.

3   Methodology

Aim of this study was a comparison to the original study of Wash [9] and thereby to re-run the study of Wash as similarly as possible. The interviews were conducted face-to-face or via Skype in two rounds that followed each other with about four weeks break in between. Within this break, the interview data of the first round was analyzed and scenarios were deduced that focused on critical results from round one. It was tried to interview as different people as possible (e.g. level of education, age, security knowledge, social background) in order to reach a wide degree of variation in the folk models.

In round one 17 people participated and in round two 9 people participated in the interviews. About 25% of the participants were female. They were aged between 18 and 60 years. As in the original study, those participants represent a part of the German population but are by no means representative.

The first interview round focused on all kinds of general home computer security risks. Participants were first asked about their security behavior in general (use of passwords, updating software, using security software), followed by questions about their knowledge about security threats (known threats, countermeasures, source of security problem) and ended with questions about specific security threats (viruses, trojans, etc.). Each interview took about 90 minutes. Based on the results of the first round, a second interview was developed which included three different scenarios about general and current home computer security risks that were derived from critical aspects and misunderstanding in interview round one. Those scenarios were:

1. A friend tries to log on into Facebook on their computer and recognizes malicious software on their PC.
2. They became a victim of a hacker attack.
3. The police notified them about a theft of their identity.

For all three scenarios, participants were asked what they would do, if they believe the scenarios can be true and why they were a targeted. Additionally, the questions about specific threats from interview round one were asked. Each interview took about 90 minutes.

For data analysis two matrices were built that categorized the answers of the participants given in the interviews and summarized them into groups. Then, two matrices were created extracting the mental models from the interview results and describing them shortly to get an impression about each mental model. To avoid subjective notions, statements were not categorized as correct or false. It is believed that mental models are simplified representations of the environment that are helpful for the person who holds them and it is seldom the case that a mental model is either correct nor false, but often partially both. In a final step, the results of this study were compared to the results of the original study. Note, pseudonyms are used in this paper.

4   Results: Folk Models of Security Threats

Folk models were categorized into models about Models of Viruses, Malware, Spyware and other malicious types of software and models of hackers and break-ins. Models were categorized as dealing with malicious types of software if the core of the model was about the functionality of the software. By contrast, models were categorized as dealing with hackers and break-ins if the core of the model was concerned with the person of the attacker. Each of the presented models was described by at least two participants and each of the participants had more than one folk model. Overall, 5 different models of viruses were found whereas 6 models for hackers and break-ins were identified. The next sections will present models of viruses.

4.1   Models of Viruses and Other Malware

Security threats within this group are all associated with the term "virus", but not all of the participants thought a virus is concrete software. However, they described it at least as a generic term of all kinds of software related to home computer risks like trojans, spyware, computer worms, and malware. Almost every participant mentioned at least two different folk models of home computer security, but not everyone knew how they work in detail and what they could do to decrease the potential threats. In general only a few had a lack of security consciousness, while the rest, who named more than one model, had been informed by media or more experienced friends. A majority knew what countermeasures they can use to be more secure.

Viruses Are Generically 'Bad'. The first model of viruses is based upon users' opinion that viruses are bad in general. The respondents described them as negative or annoying effects on their computers. All participants with this model were not sure how they can be infected by viruses, but mostly believed they could only catch a virus by visiting malicious or suspect websites or getting infected by physical media like USB flash drives. In all cases users agreed they have to actively download or execute the virus. For example Uma said "viruses come from dubious websites or links at Facebook", believing that if she does not click them, she does not get infected. In Olivia's opinion she can catch a virus by opening files on "infected USB flash drives" or "malicious attachments from spam emails". Users of this model are not in great fear of getting viruses with regard to their own behavior, but unlike the original study they all use anti-virus-software even if they never had a virus before because it makes them feel more comfortable. Paula and Julia have both had a virus (trojans), but did not know what the virus did or where it came from. They got informed by their anti-virus software which removed the Trojan automatically.

Viruses Are Buggy Software. A very common folk model is "viruses behave like buggy software". They often lead to computer reboots, corrupted files or total system crashes and always slow down the computer. Users can only fix them by re-installing their operating system. Respondents of this model usually believe those viruses do not have a special purpose and are just meant to annoy. Similar to the "viruses are generically bad" model, people thought to "catch" a virus they need to actively download or "click" a virus. Therefore, users feel mostly immune if they are careful and watch out in what kind of files they trust. Some participants said that viruses are often part of games or related things. For example, Xander, told us he can "catch viruses as part of game cracks, but thought they are not as bad as "normal" viruses so he will not stop downloading those programs. People who think viruses as some kind of "buggy software" are not sure about the purpose they have. Again, they all use anti-virus software and sometimes firewalls, because it makes them feel more comfortable.

Viruses Cause Mischief. The most frequent model is "viruses causing mischief". These mischief activities have a very wide spectrum of how they affect computers and what their intentions are. Some of the respondents named unusual pop-ups with advertisements (Fiona and Neil) or massive data loss (almost everyone) as visible effects of the infection. Participants corresponding to this model have a better understanding of what viruses do and often have concrete images of who could have created them. Quinn mentioned an interesting aspect: "viruses can cause damage to the computer's hardware", so he has to buy new parts like a new hard drive. To get mischievous viruses, it is not necessary to actively download and execute them. Users can also get them passively by "visiting suspect websites like pornographic sites" (Lewis) or "sites with manipulated scripts" (Walter). Respondents with this folk model use security software, but do not totally rely on it, because "anti-virus tools do not know every virus " (Gerrit).

Viruses Support Crime. Some of the respondents had the idea that viruses are part of criminal intents supporting organized criminals. The main goals of those viruses are identity theft, collecting personal data, opening backdoors for hackers and also extortionate robbery. Frequently this is combined with spyware like keyloggers to send the attackers passwords and other login information (Matt, Arthur). The model is directly connected to the models of hackers as professionals of criminal organizations. Most of the participants are worried about becoming victim of monetary robbery, but still Online-Banking is seen as very beneficial. Bob believed viruses often "take over [..]online banking or other financial accounts and automatically transfer money to criminals". Also if they got robbed by viruses most of them thought it would be their own fault and not the fault of Online-Banking in general (Xander, Walter). Participants in this group have a distinct sense of privacy and are afraid of someone stealing and abusing their identity. This abuse was defined in multiple ways: a lot of the attendees only think about collected addresses, names and various personal data (e.g. Xander), while others also believe Online-Banking accounts are real parts of their identity(Robert). A last aspect of identity theft is creating digital movement profiles which do not directly harm them, but lead to more individual advertisements on websites or, combined with collected/stolen addresses, to more precise spam. Thomas came up with viruses which can "encrypt important files" on computers, which can only be decrypted if you send the authors of the viruses money ("extortion"). Neil had the idea that some viruses were directly created by anti-virus software producers to convince more people to buy their security software.

Viruses Are Governmental software. A completely new aspect which did not occur in the original study, were viruses created by governments or secret services. These types of viruses "will be installed on your computer by policemen at house searches" (Robert) or "secretly placed by police hackers" (Bob). Those viruses are not easily categorized as good or bad. David had the opinion only criminals such as terrorists will be a target to find potential risks for mankind or illegal activities. Steven thought that governmental viruses are looking for people who are tax dodging, while Robert believed those viruses could target every citizen to observe them. As an example for this extreme point of view, he referred to the "Bundestrojaner" and "Staatstrojaner" (engl. Federal Trojan horse), which are tools from German police to possibly monitor everyone, even if they have not done any criminal activity at all. A different threat Robert had in mind when thinking of the "Staatstrojaner" was its abuse by criminals due to badly written software. He stated it would be possible to take over or put mischievous files to computers.

4.2   Models of Hackers and Break-ins

The second important category of folk models deals with "Hackers and Break-ins". All participants had an – more or less concrete - idea of what a hacker is and what he does. A hacker can be any kind of person who can somehow get access to a system to which no access permission is granted. It is often not obvious which person it exactly is or what things he does in order to break into a computer system. In any case, hackers are considered to be persons who break into a system and do something. Most of the participants thought about several types of hackers. For some of them it was really difficult to clearly separate different hacker models, because they often did not exactly know how hackers operate and where they come from. Even though most of the participants had no idea how a hacker can break into a system, they all believed it is possible. In their opinion, after a hacker has gained access to their computer, he can do whatever the users could do with their computer. Within this study six folk models for hackers were found. They describe who is believed to be the attacker, what his motivation could be and how they chose their targets.

Hackers Practice Their Hobby. One group of participants considered hackers to mainly be young technical "nerds" (i.e. Victor) and often "hobby hackers"(i.e. Kevin). When asked about the meaning of "nerds" participants described them as persons with a very good knowledge of computers and an addiction to them. The term "very good knowledge" was very generic but implied whatever it needs to break into a computer. Furthermore, they are very talented and intelligent (Olivia, Julia) and may be isolated, only having "little social competence" (Victor). Therefore they operate alone or only in small groups with only one or two other people. A "Hobby hacker" can be a "nerd" as well as a normal person who was not clearly specified. Some of the respondents believed that hackers break into systems in order to impress others, which was interpreted as a sign of their social incompetence. Some hackers (hobby hackers) were described to only break into systems "just for fun". Many participants also stated that hackers want to test their own skills and consider their break-in as a challenge. Olivia said "they hack into the school computer to delete or change grades". The effects of hackers' break-ins can cause annoying computer behavior or theft of personal data. Claus believed hackers always do damage and told us that damage does not implicitly mean "physical" damage, but rather theft of personal information. Stealing of personal files like photos is considered a threat which "happens in the background"(Paula) and is thereby hard to detect. In Steven's and Claus's case they had a look at their router logs and noticed that something undefined has gained access from the Internet. Often, victims do not know they are actually targeted, meaning they only discover any harm caused afterwards. Thus it is very important to prevent a break-in. In this model, hackers choose their victims by accident or people they personally know. Participants claim "it is very unlikely to become a target if the hacker doesn't know me". Most of them do not know how to protect themselves from hackers, because they do not know how a break-in works.

Hackers Are Intruders Who Break into Computers for Criminal Purposes. Another set of respondents believed hackers are criminal professionals that operate solo as well as in groups. They can be persons of all ages. Robert described them as "men from the 70s with long hair", whereas Ilias imagined "younger persons". Often a hacker was considered to be a male person. Some participants even believed that hackers come from a specific region. For example, Xander thought hackers are Asian or East-European people, whereas Neil believed they come from Russia. The hackers in this model are clearly criminal and very skilled. They are specialized persons with extensive computer knowledge. Break-ins are always conducted for criminal purposes, for that reason some participants stated "hackers operate solo so they don't attract attention" (Olivia, Fiona). These hackers often create software which can help them to gain access or is placed on the compromised computer. Some attendees reckoned that hackers develop and distribute their own viruses and afterwards break into the infected systems. Attacked persons are always victims of a crime. These crimes are mostly personal information theft and sometimes system damage. Personal information theft is always associated with stealing of sensitive information (mainly banking information like credit card or online banking account) which the hacker uses to come into money. Identity theft is also possible. Kevin said "hackers steal personal information to buy something online with someone else's identity". Few participants believed that hackers intentionally cause system harm. They break into the computers and intentionally delete files or cause the systems to crash. Even though it is not clear why the hackers do this, some participants thought it to be likely. Users with this folk model consider everyone to be a potential victim. Nonetheless they think it is very unlikely they could be a target because they do not think they have valuable information on their PC (Fiona). About half of the participants did not know what to do if they become a victim. The only thing they would do while they are under attack was to disconnect from the Internet or to shut down their computers.

Hackers Are Professionals of Criminal Organizations. This model is conceptually similar to "Hackers are intruders" and is also about hackers who steal users' personal information or intentionally harm computers. The difference lies in the way the hackers select their victims. Within this model, hackers are part of criminal organizations. They operate in organized groups with hierarchical structures. Four respondents called one of these organizations "the Internet Mafia"(Neil, Fiona, Lewis, Quinn). They had never heard whether an "Internet Mafia" exists, thus it is more their imagination of a structured criminal institution. Such criminal organizations consist of professional hackers and other criminal persons without computer knowledge. The "professionals" select their victims according to their expected value. "Stealing precious company secrets" was said by Lewis. Julia also believed they focus on "industrial spying or sabotage". But also "rich people with a lot of money" (Robert and Lewis) might be targets of those hackers. Additionally, groups of individuals who perfectly fit the criminal intentions, like: "building a network [botnets] for spam mails with home computers" (Kevin) might be attacked. Another reason given by Olivia was to "cripple public authorities". Subjects describing this folk model did not worry about these hackers because they did not consider themselves as worthy target and therefore did not aim to protect themselves.

Hackers Are Contractors Who Support Criminals. In this folk model hackers are contractors supporting criminals. They aim not at harming others but to make profit by selling stolen information or are engaged by criminal groups. While some of our participants thought "hackers are absolute computer-freaks acting solo"(Julia), some others perceived "hackers are small groups operating for big companies" (Neil). It is not distinct who they are exactly, but at least a combination of hobby hackers and intruders. The main reason why these hackers break into systems is to collect big amounts of personal and financial information which they resell to spammers or other criminal organizations. Zelda, for example, described the hack of the "Playstation Network" as a hack by a small group gathering credit-card information for some masterminds behind. Participants with this model mostly did not think they are directly a target, rather having an account on a big website which gets hacked (Lewis, Yvonne). For example contractors attack e-commerce companies like Amazon and eBay or financial institutions like PayPal or Online-Banking in general. Those who thought they could be a victim also believed they were only randomly selected (Eve, Paula). Hence the majority of the users are very careful about the private data they publish to online services, and use different passwords for each website to minimize the risk for more services to get compromised.

Hackers Are Governmental Officials. An additional folk model was the model "hackers engaged by governments and secret services". It is directly associated with the "viruses are governmental software" folk model. People with this mental model are often more deeply interested in computer security and politics. Due to the rising attention by reading about it in the news, also "normal" computer users are into this topic. Almost all of them had a raised concern about hacker groups working for their own government "to observe citizens" (Steven) and also supposed to defend against "cyber-war" (Robert) and online-terrorism(David), while Xander and Bob believed that governmental hackers also were the attacking party. In summary, all participants said that they only act if any type of suspicion of crime is going on. When asked about the term "government hackers", the majority responded they do not imagine very skilled hackers, but rather normal policemen with some kind of additional training in computer security and hacking. If people are concerned that they could be observed by their government, police or secret services, they only thought these hackers would create profiles and collect personal data. Neil had the idea that they could also hack into smartphones to produce movement profiles.

Hackers Are Stakeholders with Individual and Opportunistic Purposes. The last hacker folk model was hackers with opportunistic goals and targets. Those hackers are driven by their individual view on how the world should be, but may not be distinctly legal in all cases. Arthur and Kevin for example referred to "Anonymous" and "LulzSec" as stakeholders with arguable aims, but agreed they often operate in grey areas of law which may not be reasonable for everyone, "especially for governments". Another group of stakeholders named by Eve and Walter is the German lobby association "Chaos Computer Club" (abbr. "CCC"). This organized collective of hackers were described as primarily good people who want to help mankind by finding critical security vulnerabilities in administration or business systems without abusing them and "to point out deplorable circumstances in politics" (Claus).Although noted by a lot of participants, none of them were in fear to be targeted by stakeholders, since they are more interested in media-effective targets.

5   Discussion and Outlook

The participants of this study were widely interested in how they can protect themselves. But, "the vulnerability of home computers is a security problem for many companies and individuals who are the victims of these crimes, even if their own computers are secure." Within this study eight out of the eleven folk models were equal to those from the original study [8]. But additionally, three new folk models were discovered during the re-run of the study in Germany. Those models were "viruses are governmental software", "hackers are governmental employees", and "hackers are stakeholders with individual opportunistic purposes". It can be assumed, that those new models evolved due to the higher presence of the topic computer security in media during the last three years. For example, some well noticed events of the past few years were: governmental spyware, Wiki-leaks, Stuxnet (virus by a secret service), changing Facebook privacy and the German "Staatstrojaner". This indicates that users are concerned with current developments in IT security and the associated risks. Additionally, the new models show that this concern leads to new ideas about threats and that it is possible to influence the ongoing folk model by accurate reporting in the media. This fact could be used to actively change the folk models on computer security and thereby, not only promote more correct models but also promote appropriate countermeasures. Another source of those differences might be simple accounted for by the different cultural backgrounds in which the two studies were conducted. A good summary was mentioned by Politics & Policy: "[..] the E.U. generally allowing more rights to the individual. With no single law providing comprehensive treatment to the issue, America takes a more ad-hoc approach to data protection, often relying on a combination of public regulation, private self-regulation, and legislation." [4] Also the ongoing discussion in Germany about privacy policies of Facebook and Google may play a bigger role in the way the participants described their mental models. Seeing it from a cultural point of view there might be additional folk models out of the U.S. and Europe.

To develop the best possible security software it is necessary to consider those folk models to prevent misuse of it. The authors of this paper would suggest a two-step procedure: 1) Use media to arouse interest in computer security. In this step, it might be helpful to especially address those people who think that they do not need security software (e.g. people with the "hackers are professionals of criminal organizations" or "hackers are stakeholders" models) and inform about threats that might occur that are not person specific (e.g. botnets). 2). Design security software that emphasizes the potential dangers, gives action advices and supports self-reflection of security behavior.

Acknowledgements. We would like to thank Rick Wash, author of the original study, and our participants.

References

1. Asgharpour, F., Liu, D., Camp, L.J.: Mental models of computer security risks. In: Workshop on the Economics of Information Security (WEIS) (2007)
2. Balfanz, D., Durfee, G., Smetters, D.K., Grinter, R.E.: In Search of Usable Security: Five Lessons from the Field. In: IEEE Security & Privacy, pp. 19–24 (2004)
3. Camp, L.J., Wolfram, C.: Pricing security. In: Proc. of the Information Survivability Workshop (2000)
4. Hudson, K., Herr, T., Blanche, A., Cross, A.: The european union and internet data privacy. Politics & Policy publication, http://politicsandpolicy.org/article/european-union-and-internet-data-privacy
5. Johnson-Laird, P., Girotto, V., Legrenzi, P.: Mental models: a gentle guide for outsiders (1998), http://icos.groups.si.umich.edu/gentleintro.html
6. Liu, D., Asgharpour, F., Camp, L.J.: Risk communication in Security Using Mental Models (2008)
7. Raja, F., Hawkey, K., Beznosov, K.: Revealing Hidden Context: Improving Mental Models of Personal Firewall Users. In: Proc. of the fifth Symposium on Usable Privacy and Security, SOUPS 2009, Mountainview, CA, USA, July 15-17, pp. 1:1–1:12 (2009)
8. Wash, R.: Folk models of home computer security. In: Proc. of the Sixth Symposium on Usable Privacy and Security, SOUPS 2010, New York, NY, USA, pp. 11:1–11:16 (2010)

Health Is Silver, Beauty Is Golden?

How the Usage Context Influences the Acceptance of an Invasive Technology

Johanna Kluge and Martina Ziefle

Communication Science, Human-Computer Interaction Center RWTH Aachen University
{kluge,ziefle}@comm.rwth-aachen.de

Abstract. The acceptance of novel technology is one if not the most decisive component of the success of the technology rollout. Though, acceptance criteria differ not only across the diversity of users, but might also differ across the different usage context. This is especially valid for technologies in the health and beauty context, in which the balance between pro-using arguments and contra-using arguments is especially fragile. This paper focuses on the impact of the context towards the motivation to use an invasive technology. A survey was conducted in which 170 participants of a wide age range (17-89 years) took part. In the study, three different usage scenarios were presented (medical scenario, preventative healthcare scenario and beauty scenario). After an introduction into each scenario the participants had to evaluate usage motives and barriers. The results corroborated the impact of the situational context and the dependency of acceptance outcomes on the reasons for which technology might be used. Overall, acceptance was highest for medical technology and lowest for the beauty context. Considering the single reasons for or against the technology, we find that nature and weighing of perceived barriers and concerns are quite similar, independently of the context.

Keywords: invasive, usage context, motives and barriers, medical technology, beauty, cosmetic surgery.

1 Introduction

Acceptance is indispensable for a successful technology implementation in society. Therefore, technology acceptance research has become very important in the last years, especially in the healthcare section [1, 2].

The healthcare context is very sensitive for people, as it is connoted with attributes such as vulnerability and illness. Especially in times of demographic change, the need for technical and medical assistance is increasing. Due to increased life expectancy, more and more old and frail people will need medical care in the near future, while increasingly fewer people are able to take over the nursing [3, 4]. Thus healthcare devices have to meet many more requirements compared to e.g. conventional ICT-devices. Integration of the user in the development process of such technologies is indispensable for a successful implementation of a medical device.

L. Marinos and I. Askoxylakis (Eds.): HAS/HCII 2013, LNCS 8030, pp. 110–118, 2013.
© Springer-Verlag Berlin Heidelberg 2013

So far, acceptance research has provided rich information regarding the question under which circumstances users might accept information and communication technology in the working context. Regarding medical technology acceptance, there is much less information available, relating to the fact that the acceptance decision comprises more sensitive facets [5, 6]. Recent work in this area revealed that medical technology acceptance is a fragile concept, relying not only on individual factors (e.g. age, gender, culture, health status and technology experience), but also on the trade-off between perceived benefits and barriers [7-10].

Not only user aspects and perceived benefits and barriers are important to understand users' acceptance towards a technology. As several studies have shown, also the type of technology influences acceptance [11]. For example, very recently it has been shown that medical devices worn close to the body (e.g. wearables) or even implemented within the body (e.g. medical stents) are perceived controversial. One of the major reasons is a global fear of surgery and the concern about physical vulnerability [5]. When looking at the increasing frequency of cosmetic surgery, and the high willingness – especially among women – to accept surgeries for cosmetic and beauty reasons it is not easy to understand why the risk of surgery is so negatively biased in the medical invasive technology sector. It is therefore worth investigating in how far the usage context determines the refusal of invasiveness.

2   Questions Addressed

The empirical study dealt with in this paper reports on the impact of the situational usage context on technology acceptance, focusing on body-related invasive medical technology as an example. Different from previous studies, which showed the impact of user diversity [7-10], type of technology [11] and the difference between medical technology and information and communication technology [12], this study focuses on impact of using medical technology in a beauty contrasted to the health context. The aim is to show how the using context influences the evaluation of using motives and barriers taking an invasive chip as example.

Based on the fact that there is a global fear of surgery and the concern about physical vulnerability in the context of medical technology on the one hand, and an increasing frequency of cosmetic surgery on the other hand, three scenarios were chosen, in which participants had to evaluate the usefulness of one and the same technology in different scenarios: a medical scenario, second a scenario of preventative healthcare and third a beauty scenario.

Concerning the validity of the finding, it is of pivotal importance whether the acceptance towards a technology is examined in a sample with people who have already had a cosmetic surgery, because one could otherwise argue critically that people without would evaluate an invasive technology in a beauty context in a different way. This refers also to chronically ill patients, or patients who already use (invasive) medical technology. In order to get a valid sample, healthy people, people with a chronic disease and people that already have experience with cosmetic surgery were included in the sample. Thus the influence of users experience could be controlled.

3   Methodology

3.1   Procedure and Approach

A survey was conducted to evaluate the influence of different usage contexts on the motivation to use a medical device. Three scenarios relating to different situational contexts were introduced, in which participants had to evaluate the benefits and barriers of the same technical device in the respective using situations.

In the first scenario (medical scenario), participants were asked to assess their motivation to use an invasive medical stent to assist them in case of a chronic disease. The second scenario related to preventative healthcare. The participants were asked to imagine the use of an invasive chip for medical monitoring. In the third context the technology was used for beauty purposes. In this context the chip had several features for beauty purposes, e.g. to control weight or prevent hair loss.

3.2   Sample

170 participants (60% female) of a wide age range (17-89 years) took part in the survey. They responded to 16% of the participants had already had a cosmetic surgery and 17% of the sample reported to be chronically ill. The participants—invariably native German speakers—were recruited by means of posters in public places and partially by word of mouth using our existing social networks. Even though education levels across participants varied, the majority of the sample reported to be well-educated (high school level and above).

3.3   Questionnaire

The original questionnaire included a larger number of items. Here, just the relevant variables will be presented.

Independent variables The independent variables included mainly the demographic data, including age, gender, level of education, chronically diseases and if one has already had a cosmetic surgery.

Dependent variables The dependent variables consisted of using motives and barriers. The section 'using motives' comprised 14 statements that had to be answered on a six-point-scale Likert-scale (1 = total disagreement to 6 = total agreement). Items regarded different motives for the use of a chip in each scenario (e.g. absolute necessity, quality of living, staying mobile and safety aspects).

The section 'using barriers' comprised 13 items, which also had to be answered on a six-point-scale (1 = total disagreement to 6 = total agreement). The using barriers included a wide range of different aspects against the use of an invasive chip, such as worries about side effects, the fear of increasing dependency on the technology, and long-term risks.

The different motives were taken from focus groups interviews, which were carried out prior to this study. As the sensitive topic might be very controversial, evoking both, benefits and barriers at the same time, we were interested in gathering deeper insights in order to reveal individual argumentation and cognitions, which are more likely to be reflected in focus groups barriers [5, 7].

4   Results

The results of this study were analyzed by multivariate analyses of variance with a level of significance set at 5%. In order to control the influence of experience with cosmetic surgeries and chronic diseases, these two subgroups were compared with the results of the whole sample. For this reason, an analysis of variance was conducted. Comparing the results of evaluation of motives and barriers between the subgroups and the whole sample, results revealed no significant differences. Because of that, in the result section the whole sample is considered.

The result section has three main parts: at first, using barriers and motives were analyzed for the whole sample for which we summed up the single items of each context. Second, the single items of using motives and barriers were considered. Third, the influence of age and gender was assessed for all contexts.

4.1   Motives and Barriers

For the analyses of the using motives and barriers, first the sum of the single items was calculated for each context (see fig.1).

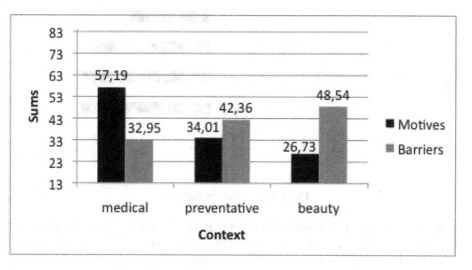

Fig. 1. Sums of motives and barriers in all contexts

As can be seen there, the using motives in the medical context show the highest agreement in average (M = 57.19; SD = 11.1), while the beauty context shows the lowest agreement (M = 26.73; SD = 13.0; N = 137). On the other side, the refusal as measured by the agreement to the barriers is highest in the beauty context (M = 48.54; SD = 13.3 N = 118) and lowest in the medical context (M = 32.95; SD = 10.3; N = 107). It therefore follows, that the using motivation in total is highest for the medical context and lowest in the beauty context.To answer the question if there is a general tendency to agree to the motives or the barriers independently of the context, an ANOVA (repeated measurements) was performed, showing a significant difference in the using motives depending on the context F(2,117) = 194.38, p =.00). The same significant result was obtained for the barriers F(2,120) = 71.37,p = 00).

4.2   Single Reasons for and against the Technology

Considering the single reasons for or against the technology, we find that nature and weighing of perceived barriers and concerns are quite similar, independently of the context (see fig. 2).

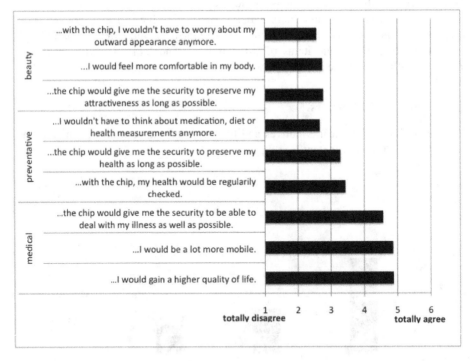

Fig. 2. Most important barriers

Across all contexts, it appears that worries about side effects (medical: M = 3.6, SD = 1.27, N = 137; preventative scenario: M = 4.1, SD = 1.31, N = 118; beauty scenario: M = 4.6; SD = 1.36, N = 107) and assumed long-term risk (medical: M = 3.4, SD = 1.36, N = 137; preventative scenario: M = 4, SD = 1.35, N = 119; beauty scenario: M = 4.5, SD = 1.36; N = 107) are the strongest arguments against using the chip. In the beauty and preventative scenario, another important using barrier is the fact that the chip is not evaluated as especially useful (preventative scenario: M = 4.56; SD = 1.35; N = 117; beauty scenario: M = 4.9; SD = 1.26, N = 107). In the medical context the fear of dependency on the technology is an important barrier for the test persons (M = 3, SD = 1.31; N = 136).

In contrast, the perceived benefits and hopes for technology usage differed considerably across using contexts. While in the medical context the most important using motives relate to the quality of living (M = 4.8, SD = 0.89; N = 136), staying mobile (M = 4.8, SD = 0.9; N = 136) and safety aspects (M = 4.66, SD = 0.96; N = 136), in the context of preventive healthcare health control (M = 3.44, SD = 1.51; N = 117) and the decreasing need of thinking about healthcare monitoring (M = 3.44, SD = 1.51; N = 117) are most important (see fig. 3).

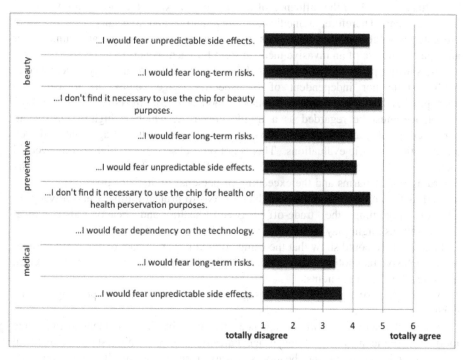

Fig. 3. Most important motives

Finally, in the beauty context, the most important usage motive are safety aspects (M = 2.77, SD = 1.62; N = 105), well-being (M = 2.74, SD = 1.66; N = 105) and decreasing worry about attractiveness (M = 2.57, SD = 1.15; N = 103). These results show that the worries and barriers about the technology are independent of the context. However, the ranking of the motives and benefits depends on the using context.

4.3   Impact of Gender and Age on Acceptance

Taking account the different user characteristics, we investigated the influence of age and gender regarding the evaluation of using motives and barriers in each context.

The analyses of variance showed that there is no significant influence of gender on the agreement with the using motives in each context. The same result was found for the using barriers. However, a correlation analyses showed a significant correlation between age and the using barriers in the preventative scenario ($r = -. 191$, $p < 0.05$). Thus, the younger participants of the sample reach higher values in the evaluation of the using barriers in the preventative scenario.

5   Discussion and Conclusion

This study focused on the influence of the usage context on the motivation to use an invasive stent. Therefore, a medical, a preventative and a beauty scenario were presented in a survey. The participants were asked to evaluate potential arguments for and against the use of an invasive medical stent for each scenario.

The starting point of the study was the assumption that technology acceptance is neither static nor independent of the specific usage context as it had been conceptualized in traditional acceptance models [15]. In contrast, technology acceptance must be regarded as a fragile construct, which is highly sensitive to perceived benefits and barriers of a diverse user group as well as usage-context driven and situation-specific evaluations. This is not only observable in highly controversial technologies, but also and especially in the medical sector. Here, humans' vital fears regarding bodily harms and the exceeding of personal limits is of pivotal importance as well as the consideration of individuals' needs to protect intimacy and privacy. In addition, regarding the trade-off between health and beauty, also ethical considerations might play a role.

In general we could show that the using context has an impact on the motivation to use an invasive technology. This applies for the using motivation and barriers overall, as well as for the single items.

As found, participants evaluate usage motives and barriers depending on the context.

It could be shown that the acceptance, measured by the agreement to the usage motives and the negation of the usage barriers, is overall highest in the medical scenario and lowest in the beauty scenario. Hence, the results show that the respondents were most willing to accept bodily harms and violation of body limits when this was necessary for the treatment of a chronic disease. Considering the evaluation of the single items, the most important arguments for the use of the invasive chip are security issues. Security was also the most important barrier, including the fear of bodily harms by a medical technology.

Considering the impact of gender, no significant influence was found. However, we found that age and the using barriers in the preventative scenario correlate significantly. From this it follows that younger persons are more likely to agree with the arguments against the use of a medical invasive stent for preventative purposes than older adults. This is probably due to the fact that younger people may not be as familiar with preventative issues as older people.

6   Limitations and Future Research

As the present study had a strong exploratory character, a number of research questions were uncovered. Still this kind of research, touching social and technical issues in the medical sector, is just at the beginning with many possible influential factors that have not been regarded so far. Even if the presented results are insightful, a cautionary note has to be considered regarding methodological specificity, and the basic vulnerability to artifacts. The results described and discussed here are based on a questionnaire method. Being asked evokes attitudes, which might reflect cognitions, and attitudes of participants, however, the gap between what humans think and what humans actually do is a well-known and vastly documented psychological phenomenon [16]. Future work should therefore integrate more experienced users of both contexts (i.e. older users and frail persons as well as people with experience in beauty surgery) in order to supplement the investigation of "anticipated usage scenarios" by "actual usage experience".

Another limitation regards the comparatively high education level. We cannot exclude that the findings can be transferred to persons with a lower education, and different values, norms and attitudes as well as another economic status which might impact the openness to medical technologies in both contexts, health and beauty.

In addition, the findings must be regarded as strongly culture-specific. The role of the body, the value of medical treatment or the possibility of beauty surgeries must be related to cultural and societal norms which are not only impacted by the mechanization level of a society, but also on the economic status and the well-being of citizens. Furthermore, even if gender was not revealed as a decisive factor in the sample studied here, it should be taken into account that gender roles and the conceptualization of interdependence and relatedness do considerably differ across countries and cultures, respectively. Finally, the extent of religiousness and the normative power of responding to religious norms in cultures could also represent a valuable research topic.

Acknowledgements. Authors thank volunteers for their participation in the survey. Thanks also to Sylvia Kowalewski, Kathrin Hippmann, Jutta und Martin Kluge, Victoria Wilkowska and Caroline Rordorf for research support.

References

1. Webster, A.: Innovative Health Technologies and the Social: Redefining Health, Medicine and the Body. Current Sociology 50(3), 443–457 (2002)
2. Jähn, K., Nagel, E.: E-Health. Springer, Berlin (2004)
3. Wittenberg, R., Malley, J.: Financing long-term care for older people in England. Ageing Horizons 6, 28–32 (2007)

4. Warren, S., Craft, R.L.: Designing smart health care technology into the home of the future. Engineering in Medicine and Biology 2, 677 (2007), http://www.hctr.be.cua.edu/HCTworkshop/HCT-pos_SW-FutureHome.htm

5. Wilkowska, W., Ziefle, M.: User diversity as a challenge for the integration of medical technology into future home environments. In: Ziefle, M., Röcker, C. (eds.) Human-Centred Design of eHealth Technologies. Concepts, Methods and Applications, pp. 95–126. IGI Global, Hersehy (2011)

6. Stronge, A.J., Rogers, W.A., Fisk, A.D.: Human factors considerations in implementing telemedicine systems to accommodate older adults. Telemedicine & Telecare 13, 1–3 (2007), doi:10.1258/135763307779701158

7. Ziefle, M., Schaar, A.K.: Gender differences in acceptance and attitudes towards an invasive medical stent. Electronic Journal of Health Informatics, 6(2), e13, 1–18 (2011)

8. Ziefle, M., Bay, S.: Mental models of Cellular Phones Menu. Comparing older and younger novice users. In: Brewster, S., Dunlop, M.D. (eds.) Mobile HCI 2004. LNCS, vol. 3160, pp. 25–37. Springer, Heidelberg (2004)

9. Alagöz, F., Wilkowska, W., Roefe, D., Klack, L., Ziefle, M., Schmitz-Rode: Technik ohne Herz? Nutzungsmotive und Akzeptanzbarrieren medizintechnischer Systeme aus der Sicht von Kunstherzpatienten. Deutscher AAL-Kongress "Assistenzsysteme im Dienste des Menschen. Zu- hause und unterwegs. In: Proceedings of the Third Ambient Assisted Living Conference (AAL 2010), January 26-27. VDE Verlag, Berlin (2010)

10. Searight, H., Gafford, J.: Cultural Diversity at the End of Life: Issues and Guidelines for Family Physicians. American Family Physician 71(3), 515–525 (2005)

11. Berger, J.T.: Cultural discrimination in mechanisms for health decisions: a view from New York. Journal of Clinical Ethics 9, 127–131 (1998)

12. Busch, T.: Gender differences in self efficacy and attitudes toward computers. Journal of Educational Computing Research 12, 147–158 (1995)

13. Ziefle, M., Schaar, A.K.: Technical Expertise and its Influence on the Acceptance of Future Medical Technologies. What is influencing what to which extent? In: Leitner, G., Hitz, M., Holzinger, A. (eds.) USAB 2010. LNCS, vol. 6389, pp. 513–529. Springer, Heidelberg (2010)

14. Arning, K., Ziefle, M.: Different Perspectives on Technology Acceptance: The Role of Technology Type and Age. In: Holzinger, A., Miesenberger, K. (eds.) USAB 2009. LNCS, vol. 5889, pp. 20–41. Springer, Heidelberg (2009)

15. Arning, K., Ziefle, M., Arning, J.: Comparing apples and oranges? Exploring users' acceptance of ICT and eHealth applications. In: International Conference on Health Care Systems, Ergonomics, and Patient Safety (HEPS) (2008)

16. Venkatesh, V., Davis, F.D.: A Model of the Antecedents of Perceived Ease of Use: Development and Test. Decision Sciences 27, 451–481 (1996), doi:10.1111/j.1540-5915.1996.tb01822.x

17. Festinger, L.: Theory of Cognitive Dissonance. Huber, Stuttgart (1978)

A Study Using TAM on the Recognition of Individuals' Privacy and the Acceptance of Risk

—The Case of Japanese Internet Users—

Ayako Komatsu

Security Economics Laboratory,
Information-Technology Promotion Agency,
The Research Institute of Economy and Trade Industry, Tokyo, Japan
`a-koma@ipa.go.jp`

Abstract. In this paper, a survey was conducted on the current status of social networking services (SNS) with an emphasis on privacy concerns, which are often deemed an obstruction factor in the use of such services on the Internet. Anxiety over personal privacy and other factors were analyzed based on the technology acceptance model (TAM). The results of the survey show that "perceived usefulness" scored highest with respect to SNS, although, on the demerit side, there were marked anxieties over privacy.

Keywords: TAM, privacy risk, SNS, Trust, SEM.

1 Introduction

There are a large number of Internet services related to social life and the economy. When users access these services, information such as purchase history and usage history may be accumulated by the service provider. The service provider uses these data to offer information that can improve convenience for the user; for example, by making recommendations. On the other hand, there are feelings of public unease when data on users are accumulated. If this uneasiness is not eliminated, the use of services that profit from such information may not advance, which in turn would hinder the creation of further new services and the development of a networked society. By clarifying attitudes and actions concerning the security and privacy of users, the Internet service environment can provide a sense of relief to users, and enhance the use of Internet services.

Privacy issues arise when information belonging to individuals (personal information) is used or provided to external entities in an undesired or unexpected way. The loss of privacy leads to the violation of three rights: "seclusion," the right to be invisible (not to be recognized) to others; "solitude," the right to be left alone; and "self-determination," the right to control one's personal information [1][2].

In Japan, the "Protection of Personal Information Act" was enacted in 2005. To comply with this law, many enterprises have imposed strict rules governing personal

L. Marinos and I. Askoxylakis (Eds.): HAS/HCII 2013, LNCS 8030, pp. 119–126, 2013.

information. As a result, some Japanese businesses have encountered difficulties in the appropriate use of personal information. In "Secure Japan 2008" by the National Information Security Center, it was stated that enterprises are exhausted by implementing and carrying out security measures [3]. Another aspect of privacy concerns is the recognition of the risks of providing personal data by the subject. This appears in the study on unease in the "White Paper on Telecommunications" published by the Ministry of Internal Affairs and Communications, which deals with consumers' anxiety regarding Internet privacy. It was reported that, in terms of Internet usage, "There is uneasiness regarding the protection of privacy information," and that this is a major concern (71.2%). Given this situation, it is essential to alleviate the privacy concerns of individuals, thereby enabling them to agree to the use of personal information. It is also very important for users and the service providers to trust each other, which could be achieved by clarifying the status of an individual's perception and acceptance of risks related to privacy.

2   Related Studies

Many studies have been made concerning aspects of privacy, such as privacy enhancement technology, privacy from legal or economic perspectives, and sociology, as listed in documents from a prime life project [4][5][6]. Privacy protection is also described in research documents from the viewpoint of recognition by the individual when using the Internet. There are several studies such as [7], which conducted a survey covering four countries, including Japan, that revealed that, compared to people from other countries, Japanese people consider it more risky to disclose individual information. The privacy concern of individuals with regard to direct marketing has also been investigated [8]. In return for the reporting of financial news, the consumer may willingly offer demographic data. In addition, there are situations in which an individual may offer information with pleasure if it saves time. Another survey has indicated that the media flair of the Internet has a negative influence on the recognition of risks in online purchases and that the recognition of privacy influences online transactions [9]. The European Union [10] conducted an informative survey in terms of a user's recognition of using new emerging services such as social networking services (SNS). This survey discusses four paradoxes: the privacy paradox, the control paradox, the responsibility paradox, and the awareness paradox. It is noted that paradoxes exist in cases in which individuals must select a service despite privacy concerns. Individuals solve such contradiction themselves and decide their preferences regarding privacy and other factors. This situation must be made clear for the efficient promotion of the use of personal data. To solve this issue, two main standpoints can be outlined: one focusing on personal interest, and the other on economic interest. Studies on privacy and economics have been conducted from the perspective of individual behavior, and research in this area, called privacy economics, has been performed [11][12]. [13] reveals the way in which people recognize risks by using the theories of time inconsistency, hyperbolic discounting, and self-control bias. In a case related to eID, the research [14] is an investigation of the relationship between the level of authentication technology and economic value. There is a study in which people are classified into three categories: privacy guardians, information sellers, and convenience seekers [15]. Another study [16] is a survey of the attitudes of Internet users, in which people disclose personal information in a trade-off against economic value. Unfortunately, few research has been conducted that scientifically conducts an investigative analysis on the privacy concerns of individuals in the Japanese online environment, as far as the author knows[17]. It is necessary to have knowledge of the recognition of privacy concerns, which varies from country to country, to investigate the state of privacy concerns in Japan.

2.1   Technology Acceptance Model

When a company deploys a new technology, it is important to analyze what kind of action is taken, and whether the action is regularity and modeled by users. The technology acceptance model (TAM) is widely accepted as being effective in this regard. "Perceived Usefulness" is the subjective expectation of the user who expects that use of a specific application system will raise the performance of work for a certain organization. "Perceived Ease of Use" means the extent of expectation not to take specific efforts regarding the use of the object system. "Intention" contains two factors, one is the extent to evaluate the willingness to use the system and the other is the intention to carry out the action.

Kim et.al conducted study of how a risk and a trust influence users' intention in e-commerce [18]. There, although a trust has influence of positive to intention, it is shown clearly that risk has influence with a negative as a result of investigation. In this paper, a hypothesis is built to unify a risk and a trust to TAM as shown Fig.1. In the hypothesis, we add confidence on the internet because it is considered that a new service such as SNS is influenced not by trust in specific service but by confidence on the Internet.

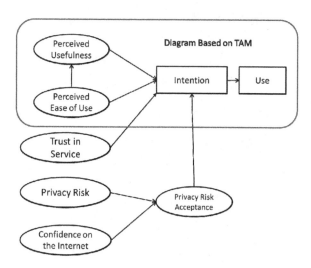

Fig. 1. Hypothesis Model and TAM

3   Survey on Recognition of Privacy Risk

According to TAM, it is necessary that a new technology has enough efficiency and ease of use to appeal to users. These factors mainly pertain to the user. However, environmental factors such as privacy risks and trust on the Internet are considered to influence a subject's use of new technology. This paper focuses on SNS, which are spreading throughout the Internet, and seeks to clarify the cognitive elements on using SNS by analyzing the results of a questionnaire conducted over the Internet.

3.1   Scenario and Questionnaire

Scenario

Following Scenario was shown to respondents   before questionnaires.

Aoi, your friend, is 16 and always busy hanging out with her friends. A company offers her a service to keep in touch with her friends and get to know new people who are interested in the same things in her neighborhood (bars, clubs, gyms and high school). However, this service requires some personal data, such as age, gender and location. The service is accessible via her mobile phone, and if Aoi activates the service, her whereabouts and current activities are charted to match other people's whereabouts. What would you recommend she does?

Mock-Up Site

The mock-up of the site shown in Fig. 2 was prepared so that it was easier for respondents to understand the scenario.

Fig. 2. Mock-up site shown in questionnaire

Questionnaire

Respondents are asked questionnaire   shown in Table 1 after reading the scenario .

Table 1. Questionnaire

		Metrics
Ease of Use: To what extent do you agree with the following description of the service?		
Q1	Learning to use such a service would be easy for me	Strongly disagree (1) to
Q2	I would find this service easy to use	Strongly agree (7)
Usefulness: To what extent do you agree with the following description of the service?		
Q3	I show my profile to close friends by any method I like	Strongly disagree (1) to
Q4	Using this system would fit my lifestyle	Strongly agree (7)
Q5	The benefits of using this system are apparent to me	
Trust in the service		
Q6	I would trust the system	Strongly disagree (1) to
Q7	I think the service would be reliable	Strongly agree (7)
Potential Risks: What are the potential risks you would mention to your friend?		
Q8	Your activities may be monitored	Strongly disagree (1) to
Q9	Information may be collected that could be used against you in future life	Strongly agree (7)
Q10	Someone may hack into the system and steal your personal information	
Internet confidence: More generally, concerning the Internet, would you say that:		
Q11	The Internet has enough safeguards to make me feel comfortable giving my personal details online	Strongly disagree (1) to
Q12	The Internet is now a robust and safe environment in which to conduct transactions	Strongly agree (5)
Q13	The Internet is safe enough to preserve my privacy as I carry out leisure, business and personal activities	
Q14	I am confident that I can protect my privacy online	
Intention of Use: Overall, do you think that:		
Q15	Using this service would be:	A good idea (1) to A bad idea (5)
Q16		A wise idea (1) to A foolish idea (5)
Q17	The idea of using this service is:	Attractive (1) to Not attractive (5)
Q18	You like it (1) to You dislike it (5)	

3.2   Data Collection and Analysis

The survey titled "A survey of awareness on Internet Usage" was carried out from March 12 to March 16, 2010 by NTT Resonant. The age of the respondents was from 15 to over 60, split into age groups spanning 10 years. A total of 1000 valid responses was obtained.

In order to test how the proposed factors influence to the intention to use SNS, structural equation model(SEM) is used .We draw a path diagram using the observed variables shown in Fig. 3 based on a hypothesis model. The accuracies of the diagram are 0.957 and 0.930, GFI and AGFI respectively, which shows the path diagram, is highly representative. Red lines are paths those did not appear in the hypothesis.

Although "usefulness" and "ease of use" is defined as affecting use intention in TAM, "ease of use" did not form a path to the use intention.

The "Trust in Service" that this hypothesis defined, influenced the action intention a little, and influenced usefulness to a rather higher degree. We constructed a hypothesis that the concern of privacy risk drew a path from risk concern and acceptance to an action intention with trust on the Internet. However, the relation between privacy risk and trust on Internet is not recognized. The privacy risk had a negative influence on use intention. Confidence on the Internet affected strongly to perceived usefulness.

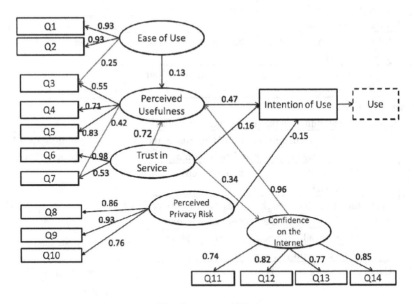

Fig. 3. Result of SEM

4   Conclusion

In this study, the privacy risk, trust on the service and confidence on the Internet are added to TAM, and the responses to a questionnaire were analyzed to determine what elements influenced a user's intention to use SNS. A questionnaire was carried out and verification analysis was conducted by SEM. As a result, a part of TAM could be verified and it was found that usefulness affected use intention most highly. Moreover, although concern over privacy risk was significant, it was not a strong influence on the decision to use SNS.

Acknowledgments. The author would like to express their appreciation to Associate Prof. H.Okada , Prof. Vatchara, Assistant Prof. M.Ueda and Esq I.Takahashi for their contribution to carrying out the survey. Further, special recognition is extended to Dr. Compano and Dr. Lusoli of IPTS for their kindly acceptance of the use of the same questionnaires in JAPAN.

References

1. Holtzman, D.H.: Privacy Lost: How Technology Is Endangering Your Privacy. Jossey-Bass (October 13, 2006)
2. Goodwin, C.: Privacy: Recognition of a Consumer Right. Journal of Public Policy & Marketing 10(1), 149–166 (1991)
3. Ministry of Internal A and Communication: White Paper on ICT in JAPAN 2010, p. 168 (June 2010),
   http://www.soumu.go.jp/johotsusintokei/whitepaper/ja/h22/
   pdf/m4010000.pdf
4. Camenish, J., Samarati, P.: First Report on mechanism, PrimeLife (February 27, 2009),
   http://www.primelife.eu/images/stories/deliverables/
   d2.1.1-first_report_on_mechanisms-public.pdf
5. Sommer, D., Zwingelberg, H.: Second Report on mechanisms, Primelife (February 28, 2010),
   http://www.primelife.eu/images/stories/deliverables/
   d2.3.1-second_report_on_mechanisms.pdf
6. Kosta, E., Dumortier, J., Ribbers, P., Fairchild, A., et al.: Requirements for Privacy Enhancing Tools, PRIME (March 20, 2008)
7. Rosa, C.D., et al.: Sharing Privacy and Trust in Our Networked World. Online Computer Library Center, Dublin (2008)
8. Phelps, J., Nowak, G., Ferrell, E.: Privacy Concerns and Consumer Willingness to Provide Personal Information. Journal of Public Policy & Marketing 19(1), 27–41 (2000)
9. Miyazaki, A.D., Fernandez, A.: Consumer Perceptions of Privacy and Security Risks for Online Shopping. Journal of Consumer Affairs 35(1), 27–44 (2001)
10. Lusoli, W., Miltgen, C.: Young People and Emerging Digital Services–An exploratory Survey on Motivations, Perceptions and Acceptance of Risks (2009),
    http://ftp.jrc.es/EURdoc/JRC50089.pdf
11. Varian, H.: Economic Aspects of Personal Privacy. In: U.S. Dept. of Commerce, Privacy and Self-Regulation in the Information Age (1996)
12. Acquisti, A.: Nudging Privacy- Behavioral Economics of Personal Information. IEEE Security & Privacy (November/December 2009)
13. Acquisti, A.: Privacy in Electronic Commerce and the Economics of Immediate Gratification. In: Proceedings of the 5th ACM Conference on Electronic Commerce, pp. 21–29. ACM (2004)

14. Robinson, N., et al.: Security, At What Cost? Quantifying people's trade-offs across liberty, privacy and security. RAND Corporation (2010)
15. Hann, H., Hui, K.-L., Lee, T.S., Png, I.P.L.: Online Information Privacy: Measuring the Cost-Benefit Trade-off. In: Proc. of Twenty-Third International Conference on Information Systems (2002)
16. Faja, S.: Privacy in e-commerce: Understanding User Trade-offs, vol. VI(2), pp. 83–89 (2005) (Issued in Information Systems)
17. Komatsu, A.: Tsutomu Matsumoto, Empirical Study on privacy Concerns and the Acceptance of e-Money in Japan. Journal of Information Processing 19, 307–316 (2011)
18. Kim, D.J., Ferrin, D.L., Rao, H.R.: A trust-based consumer decision-making model in electronic commerce: the role of trust, perceived risk, and their antecedents. Decision Support Systems 44(2), 544–564 (2008)

Personality's Influence on Facebook's Privacy Settings: A Case of College Students in Taiwan

Tingya Kuo [1] and Hung-Lian Tang [2]

[1] Chung Hwa University of Medical Technology, Tainan, Taiwan
[2] Eastern Michigan University, Ypsilanti, USA
n97b0004@stust.edu.tw, htang@emich.edu

Abstract. Social networking sites such as Facebook have been experiencing tremendous growth for the last several years. In order to get connected with people, Facebook users have to create personal profile with real data about themselves, such as name, home address, email address, phone numbers, relationship status etc. However, there have been ongoing concerns about information disclosure and privacy. Research has indicated personality is one of many factors may have some influence on Facebook's usage, information disclosure, and privacy. The purpose of this research was to investigate possible influence of personality on Facebook privacy settings. Five hypotheses about personality and Facebook privacy settings were developed. Data were collected from 500 college students in Taiwan, with 441 valid data. Four hypotheses about personality and privacy settings were partial supported. People with high extraversion had low privacy settings on family and relationships, religious and political view, and birthday. People with high agreeableness had high privacy settings on wall, photos and videos, religious and political view, birthday, and comments. People with high continuousness had high privacy settings on browsing personal profile and searching personal profile. People with high emotional stability had high privacy settings on religious and political views, and birthday. However, one hypothesis about openness and privacy settings was not supported.

Keywords: Personality, Facebook's privacy settings, Taiwan.

1 Introduction

Facebook have been experiencing tremendous growth for the last several years. In 2006, there were around 1.2 million users, but there were 1.01 billion monthly active users as of September 30, 2012. Taiwan ranked 19th in the world with 13.23 million users (57.79% of population, the highest penetration rate in the world).

To open a Facebook account, users have to create personal profile with real data about themselves, such as name, home address, email address, phone numbers, relationship status etc. However, there have been ongoing concerns about information disclosure and privacy. Researches have indicated personality is one of many factors may have some influence on Facebook's usage, information disclosure, and privacy.

L. Marinos and I. Askoxylakis (Eds.): HAS/HCII 2013, LNCS 8030, pp. 127–134, 2013.

However, most of these researches are based on data collected from North America college students. The findings of these researches may not be applicable to users with different culture and languages.

The purpose of this research was to explore possible personality influence on Facebook's privacy settings of college students in Taiwan. Analyzing Taiwanese college students' personality influence on privacy settings may provide insights about Facebook's usage in a different culture and language.

2   Literature Reviews

2.1   Personality

There are many personality models for determining individuals' personality traits and types. One of the popular models is the Big Five Factors Model, which classified personality traits into five types: extraversion, conscientiousness, agreeableness, neuroticism and openness (McCrae & John, 1992). Many instruments for assessing the Big Five Factors have been developed with various numbers of questions (from 240 questions to 10 questions). If a research's focus is about relationship between personality and other constructs, then an instrument with a small number of questions would be suitable (Gosling, Rentfrow & Swann, 2003).

2.2   Personality and Facebook's Usages

Ross et al. (2009) indicated that users with different personality types did use different aspects of Facebook. High extraversion people joined more groups than low extraversion people, high openness people liked to be sociable on Facebook, and high neuroticism people liked to use the Facebook's Wall, but low neuroticism people preferred posting photos. Amichai-Hamburger and Vinitzky (2010) discovered a strong link between personality and Facebook uses. High extraversion people tended to have more friends and groups than low extraversion people. High neuroticism people tended to be willing to show more personal information and use private messages. High agreeableness people liked to post more pictures on Facebook. High openness people would use more features of the Facebook. High conscientiousness people tended to have more friends but less pictures loaded in the Facebook. Ryan and Xenos (2011) found out that Facebook users are likely to be extraverted, but less conscientious. Gosling, Gaddis, and Vazire (2007) found out that personality impressions from Facebook users' profiles are correlated with personality perceived by users themselves and by their friends. Gosling et al. (2011) also discovered that high extraversion and agreeableness people had more Facebook usages then other three types of personality.

2.3   Facebook's Privacy Settings

Facebook's users have revealed a large amount of personal information, but most users are not aware of privacy options and allow others to view and search their personal profiles (Acquisti & Gross 2006; Lampe, Ellison &Steinfield, 2007; Stutzman, 2006). Lewis, Kaufman and Christakis (2008) found out that a student' gender, Facebook activity level, friends have influence on the student's private profile. Grubbs and Milne (2010) investigated gender differences in young adult Facebook users' privacy beliefs and privacy protection behaviors, and found out that women are more concern about their privacy and more likely to protect their privacy than men. Taraszow et al. (2010) analyzed Facebook profiles of 131 young people, and found out that young people between the age of 18 and 22 entered their real personal and contact information and accepted strangers' requests for friendship without knowing potential dangers of revealing private profile.

3   Research Methodologies

3.1   Hypotheses

The above researches indicated possible relationships between personalities and Facebook usages, and influence of gender, friends, and culture on private profiles; however, there is no discussion about possible personality influence on Facebook's privacy settings. The main purpose of this study was to explore possible relationships between personalities and Facebook's privacy settings. It was assumed that different personality traits may have influence on Facebook's privacy settings. Five hypotheses with five personality traits were developed.

1. High extraversion people's privacy settings are different from those of low extraversion people,
2. High agreeableness people's privacy settings are different from those of low agreeableness people,
3. High conscientiousness people's privacy settings are different from those of low conscientiousness people,
4. High emotional stability people's privacy settings are different from those of low emotional stability people,
5. High openness people's privacy settings are different from those of low openness people.

3.2   Survey Instrument

Personality data were collected with the TIPI (Ten-Item Personality Inventory) instrument to avoid negative feeling of using lengthy instrument (Gosling et al., 2003). It was used to assess personality with Big five personality traits of Openness (open to new experiences, complex vs. conventional, uncreative), Conscientiousness (dependable, self-disciplined vs. disorganized, careless), Extraversion (extraverted, enthusiastic vs. reserved, quite), Agreeableness (sympathetic, warm vs. critical, quarrelsome), and Emotional stability (anxious, easily upset vs. calm, emotionally stable). The instrument used a seven-point Likert scale with rating from 1 (strongly disagree) to 7 (strongly agree).

Data about Facebook's privacy settings such as browsing my profile, searching my profile, my status, photo, and posting, walls, family and relationship, photos and videos, religious and political views, birthday, messages, email and instant message, phone and address were collected with three categories (1. Everyone, 2. Friends of friends, 3.Friends only).

3.3   Participants

Surveys were distributed to 500 college students in Taiwan, with 441 valid data sets. The data sets were analyzed with SPSS. Among the 441 students, 92 students were male (20.9%), and 349 students were female (79.1%). 100 students were freshmen (22.7%), 126 students were sophomore (28.6%), 145 students were junior (32.9%), 66 students were senior (15%), and 4 students were graduate (0.9%).

4   Results

4.1   Descriptive Statistics

10 items of personality's data were combined into 5 personality traits. Among the five personality traits, Openness has the highest mean of 5.02, and Extraversion has the lowest mean of 4.02.

Table 1. Descriptive Statistics of Personalities (N=441)

Item	Mean	Std. Dev.
Extraversion	4.24	1.45
Agreeableness	4.98	1.11
Conscientiousness	4.58	1.32
Emotional stability	4.31	1.42
Openness	5.02	1.07

Table 2 depicted means and frequency distributions of 10 privacy settings. Phone number and address has the highest mean of 2.37, and Search my personal information has the lowest mean of 1.79. Though the means were in the range between 1.79 and 2.37, frequency distributions showed that most users chose to disclose private information to either everyone or friends only. In addition, majority of users disclosed their birthday to everyone, and allowed everyone to browse and search their personal information. On the contrary, majority of users disclosed contact information such as email, phone number and address to friends only.

Table 2. Descriptive Statistics of Privacy Settings (N=441)

Item	Mean	Std. Dev.	Frequency Dist.*		
			1	2	3
Browse my personal information	1.89	.963	230	28	183
Search my personal information	1.79	.945	252	29	160
Status, Photos, and Posts	1.98	.957	205	38	198
Wall	1.96	.954	209	40	192
Family and relationships	2.05	.962	193	33	215
Photos and videos	2.04	.960	194	35	212
Religious and political views	1.97	.971	215	26	200
Birthday	1.87	.962	237	26	178
Comments	1.97	.957	208	38	195
Email and instant message	2.09	.965	187	28	226
Phone number and address	2.37	.900	127	24	290

*1: Everyone, 2: friends of friends, 3: friends.

4.2   Hypotheses Testing

In order to compare the "purer" personality differences, Ross et al. (2009) used a method of dividing the five personality's data into three groups, namely, low score, medium score, and high score, then compare data between the high and low groups only. This research used the same method, thus only the privacy data from the low and high groups were used to analyze possible personality influence on privacy settings.

Five hypotheses were tested with the independent sample t test method. Table 3 depicted only those personalities and privacy settings tested with significant differences. People with high extraversion were significantly different from people with low extraversion in 4 areas (family and relationships, religious and political view, birthday and comments). People with high agreeableness were significantly different from people with low agreeableness in 5 areas (wall, photos and videos, religious and political view, birthday, and comments). People with high conscientiousness were significantly different from people with low conscientiousness in 2 areas (browse my personal information, search my personal information). People with high emotional stability were significantly different from people with low emotional stability in 2 areas (religious and political view, birthday). However, people with high openness were not significantly different from people with low openness in any of 10 privacy settings.

Table 3. Hypotheses Testing of Personalities and Privacy Settings

Personality	Privacy Settings	Scores	Mean	Std. Dev.	t value	p value
Extraversion	Family and relationships	low	2.11	.956	1.966 *	.047
		high	1.89	.956		
	Religious and political view	low	2.07	.971	2.050*	.041
		high	1.84	.955		
	Birthday	low	1.99	.973	2.899**	.004
		high	1.67	.921		
	Comments	low	2.08	.956	2.514*	.012
		high	1.80	.938		
Agreeableness	Wall	low	1.83	.940	-2.235*	.026
		high	2.12	.943		
	Photos and videos	low	1.91	.957	-2.062*	.040
		high	2.17	.925		
	Religious and political view	low	1.86	.966	-2.666**	.008
		high	2.20	.937		
	Birthday	low	1.72	.939	-2.957**	.003
		high	2.10	.954		
	Comments	low	1.84	.940	-2.067*	.040
		high	2.11	.958		
Conscientiousness	Browse my personal information	low	1.84	.948	-2.135*	.034
		high	2.11	.974		
	Search my personal information	low	1.68	.900	-2.528*	.012
		high	1.99	.976		
Emotional stability	Religious and political view	low	1.78	.944	-2.781**	.006
		high	2.10	.971		
	Birthday	low	1.70	.931	-2.610**	.010
		high	2.00	.968		

Sig. level *p<.05, **p<.01, ***p<.001.

5   Discussions

Previous researches about personality and Facebook's usages (Ross et al. 2009; Amichai-Hamburger & Vinitzky, 2010) showed that high extraversion people had more groups, more friends and more usage than low extraversion people, and Facebook users were more likely to be extraverted (Ryan & Xenos, 2011). This research discovered high extraversion people disclosed family and relationships, religious and political view, birthday, and comments to everyone. Therefore, the results about people with high extraversion were similar with findings of previous researches. However, it was surprised to see that high agreeableness people did not disclose their walls, photos and videos, religious and political views, birthday, and comments to everyone. People with high continuousness did not allow everyone to browse or search their personal profile. People with high emotional stability have high privacy settings on religious and political views, and birthday. There were three privacy settings, namely, 1) status, photo and posts, 2) email and instant message, and 3) Phone number and address, were not significantly different for all 5 types of personality. This means that people prefer to disclose their contact information only to their friends regardless of their personality types.

6   Conclusions

Previous researches indicated people with different personality types did use different aspects of Facebook, and genders and friends had influences on privacy settings, but the results were not conclusive. There was no research about possible influence of personality on privacy settings. This research investigated possible connections between 5 personality types and privacy settings. The findings only partially supported that 4 personality types, namely, extraversion, agreeableness, conscientiousness, and emotional stability, had some influences on privacy settings, but openness did not have any influence on privacy settings.

References

1. Amichai-Hamburger, Y., Vinitzky, G.: Social network use and personality. Computers in Human Behavior 26(2010), 1289–1295 (2010)
2. Acquisti, A., Gross, R.: Imagined Communities: Awareness, Information Sharing, and Privacy on the Facebook. In: 6th International Workshop on Privacy Enhancing Technologies (June 2006)
3. Gosling, S., Augustine, A., Vazire, S., Holtzman, N., Gaddis, S.: Manifestations of Personality in Online social Networks: Self-Reported Facebook-Related Behaviors and Observable Profile Information. Cyberpsychology, Behavior, and Social Networking 14(9), 483–488 (2011)
4. Gosling, S., Gaddis, S., Vazire, S.: Personality Impressions Based on Facebook Profiles. In: International Conference on Weblogs and Social Media, Boulder, Colorado, March 26-28 (2007)
5. Gosling, S., Rentfrow, P., Swann, W.: A very brief measure of the Big-Five personality domains. Journal of Research in Personality 37, 504–528 (2003)
6. Grubbs, M., Milne, G.: Gender Differences in Privacy-related Measures for Young Adult Facebook Users. Journal of Interactive Advertising 10(2), 28–45 (2010)
7. Lampe, C., Ellison, N., Steinfield, C.: A Familiar Face(book): Profile Elements as Signals in an Online Social Network. In: CHI 2007 Proceedings, pp. 435–444 (2007)
8. Lewis, K., Kaufman, J., Christakis, N.: The Taste for Privacy: An Analysis of College Student Privacy Settings in an Online Social Network. Journal of Computer-Medicated Communication 14(2008), 79–100 (2008)
9. McCrae, R., John, O.: An introduction to the Five-Factor model and its applications (special edition). Journal of Personality 60, 175–215 (1992)
10. Ross, C., Orr, E., Sisic, M., Arseneault, J., Simmering, M., Orr, R.: Personality and motivations associated with Facebook use. Computer in Human Behavior 25(2009), 643–654 (2009)

11. Ryan, T., Xenos, S.: Who uses Facebook? An investigation into the relationship between the Big Five, shyness, narcissism, loneliness, and Facebook usage. Computers in Human Behavior 27(2011), 1658–1664 (2011)
12. Stutzman, F.: An Evaluation of Identity-Sharing Behavior in Social network Communities. International Digital and Media Arts Journal 3(1), 10–18 (2006)
13. Taraszow, T., Aristodemou, E., Shitta, G., Laouris, Y., Arsoy, A.: Disclosure of Personal and Contact Information by Young People in Social Networking Sites: An Analysis using Facebook profiles as an example. International Journal of Media and Cultural politics 6(1), 81–101 (2010)

An Influence of Self-evaluated Gender Role on the Privacy Management Behavior in Online Social Networks

Kijung Lee and Il-Yeol Song

The iSchool at Drexel, College of Information Science and Technology
Drexel University
3141 Chestnut Street, Philadelphia, PA 19104
{kl324,song}@drexel.edu

Abstract. The primary goal of this paper is testing a causal model of privacy management indicating the influence of gender on the user behavior of privacy management in OSNs. We adopted communication privacy management theory and the theory of planned behavior, developed a causal model showing the influence of self-evaluated gender role on the behavior of privacy management in online social networks, and tested a set of hypotheses using structural equation modeling (SEM). The results of SEM indicate that self-evaluation of masculinity and femininity did not have significant relationship with user's behavior of privacy management in OSN.

Keywords: privacy, privacy management, gender role, bem sex role inventory, online social networks, causal modeling, confirmatory factor analysis, structural equation modeling.

1   Introduction

The exponential growth of OSNs, while offering a greater range of opportunities for communication and information sharing, raises issues in privacy, especially, managing private information while communicating with others. Oftentimes, identity in OSNs is identical to the one in a real life because communication in OSN is based on experience of the real life. Many users consider OSNs as an extension of social interaction in real life. Unlike the real life, however, personal information in OSNs is extremely difficult to be under control of the information owner. The profile information in OSN can be collected by entities that are capable of endangering privacy, e.g., data miners and cybercriminals. It is not only the profile but also published communication that can reveal about a user. Sometimes form-free information can tell much more than profile information if the information is inferred correctly. Information can be revealed from what the user posts or from what others post on the user's page. Written communication in OSN, once published, can be read, copied, and reproduced by other users who have access to the published message. Since most OSN websites provide coarse categorization of social groups, it is difficult for users to control their privacy by posting messages only for intended audience. In other words, it is possible

L. Marinos and I. Askoxylakis (Eds.): HAS/HCII 2013, LNCS 8030, pp. 135–144, 2013.
© Springer-Verlag Berlin Heidelberg 2013

that your boss can see conversation between you and your coworker gossiping about her in OSNs. Although some threats are unavoidable in order to register for and use the service, majority of threats are caused from user's voluntary disclosure.

According to Petronio [1], individuals manage privacy boundaries using a rule-based system that guide all facets of the disclosure process, including how boundaries are coordinated between individuals. CPM clearly delineates that people have distinct set of attributes when they make decisions about managing their privacy. CPM maintains that five factors play into the way we develop our own privacy rules: culture, gender, motivation, context, and risk/benefit ratios. In our study, we focus on the gender factor and investigate the causal relationship between gender and user's behavior of privacy management in OSNs.

Although there has been disagreement on which gender is more sensitive to privacy [2-5], generally, researchers believe that the gender is one of the primary factors influencing user's behavior of privacy management. In this study, we particularly examine the relationship between the self-perception of gender role and the user behavior of managing the amount of private information being shared.

This paper is organized as follows: In the background section, we discuss theories constituting the idea and construct structure of our model. In the methods section, we describe a general procedure of methods in studies utilizing SEM technique, and demonstrate our research problem using structural equation modeling technique. Primarily, we discuss creation of a model, survey implementation and data collection, and analysis of the models for our study. In analysis section, our discussion presents evaluations and potential revisions of the model while providing interpretations of the analytical results of the study. In the discussion section, we briefly discuss implications of the paper in theory development and application and in practical application to system design. Then we summarize our findings and identify future plans in the conclusion section.

2   Theoretical Background

Theories fundamental to this dissertation are Communication Privacy Management (CPM) theory [1] and Theory of Planned Behavior (TPB) [6-8]. First, we borrow the basic idea of CPM theory to show the backbone of our model. CPM theory identifies that people control their private information based on the use of personal privacy rules. Through developing, learning, and negotiating rules depending on culture, gender, motivation, context, and risk / benefit ratio, people coordinate boundary linkages, boundary permeability, and boundary ownership. The primary focus in this paper, however, is the influence of gender. Second, behavioral mechanism embedded in our model is borrowed from TPB. The theory explicates a mechanism of human decision-making process, i.e., a causal link constituting, "a person's salient beliefs and evaluations, attitude toward a behavior, and behavioral intentions." The theory also states that subjective norms, perceived behavioral control and attitude toward a behavior jointly determine the behavioral intention. In this section, we discuss how the two theories are used in constituting the models of privacy management in OSNs.

2.1   Communication Privacy Management Theory

The CPM theory emphasizes that it is necessary to consider communicative interactions between people to grasp disclosure of private information. The theory offers concepts and conceptual structures to help identify the way people coordinate the influencing factors on their privacy. According to Petronio [1], communication privacy management theory deals with how individuals make decisions to disclose private information to others and how this relational process is coordinated. She argues that "boundaries" serve as a useful metaphor illustrating that, although there may be a flow of private information to others, borders mark ownership lines such that issues of control are clearly understood by the communicating partners. CPM supposes that both the discloser and the recipient of the disclosure have a degree of agency during the process of revealing private information. Boundaries are coordinated by both parties, and once a successful disclosure is made, the individuals involved coordinate their boundaries so that the private information is co-owned and co-managed appropriately. When disclosures occur, the discloser is willingly giving up a degree of control and ownership over the private information. Consequently, people make choices to reveal or to conceal private information based on criteria and conditions that they perceive as salient.

The primary idea of CPM is that people have a desire for privacy and the dynamic process of revealing and hiding private information constitutes the process of fulfilling the desire. Whenever we share a portion of that information with someone, we are reshaping a privacy boundary. Having a mental image of protective boundaries is central to understanding the five core principles of Petronio's CPM.

Gender criteria potentially influence the way different gender perceives the nature of their privacy. Hence, research argues that men and women use different sets of criteria to define ownership of private information and how they are managed [9, 10]. Therefore, based on the research, we can infer that men and women develop distinct rules for managing privacy boundaries.

Sex role and sex role identity has been studied resulting in more complex analyses of gender influence on the management of privacy boundary. Derlega et al [11] discusses relationship between sex typing and disclosure topics. They argue that men, than women, are more willing to disclose about private information generally perceived as masculine, while women are more willing to reveal about private information in relation to feminine topics than men. Particularly, in US culture, men are characterized in terms of achievement, competition, and success, whereas women are viewed in attributes of emotionality and sensitivity [12-14].

2.2   The Theory of Planned Behavior

Intentions to perform behaviors of different kinds can be predicted from attitudes toward the behavior, subjective norms, and perceived behavioral control; according to Ajzen and Fishbein [6] and Fishbein and Ajzen [7], these intentions, together with perceptions of behavioral control, account for considerable variance in actual behavior.   It can be briefly represented in a mathematical function as;

$$BI = (A_B)\omega1 + (SN)\omega2 + (PBC)\omega3 \qquad (1)$$

where BI refers to behavioral intentions, AB is attitude towards the behavior, SN denotes subjective norm, PBC represents perceived behavioral control and $\omega1$, $\omega2$, $\omega3$ indicate weights for each component. Including background factors and actual behavioral control, the model of TPB can be presented as in Figure 1 below.

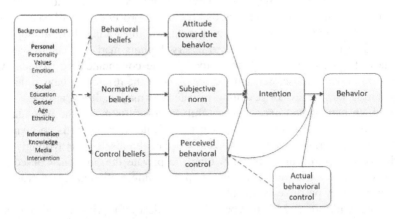

Fig. 1. The theory of planned behavior as illustrated in Fishbein and Ajzen [8]

Although there is not a perfect relationship between behavioral intention and actual behavior, intention can be used as a proximal measure of behavior. This observation was one of the most important contributions of the TPB model in comparison with previous models of the attitude-behavior relationship. Thus, the variables in this model can be used to determine the effectiveness of implementation interventions even if there is not a readily available measure of actual behavior.

3   Methods

The method of this study follows generic steps suggested by most studies that facilitate SEM techniques as their analytical approach. First, using a qualitative approach, a conceptual model is created. Then, measurement items for research variables and constructs are created and/or adopted and modified depending on availability. Using the identified model and measurement items, a user survey is designed and implemented to collect user responses. Lastly, the conceptual model is redrawn using AMOS software with the connection to the collected user responses.

3.1   Research Questions

Research questions are formulated in order to examine models of user experience regarding their privacy management in OSNs. Questions are organized to identify salient research constructs, develop models based on the research constructs and test them for fitness to user data, and define and test statistical significance of interrelationship among the research constructs. Two primary questions are formulated as below;

RQ1: Can we identify quantitative models of user's privacy management in OSNs?

RQ2: What are the significant relationships among research constructs within the model?

3.2   Model Composition

Combining the CPM theory and TPB, a model of our interest can be represented as below in Figure 2. The diagram shows the overall model including all factors from CPM and TPB. The rectangle on the left shows foundations for privacy rule management (derived from CPM), while the rectangle on the right contains factors that are related to behavioral decision (originated from TPB). Behavioral component of endogenous measure is analyzed as a set; for example, "intention to control boundary permeability" is analyzed along with "attitudes towards controlling boundary permeability", "subjective norm about controlling boundary permeability", and "behavioral control of controlling boundary permeability". Controlling permeability is operationally defined in the later section as "Controlling how much private information to reveal"

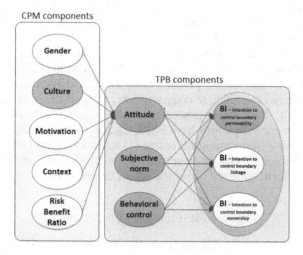

Fig. 2. A combined model of CPM theory and TPB represented in a model

3.3   Data Collection

The survey was implemented using a paid service from Surveygizmo.com. The sample (N=400) was collected mostly from United States (93.2%). Caucasian was the most participated race (65.2%, African American 11.3%, and Asian 8.5%), and gender proportion was male, 54.7%, and female, 45.3%. Also, more than 80% of participants had higher than college education. Ages between 30 and 39 were the most frequent age group (27.5%) and twenties and forties followed in the proportion of 24.3% and 19.8%, respectively.

3.4   Questionnaire Construction

The impact of gender on privacy rule management is based on the idea that different degree of gender orientation is accounted for idiosyncratic patterns of boundary management for each gender. For example, ownership of private information can be defined by different sets of criteria by different gender [9, 10]. Consequently, they have distinct understanding of advantage and disadvantage in concealing and revealing. Other studies [11, 15] seek difference in the pattern of disclosure from sex role. This is more complex line of research than simple comparison between the amount of disclosing between men and women in that the mechanism of privacy is explained in relation to types of disclosing information as well as social evaluation and expectation of gender role.

There are number of measurements for sex role [12, 14, 16]. Gender is a frequently discussed topic of research when it comes to social characterizations and behavioral decisions consequential to such biological dichotomy. One controversial issue in such research is classification based on biological characteristics of gender. In this project, therefore, gender is measured in terms of continuous score based on existing measure, Bem Sex Role Inventory [12, 13], i.e., BSRI. The BSRI is a self-report measure of sex role orientation. We especially adopted short form BSRI [14, 17]. The short form of the BSRI contains 30 items. The Masculinity scale consists of 10 traits traditionally viewed as more desirable for a man than for a woman. The Femininity scale consists of 10 traits traditionally viewed as more desirable for a woman. Sample items from the Masculinity scale include independent, competitive, and aggressive; sample items from the Femininity scale include compassionate, sympathetic, and sensitive to the needs of others [14]. To measure gender traits, survey participants are asked to rate a set of gender characterizing words from BSRI, e.g., aggressive or tender, in a 7 point Likert scale spanning from Almost never true (1) to Almost always true (7). Note that the context of this self-evaluation is interaction on online social networks. A simple equation can be identified to show that the gender criteria can be combination of two sub-factors;

$$GC = (MSE)\omega 1 + (FSE)\omega 2 \tag{2}$$

where MSE represents self-evaluation of Masculinity, and FSE represents self-evaluation of Femininity.

4   Analysis

In this section, we discuss results of statistical analyses manifesting research questions and hypotheses. A two-step process is described in terms of analyzing measurement models and structural models.

In order to analyze measurement models, a series of factor analyses are conducted. In our approach, we use both Exploratory Factor Analysis (EFA) and Confirmatory Factor Analysis (CFA). The two statistical techniques serve different purposes. First, EFA is used for finding hidden construct out of a set of variables. Using this analysis, we identify factor structures (a grouping of variables based on strong correlations), compare them with foundational theories and models, and interpret emerged structures. During this process, we also detect "misfit" variables. In general, an EFA prepares the variables to be used for cleaner structural equation modeling. In contrast, the purpose of CFA is validating the identified structure of theoretical components. Therefore, models are defined first and then tested whether the data support them. However, we use it for both exploratory and confirmatory purposes since our research is somewhat exploratory in the sense that we develop a quantitative model based on an interpretive theory by examining quantitative measures to best describe behavioral models. Based on the structures identified as a result of EFA, in the second step, we conduct CFA to see how observed variables are related to latent variables and how appropriate the measurement models are.

In the second step of analysis, structural models are identified and estimated. In this step, a set of causal relationships are hypothesized in the models and tested against the collected data while the models are evaluated for their fitness to the data.

4.1   A Measurement Model of Gender Criteria

To measure and analyze privacy rule development of gender criteria, we used short form Bem Sex Role Inventory (BSRI), a measurement scale of self-reported sex role perception. The original sample (N=400) was treated for univariate and multivariate outliers. For the analysis of gender criteria, sample size was N=348 after screening.

In order to identify factor structure, first, EFA was conducted. However, EFA produced factor structure that is difficult to interpret. Some items were cross loaded and other items were loaded on factors that are not claimed in the original theory. In order to keep the factor structure identified in Bem's theory, we conducted a CFA using all observed variables. As a result of the CFA, 5 items from male and 5 items from female were removed. From the female factor, "Affectionate", "Warm", "Gentle", "Tender", and "Loves children" were removed while, from the male factor, "Aggressive", "Independent", "Forceful", "Dominant", and "Assertive" were removed. Fit indices indicated a good fit of the model to the data because most of the indices were within the recommended thresholds.   Fit indices of the measurement model of gender construct ($\chi2$ (25) = 91.868, p<.001) were as follows: CMIN/DF = 3.68, RMSEA = .09, NFI = .96, CFI = .97, GFI = .95, AGFI = .90, TLI = .95. With this result, we conducted CFA again on the gender factors with behavioral constructs from TPB. Fit indices of the measurement model of gender construct with TPB constructs ($\chi2$ (206) = 420.617, p<.001) were as follows: CMIN/DF = 2.04, RMSEA = .05, NFI = .96, CFI = .95, GFI = .90, AGFI = .88, TLI = .94.

Two hypotheses are formulated in operational level;

H1: In OSNs, self-reported measure of user's masculinity has influence on the attitude towards controlling the amount of private information being shared.

H2: In OSNs, self-reported measure of user's femininity has influence on the attitude towards controlling the amount of private information being shared.

4.2   A Structural Model of Gender Criteria

We tested the causal model using the SEM technique. Figure 3 reports the results of SEM analysis. Fit indices indicate that the model ($\chi 2(214) = 573.866$, p<.001) is a good fit to the data; CMIN/DF = 2.68, RMSEA = .065, NFI = .90, CFI = .94, GFI = .89, AGFI = .86, TLI = .92.   We found that influence of masculinity on attitude towards a behavior was not statistically significant. . (β = .06, N/S, Hypothesis 1 not supported). Also, effect of femininity on attitude towards a behavior was not statistically significant. (β = .17, N/S, Hypothesis 2 not supported). In the population, whether a user has female trait or male trait does not have influence on the attitude towards controlling the amount of private information being shared.

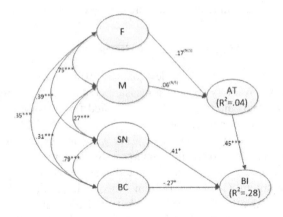

Fig. 3. A structural model of gender criteria

5   Discussion and Conclusion

This study explores how gender role influence processes and patterns of user's behavior of privacy coordination in OSNs. A causal model is identified so that; 1) causality functions between criteria of privacy rules, i.e., gender, and user behavior of privacy coordination, i.e., information sharing behavior in particular, are measured and analyzed, and 2) user traits and perceptions are examined and tested in relation to privacy management in OSNs. The findings indicate that whether a user has female trait or male trait does not have influence on the attitude towards controlling the amount of private information being shared.

Messy structure of factors implies that some items in original BSRI may not be suitable for representing gender roles in OSNs. Also, causal links from gender roles to behavioral components resulted statistically not significant. It needs more investigation to see whether measuring gender role is appropriate (rather than measuring simply gender), whether BSRI is appropriate in the research context, and whether the size difference, between masculinity and femininity, of the effects on the behavioral components mean anything substantial.

Implications of this paper can be discussed in the perspective of theory in terms of "quantification" and "systemization". First, quantitative measurements and metrics are applied to get a grasp of privacy in OSNs. Communication privacy management (CPM) theory, with its interpretive nature, describes fundamental idea of which rules are developed and how they influence the mode of communication and decision of private boundary. While CPM offers a solid view for understanding and interpreting social interactions, this paper, based on the CPM, tests hypotheses, looks at cause and effects, and identifies models of prediction. Second, the paper provides systematic investigation of user's privacy behavior based on widely accepted theories. In particular, foundations of privacy rule and coordination behavior investigated in CPM are applied in the framework of the theory of planned behavior (TPB) for reliable prediction model. Therefore, the model will serve as basis for further examination of user behavior in regards to their privacy management in OSNs.

References

1. Petronio, S.S.: Boundaries of privacy: dialectics of disclosure. State University of New York Press, Albany (2002)
2. Acquisti, A., Gross, R.: Imagined Communities: Awareness, Information Sharing, and Privacy on the Facebook. In: Danezis, G., Golle, P. (eds.) PET 2006. LNCS, vol. 4258, pp. 36–58. Springer, Heidelberg (2006)
3. Caverlee, J., Webb, S.: A Large-Scale Study of MySpace: Observations and Implications for Online Social Networks. In: Association for the Advancement of Artificial Intelligence, Chicago, IL (2008)
4. Joinson, A.N.: 'Looking at', 'Looking up' or 'Keeping up with' People? - Motives and Uses of Facebook. In: CHI 2008, Florence, Italy, pp. 1027–1036 (2008)
5. Lewis, K., Kaufman, J., Christakis, N.: The Taste for Privacy: An Analysis of College Student Privacy Settings in an Online Social Network. Journal of Computer-Mediated Communication 14, 79–100 (2008)
6. Ajzen, I., Fishbein, M.: Understanding attitudes and predicting social behavior. Prentice-Hall, Englewood Cliffs (1980)
7. Fishbein, M., Ajzen, I.: Belief, attitude, intention, and behavior: An introduction to theory and research. Addison-Wesley, Reading (1975)
8. Fishbein, M., Ajzen, I. (eds.): Predicting and changing behavior: The reasoned action approach. Psychology Press, New York (2010)
9. Petronio, S.S., Martin, J.: Ramifications of revealing private information: A gender gap. Journal of Clinical Psychology 42, 499–506 (1986)
10. Petronio, S.S., Martin, J., Littlefield, R.: Prerequisite conditions for slef-disclosure: A gender issue. Communication Monographs 51, 268–273 (1984)
11. Derlega, V.J., Durham, B., Gockel, B., Sholis, D.: Sex differences in self-disclosure: Effects of topic content, friendship, and partner's sex. Sex Roles 7, 433–447 (1981)

12. Bem, S.L.: The measurement of psychological androgyny. Journal of Consulting and Clinical Psychology 42, 155–162 (1974)
13. Bem, S.L.: Theory and measurement of androgyny: A reply to the Pedhazur-Telenbaum and Locksley-Colten critiques. Journal of Personality and Social Psychology 37, 1047–1054 (1979)
14. Bem, S.L.: Bem sex role inventory professional manual. Consulting Psychologists Press, Palo Alto (1981)
15. Hill, C.T., Stull, D.: Gender and self-disclosure: Strategies for exploring the issues. In: Derlega, V.J., Berg, J.H. (eds.) Self-disclosure: Theory, Research, and Therapy, pp. 81–96. Plenum Press, New York (1987)
16. Spence, J.T., Helmreich, R.L., Strapp, J.: Ratings of self and peers on sex-role attributes and their relation to self-esteem and conceptions of masculinity and femininity. Joural of Personality and Social Psychology 32, 29–39 (1975)
17. Colley, A., Mulhern, G., Maltby, J., Wood, A.M.: The short form BSRI: Instrumentality, expressiveness and gender associations among a United Kingdom sample. Personality and Individual Differences 46, 348–387 (2009)

A Taxonomy of Cyber Awareness Questions for the User-Centered Design of Cyber Situation Awareness[*]

Celeste Lyn Paul and Kirsten Whitley

Department of Defense, United States
clpaul@tycho.ncsc.mil, visual@tycho.ncsc.mil

Abstract. This paper offers insights to how cyber security analysts establish and maintain situation awareness of a large computer network. Through a series of interviews, observations, and a card sorting activity, we examined the questions analysts asked themselves during a network event. We present the results of our work as a taxonomy of cyber awareness questions that represents a mental model of situation awareness in cyber security analysts.

Keywords: Computer security, situation awareness, user-centered design.

1 Introduction

This paper presents a taxonomy of cyber awareness questions derived from a series of user-centered research activities that can be used to inform the design and development of cyber situation awareness technology. One of the most important responsibilities of a cyber security analyst is to watch over and protect his network from harm. Maintaining situation awareness of the wide variety of events that occur and massive amounts of data generated is one of many analytic challenges. Situation awareness technology aims to reduce the data overload burden placed on the analyst. Good situation awareness technology requires good design, and good design requires a good understanding of the user and a focus on the user during the design process.

In the case of a cyber security analyst, the practice of good user-centered design is focused on his security-related work processes on a large computer network. One way of understanding how a cyber security analyst accomplishes situation awareness on a large computer network is to study the questions he may ask himself during the course of a network event. Studying the relationships between these questions will lead to a better understanding of the analysts' mental model of cyber situation awareness. A mental model of cyber situation awareness is a valuable tool in the user-centered design of cyber-related technology and to researchers who cannot always study cyber security analysts in the field.

L. Marinos and I. Askoxylakis (Eds.): HAS/HCII 2013, LNCS 8030, pp. 145–154, 2013.
© Springer-Verlag Berlin Heidelberg 2013

2   Background

There is a growing body of work within the cyber security field that is focused on understanding the work processes of cyber security analysts. For example, the results of a series of interviews with a wide variety of cyber security analysts by Werlinger et al. [8] described three stages of computer network incident response activities: preparation; anomaly detection; and, anomaly analysis. Work by Goodall et al. [5] discussed the work process for network intrusion detection analysts in four task stages: monitoring the network for events; triaging an event; analysis of an event; and, response to an event. Thompson et al. [7] expanded Goodall et al.'s work to include a pre-processing stage before the monitoring stage that involves intrusion detection system preparation, as well as expanding the triage stage to include activities for determining the cause of an event and deciding if the event should be escalated to analysis. Although individually these studies describe different phases of activities within the cyber analytic work process, together they infer a general cyber analysis work process model: preparation, monitoring, detection, analysis, and response to network events.

Few researchers have specifically focused on situation awareness during the cyber analysis work process. Situation awareness is a state of knowledge within the context of a dynamic system, often with three stages: perception, comprehension, and projection [4]. Work by D'Amico et al. [2] examined the analytic questions of intrusion detection analysts to understand how they fused complex data during different stages of situation awareness. They developed a model of situation awareness that extended and overlapped with the model for the cyber analysis work process: event detection (monitoring and detection); situation assessment (analysis); and, threat assessment (response). Later research by D'Amico et al. [3] added role-based work processes that corresponded to their model of situation awareness, such as: triage analysis; escalation analysis; correlation analysis; threat analysis; incident response; and, forensic analysis.

However, there is still a general lack of information on cyber security analysts, their work processes, and how they establish and maintain situation awareness. Conducting empirical and ethnographic research with cyber security analysts is often difficult. There are a number of challenges to involving cyber security analysts in research, such as establishing contact with cyber security analysts who have the time to participate in research and are willing to share potentially sensitive information related to their jobs [1]. Additionally, the role of a cyber security analyst is difficult to define and ranges from a system administrator, intrusion detection analyst, to an incident responder. Cyber security analysts may take on the same, different, or overlapping responsibilities depending on the scope of the job role or size of the organization [3]. As computer networks become larger and more complex, understanding how cyber security analysts manage the large amounts of information generated by these networks and maintain awareness of the increasing number of events on these networks will be critical to future technology design and development.

3   Methodology

A combination of ethnographic research methods were used to understand the mental model of cyber security analysts responsible for a large network. First, interviews and observations were conducted to gain an understanding of analysts' work environment. Then, a card sorting activity was conducted to understand analysts' conceptual models of situation awareness on a network. Analysts in our study were primarily responsible for intrusion detection and not incident response.

3.1   Interviews and Observations

Interviews were conducted with six cyber security experts. Participants had at least one year of previous or current experience working in support of a network operations center as well as additional experience in cyber security. The interviews were open-ended with no structured topics except for the overall purpose of the interview. Participants were asked to discuss their experiences in cyber security and within the operations center. Participants were asked to talk freely, and were only interrupted with follow-up and clarification questions. If the topic did not come up during the initial discussion, participants were prompted to discuss their experiences with cyber situation awareness and the types of high level orientation questions they ask themselves during a new or ongoing event. Interviews lasted between 45 minutes to 1.5 hours. To supplement the interviews, approximately 25 additional hours of observations of a round-the-clock network operations center were conducted. This included general observations of analyst work during normal operations, attending operations center meetings, and observing two training exercises. Participant interruptions were minimal and participants were available to answer questions and discuss their activities. Observation sessions lasted between one and four hours each.

3.2   Card Sorting Activity

Card sorting is a knowledge elicitation method that helps people describe relationships between and hierarchy among concepts [6]. An open card sorting study was conducted with 12 cyber security analysts using 44 cyber situation awareness questions. Participants had at least one year of previous or current experience working in a round-the-clock network operations center and were primarily responsible for network intrusion detection. Participants were not responsible for incident response.

Cyber Awareness Questions. A list of questions was derived from the interview and observation data. These were questions analysts reported asking themselves to establish and maintain awareness of new and ongoing network events. The informality and similarity between questions was not edited to preserve any nuance that existed in question phrasing. Table 1 provides a list of the cyber awareness questions derived from interviews and observations of cyber security analysts and used in the card sorting study.

Procedure. Participants sorted the 44 cyber awareness questions into groups that best reflected their understanding of the questions. Once the questions were sorted into groups, participants labeled each group with a descriptive word or phrase. At the end of the activity the study moderator debriefed the participants' work by asking them to explain how they sorted the questions and why. Card sorting sessions lasted between 45 minutes and one hour.

Table 1. Cyber awareness questions used in card sorting study

1. Are there more or less bad guys attacking my network than normal?	23. What did the bad guys take?
2. Can I see the attack I know is happening?	24. What do I do about the attack?
3. Does the attack have a negative effect on other business operations?	25. What do I not see happening on my network?
4. Does this attack matter?	26. What does my network look like to the bad guys?
5. Have I seen an attack like this before?	27. What does my network look like?
6. How did the bad guys get into my network?	28. What does the attack look like?
7. How is my network being attacked?	29. What does the event on my network mean?
8. How is my network different from last week?	30. What happened on the network last night?
9. How serious is the attack?	31. What is different on my network from last week?
10. How successful was the attack?	32. What is happening on my network now?
11. Is anything different happening on my network than normal?	33. What is happening with my network?
12. Is anything interesting happening on my network?	34. What is normal for my network?
13. Is it a good day on the network?	35. What is not normal for my network?
14. Is my network configured correctly?	36. What is the most important event happening on my network?
15. Is my network healthy?	37. What is the status of my network?
16. Is something bad happening on the network?	38. What malware have been detected on my network?
17. Is something happening on the network?	39. What systems are up or down on my network?
18. Is the event on my network good, bad, or just different?	40. Where are the bad guys attacking from?
19. Is there more or less traffic on my network than normal?	41. Where on my network am I being attacked?
20. Is this a new attack I have not seen before?	42. Who is attacking my network?
21. What are the bad guys doing on my network?	43. Why is my network being attacked?
22. What did the bad guys do?	44. Why are computers on my network not available?

3.3   Analysis

An analysis of the top question pairs based on descriptive statistics and question co-occurrence provided insights to the most critical cyber situation awareness questions. Co-occurrence was calculated as the number of participants who sorted two questions together independent of the group the questions were sorted into during the card sorting activity. Graph visualization of question co-occurrence was then used to analyze clusters of questions. Graph features such as, network weight, clusters, and bridges were used to identify topic areas. Content analysis of the clusters provided insight to topic areas that shape an analyst mental model for cyber situation awareness. Knowledge from the interviews and observations provided additional context and was integrated into the interpretation and understanding of the results.

3.4   Limitations

Cyber security analysts are often difficult to involve in research [1]. Only a limited number of cyber security analysts were available to participate in this study. Card sorting studies can be run with a large number of participants using quantitative analysis methods or a small number of participants using qualitative analysis methods [6]. We chose to conduct a small qualitative card sorting study because of the benefits of in-depth qualitative analysis and the challenges recruiting cyber security analysts. To compensate for a smaller study, we triangulated our results with graph visualization analysis and the results from observations and interviews.

4   Results

4.1   Top Question Pairs

There were 144 card pairs with 50% (6/12 participants) co-occurrence representing 98% (43/44) of the questions in the study. There were 21 question pairs with 75% (9/12 participants) co-occurrence representing 52% (23/44) of the questions in the study. Overall, there was good representation of all the questions in the study within the highest co-occurrence pairs. Table 2 provides a list of the cyber awareness question pairs with 75% co-occurrence. Additionally, we found three types of relationships between the highest co-occurrence question pairs that we define as: question similarity, question sets, and question order. The question types were derived from qualitative analysis of the question relationships.

Similarity. The first type of question pair relationship was based on *similarity* (A is the same as B) in which two questions are asking the same thing. These questions are essentially the same, just asked differently depending on the situation:

"How is my network different from last week?"
"What is different on my network from last week?" (9/12 participants)

Set. The second type of question pair relationship was a *logical set* (A and B are the same type) in which questions are distinctly different but related in purpose or goal:

"Is anything different happening on my network than normal?"
"Is anything interesting happening on my network?" (10/12 participants)

Table 2. Top 75% co-occurrence (9/12 or more participants) cyber awareness question pairs

CO	Question	Question
92%	Is anything interesting happening on my network?	Is something bad happening on the network?
92%	What did the bad guys take?	How successful was the attack?
83%	What happened on the network last night?	What is different on my network from last week?
83%	Is something happening on the network?	Is anything interesting happening on my network?
83%	Is anything interesting happening on my network?	Is anything different happening on my network than normal?
83%	What does the attack look like?	Have I seen an attack like this before?
75%	How is my network different from last week?	What is different on my network from last week?
75%	Is anything different happening on my network than normal?	Is something happening on the network?
75%	Is anything different happening on my network than normal?	Is something bad happening on the network?
75%	Is anything different happening on my network than normal?	What is happening with my network?
75%	Is anything different happening on my network than normal?	Is there more or less traffic on my network than normal?
75%	Is something happening on the network?	Is something bad happening on the network?
75%	What is happening with my network?	What do I not see happening on my network?
75%	Is it a good day on the network?	Is my network healthy?
75%	Is it a good day on the network?	What is the status of my network?
75%	What is the status of my network?	What is normal for my network?
75%	What is the status of my network?	What systems are up or down on my network?
75%	What does the attack look like?	Who is attacking my network?
75%	Have I seen an attack like this before?	Who is attacking my network?
75%	Does this attack matter?	How serious is the attack?
75%	What did the bad guys do?	What did the bad guys take?

While the framework of this question pair is very similar, e.g., "Is anything ... on my network?", the use of "different" and "interesting" make the questions distinct. Based on the knowledge gained from the interviews and observations, "different" is not always "interesting" but both are equally important and asked.

Order. The third type of question pair relationship was a *logical order* (A comes before B) in which a question was a logical follow-up or a requirement to the previous question. For example, the order of these questions implies an analytic process, including the priority or requirement to answer certain questions before others:

"What does the attack look like?"
"Have I seen an attack like this before?" (10/12 participants)

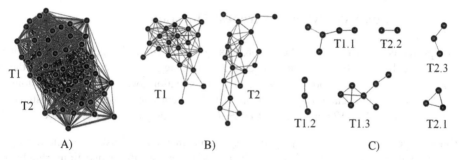

Fig. 1. Graph visualizations of question co-occurrence with potential topics. A) Base network with 50% (6/12 participants) co-occurrence highlighted revealing two topic areas; B) 50% co-occurrence network with two main topic areas; C) 75% (9/12 participants) co-occurrence network revealing six sub-topic areas.

4.2   Graph Visualization and Content Analysis

The most interesting graph visualizations were those that were expressed by the highest number of participants. Figure 1 shows graph visualizations for all question pairs (Fig.1-A), 50% co-occurrence (Fig.1-B) that represented questions paired by at least half of the participants in the study, and 75% co-occurrence (Fig.1-C) that represented questions paired by a majority of participants.

An overlay of the 50% co-occurrence question pairs on the base network visualization showed two question co-occurrence clusters, potentially revealing two main topic areas (Fig.1-A). A visualization of the 50% co-occurrence question pairs (Fig.1-B) showed the two clusters found in the base network (Fig.1-A) as well as graph features such as sub-clusters and bridges that identify possible sub-clusters. A visualization of the 75% co-occurrence question pairs (Fig.1-C) showed six small clusters that are a sub-set of the two 50% co-occurrence clusters (Fig.1-B).

Content analysis of the questions in the two clusters (Fig.1-B) revealed potential topics in Event Detection (T1) and Event Orientation (T2). Further content analysis of the six clusters from the 75%+ co-occurrence question pairs (Fig.1-C) revealed potential sub-topics such as Network Baseline (T1.1), Change Detection (T1.2), Network Activity (T1.3), Event Identification (T2.1), Mission Impact (T2.2), and Damage Assessment (T2.3).

Further analysis of different levels of co-occurrence visualization disambiguated the relationships between question pairs that were not clearly from one of the six 75%+ co-occurrence clusters. For example, several additional questions can be classified in one of the six topics by examining the visualization for the 67% co-occurrence question pairs (8/12 participants) and 58% co-occurrence question pairs (7/12 participants). These additional questions are included in Table 3 taxonomy of cyber awareness questions.

5   Taxonomy of Cyber Awareness Questions

The presented taxonomy of cyber awareness questions offers insights into different stages of cyber situation awareness (Table 3). The categories were derived from the results of the study and previous work in cyber situation awareness. The questions were organized into categories based on their co-occurrence score from our study, ranging from 58% (7/12 participants) to 92% (11/12 participants) co-occurrence.

Event Detection. This category contains questions that analysts ask prior and during initial awareness of a network event. In Event Detection, these questions roughly align with the perception phase of situation awareness.

Network Baseline. A network baseline is a model or snapshot of the network when it functioning in a "normal" state, in which "normal" is often the best approximation of healthy, acceptable operation. Comparison to their mental baseline was a common way analysts in this study articulated how their analytic needs precede cyber events.

Change Detection. Change detection is the ability to compare states of the network to identify differences and trends. The concept differs only slightly from network Baseline in that, here, analysts focus on the comparison between two network states.

Network Activity. Network activity reflects a shift from "normal" to "not normal" network activity that acts as a cue for the analyst to narrow his attention for in-depth analysis. These questions relate closest to the situation awareness concept of perception as well as allude to the transition between Change Detection and Event Identification.

Event Orientation. This category contains questions that analysts ask and are most closely aligned with the comprehension stage of situation analysis. In Event Orientation, analysts are working to maximize insight into an identified cyber event.

Identification. Identification is the recognition that a subset of network activity warrants analytic attention. This category is the detailed analysis of an event to identify who, what, when, where, and why and attack is happening and to possibly link the activity to familiar threats.

Mission Impact. Mission impact is analysis to prioritize the importance of an identified threat. Analysts must judge the severity of the threat to business operations, such as personnel necessary to respond to the threat, to help determine how to distribute limited resources for investigating and responding to the threat.

Damage Assessment. Damage assessment is analysis to inform a response to an identified threat. These questions differ somewhat from Mission Impact; here, the goal is to understand the full effects of the attack on the internal network.

Table 3. Taxonomy of Cyber Awareness Questions for Cyber Situation Awareness

Event Detection	Event Orientation
Network Baseline	*Event Identification*
• Is it a good day on the network?	• Have I seen an attack like this before?
• Is my network configured correctly?	• Is this a new attack I have not seen before?
• Is my network healthy?	• How is my network being attacked?
• What does my network look like?	• What are the bad guys doing on my network?
• What is happening on the network now?	
• What is normal for my network?	• What does the attack look like?
• What is not normal for my network?	• Where on my network am I being attacked?
• What is the status of my network?	• Who is attacking my network?
• What systems are up or down on my network?	• Where are they bad guys attacking from?
	• Why is my network being attacked?
Change Detection	*Mission Impact*
• How is my network different from last week?	• Does this attack matter?
• What happened on the network last night?	• How serious is the attack?
• What is different on my network from last week?	• What do I do about the attack?
Network Activity	*Damage Assessment*
• Is anything different happening on my network than normal?	• Does the attack have a negative effect on other business operations?
• Is anything interesting happening on my network?	• How successful was the attack?
	• What did the bad guys do?
• Is something bad happening on the network?	• What did the bad guys take?
• Is something happening on the network?	
• Is the event on my network good, bad, or just different?	
• Is there more or less traffic on my network than normal?	
• What do I not see happening on my network?	
• What does the event on my network mean?	
• What is happening with my network?	
• What is the most important event happening on my network?	
• Why are computers on my network not available?	

6   Conclusion

In this paper we utilized user-centered and ethnographic research methods to explore and understand the mental model of cyber security analysts responsible for a large network. Our results lead to the contribution of a taxonomy of cyber awareness questions that describes a set of questions analysts ask themselves while they establish and maintain situation awareness during a network event.

This taxonomy provides valuable information about the cyber security analyst and will support the user-centered design and development of cyber situation awareness technology. For example, the taxonomy could be used during the design of cyber situation awareness visualization. Good design is especially important for large-scale visualizations that display large amounts of data. This taxonomy of cyber awareness questions would help inform the design of visualizations that would help analysts better establish and maintain situation awareness of a large computer network.

However, this study only addresses part of the picture. Our taxonomy does not include questions related to incident response while other models of cyber situation awareness do. The cyber security analysts in our study were specialized and only responsible for intrusion detection related activities as opposed to other research that studied generalists (e.g., [8]) or specific types of cyber security analysts (e.g., [2, 5, 7]). This may explain the lack of incident response topic area and questions in our taxonomy. Additional work in this cyber situation awareness will contribute additional questions and topic areas to the taxonomy.

References

1. Botta, D., Werlinger, R., Gagné, A., Beznosov, K., Iverson, L., Fels, S., Fisher, B.: Towards Understanding IT Security Professionals and Their Tools. In: ACM Symposium on Usable Privacy and Security, pp. 100–111 (2007)
2. D'Amico, A., Whitley, K., Tesone, D., O'Brien, B., Roth, E.: Achieving Cyber Defense Situational Awareness: A Cognitive Task Analysis of Information Assurance Analysts. In: Human Factors and Ergonomics Society Annual Meeting, pp. 229–233 (2005)
3. D'Amico, A., Whitley, K.: The Real Work of Computer Network Defense Analysts. In: Symposium on Visualizations for Computer Security, pp. 19–37 (2007)
4. Endsley, M.R.: Toward a Theory of Situation Awareness in Dynamic Systems. Human Factors 37(1), 32–64 (1995)
5. Goodall, J.R., Lutters, W.G., Komlodi, A.: Developing expertise for network intrusion detection. Information Technology & People 22(2), 92–108 (2009)
6. Hudson, W.: Card Sorting. In: Soegaard, M., Dam, R. (eds.) The Encyclopedia of Human-Computer Interaction, 2nd edn. The Interaction Design Foundation, Aarhus (2013)
7. Thompson, R.S., Rantanen, E.M., Yurcik, W.: Network Intrusion Detection Cognitive Task Analysis: Textual and Visual Tool Usage and Recommendations. In: Human Factors and Ergonomics Society Annual Meeting, pp. 669–673 (2006)
8. Werlinger, R., Muldner, K., Kawkey, K., Beznosov, K.: Preparation, detection, and analysis: the diagnostic work of IT security incident response. Information Management & Computer Security 18(1), 26–42 (2010)

Click Me If You Can!
When Do Users Follow a Call to Action in an Online Message?

Thomas Pfeiffer[1], Heike Theuerling[2], and Michaela Kauer[2]

[1] Center for Advanced Security Research Darmstadt, Germany
thomas.pfeiffer@cased.de
[2] Technische Universität Darmstadt, Insitute of Ergonomics, Germany
{h.theuerling,kauer}@iad.tu-darmstadt.de

Abstract. Being able to predict how internet users react when confronted with a potentially dangerous call for action in an online message (such as an e-mail) is important for several reasons. On the one hand, users have to be protected from fraudulent e-mails such as phishing. On the other hand, over-cautious users would be difficult to communicate with on the internet, so senders of legitimate messages have to know how to convince recipients of the authenticity of their messages. Extensive research already exists from both of these perspectives, but each study only explores certain aspects of the complex system of factors influencing users' reactions. In this paper the results of our efforts to integrate the various existing findings into one comprehensive model are presented, along with the results of a preliminary evaluation of some of the model's predictions using quantitative as well as qualitative measures and eye-tracking.

Keywords: decision model, e-mail, phishing, social engineering, e-commerce, trust, risk.

1 Introduction

Electronic messages such as e-mails or messages on social networks like Twitter or Facebook are an important communication medium for private as well as business-to-business (B2B) and business-to-consumer (B2C) communication. However, the existence of diverse kinds of malicious messages (e.g. phishing, financial fraud, attachments containing malware) exposes users who blindly trust every message they receive and do everything the message prompts them to do (e.g. clicking a link and entering data into a web form, opening an attachment or transferring money) to serious risks. Therefore, recipients have to decide carefully which message they should trust and which calls to action they should follow, whereas senders of legitimate messages have to find ways to gain their recipients' trust and ideally make them follow their calls to action. To inform efforts both to prevent misplaced trust and to gain legitimate trust, it is important to understand which attributes of a message, its sender, its recipient or the

L. Marinos and I. Askoxylakis (Eds.): HAS/HCII 2013, LNCS 8030, pp. 155–166, 2013.

context in which the message is received increase or decrease the likelihood that the recipient trusts the message and follows the call to action contained in it.

In an approach to gain a comprehensive understanding of these attributes and processes, we have integrated current research mainly from the usable security and e-commerce disciplines into a general path-analytic model to predict a user's decision whether to follow a call to action in an online message or not.

In section 2 we summarize the existing literature on the topic and in particular the outcomes of existing empirical research. Section 3 describes the method used to create the initial version of the predictive model. The model itself is described in section 4. Section 5 illustrates an early study conducted to qualitatively explore some of the model's paths using eye-tracking.

2   Background

As described in a previous publication [1], our work draws mainly from two fields of scientific research: E-commerce and usable security. Both fields have approached users' decisions in potentially risky online environments. While e-commerce research concentrates on users' trust in legitimate websites and messages, usable security researchers focus on users' reactions to social engineering attacks such as phishing e-mails. While e-commerce research is mainly concerned with websites instead of messages, we hypothesize that findings from websites can be transferred to e-mails, since studies that used both e-mails and websites as stimuli (e.g. [2,3]) found similar effects for both.

In research from both fields, several factors affecting usage of a website or following a call to action in an e-mail have been found empirically. In accordance with the Theory of Planned Behavior [4], Kim et al. [5] found purchase on an e-commerce site to be predicted by intention to purchase. Intention to purchase in turn was found to be positively influenced by trust [5,6,7], perceived/expected benefit [8,5] and negatively influenced by perceived risk [5,8]. Aiken and Boush [9] conceptualized willingness to provide information to a website as the behavioral component of trust. Similarly, intention to adopt e-services was found to be positively influenced by expected benefit/usefulness [10], trust (directly [11] or mediated by usefulness [10]), and risk (directly [11] and via usefulness [11,10]). Hardee et al. [12] found both perceived risk and expected benefit to influence intention to engage in secure behavior.

In the studies by Blais and Weber and Figner and Weber [13,14] risk taking is seen as an evaluation of the expected benefits and the perceived risk. Chang and Chen [7] found risk perception to influence attitude towards reading commercial e-mail and thereby intention to read it. Weber and Hsee [15] postulated differences in risk preference to be caused by attitudes toward perceived risk or by different perceptions of the risk. Blais and Weber [13] found risk perception to be a good predictor of risk taking. The same applies to a study [16] where risk taking was operationalized as visiting a website with an SSL error. Depending on content and context riskiness of a situation is perceived differently between and within individuals [15,17]. A different perception of the respective risk was found to be the reason for gender differences in risk-taking [17]. According to Weber [15] there is a wide range of factors influencing these perceptions, like "outcome feedback from previous risky decisions, aspiration levels, trust, expectations, and loss functions for outcomes that deviate from expectations". More than the perceived risk Hanoch et al. [18] found the respective perceived benefit to mediate the propensity to take risk.

Furthermore, increased trust was found to decrease perceived risk [5,7] and vice versa [19,10,7]. Trust was found to increase expected benefit [10], but Fogg et al. [20] also found "usefulness of information" to be a predictor of a website's perceived credibility.

According to the model of organizational trust by Mayer et al. [21], trust is preceded by the trustee's perceived ability, benevolence and integrity. Gill et al. [22] confirmed the model empirically and found that the trustor's propensity to trust is only effective in influencing the trustor's intention to trust in a specific trustee in the absence of clear signals of the trustee's high or low ability, integrity and benevolence. However, other studies [5,23,7,24] found a general positive influence of propensity to trust on specific trust. Schlosser et al. [25] confirmed the influence of perceived ability on the intention to buy from a website (which they call "trusting intention") for users searching for specific information on a website, and the influence of perceived benevolence for users generally browsing a site. Fogg et al. [20] found a website owner's "company motive" to influence the site's perceived credibility. Implied investment into a website was found to predict trust (via perceived integrity) [25,9,26].

Many studies investigated the effects of different attributes of the website or message itself on perceived risk, expected benefit and especially on trust. The information or content quality of a website was found to have influence on trust [5,27,20,6,7,28](via perceived ability), as were spelling and grammar errors [29,30]. Language which felt persuading to readers on websites [20] or in e-mails [30,2] specifically was found to decrease trust, as was the request to enter a lot of sensitive information on a website [28]. Design and structure of websites [27,20,28,31] or e-mails [30] was found to be another factor influencing trust. The presence of a footer was found to increase trust in both websites [28,20] and e-mails [30,2] (via perceived ability), as was the presence of a third-party trust seal on websites [9,20,26,27,28] and e-mails [2]. Personalization of content was also found to increase trust in the authenticity of e-mails [30,29]. Perceived privacy and security protection is another factor that increases perceived ability, benevolence and integrity and thus trust in websites [5,28,25] and decreases perceived risk [5]. Further investigating some of the aforementioned factors, Tsow and Jakobsson [2] found that design, trust seals, URLs and HTTPS only affected trust in e-mails and websites when their narrative strength was low, leading users to focus on these secondary indicators for their trust decision, whereas high narrative strength increased trust in general.

The sender's address of e-mails was found to be an important factor influencing trust [30,29,32,3], but Vishwanath et al. [33] found that only recipients with sufficient knowledge of phishing and/or general computer self-efficacy paid attention to the e-mail's source. Classification of an e-mail by an e-mail service/program as spam was found to reduce trust in that e-mail as well [3].

Attributes of the – purported – sender of an e-mail or owner of a website have been found to play an important role in eliciting trust from recipients/users. The most prominent of these attributes is reputation or brand which was found to increase trust [5,26,6,7,3,29,28] and reduce perceived risk [5,7]. Another important factor is the recipient's/user's familiarity with the purported sender/website owner [5,20,26,32], as well as perceived similarity to the sender/owner [23,26]. Jagatic et al. [32] also found that men were more likely to follow calls to action contained in e-mails that purportedly came from women.

Three kinds of attributes of the recipient of an e-mail or user of a website were also found to affect their decisions regarding e-mails or websites: Knowledge/experience, personality traits and demographic attributes. Users with more knowledge of and/or experience with social engineering threats [34,35], or better general computer knowledge [32,35] were found to be less likely to fall for phishing e-mails. General internet experience was found to decrease vulnerability to phishing attacks [35] and have an inverted-U-shaped relation with trust in online firms [9]. A higher level of general education was found to either reduce [35] or increase [24] vulnerability to phishing attacks.

User's perceived protection from opportunism while using e-commerce was found to increase trust in e-commerce sites [26,6], whereas fear of financial risks was found to decrease their susceptibility to phishing [34,35]. Workman [24] found the personality traits commitment, obedience, and propensity to trust to positively influence susceptibility to phishing attacks. Women were found to be more susceptible to phishing attacks than men [32,35], but Sheng et al. [35] found that this effect is mostly mediated by lower technology knowledge and training. Age was found to correlate either with higher [24] or lower susceptibility to phishing [32,35], though Sheng et al. [35] found the effect to be completely mediated by higher education, exposure to anti-phishing training, internet experience and fear of financial risks.

High e-mail load was found to increase a person's susceptibility to phishing attacks, and people who perceived their computer as less vulnerable to attacks were found to perceive less risk from ignoring their browser's SSL certificate warnings [16].

3   Method

The first step in the creation of our model was the extraction of empirically found and/or verified antecedents of users' behavior in risky online scenarios from the existing literature, as well as the direction and form of their relationships among themselves and to the actual behavior. In the next step, similar constructs where merged in order to reduce the number of constructs in the model. Some of the studies we used put their findings in the context of theoretical models of intra-personal processes but others did not, making the integration of the findings non-trivial. Therefore we tried to integrate the empirical findings reported without theoretical models into the theoretical models we found, based on theoretical considerations. We then inserted the construct of "threat-Awareness" (see section 4 for details) into the model to further explain connections found in the literature. Since the model at this point was deemed too complex for easy presentation and discussion, antecedents were aggregated to groups for simplified representation of the model. This simplified representation was then discussed with two groups of scientists from the fields of user-centered trust in interactive systems and ergonomics and refined according to their comments.

4 Results

Figure 1 shows the simplified representation of the model. The predicted behavior is labeled "Follow call to action", it is preceded by "Intention to follow". The intention to follow the call to action is in turn positively influenced by the recipient's trust in the message's sender and the message itself, as well as the recipient's expected benefit from following the call. It is negatively influenced by the risk a user perceives when following the call to action, moderated by the amount of possible loss. Trust and perceived risk influence each other negatively, trust affects expected benefit positively, and perceived risk influences it negatively.

The most important group of variables influencing the aforementioned variables are the attributes of the message itself. The actual content (the call to action itself and the context in which it is embedded, as well as personalization and the narrative strength of the content) influences trust as well as perceived risk and expected benefit. Formal aspects such as design, grammar and spelling correctness, language, the presence of logos, fine-print footers or third-party trust seals all affect trust. Third-party seals also affect perceived risk.

Another important group of variables are attributes of the message's purported sender. In accordance with Gill et al. [22], trust in the sender is influenced by the sender's perceived ability, integrity and benevolence. Those are in turn influenced by the purported sender's reputation or brand, the recipient's familiarity with and perceived similarity to him or her or the sender's gender (especially male recipients are more likely to trust female senders).

We introduced the variable "threat-awareness" into the model to reflect the individual differences in the approach to trust decisions. Threat-aware recipients are both motivated and able to evaluate authenticity of a message by technical means and only factor attributes of the message's purported sender into their trust decision if they perceive the message as being authentic. Threat-unaware recipients, on the other hand, are not aware that a message's sender information and content can be forged and thus trust a message if they trust its purported sender. Threat-awareness is a combination of the knowledge of or experience with the threat of forged online messages on the one hand and the technical knowledge and/or experience necessary to effectively evaluate a message's authenticity on the other hand. This is reflected in the model as multiple moderating effects: Perceived authenticity moderates the the effect of attributes of the purported sender on trust, and that moderating effect is in turn moderated by threat-awareness. Additionally, threat-awareness moderates the effect of attributes of the message on perceived authenticity. In fact, perceived authenticity does not play any role for the decision of threat-unaware recipients. Besides knowledge and experience, current threat-awareness is also influenced by contextual factors such as time pressure or distractions affecting the recipient, or the narrative strength of the message.

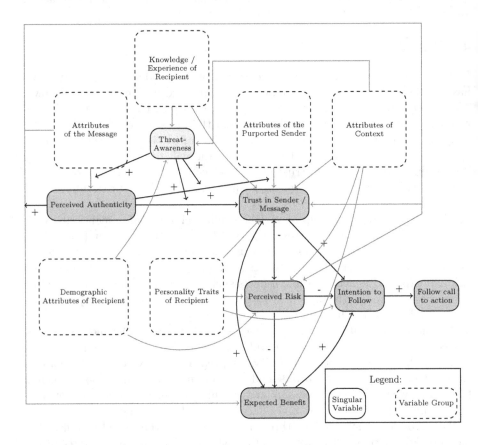

Fig. 1. Simplified representation of the model to predict whether a user follows a call to a potentially risky action contained in an online message

Another group of variables are the recipient's personality traits. For example, recipients' general propensity to trust affects their trust in the sender/message, risk-taking propensity affects risk perception. Recipients with high obedience and commitment generally show higher intention to follow calls to action.

Attributes of the context in which the message is received influence trust in the sender/message, perceived risk, benefit, and current threat-awareness. Variables in this group are for example the contextual plausibility of the e-mail or the perceived vulnerability of the currently used computer to attacks.

Demographic attributes of the recipient such as age, gender, education or marital status correlate with perceived risk as well as threat-awareness.

5 Study

We conducted a preliminary study with a small sample in order to test whether a combination of eye-tracking and open-ended as well as closed questions can be used to evaluate the model qualitatively.

In this study, participants had to evaluate the authenticity of three e-mails. We expected participants which scored higher on a threat-awareness test to focus their attention more on aspects of the e-mail which can be used to identify authenticity more reliably (such as sender or recipient address) and less on aspects which are very easy to fake, such as design elements, than participants which scored low on the test.

Furthermore we expected the reasons given for their decisions to reflect factors found in the model.

5.1 Study Design

The study was a laboratory test taking place at the Technische Universität Darmstadt in Germany. Participants were presented with screenshots of three different e-mails in PDF format. Each e-mail was purportedly sent by PayPal Inc. One of them was authentic, the other two were phishing e-mails. All e-mails were in German, we use translated text here.

The authentic featured the usual PayPal e-mail design and informed the user about changes in their terms of service, including correct links to PayPal websites and the complete new terms of service. It was well-written, without grammatical or spelling errors, addressed the recipient by full name and was signed with "Your PayPal team".

The first phishing e-mail appeared to be from "www.paypal.de" <service@verifiedbyvisa.com> and addressed the recipient with "Dear PayPal member". It included the PayPal logo and some yellow and light-blue elements, but not the original PayPal design. It told recipients that PayPal's danger prevention system had detected suspicious credit card charges in the recipients' account and therefore the recipients should log into their account to regain access, followed by link. A sidebar contained security advice, asking recipients not to give their password to fraudulent websites. The language was of very bad quality, to the point that many sentences were barely understandable.

The second phishing mail appeared to be from "Pay.Pal-Sicherheit EURO" <kunde@pay-pal-sicherer-euro.be> addressed the recipient with "dear user". It told the recipient about an impending suspension of their account due to a missing data synchronization and asked them to synchronize their data by 11/08 to prevent the suspension by clicking a link (which did not contain a URL in the link text). This e-mail contained no layout elements. There were no grammatical errors and no spelling errors other than some missing spaces.

After looking at each e-mail (while their eye-movements were tracked using a remote eye-tracking device), participants were asked whether they perceived the e-mail as authentic and would follow the call to action or not. They were also asked to state reasons for their decision. After the task was completed, the participants took a threat-awareness quiz which consisted of questions covering both knowledge of threats encountered online and knowledge of technical aspects of internet security. The answers to both sets of questions are added to a general threat-awareness score. Furthermore information about age, gender, education, income, internet usage and experience as well as which electronic devices they owned was collected.

5.2 Results

We were able to analyze the data of ten participants, all of them male, between the age of 22 and 27, all of them were college students. All participants use the internet daily. Three participants had three to seven years of internet experience, four participants had seven to ten years and three participants had more then ten years of internet experience.

Eight participants identified all e-mails correctly. One participant perceived the first phishing e-mail as authentic and indicated that he would follow the call to action, for the reason that the e-mail advises recipients not to give away their passwords. One participant perceived the second e-mail as authentic, but indicated he would not follow the call to action because he did not perceive the reason it gave for the data synchronization as reliable. This means that in fact, no participant would have actually given his data to phishers. Therefore no influences on susceptibility to phishing could be tested.

We compared gaze dwell times for certain areas of interest from the eye-tracker between participants which scored low on the threat-awareness test and those which scored high (split at the 50th percentile). Contrary to what we expected, we found that participants who scored higher on the threat-awareness test tended to focus more on the actual content of the e-mail (49% vs. 41% of the dwell time on the legitimate mail, 40% vs. 30% for the first phishing mail and 43% vs. 33% for the second phishing mail) and less on header information (4% vs. 9%, 1% vs. 6% and 11% vs. 13%) than participants with lower scores. Both groups paid equally little attention to design elements such as logos or colored areas.

The reasons given for the perception of mails as authentic or forged were in line with our model. The phishing mails were identified as such mainly because of spelling/grammar mistakes (eight participants), attempts to persuade recipient to submit data or click a link (five participants), their design/layout (three), the poor quality of arguments (three) and lack of personalization (three). Accordingly, the authentic mail was identified as such mainly because it did not ask recipients to enter any information or click any link (five participants), because it mentioned legal matter such as terms of service and relevant laws (four participants), because of its elaborateness (three), its design/layout (three), its language quality (two) and because it contained a personalized salutation (two participants).

5.3 Discussion

The reasons participants stated for their authenticity judgments were all in line with the previous research our model is based on. All of the reasons were related to the content of the e-mails, to their language or their design. In the case of our study, these criteria actually lead to correct decisions, since the phishing mails we used were only poor imitations of authentic PayPal e-mails. However, all the criteria mentioned except for not asking to click any link or submit any information can be spoofed relatively easily by having a native speaker write the text and by copying the design and layout of authentic e-mails. The fact that none of the participants mentioned a suspicious sender or recipient address as the reason for their decision to judge an e-mail as fraudulent, and that participants who scored higher on the threat-awareness test actually spent less time looking at the header area of the e-mails seems counter-intuitive at first. On the other hand, these participants may have known that even a sender address can be spoofed (which wasn't the case in our examples, though), and since they did not have the chance to check out for example the more reliable return-path header (it was not included in the screenshot), they may have dismissed the header information as unreliable. It also has to be noted that the high/low threat-awareness groups were based only on relative scores, since standardized scores do not yet exist for the quiz we used.

Limitations. Since our stimuli turned out to be too easy to identify correctly, we cannot draw any conclusions regarding effectiveness of different decision strategies from our study. To this end, stimuli with more subtle differences between authentic and fake ones would have to be used. We cannot explore the effects of demographic attributes based on our sample either, since it was very small and very homogeneous, so in further studies we would try to recruit larger and more heterogeneous samples.

The insights we gained from our very limited preliminary study holds the promise that eye-tracking, combined with qualitative and quantitative measures of decision strategies and influencing factors can give valuable information for understanding recipients' behavior when facing potentially fraudulent and dangerous online messages.

6 Conclusion and Outlook

The model presented here integrates as well as extends previous decision models for user reactions to potentially dangerous websites or online messages in order to provide increased predictive power as well as generalizability compared to previous models. This model constitutes basic/fundamental research with various ways of application. Plans already exist to use it to inform algorithms which will warn users about potentially dangerous actions, or prevent cues used to evaluate trustworthiness, risk and usefulness of an electronic message from misleading users. Knowledge about factors influencing users' decisions is also useful when creating material to teach users to improve their decision-making process: They should be taught to apply decision criteria which often lead to good decisions and avoid those which often lead to bad decisions. Since the model encompasses both malicious and legitimate messages, it can also guide the design of online messages which legitimately attempt to call users to appropriate action (e.g. in commercial or official communication).

The next step is a larger-scale quantitative empirical evaluation of the model using structural equation modeling techniques to verify the predicted influence paths and determine their relative strengths. Further qualitative studies using eye-tracking could additionally provide further insights into the detailed processes underlying the influence of the different factors.

Acknowledgements. We thank Kathrin Tello and Julian Eurich for conducting the study, and Isabel Klinkigt for proof-reading.

References

1. Pfeiffer, T., Kauer, M., Bruder, R.: Integrating e-commerce and social engineering perspectives on trust in online communication. In: Workshop "User-centered Trust in Interactive Systems" at NordiCHI 2012, Copenhagen (2012), http://tuprints.ulb.tu-darmstadt.de/id/eprint/3249
2. Tsow, A., Jakobsson, M.: Deceit and deception: A large user study of phishing (retrieved September 9, 2007)
3. Kumaraguru, P., Acquisti, A., Cranor, L.F.: Trust modelling for online transactions: a phishing scenario. In: Proceedings of the 2006 International Conference on Privacy, Security and Trust: Bridge the Gap Between PST Technologies and Business Services, PST 2006, pp. 11:1–11:9. ACM, New York (2006)
4. Ajzen, I.: The theory of planned behavior. Organizational Behavior and Human Decision Processes 50(2), 179–211 (1991)
5. Kim, D.J., Ferrin, D.L., Rao, H.R.: A trust-based consumer decision-making model in electronic commerce: The role of trust, perceived risk, and their antecedents. Decision Support Systems 44(2), 544–564 (2008)
6. Harrison McKnight, D., Choudhury, V., Kacmar, C.: The impact of initial consumer trust on intentions to transact with a web site: a trust building model. The Journal of Strategic Information Systems 11(3-4), 297–323 (2002)
7. Chang, H.H., Chen, S.W.: The impact of online store environment cues on purchase intention: Trust and perceived risk as a mediator. Online Information Review 32(6), 818–841 (2008)
8. Glover, S., Benbasat, I.: A comprehensive model of perceived risk of e-commerce transactions. International Journal of Electronic Commerce 15(2), 47–78 (2010)
9. Aiken, K., Boush, D.: Trustmarks, objective-source ratings, and implied investments in advertising: Investigating online trust and the context-specific nature of internet signals. Journal of the Academy of Marketing Science 34(3), 308–323 (2006)
10. Horst, M., Kuttschreuter, M., Gutteling, J.M.: Perceived usefulness, personal experiences, risk perception and trust as determinants of adoption of e-government services in the netherlands. Computers in Human Behavior 23(4), 1838–1852 (2007)
11. Featherman, M.S., Pavlou, P.A.: Predicting e-services adoption: a perceived risk facets perspective. International Journal of Human-Computer Studies 59(4), 451–474 (2003)

12. Hardee, J., Mayhorn, C., West, R.: I downloaded what?: An examination of computer security decisions. In: Proceedings of the Human Factors and Ergonomics Society Annual Meeting, vol. 50, pp. 1817–1820 (2006)
13. Blais, A.R., Weber, E.U.: A domain-specific risk-taking (DOSPERT) scale for adult populations. Judgment and Decision Making 1(1), 33–47 (2006)
14. Figner, B., Weber, E.U.: Who takes risks when and why? Current Directions in Psychological Science 20, 211–216 (2011)
15. Weber, E., Hsee, C.: Cross-cultural differences in risk perception, but cross-cultural similarities in attitudes towards perceived risk. Management Science, 1205–1217 (1998)
16. Sunshine, J., Egelman, S., Almuhimedi, H., Atri, N., Cranor, L.F.: Crying wolf: an empirical study of SSL warning effectiveness. In: Proceedings of the 18th Conference on USENIX Security Symposium, SSYM 2009, pp. 399–416. USENIX Association, Berkeley (2009)
17. Weber, E., Blais, A., Betz, N.: A domain-specific risk-attitude scale: Measuring risk perceptions and risk behaviors. Journal of Behavioral Decision Making 15(4), 263–290 (2002)
18. Hanoch, Y., Johnson, J.G., Wilke, A.: Domain specificity in experimental measures and participant recruitment an application to risk-taking behavior. Psychological Science 17(4), 300–304 (2006)
19. Evans, A.M., Krueger, J.I.: Elements of trust: Risk and perspective-taking. Journal of Experimental Social Psychology 47(1), 171–177 (2011)
20. Fogg, B.J., Soohoo, C., Danielson, D.R., Marable, L., Stanford, J., Tauber, E.R.: How do users evaluate the credibility of web sites?: a study with over 2,500 participants. In: Proceedings of the 2003 Conference on Designing for User Experiences, DUX 2003, pp. 1–15. ACM, New York (2003)
21. Mayer, R.C., Davis, J.H., Schoorman, F.D.: An integrative model of organizational trust. Academy of Management Review, 709–734 (1995)
22. Gill, H., Boies, K., Finegan, J.E., McNally, J.: Antecedents of trust: Establishing a boundary condition for the relation between propensity to trust and intention to trust. Journal of Business and Psychology 19(3), 287–302 (2005)
23. Bekmeier-Feuerhahn, S., Eichenlaub, A.: What makes for trusting relationships in online communication? Journal of Communication Management 14, 337–355 (2010)
24. Workman, M.: Wisecrackers: A theory-grounded investigation of phishing and pre-text social engineering threats to information security. Journal of the American Society for Information Science and Technology 59(4), 662–674 (2008)
25. Schlosser, A.E., White, T.B., Lloyd, S.M.: Converting web site visitors into buyers: How web site investment increases consumer trusting beliefs and online purchase intentions. Journal of Marketing 70(2), 133–148 (2006)
26. Walczuch, R., Lundgren, H.: Psychological antecedents of institution-based consumer trust in e-retailing. Information & Management 42(1), 159–177 (2004)
27. Yang, Y., Hu, Y., Chen, J.: A web trust-inducing model for e-commerce and empirical research. In: Proceedings of the 7th International Conference on Electronic Commerce, ICEC 2005, pp. 188–194. ACM, New York (2005)
28. Lin, E., Greenberg, S., Trotter, E., Ma, D., Aycock, J.: Does domain highlighting help people identify phishing sites? In: CHI 2011, pp. 2075–2084. ACM, New York (2011)
29. Downs, J.S., Holbrook, M.B., Cranor, L.F.: Decision strategies and susceptibility to phishing. In: Proceedings of the Second Symposium on Usable Privacy and Security, SOUPS 2006, pp. 79–90. ACM, New York (2006)

30. Karakasiliotis, A., Furnell, S., Papadaki, M.: Assessing end-user awareness of social engineering and phishing. In: Information Warfare and Security Conference, pp. 60–72 (2006)
31. Dhamija, R., Tygar, J.D., Hearst, M.: Why phishing works. In: Proceedings of the SIGCHI Conference on Human Factors in Computing Systems, CHI 2006, pp. 581–590. ACM, New York (2006)
32. Jagatic, T.N., Johnson, N.A., Jakobsson, M., Menczer, F.: Social phishing. Commun. ACM 50(10), 94–100 (2007)
33. Vishwanath, A., Herath, T., Chen, R., Wang, J., Rao, H.R.: Why do people get phished? testing individual differences in phishing vulnerability within an integrated, information processing model. Decision Support Systems 51(3), 576–586 (2011)
34. Downs, J.S., Holbrook, M., Cranor, L.F.: Behavioral response to phishing risk. In: Proceedings of the Anti-Phishing Working Groups 2nd Annual eCrime Researchers Summit, eCrime 2007, pp. 37–44. ACM, New York (2007)
35. Sheng, S., Holbrook, M., Kumaraguru, P., Cranor, L.F., Downs, J.: Who falls for phish?: a demographic analysis of phishing susceptibility and effectiveness of interventions. In: Proceedings of the 28th International Conference on Human Factors in Computing Systems, CHI 2010, pp. 373–382. ACM, New York (2010)

Increasing Trust Perceptions in the Internet of Things

Trenton Schulz and Ingvar Tjøstheim

Norsk Regnesentral – Norwegian Computing Center,
Gaustadalléen 23a/b, Kristen Nygaards hus, NO-0373 Oslo, Norway
{Trenton.Schulz,Ingvar.Tjostheim}@nr.no
http://www.nr.no

Abstract. When interacting with objects and services in the Internet of Things, people will need to trust that their data is safe, and that "things" will do what they promise they will do. As part of a user evaluation of a toolkit for providing security and privacy information to users, we created two models to find a pattern in changes in the perception of trust in the participants. The model based on demographics was not very descriptive. But, the model based on participants' privacy concerns and trust traits revealed a good match between changes in trust based on information from our toolkit. While there were some limitations in the current study, it showed how TFT can be improved for future evaluations.

1 Introduction

We interact with many different objects, portable, stationary or virtual, to accomplish tasks throughout the day. In the future, these objects will communicate with other objects, either locally or over the Internet. The result of this phenomenon is the *Internet of Things* (IoT) [1]. Users in the IoT will need to know that their data is protected and that their privacy is protected. This can be difficult when users are traveling in different environments and some interactions happen automatically. In short, it is desirable for users to look at privacy and security information and decide whether or not to *trust* the IoT.

Our work involves creating a Trust Feedback Toolkit (TFT) that can present information to users about the security of their connection, what data is collected, how long it is stored, and what is done with it. We have targeted smartphones and tablets for presenting this information as they are likely mobile objects that might participate in different IoT environments. We wanted to study how this information would affect users' trust of the system. Would this information make users more likely to trust or distrust a system? What sort of information makes users trust a system?

To answer these questions, we developed a user evaluation where participants interacted with several IoT environments with the aid of the TFT. We analyzed the results from the evaluations using the partial least squares (PLS) method with emphasis on the impact of the TFT. We found that for certain groups of users, the TFT did alter these users' perception of trust in the system. The impact was not always as expected, for some the effect was a decrease in trust in the system.

The contribution of this paper is to highlight a model that can find patters in changes in trust perception for users of our TFT. The paper is organized as follows. Section 2

L. Marinos and I. Askoxylakis (Eds.): HAS/HCII 2013, LNCS 8030, pp. 167–175, 2013.

provides some background and information about the terminology used in our study and how we use it; Section 3 describes how the study was carried out; Section 4 presents the results and how we created our models; Section 5 discusses these models; Finally, Section 6 provides a conclusion, lessons learned, and possible future work.

2 Background

The idea behind the IoT has been around for a while and was first used in 1999 by Ashton [1]. The IoT refers to uniquely identifiable *things*—either real or virtual—and their representation in an Internet-like infrastructure. As technology progresses, other definitions of the IoT have emerged. Here, we are looking at various things that might appear in smart environments, such as smart homes, smart offices, or e-voting. The scenarios can also be used for ambient assisted living (AAL). The things in these environments are "smart" versions of everyday objects—for example, like doors, medicine cabinets, elevators, and receptionists—and the infrastructure that is necessary for these things to work.

Trust is a concept that has many different meanings depending on the context (e.g., sociology, psychology, ethics, economics, management, and computer science). There are many reviews of trust. For example, Steinke et al. [2] take a look at trust specifically in the AAL settings. Yan et al. [3] have looked at theoretical issues when studying trust in Human-Computer Interaction. Other articles have looked at different ideas about trust in the IoT. Leister and Schulz [4] provide a summary of definitions and categories of trust while proposing an indicator for trusting a thing and its information. Even restricting the search to computer security shows differing definitions of trust [5]. There are many examples of studies that are concerned with trust perception related to the use of a particular service, for instance online banking. It is also typical to study trust at a single point in time. In contrast, Joinson and Reips [6] designed a study that looked at changes in users' trust and privacy on the Internet over a 6-week period.

While the definition of trust generated lots of discussion for us, our focus is on the user's trust. We settled on the definition presented by Döbelt et al. [7], "A user's confidence in an entity's reliability, including that user's acceptance of vulnerability in a potentially risky situation."

3 Study

The TFT has two parts: a framework for integrating into devices that catches security events and a user interface that presents information to the user and allows them to decide if they will continue with an action or not (see Fig. 1). Example information that the TFT provides is if the user is connecting to an unencrypted network, what sort of information the system wishes to store, or if a purchase will be over a certain amount. We designed an evaluation that focused on the user interface part of the TFT, and how well the information provided by the TFT aids the user in making decisions and affecting trust.

Very few have first-hand experience with the IoT. Therefore, we created two virtual reality (VR) environments to carry out user tests. One was a smart office building with

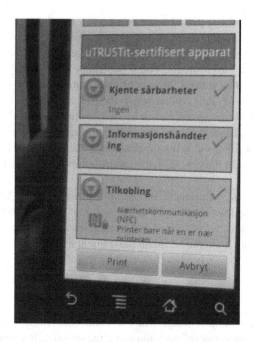

Fig. 1. An example of a TFT screen on a smartphone during the evaluations

multiple floors, meeting rooms, and break rooms. The second was a smart home environment that focused on AAL with a smart medicine cabinet that reminded users to take their medicine and door access for caregivers.

We recruited participants with different backgrounds in two different countries (Norway and Germany) to evaluate the interfaces. We followed the ethical guidelines [8] and participants filled in a consent form. Before entering the virtual environment, participants were asked to fill out questionnaires. Topics included questions about demographics (e.g., age, education level, and gender), how participants judged their own ICT abilities, their knowledge of the IoT, how they felt about certain privacy issues, and their *trust traits* [9]. The trust traits consisted of a survey where participants used a Likert scale to indicate how much they agreed or disagreed with statements about trust and security issues with the Internet, new devices, and ICT in general.

Once they had completed the questionnaires, participants were given a training session in navigation and interaction in a sample virtual environment. After participants were comfortable with the interaction (some chose not to continue), they started the evaluation in either the smart home or the smart office environment. Participants would navigate in the environment and perform tasks by interacting with the different objects using either a smartphone or a tablet. Participants were filmed during their interactions (both themselves and the screen for the smartphone or tablet), and their heart rate and skin conductivity were monitored. In total, there were 16 different tasks that the users had to perform. Four tasks were set up with the participant doing the task one time without the TFT and another time with the TFT. These tasks were: *a*) entering the break room, *b*) purchasing coffee, *c*) purchasing perfume, and *d*) ordering medicine.

After participants had completed a task, they were asked questions about their *trust state*; this consisted of four statements about trust. Participants would rate on a scale of one to four how much they agreed or disagreed with the statements (one is total disagreement, 4 is total agreement). These questions were if they felt their personal data was protected, if they trusted the security mechanisms in the system, if there was enough information about their connection to the IoT, and if they felt the network was well structured. In addition, participants needed to rate on a scale from one to four how much they trusted the things in the completed task and why. After completing all tasks, participants filled out a final questionnaire about the tasks and their experiences in virtual reality. In the end, 35 participants completed the tasks and the pre- and post-questionnaires.

After the evaluations, we created the *change in trust* variable based on four tasks that were done with and without the TFT. The variable shows a change in trust: either positive (coded as 3), no change (coded as 2), or negative (coded as 1). We designed the study to find the factors that could explain the influence of the TFT in changing trust.

4   Results

The study used a within subject design with two conditions. In condition one, the system acted without any warnings or information about the security. In condition two, the user received warnings and relevant information from the TFT regarding security. The goal was to increase trust when it is appropriate based on the information presented to the participants. Of the 35 participants, 14 felt an increase in trust in the system after using the TFT, eight felt a decrease in trust in the system, and 13 experienced no change. We will focus on those that experienced a change in trust perception.

Partial least squares (PLS) is the statistical analysis technique used to interpret data from the study and to test the two models. PLS is a structural equation modeling technique that can simultaneously estimate measurement components and structural components that are the relationships among these constructs. PLS does not require a large sample size [10, 11].

We investigated two models that could explain the influence of the TFT in changing trust. Model 1 looked at demographics—age, gender, and education—and the user's assessment of technical skills. Model 2 focused on privacy concerns and trust traits. The PLS Path Modeling for these models are shown in Fig. 2 and Fig. 3, respectively.

Model 1 showed that older people would have lower trust after seeing the information from the TFT. This was also the case for high education and high ICT skills. However, the R^2 value for this model was low (0.15) and was not very predictive. This implies that if the goal is to understand the impact of the TFT, we should look for something other than demographics.

Literature showed that privacy can be a factor that influences trust [12, 13, 14], but there is not necessarily a straightforward relationship between privacy concerns and actual behavior [6]. Another approach is to study differences caused by trust traits. We looked at both privacy and trust traits [15, 16]. We made a variable based on answers to the questions that were asked about the privacy concerns and the trust traits before participants entered the VR environment and created a new model called Model 2.

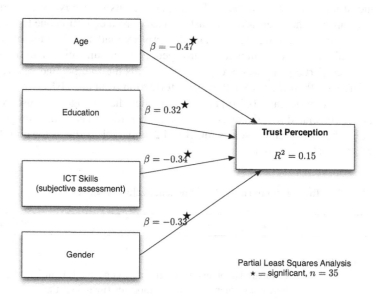

Fig. 2. Predicting change in trust perception based on demographics

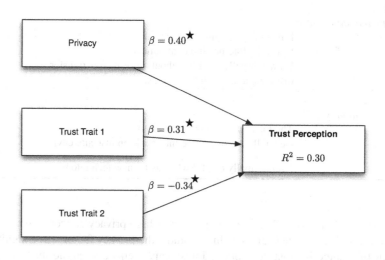

Fig. 3. Predicting change in trust perceptions based on opinions of privacy and security

Model 2 shows that the three variables show a pattern about change in the perception of trust due to information from the TFT. The participants with privacy concerns had a tendency to answer that their level of trust increased from condition one to condition two. According to this finding we can state that privacy matters. The same is true for participants that tend to be optimistic towards people, communication, and transfer of information. Yet, participants who are skeptical towards the Internet and new technology do not increase their trust when they get information from the TFT.

The R^2 value is moderate (0.30) [17]. This implies that changes in trust from the TFT are better correlated by privacy concerns and trust traits than from demographics. Table 1 shows the measurement scales for Model 2, and Table 2 shows the correlations between Model 2's latent variables.

Table 1. Summary of Measurement Scales for Model 2

Construct	Measure	Factor Loading
Privacy *composite reliability*: 0.82		
PC2	Compared to others, I am genuinely concerned about how companies and other authorities (including the Internet) process my personal data.	0.74
PC5	Compared to other topics, my private life and privacy are very important.	0.80
PC6	I am concerned about things that can threaten my private life and privacy.	0.78
Trust Trait 1 *composite reliability*: 0.87		
TT7	I trust people in most circumstances.	0.83
TT8	I trust the Internet and communication.	0.90
TT9	I am normally positive about information transfer that happen through IT systems.	0.76
Trust Trait 2 *composite reliability*: 0.75		
TT12	The Internet is an unsafe medium.	0.72
TT13	Generally, I feel that the Internet is an insecure environment.	0.77
TT4	I am normally careful when using new technology.	0.65

Joinson and Reips write that many people report high privacy concernts when faced with a specific threat to their privacy. In our study, the privacy factor was a significant predictor of change in trust perception. Joinson and Reips also argue that users rely "...heavily on situational cues to make a decision rather than their preexisting attitudes" [6, p.18].

Based on this, we interpret our findings as follows: both attitudinal factors—such as privacy and trust traits—matter in determining change in trust. But, a model with these factors cannot fully explain why trust increases, decreases, or does not change.

Table 2. Correlation between latent variables for Model 2

	Change in Trust Perception	Privacy	Trust Trait 1	Trust Trait 2
Change in Trust Perception	1.00			
Privacy	0.29	0.77		
Trust Trait 1	0.37	0.08	0.83	
Trust Trait 2	−0.21	0.41	0.10	0.71

Our findings also indicate that situational cues—for instance, information presented by the TFT—matter. So, the TFT is a tool that can be used to increase awareness in trust and security issues.

5   Discussion

The second structural model contains the paths between the three independent variables (constructs) and the dependent variable, the TFT. An examination of the structural model using PLS indicates that the model explains approximately 40 percent of the variability in trust perception ($R^2 = 0.30$).

According to Chin [17], R^2 values of 0.19, 0.33, and 0.67 can be described as weak, moderate, and strong, respectively. Consider also the principle of parsimony where we try to explain the most with the least. This principle favors a research model with fewer explanatory variables, assuming that this model explains the dependent variable almost as well as a model with additional variables. With the limited number of participants, it not acceptable to create many explanatory variables for a model.

In our study, the model based on demographics is weak and shows no pattern to explain trust perceptions. The model based on privacy and trust traits did show predictive power; participants having concerns about privacy and the safety of the network were influenced by the TFT and changed their perception of trust in the IoT. This helps inform designers what type of information needs to be conveyed when designing trustworthy systems for the IoT.

There are limitations with Model 2. One limitation is that it is not a comprehensive model and it has very few variables. In addition, this model is only linked to people with certain privacy concerns and trust traits. It is also difficult to say how the usability of the TFT affected the perception of trust. Usability will be included in the next evaluation.

Another limitation is the number of participants in the study. With only 35 participants it is difficult to say how our results compare to a larger sample. However, our study provides a much richer understanding of trust perception for these participants than a large questionnaire-based study. The evaluation took place in a controlled environment where the participants had context and meaningful tasks to perform. The study was designed to reveal change in trust perception because we kept other variables stable, and we measured the trust state right after completion of each task. We feel that the PLS method is helpful in showing that we get meaningful results despite a small number of participants.

Some participants reacted negatively to the TFT: they distrusted things that should have been trusted and trusted things that should have been distrusted. Sometimes, when not reflecting on what is happening, providing information may cause some participants to think there is something they need to be concerned about. In this case, suddenly getting security information—even if it shows that things are safe—when they previously received no information might cause this reaction. Ideally, the TFT should provide information so that everyone can make the right decision. Still, we see that participants with privacy concerns and certain trust traits are helped by the TFT.

Finally, skeptical users can be a difficult to serve. The findings indicate that even though we present relevant security and privacy information, skeptical users are skeptical of *that* information. It seems necessary for users to trust the TFT itself before the TFT can be play a role in informing users' trust perception.

6 Conclusion

We have created two models based on the responses that were given by participants. Model 2 gives an indication of a possible model that can be used to correlate change in trust perception. We also can see that while a survey about trust or privacy concerns can give us some information about the topic of trust, our study with virtual reality and multiple checks of the trust state allowed us to get a deeper understanding of what might cause changes in trust perception.

The evaluations provided valuable feedback on how the TFT could be improved. This resulted in a new UI for presenting security and privacy information to the user. This new UI will be tested in an upcoming evaluation in both virtual reality and the real world. The next evaluation will include more participants and focus specifically on the usability of the TFT. We expect that the next evaluation will give us a deeper understanding of what causes changes in trust perception and also lead to a better TFT that can benefit everyone.

Acknowledgments. This research is funded as part of the uTRUSTit project. The uTRUSTit project is funded by the EU FP7 program (Grant agreement no: 258360). Thanks to Wolfgang Leister and Mark Summerfield for proofreading the article.

References

1. Ashton, K.: That 'Internet of Things' Thing. RFID Journal (2009),
   http://www.rfidjournal.com/article/view/4986
2. Steinke, F., Fritsch, T., Silbermann, L.: Trust in Ambient Assisted Living (AAL) – A Systematic Review of Trust in Automation and Assistance Systems. International Journal of Advances in Life Sciences 4(3), 77–88 (2012),
   http://www.iariajournals.org/life_sciences/tocv4n34.html
3. Yan, Z., Kantola, R., Zhang, P.: Theoretical Issues in the Study of Trust in Human-Computer Interaction. In: IEEE 10th International Conference on Trust, Security and Privacy in Computing and Communications, pp. 853–856. IEEE (November 2011)
4. Leister, W., Schulz, T.: Ideas for a Trust Indicator in the Internet of Things. In: Leister, W., Dini, P. (eds.) The First International Conference on Smart Systems, Devices and Technologies, SMART 2012, pp. 31–34. IARIA, Stuttgart (2012)

5. Hornák, Z., Nyilas, I., Schrammel, J., Wolkerstorfer, P., Ellensohn, L., Geven, A., Fritsch, L., Schulz, T., Abie, H., Pürzel, F., Wittstock, V.: D.3.1 Technology and Standard Report (2010), http://www.utrustit.eu/uploads/media/utrustit/utRUSTit_D3.1_TechnologyReport_Final.pdf

6. Joinson, A., Reips, U.: Privacy, Trust, and Self-Disclosure Online. Human Computer Interaction 25(1), 1–24 (2010)

7. Döbelt, S., Busch, M., Hochleitner, C.: Defining, Understanding, Explaining TRUST within the utRUSTit Project. Tech. rep., CURE, Vienna, Austria (2012)

8. Fuglerud, K.S., Solheim, I., Ellensohn, L., Pürzel, F., Schulz, T.: utRUSTit Deliverable D7.4 Ethics manual. Tech. rep., Norwegian Computing Center (2011), http://www.utrustit.eu/uploads/media/utrustit/utRUSTit_D7.4._Ethics_Manual_Final_2.0.pdf

9. Busch, M., Döbelt, S., Hochleitner, C., Wolkerstorfer, P., Schulz, T., Fuglerud, K.S., Tjøstheim, I., Pürzel, F., Wittstock, E., Dumortier, J., Vandezande, N.: utRUSTit Deliverable D6.2. Design Iteration I: Evaluation Report. Tech. rep., CURE–Center for Usability Research and Engineering (2012), http://www.utrustit.eu/uploads/media/utrustit/utRUSTit_D6.2-Evaluation_Report_final.pdf

10. Fornell, C., Larcker, D.F.: Evaluating Structural Equation Models with Unobservable Variables and Measurement Error. Journal of Marketing Research 18(1), 39–50 (1981)

11. Barclay, D., Higgins, C., Thompson, R.: The Partial Least Squares (PLS) Approach to Causal Modeling: Personal Computer Adoption and Use as an Illustration. Technology Studies 2(2), 285–309 (1995)

12. Moncrieff, S., Venkatesh, S., West, G.: Dynamic privacy assessment in a smart house environment using multimodal sensing. ACM Transactions on Multimedia Computing, Communications, and Applications 5(2), 1–29 (2008)

13. Yousafzai, S.Y., Pallister, J.G., Foxall, G.R.: Strategies for building and communicating trust in electronic banking: A field experiment. Psychology and Marketing 22(2), 181–201 (2005)

14. Nixon, P., Wagealla, W., English, C., Terzis, S.: Security, Privacy and Trust Issues in Smart Environments. In: Smart Environments: Technology, Protocols and Applications, pp. 220–240. Wiley, London (2004)

15. Mooradian, T., Renzl, B., Matzler, K.: Who Trusts? Personality, Trust and Knowledge Sharing. Management Learning 37(4), 523–540 (2006)

16. Rotter, J.B.: A new scale for the measurement of interpersonal trust. Journal of Personality 35(4), 651–665 (1967)

17. Chin, W.W.: The Partial Least Squares Approach to Structural Equation Modeling. In: Modern Methods for Business Research, pp. 294–336. Laurence Wrlbaum Associates, Hillsdale (1998)

Perception of Risky Security Behaviour by Users: Survey of Current Approaches

Lynsay A. Shepherd, Jacqueline Archibald, and R.I. Ferguson

University of Abertay Dundee, School of Engineering, Computing and Applied Mathematics,
Dundee, DD1 1HG
{lynsay.shepherd,j.archibald,i.ferguson}@abertay.ac.uk

Abstract. What constitutes risky security behaviour is not necessarily obvious to users and as a consequence end-user devices could be vulnerable to compromise. This paper seeks to lay the groundwork for a project to provide instant warning via automatic recognition of risky behaviour. It examines three aspects of the problem, behaviour taxonomy, techniques for its monitoring and recognition and means of giving appropriate feedback. Consideration is given to a way of quantifying the perception of risk a user may have. An ongoing project is described in which the three aspects are being combined in an attempt to better educate users to the risks and consequences of poor security behaviour. The paper concludes that affective feedback may be an appropriate method for interacting with users in a browser-based environment.

Keywords: End-user security behaviours, usable security, affective computing, user monitoring techniques, user feedback, risk perception, security awareness.

1 Introduction

Despite the widespread availability of security tools such as virus scanners and firewalls, risky behaviour exhibited by the end-user has the potential to make devices vulnerable to compromise [1]. This paper aims to identify what constitutes risky security behaviour, review current methods of monitoring user behaviour, and examine ways in which feedback can be provided to users with a view to educating them into modifying their behaviour when browsing the web. Previous work has indicated users need to learn and recognise patterns of risky behaviour themselves [21] [22], thus improving system security.

2 Background

Users often regard system security as obtrusive and restrictive of their ability to perform tasks. Owing to this, they often attempt to circumvent these measures, at the risk of breaching system security [2]. It is possible to place risky security behaviours into categories, allowing monitoring techniques to be developed which attempt to capture the behaviour.

L. Marinos and I. Askoxylakis (Eds.): HAS/HCII 2013, LNCS 8030, pp. 176–185, 2013.
© Springer-Verlag Berlin Heidelberg 2013

2.1 Types of Behaviour

There are a number of ways in which user behaviour could be perceived as risky e.g. interaction with poorly constructed web-based applications may place users at risk from coding vulnerabilities [11]. Other risky behaviours include creating weak passwords, sharing passwords [3] [12] and downloading data from unsafe websites [13].

The problem can be exacerbated by misplaced trust in a comfortable computing environment: if a user interacts with a device regularly, they may form a knowledge-based trust relationship with it [24] (as cited in [25]) whereby, based upon their history with the device, they become accustomed to its peculiarities. Such familiarity may cause the user to be over trustful of interactions performed on it. Knowledge-based trust is said to be persistent and even if performance differs, the trust relationship remains.

2.2 Monitoring Techniques/Measuring Awareness

It is possible that risky security behaviour can be automatically recognised through user monitoring. Previous studies [4] [5] refer to the use of an event-based system, allowing user's actions to be monitored across a range of applications running on the operating system. Video monitoring is also a technique which has been used successfully. In particular, it has been used to record eye movements of users, thus determining the affective state of the end-user [6]. When used in combination with a task-based approach, video monitoring can provide a detailed overview of end-user behaviour, in comparison to approaches monitoring a singular type of interaction [7].

Monitoring techniques are just one component which can be investigated when exploring the issue of end-user security behavior. When measuring awareness it is useful to record the perception of risk which users have. Several pieces of research have been conducted in the area, investigating suitable metrics for describing the perception of risk. Previous studies have employed questionnaires to assess how the user perceives their behavior [8]. This concept can be extended to make use of both questionnaires and psychometric models, providing an overview of perceived risky behaviour [14] [15].

2.3 Types of Feedback

There are many methods of providing user feedback. These include pieces of textual information, where specific words are used e.g. describing a password as "weak" [9]. Colour can be used in combination with text, or alone in a bar meter, displaying either green/blue to imply "good" or red for "bad" [9]. Furthermore, dialogue, colours and sounds can be used together to alter the affective state of a user [18].

Avatars have been widely implemented to change the affective state of the user, particularly in the field of intelligent tutoring agents. In a number of instances the introduction of avatars has proved beneficial and has helped users in educational environments [18] [19] [20].

3   Analysis

This section explores previous research, to provide a comparison of terminology used when describing risky security behaviour. Applying monitoring techniques to users can capture such behaviour and allow perception of risk to be measured. Potentially, user behaviour could be influenced by feedback provided.

3.1   Risky Behaviour – A Taxonomy

There have been several attempts to categorise behaviours displayed by users which could be classified as risky (summarised in Table 1), including a 2005 paper by Stanton et al. [3]. Following interviews with both security experts and IT experts, and a study involving end-users in the US, across a range of professions, a taxonomy of 6 behaviours was created: intentional destruction, detrimental misuse, dangerous tinkering, naïve mistakes, aware assurance and basic hygiene.

Padayachee [26] provides a breakdown of compliant security behaviours whilst investigating if certain users had a predisposition to adhering to security behaviour. A taxonomy was developed, highlighting elements which may influence security behaviours in users i.e. extrinsic motivation, identification, awareness and organisational commitment. The paper acknowledges the taxonomy does not present a complete overview of all possible motivational factors regarding compliance with security policies. Despite this, it may provide a basis as to how companies could start to improve their security education, with a view to gaining the attention of end-users.

In terms of common risky behaviours, passwords can be problematic with a trade-off existing between the usability of passwords and the level of security they provide [12]. Usable passwords are easier for users to remember however, this can mean they are short and therefore less secure. Users may also engage in questionable behaviour e.g. sharing passwords. Whilst exploring the issue of basic security hygiene, Stanton et al. [3] touched on the subject of passwords. A survey of 1167 end-users highlighted several instances of risky security behaviour e.g. 27.9% of participants wrote their passwords down and 23% revealed their passwords to colleagues.

Another of these categories is related to how users perceive technology flaws, e.g. vulnerability to XSS attacks or session hijacking. Social engineering can also be considered to fall into this category: e.g. An attacker could potentially clone a profile on a social networking site and use the information to engineer an attack against a target(eg via the malicious link technique) [11]. Such attacks can be facilitated by revealing too much personal information on social networking sites [10].

Downloading illegal files such as music/software can be classed as risky behaviour: in addition to breaking the law, users are potentially exposing their system to viruses or malware that the downloaded files may contain [13].

Table 1. - Comparison of terminology describing risky security behaviours

[3] Stanton, J.M. et al.	[26] Padayachee, K.	[12] Payne, B. and Edwards, W	[10] Balduzzi, M.	[11] Hadnagy, C.	[13] Fetscherin, M.	[29] Herath, T. and Rao, H.R.
Intentional destruction: intention to harm IT resources in a company	Amotivation	-	-	-	-	-
Detrimental misuse: using IT for inappropriate purposes	Amotivation	-	-	-	Download -ing illegal files	-
Dangerous tinkering: accidentally configuring IT resources with security flaws	-	-	-	-	-	-
Naïve mistakes: user doesn't realise their behaviour is flawed	-	Password usability	Sharing too much on social networks	Sharing too much on social networks	-	-
Aware assurance: wants to protect company IT systems- recognises security issues.	Extrinsic motivation	-	-	-	-	Intrinsic motivation : perceived effectiveness
Basic hygiene: user is educated about security issues and adheres to security policies	Extrinsic and intrinsic motivation	Password usability	-	-	-	Extrinsic motivation :social pressures

3.2   Monitoring Risky Behaviour

Multiple approaches have been used in the past to monitor user behavior. Fenstermacher and Ginsburg [5] have experimented with the use of a system event-based approach (originally designed for gathering usability information) which linked applications running across the operating system. Each application invoked several method calls and functions, making use of Microsoft's Component Object Model and Python. An XML-based log file was then generated based-upon the actions of the user, containing information such as a timestamp, the application used and which event was triggered. This suggests a similar technique could be applied when monitoring risky security behaviour.

Additionally, a combination of video and task monitoring could be used to view user behavior [6]. In a study by Heishman, the eye movement of participants was monitored to interpret the affective state of the user. Results of the study found it was possible to detect the affective and cognitive states of users and that such a technique may be used when exploring further HCI concepts.

Doubleday et al. also successfully used both video and task monitoring to observe behavior [7]. In this study, users were given a series of tasks to complete e.g. retrieving information from a database. Whilst completing the assigned tasks, users were asked to provide a running commentary of their thoughts. They were observed via a video camera during this process to gauge their level of interaction with the system. Additionally, they were provided with a questionnaire on completion, comprising of a 7-point Likert scale regarding usability aspects of the system e.g. the appeal of the system used. The research highlights that when monitoring risky behaviour, a multimodal approach is useful, allowing a comparison of results from each monitoring method.

3.3   Measuring Perception of Risk

It can be hard for the user to recognise their security behaviour as risky. A number of techniques have been used to gauge the perception of risk (summarised in Table 2). Farahmand et al. [14] explored the possibility of using a psychometric model originally developed by Fischoff et al. [15] in conjunction with questionnaires, allowing a user to reflect on their actions and gauge their perception, providing a qualitative overview.

Takemura [27] also used questionnaires when investigating factors determining the likelihood of workers complying with information security policies defined within a company, in an attempt to measure perception of risk. Participants were asked a hypothetical question regarding whether or not they would implement an anti-virus solution on their computer if the risk of them getting a virus was 10%, 20% and etc. Results revealed that 52.7% of users would implement an antivirus solution if the risk was only 1% however, 3% of respondents still refused to implement antivirus, even when the risk was at 99% which displays a wide range of attitudes towards risk perception. The study concluded that risk perception was a psychological factor with the potential to influence problematic behaviours.

San-José and Rodriguez [28] used a multimodal approach to measure perception of risk. In a study of over 3000 households with PCs connected to the internet, users were given an antivirus program to install which scanned the machines on a monthly basis. The software was supplemented by quarterly questionnaires, allowing levels of perception to be measured and compared with virus scan results. Users were successfully monitored and results showed that the antivirus software created a false sense of security and that users were unaware of how serious certain risks could be.

Ng, Kankanhalli and Xu [16] examined the use of a health belief analogy when explaining the perception of risk in terms of cyber security. The perception of falling ill was directly related to a) the perceived susceptibility of falling ill and b) how severe the illness is perceived to be. When translated to the field of cyber security, it was discovered these factors along with perceived benefits, perceived barriers, cues to action, general security orientation and self-efficacy can help to determine the riskiness of user behaviour. Experiments were conducted with an example based upon email attachments. It was concluded that users security behaviour could be determined via perceived susceptibility, perceived benefits, and self-efficacy.

Table 2. - Comparison of methods used for measuring perception of risky behaviour

Technique	Description
Psychometric model	Used the models to determine characteristics relating to gauging perception of security and privacy risks [14].
Questionnaires	Subjects were assigned questionnaires to allow them to reflect on their perception of risk [14].
	Used to determine the likelihood of workers complying with information security policies [27].
	Used quarterly questionnaires to gauge perception of risk. Compared these to anti-virus scan results [28].
Technology-based	Installed antivirus software on over 3000 internet connected PCs which were scanned on a monthly basis [28].
Health belief model	The model was used as an analogy to explain perception of risk [16].

3.4   Feedback

Several methods can be deployed to inform the user that they are exhibiting risky behaviour (summarised in Table 3). Ur et al. [9] investigated ways in which feedback could be given to users, in the context of aiding a user in choosing a more secure password. Research conducted found that users could be influenced into increasing their password security if terms such as "weak" were used to describe their current attempt. In the research, colour was also used as a factor to provide feedback to users. When test subjects were entering passwords into the system, a bar meter was shown next to the input field. Depending upon the complexity of the password, the meter displayed a scale ranging from green/blue for a good/strong password to red, for a simplistic, easy to crack password. Data gathered from the experiments showed that the meters also had an effect on users, prompting them to increase system security by implementing stronger passwords.

Multimedia content such as the use of colour and sound [18] can also be used to provide feedback to the user. In a game named "Brainchild" developed by McDarby et al., users must gain control over their bio-signals by relaxing. In an attempt to help users relax, an affective feedback mechanism has been implemented whereby the sounds, colours and dialogues used provides a calming mechanism.

Textual information provided via the GUI can be used to communicate feedback to the user [17]. Dehn and Van Mulken conducted an empirical review of ways in which animated agents could interact with users. In doing so, they provided a comparison between the role of avatars and textual information in human-computer interaction. It was hypothesised that textual information provided more direct feedback to users however, avatars could be used to provide more subtle pieces of information via gestures or eye contact. Ultimately it was noted multimodal interaction could provide users with a greater level of communication with the computer system.

Previous research has indicated that affective feedback can be utilised when aiding users in considering their security behaviour online, since it can detect and help users alter their internal states [18]. Work conducted by Robison et al. [19] used avatars in an intelligent tutoring system to provide support to users, noting that such agents have to decide whether to intervene when a user is working, to provide affective feedback. However, there is the danger that agents may intervene at the wrong time and in doing so, may cause some negative affects when attempting to aid a student.

Hall et al. [20] concurs with the notion of using avatars to provide affective feedback to users, indicating that they influence the emotional state of the end-user. Avatars were deployed in a personal social and health education environment, to educate children about the subject of bullying. Studies showed that the avatars produced an empathetic effect in children, indicating that the same type of feedback could be used to achieve the same result in adults.

Table 3. - Comparison of feedback techniques

Technique	Description
Textual	Specific words were chosen to persuade participants to consider password security i.e. participants would not want a password to be described as "weak" [9].
	Textual data can provide more direct feedback [17].
Colour	Used colours in bar meters to indicate password strength [9].
	Specific colours used to allow users to control their state [18].
Sound	Specific music used to allow users to control their state i.e. calming music [18].
Avatars	General overview of the role of animated agents in HCI [17].
	Avatars were utilised in an intelligent tutoring system, to support users learning about microbiology and genetics [19].
	Avatars were deployed in a personal social and health environment to provide education on bullying [20].

4   Conclusion/Future Work

It has been observed that educating users about security issues is key to reducing risky behaviour however this is notoriously difficult [21] [22]. Ng, Kankanhalli and Xu concur with this sentiment [16], specifically stating that users should be trained about various security controls, and what they are used for, therefore improving the user's understanding and level of self-efficacy. Ultimately, this will improve system security.

Work currently being undertaken by Shepherd [23] seeks to advance the field by exploring the role of affective feedback in enhancing security risk awareness, focussing on a browser-based environment. Previous research has indicated that affective computing may serve as a method of educating users about risky security behaviours. The project seeks to develop an initial software prototype (in the form of a Firefox extension) to monitor user interaction within a web browser, comparing captured behaviour to models of known risky behaviours. The prototype will then be developed further, with the addition of feedback agents, featuring affective feedback techniques in an attempt to investigate a) if security risk awareness improves in end-users and b) if system security improves through the use of affective feedback.

References

1. Li, Y., Siponen, M.: A call for research on home users information security behaviour. In: PACIS 2011, Proceedings (2011) (paper 112)
2. Pfleeger, S., Caputo, D.: Leveraging behavioral science to mitigate cyber security risk, Computers & Security (2012), doi:10.1016/j.cose.2011.12.010 (accessed October 29, 2012)
3. Stanton, J.M., et al.: Analysis of end user security behaviors. Computers and Security 24, 124–133 (2005)
4. Hilbert, D., Redmiles, D.F.: Extracting usability information from user interface events. ACM Computing Surveys, 384–421 (December 2000)
5. Fenstermacher, K.D., Ginsburg, M.A.: Lightweight framework for cross-application user monitoring. IEEE Computer, 51–58 (2002)
6. Heishman, R., Duric, Z., Wechsler, H.: Understanding cognitive and affective states using eyelid movements. In: First IEEE International Conference on Biometrics: Theory, Applications, and Systems, BTAS 2007, September 27-29, pp. 1–6 (2007), http://dx.doi.org/10.1109/BTAS.2007.4401944 (accessed November 2, 2012)
7. Doubleday, A., et al.: A comparison of usability techniques for evaluating design. In: Coles, S. (ed.) Proceedings of the 2nd Conference on Designing Interactive Systems: Processes, Practices, Methods, and Techniques, DIS 1997, pp. 101–110. ACM, New York (1997), http://doi.acm.org/10.1145/263552.263583 (accessed November 2, 2012)
8. Staddon, J., et al.: Are privacy concerns a turn-off?: engagement and privacy in social networks. In: Proceedings of the Eighth Symposium on Usable Privacy and Security, SOUPS 2012, Article 10, 13 pages. ACM, New York (2012), http://doi.acm.org/10.1145/2335356.2335370 (accessed November 2, 2012)
9. Ur, B., et al.: How does your password measure up? The effect of strength meters on password creation. In: Security 2012 Proceedings of the 21st USENIX Conference on Security Symposium, Berkeley, CA, USA (2012); Also presented at Symposium On Usable Privacy and Security, July 11-13, pp. 462–469. ACM, Washington, DC (2012), https://www.usenix.org/conference/usenixsecurity12/how-does-your-password-measure-effect-strength-meters-password-creation (accessed November 2, 2012)
10. Balduzzi, M.: Attacking the privacy of social network users. HITB Secconf 2011 Malaysia (2011), http://conference.hitb.org/hitbsecconf2011kul/materials/D1T1%20%20Marco%20Balduzzi%20-%20Attacking%20the%20Privacy%20of%20Social%20Network%20Users.pdf (accessed September 21, 2012)
11. Hadnagy, C.: Social engineering: the art of human hacking, pp. 23–24. Wiley Publishing, Indianapolis (2011)
12. Payne, B., Edwards, W.: A brief introduction to usable security, pp. 13–21 (May/June 2008)
13. Fetscherin, M.: Importance of cultural and risk aspects in music piracy: A cross-national comparison among university students. Journal of Electronic Commerce Research (January 2009), http://www.csulb.edu/journals/jecr/issues/20091/Paper4.pdf (accessed October 30, 2012)

14. Farahmand, F., et al.: Risk perceptions of information security: A measurement study. In: Proceedings of the 2009 International Conference on Computational Science and Engineering, CSE 2009, vol. 3, pp. 462–469. IEEE, Washington, DC (2012), http://dx.doi.org/10.1109/CSE.2009.449 (accessed November 2, 2012)
15. Fischoff, B., et al.: How safe is safe enough? A psychometric study of attitudes towards technological risks and benefits. Policy Sciences 9(2), 127–152 (1978)
16. Ng, B., Kankanhalli, A., Xu, Y.: Studying users' computer security behavior: A health belief perspective. Decision Support Systems 46(4), 815–825 (2009), http://dx.doi.org/10.1016/j.dss.2008.11.010, doi:10.1016/j.dss.2008.11.010 (accessed December 6, 2012)
17. Dehn, D., Van Mulken, S.: The impact of animated interface agents: a review of empirical research. International Journal of Human– Computer Studies 52(1), 1–22 (2012), http://dx.doi.org/10.1006/ijhc.1999.0325 (accessed May 30, 2012)
18. McDarby, G., et al.: Affective feedback. Media Lab Europe (2004), http://medialabeurope.org/mindgames/publications/publicationsAffectiveFeedbackEnablingTechnologies.pdf (accessed May 22, 2012)
19. Robison, J., McQuiggan, S., Lester, J.: Evaluating the consequences of affective feedback in intelligent tutoring systems. In: Proceedings of International Conference on Affective Computing and Intelligent Interaction, ACII 2009, Amsterdam, pp. 37–42. IEEE (2009), http://www4.ncsu.edu/~jlrobiso/papers/acii2009.pdf (accessed May 22, 2012)
20. Hall, L., Woods, S., Aylett, R.S., Newall, L., Paiva, A.C.R.: Achieving empathic engagement through affective interaction with synthetic characters. In: Tao, J., Tan, T., Picard, R.W. (eds.) ACII 2005. LNCS, vol. 3784, pp. 731–738. Springer, Heidelberg (2005)
21. Jakobsson, M., Ramzan, Z.: Crimeware: understanding new attacks and defenses, p. 400. Addison-Wesley, Upper Saddle River (2008)
22. Ed Team. Social. HITB Magazine 1(6), 44–47 (2011), http://magazine.hitb.org/issues/HITB-Ezine-Issue-006.pdf (accessed September 21, 2012)
23. Shepherd, L.: Enhancing security risk awareness in end-users via affective feedback. PhD Proposal, University of Abertay, Dundee (2012) (unpublished)
24. Lewicki, R.J., Bunker, B.B.: Developing and maintaining trust in work relationships. In: Kramer, R., Tyler, T. (eds.) Trust in Organizations: Frontiers of Theory and Research, pp. 114–139. Sage Publications, Thousand Oaks (1996)
25. Mcknight, D., et al.: Trust in a specific technology: An investigation of its components and measures. ACM Transactions on Management Information Systems 2(2), Article 12 (2012), http://dx.doi.org/10.1145/1985347.1985353 (accessed December 6, 2012)
26. Padayachee, K.: Taxonomy of compliant information security behavior. Computers & Security 31(5), 673–680 (2012), http://dx.doi.org/10.1016/j.cose.2012.04.004 (accessed December 6, 2012)
27. Takemura, T.: Empirical analysis of behavior on information security. In: Proceedings of the 2011 International Conference on Internet of Things and 4th International Conference on Cyber, Physical and Social Computing, ITHINGSCPSCOM 2011, pp. 358–363. IEEE Computer Society, Washington, DC (2011), http://dx.doi.org/10.1109/iThings/CPSCom.2011.8 (accessed January 7, 2013)

28. San-José, P., Rodriguez, S.: Study on information security and e-Trust in Spanish households. In: Proceedings of the First Workshop on Building Analysis Datasets and Gathering Experience Returns for Security, BADGERS 2011, pp. 1–6. ACM, New York (2011), http://doi.acm.org/10.1145/1978672.1978673 (accessed January 7, 2013)
29. Herath, T., Rao, H.R.: Encouraging information security behaviors in organizations: Role of penalties, pressures and perceived effectiveness. Decision Support Syst. 47(2), 154–165 (2009), http://dx.doi.org/10.1016/j.dss.2009.02.005 (accessed January 31, 2013)

Understanding People's Preferences for Disclosing Contextual Information to Smartphone Apps

Fuming Shih and Julia Boortz

Massachusetts Institute of Technology
{fuming,jboortz}@mit.edu

1 Introduction

Smartphones have become the primary and most intimate computing devices that people rely on for their daily tasks. Sensor-based and network technologies have turned smartphones into a "context-aware" information hub and a vehicle for information exchange. These information provide apps and third party with a wealth of sensitive information to mine and profile user behavior. However, the Orwellian implications created by context-awareness technology have caused uneasiness to people when using smartphone applications and reluctance of using them [6]. To mitigate people's privacy concerns, previous research suggests giving controls to people on how their information should be collected, accessed and shared. However, deciding *who* (people or the application) gets to access to *what* (types of information) could be an unattainable task. In order to develop appropriate applications and privacy policies it is important to understand under what circumstances people are willing to disclose information.

In this work, we explore people's willingness to disclose their personal data, especially contextual information collected on smartphones, to different apps for specific purposes. The goal is to identify the factors that affect people's privacy preferences. For example, study of location-sharing apps shows that user preferences vary depending on the recipients and the context (e.g. place and time). However, previous studies that used surveys and interview methods [11,4] have the limitations in capturing the real causes for people's privacy concerns [2].

We used a hybrid approach of the experience sampling method [10] and the diary study to solicit people's willingness for disclosing information in different contexts. Specifically, we looked at possible contextual factors such as location, time and people's activities at the moment they are asked to disclose the data. Additionally, we tackled the following challenges when conducting the study:

1. How do we collect information that can sufficiently represent people's contexts throughout the day?
2. How do we effectively solicit people's preferences for information disclosure that are related to their contexts?
3. What are the possible and common confounding factors introduced by people other than their contexts?

L. Marinos and I. Askoxylakis (Eds.): HAS/HCII 2013, LNCS 8030, pp. 186–196, 2013.

We conducted a three week-long study with 38 participants to collect contextual information and self-reported data using smartphones. In parallel to that, we also solicited people's preference for information disclosure using contextualized questions. The questions specify the type of developers of the app, their purposes for data collection, benefits of sharing, and most importantly the user context. The responses to the questions enable us to build a preference model for each participant that reflects his or her privacy concerns in different contexts. We applied J48 implementation of C4.5 algorithm, a decision tree algorithm, to generate rules that could intuitively represent most relevant contextual factors. For some participants, the resulting models showed strong correlations between their decisions of information disclosure and their context, whereas others had decisions that were strongly biased toward other external factors such as the type of the data requestor or rewarded benefits.

2   Related Work

Research has shown that different types of context can affect smartphone users' decisions to disclose information. Context can include information about the situation users are in such as location, time of day, day of the week, and what users are doing [9,5,1]. It can also include information such as whom users are sharing it with, how the information will be used, what types of information are being shared, the level of detail of the shared information [11,12].

Khalil et al. [9] explored sharing patterns of context information by using the Experience Sampling Method (ESM). Their approach relied on self-reported data to capture user contexts by asking the user to input her location and activity manually every time. This approach, as with other studies that used ESM [1,5], is subject to getting false inputs from the users or missing labels after the users get annoyed because of the frequent prompts from the ESM program. To reduce the bias introduced by human errors, we improved ESM method by automatically detecting frequently visited places and prompting the user with the same label that the user has input earlier for the same place.

Mancini et al. [11] implemented the concept of "memory triggers", a short phrase to remind the participants of the situations when data about their experiences were collected. Using the memory phrase, the interviewer could then carry out a deferred contextual interview in which the participants were brought back in memory to recall a particular experience and the context of previous actions. We used the similar approach with some enhancements at creating the memory triggers. To record and reconstruct an individual's daily contexts, we used a hybrid approach similar to the Day Reconstruction Method (DRM) suggested in [8]. Our approach reconstructs the diary of the previous day automatically using user inputs of locations and activities through the enhanced ESM.

Jedrzejczyk et al. [7] investigated the effectiveness of using contextual information to model user preferences of real-time feedback in social location-tracking system. They built the predictive model by analyzing contextual information from sensor data on the smartphone. While using similar set of contextual information, we focus on exploring the effects of context on people's privacy decisions.

3   Approach

We want to accomplish the following two goals with the study approach: 1) to collect information that describes a participant's daily context, 2) to solicit people's answers that are as much contextually-bound as possible. The study lasted three weeks and was conducted in March and April of 2012. There are two tasks that the participants need to perform during the study. First, the participants were asked to install a program on their smartphone to collect sensor data, and respond to prompted questions for labeling their current location and activity. Next, the participants answered survey questions that were nightly generated and customized for each participant according to their daily contexts collected in the previous day. By the end of the study, qualified participants were called to join in-lab interviews. The interview provides more insights and details about the "contextually ground" reasons of why participants shared or not shared their information under specific contexts.

3.1   Recruitment and Demographics

We recruited 38 participants from the campus through email-lists and flyers posted on bulletin boards. Twenty-eight participants were students (19 undergraduates and 9 graduate students) and twenty were female. The participants were screened for their English proficiency and use of the Android smartphone as their primary mobile device. About half of the participants lived outside of the campus; they possessed different lifestyle and composition of daily context (e.g. commuting between work places and homes) than that of the students. Participants were compensated based on their level of participation in the study, including hours of logging context data ($2.6 per day), numbers of survey questions answered($2 per survey), and $10 for the final interview. An additional $2.6 were awarded to the participants for each week's completion of the two tasks. Besides the benefits, the participants needed to be compliant with the rules that ensure enough coverage of the self-reported data to correctly represent their daily context, or else they would not get their compensation for the day. The incentive structure was used to motivate the participants to contribute more data and stay in the study. Twenty seven participants (14 undergrads, 7 graduate students, and 6 campus staffs) completed the full study and 11 of them joined the final interview.

3.2   Pre-experiment Survey

The participants were asked to fill a pre-experiment survey before the study to capture their familiarity of using smartphone apps and their experiences with major online web services (e.g. Google services such as Gmail, social networking sites like Facebook or online shopping sites like Amazon). Table 1 summarizes the questions and the statistics of the answers in the survey. We also asked for their frequently visited local companies in three categories (e.g. banking, retail, and grocery stores) that were used later for generating personalized surveys. The

Table 1. Pre-experiment Survey

Q_1: How much time a day do you spend on using smartphone applications?	Q_2: How many Google services are you using currently?	Q_3: How many hours a day do you spend on Facebook?	Q_4: How often do you shop online on Amazon?
less than 30 minutes A_{11}: **15.7%** (6/38)	less than 3 A_{21}: **15.7%** (6/38)	less 0.5 hour A_{31}: **39.4%** (15/38)	seldom (e.g. only few times a year) A_{41}: **28.9%** (11/38)
between 30 minutes and 1 hour A_{12}: **21.1%** (8/38)	between 3 and 5 A_{22}: **34.2%** (13/38)	between 0.5 and 1 hour A_{32}: **31.5%** (12/38)	sometimes (e.g. about once a month) A_{42}: **31.5%** (12/38)
more than 1 hour A_{13}: **63.1%** (24/38)	more than 5 A_{23}: **50%** (19/38)	more than 1 hour A_{33}: **28.9%** (11/38)	very often (e.g. more than 3 times a month) A_{43}: **39.4%** (15/38)

survey results showed that more than half of the participants are heavy users of smartphone apps and Internet web services.

3.3 Data Collection: Recording a History of Daily Contexts

We used a hybrid approach of combining the experience sampling method with the diary method for acquiring in situ answers from the participants. We call the experience sampling method the *context recording* part and the diary method the *experience reconstruction* part of the study. The "context recording" part includes logging the contextual information as well as collecting annotations, tuples of location and activity, from the participants.

A data-logger program that was pre-installed in the smartphone would read various sensor data in the background to record contextual information such as location, time and proximity data (scanning of Bluetooth devices) of the participant. The data logger program, as shown in Figure 1, also detected frequently visited places and prompted the participants to provide annotations that they found meaningful to describe the moment when getting the prompt. For example, the participants received periodically a question like: *"Where are we? And what are we doing?"* They could answer the question by choosing a location and an activity label from a predefined list of choices or by creating new labels suitable for that situation. By doing so, we were able to generate a history of contexts for different events that a participant encountered during the day.

3.4 Diary Study

For the "experience reconstruction" part, we sent a customized survey to each participant everyday with questions generated from the annotations of locations and activities each participant gave in the previous day. For example, if previously the participant entered "Messeeh Dining" as the location label and "Having Lunch" as the activity label, then the questions would be generated as shown in Figure 2. Each survey contained 4 to 10 question groups, depending on how many

 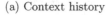
 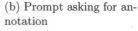

(a) Context history   (b) Prompt asking for an- (c) List of options for an-
                              notation   notation

Fig. 1. Screenshots of the data logging application

annotations the participant provided for that day. Although a participant might provide several annotations of her locations and activities within an hour, we only sampled at most one annotation from that set. We chose one-hour window because people tend to regiment their life according to work-related schedule as described in previous research of life-logging applications [3].

For each question group, we presented three questions to collect the preferences for disclosing different contents: location data, situation data, and proximity data (bluetooth scanning of the nearby devices). We ask the participants "Would you have disclosed..." to clearly indicate that we want them to think about whether or not they would disclose the information. The contextual clues (time, location and activity labels) on top of each group help the participant recall the "context" when giving the answers. The participant was asked questions about her willingness to disclose the data to a particular entity with a specified purpose of data use.

The question simulated the situation of disclosing personal data to an application developed by a particular company or entity. For each question, the developer type is selected from three categories: *academic entities*, *companies*, and *well-known large companies with web services* with equal probability. In order to limit any bias that the participant might have for particular organizations, we used multiple different organizations for each category of requestors. For the category academic entities, we used *MIT*, *Media Lab* and *Harvard Medical*. For the category local companies, we used *banking*, *retail store*, and *grocery store*. The specific grocery store, retailer, or banking company is customized to participants based on the pre-experiment survey indicating which companies they normally use. We anticipate that this customization will make users responses more representative of their actual disclosure preferences, since it brings the experiment closer in-line with their everyday life. Finally, we used *Google*, *Amazon*, *Facebook* to represent well-know large companies with web services.

For each category of requestors, we included the benefit or the purpose for collection the information. For academic requestors, the survey questions tell users that the data is being collected for research purposes. When the requestor is a company, users are asked if they would disclose the information in return for a $2 coupon. Finally, when well-known large companies with web services are asking for information, users are told that the purpose is for improving personal service. We expect that these purposes will help eliminate hesitancy to share by showing users that the information disclosed will be useful for the requestor.

4 Results

The 27 participants who completed the study answered 4781 question groups (14343 questions) in total. The participants answered an average of 24 questions per day. Those participants started but quitted the study early, their results were not taken into consideration. The overall participant rate of the study, counting those who finished both the data collection and diary survey, was 71%.

In this section, we report the main findings of our study, including both quantative data collected from the study and qualitative interview data. We start by

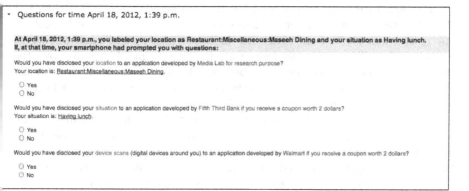

Fig. 2. Example of a personalized questionnaire based on "contextual information"

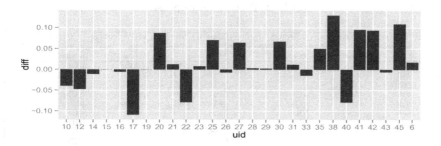

Fig. 3. The percentage of *yes* responses for disclosing locations annotated as *home* vs. the percentage of *yes* responses specifically at time slots after 6pm or before 6am

describing the general outcome from the survey questions. Then we look into the responses of each individual and how the results relate to contextual factors using outputs from the decision tree algorithm. Lastly, we use interview data to understand the privacy attitudes of participants that are often difficult to distill just from the quantitative data.

Type of Data and Context. The results showed that the participants are most likely to disclose activity data (62% yes), followed closely by location data (59% yes), but are much less likely to disclose Bluetooth data (49% yes). The interview data revealed that the participants are more reluctant to disclose Bluetooth data due to the unsureness of what information can be disclosed by Bluetooth data.

As for the general trend across individuals, we found that the preference for disclosing information are dependent on the participant's location at the time of sharing. For instance, the participants are most likely to disclose their locations when they were at places in the category *traveling* (79%), followed by *activities* (78%), *school* (65%), *work* (62%), *fun stuff* (58%), *on the go* (58%), *restaurant* (57%), *other* (54%), and lastly *home* (52%). The places that are deemed to be more private for personal activities such as *home* and the places in the *restaurant* category were shared less than public places such as *bus stops* in the *traveling* category or different classrooms in the *school* category. In contrast, our results also showed the difference in time did not significantly affect the participant's willingness to disclose location. For example, Figure 3 shows that there is only a small difference (10%) between the percentage of all *yes* responses for disclosing locations annotated as "home" and the *yes* responses for locations if the timestamps were after 6pm or before 6am.

When considering the data requestor, the participants are most likely to disclose their data to academic entities (44%), followed by local companies (36%), and least likely to large companies with web services (20%). These results show that users are more willing to disclose information to people who they are closer to – in this case local businesses as opposed to larger web services.

Individual Preference Model. We ran C4.5 decision tree algorithm and produced rules from each participant's responses. Our results showed that about

Table 2. Participant responses

User ID	Number of responses	Percentage of saying yes (%)	Affected by requestor type(R) or context(C)	User ID	Number of responses	Percentage of saying yes (%)	Affected by requestor type(R) or context(C)
P6	753	67	(C)	P10	819	38	(C)
P14	480	64	(R)	P12	1024	76	(C)
P15	363	100		P16	645	88	(C)
P20	555	59	(C)	P17	240	51	(C)
P22	522	76	(C)	P19	318	100	
P25	666	23	(R)	P21	579	10	(C)
P27	840	66	(R)	P26	438	79	(R)
P33	642	71	(C)	P29	585	35	(R)
P35	732	45	(R)	P30	771	36	(C)
P45	381	32	(R)	P31	210	69	(R)
P42	279	31	(C)	P38	675	78	(R)
P23	279	90		P41	333	36	(R)
P28	615	1		P43	390	99	
P40	210	76	(C)				

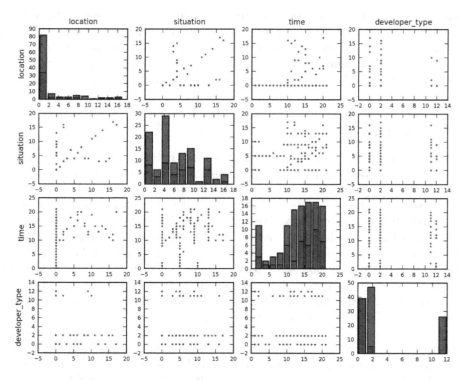

Fig. 4. Responses (··· Deny; ··· Allow) showing privacy preferences are biased towards certain companies (*developer type*)

81% (22/27) of the study participants have obvious patterns in their responses. Table 2 summarizes the results of participants' reponses, and it shows that some participants are what Westin called "privacy fundamentalist" and "privacy unconcerned" [13] such that they either rejected or accepted most of the data requests in the survey questions. About 54% (12/22) of these participants have decision rules that are related to contextual factors (location, time, and their activities), while the rest have decision rules related only to the data requesters. For instance, Figure 4 shows that the participant responded with *yes* when the *developer type* was of type academic entities (specified as index 0 in the *developer_type* box in the scatter plot.[1]), and *no* in the other categories. These results suggest that people have developed default policies based on other concepts such as trust of the companies rather than contextual information.

We found that the participants who incorporated contextual factors in their decisions have patterns based on: 1) location and time, 2) time and data requestors, and 3) location and data requesters. For example, P42 rejected all data request for location *Home* after midnight and before 6am. P17 would not

---

[1] Each box represents one factor (location, situation/activity, time, and developer type) that affects the participant's responses. The x-axis represents indexes of locations, activities, hours, and developer types.

disclose her locations to data requestors from the category *grocery stores* between 12pm and 6pm. P17 later explained in the interview that she would not disclose work-related locations to a grocery store because locations from work are "unrelated" to understand her shopping behaviors. P29 would not disclose all locations labeled as *home* to requestors besides those from the category *academic entities*.

4.1 Post Interview

We invited the participants who completed the study for a focus-group interview. Each interview was held in a conference room and lasted about 30 minutes with 3 participants attending. We asked questions concerning their reasons for rejecting or allowing the data requests, and details about the conditions (context) that triggered their privacy concerns. We first asked the participant to describe what were they thinking when they were answering the questions. Then we asked them to recall their rules, if any, for sharing their information. We identified three characteristics of how some participants evaluate privacy risks based on their privacy expectations that are shaped by context: 1) private or public of their context, 2) sensitivity of the disclosed information, and 3) relations between the purpose of data collection and the context.

One of the deciding factors for disclosing personal information is to consider whether its context is private or public [11]. However, people have different interpretations of what is public and what is private. P30, for example, considered any location with "hanging out with friends" as its activity label a public context. On the contrary, P20 decided that all activities "hanging out with friends" are private. These two different views on the concept of "privateness" for a specific context resulted in two opposite rules in the decision tree algorithm. Second, failure in communicating what to disclose caused misjudgments on the sensitivity of the disclosed information. For example, several participants reported that they would not disclose Bluetooth data because they thought the term "device scans" in the questions means "all information on the smartphone". However, P33 and P38 who recognized this as Bluetooth technology would always disclose this information. Because, as they pointed out, *"I think device scans give information about the devices around me, and it is not personal."* Deciding the sensitivity of information then depends on participants' knowledge about the technology used in data collection. Lastly, participants tended to reject data requests if they failed to find "reasonable" connections between data collection and its possible purposes in a specific context. For example, P17 *"can't think of why an app needs my locations at work to figure out what I like to shop for food."* Similarly, many participants said no to the companies with web services because they were unsure about how the disclosed information can be used by the data requestor.

Another interesting finding is how people developed their rules during the period of the study. Several participants reported that they started the study without obvious rules in mind, responding the questions by just their instincts. But as the study continued, rules were introduced accumulatively through relevant contexts. For example, P22 *"Before the study, I didn't think much about giving away my information. Then I realized that I would always say no when I am working in my office, so I started saying no at all places when I am working."*

5 Conclusion

Our study of people's preference for information disclosure on smartphones has addressed three challenges in mobile privacy research. Firstly, to record information that approximates an individual's daily contexts, we used an enhanced experience sampling method. The ESM program prompts the user automatically for annotations of locations and activities whenever it detects a new place or that a previous labeled place is re-visited.

Secondly, in order to investigate people's *privacy in context*, we created the personalized survey in which each participant would answer questions with the help of the contextual triggers. The participant would to give her privacy preferences while recalling the experience *in situ*. We then applied the decision tree algorithm C4.5 to generate a preference model for each participant. We found that although people have some default policies, not much can be gleaned about just how much contextual factors can affect people's decisions about data disclosure. Furthermore, both the quantitative and the qualitative data showed that other external factors such as types of the data requestors predominate over the contextual factors.

Lastly, the participants had several issues when providing their responses in the study. These issues include the lack of understanding about the privacy impacts of disclosed data and lack of connection between their decision and the purpose of the data collection. Together, these problems lead to indifferent responses during different contexts of data disclosure. Future study should inform people the capability of the technology that is used in data collection and create a sense of real use of the disclosed information for a specfic purpose instead of presenting just hypothetical questions.

References

1. Anthony, D., Henderson, T., Kotz, D.: Privacy in location-aware computing environments. IEEE Pervasive Computing 6(4), 64–72 (2007)
2. Barkhuus, L.: The mismeasurement of privacy: using contextual integrity to reconsider privacy in hci. In: Proceedings of the SIGCHI Conference on Human Factors in Computing Systems, CHI 2012, pp. 367–376. ACM (2012)
3. Blum, M., Pentland, A., Troster, G.: Insense: Interest-based life logging. IEEE MultiMedia 13(4), 40–48 (2006)
4. Castañeda, J., Montoro, F.: The effect of Internet general privacy concern on customer behavior. Electronic Commerce Research (2007)
5. Consolvo, S., Smith, I.E., Matthews, T., LaMarca, A., Tabert, J., Powledge, P.: Location disclosure to social relations: why, when, & what people want to share. In: Proceedings of the SIGCHI Conference on Human Factors in Computing Systems, CHI 2005, pp. 81–90. ACM (2005)

6. Madden, M., Boyles, J.L., Smith, A.: Privacy and data management on mobile devices. Technical Report CS-2011-02, Pew Research Center (September 2012)
7. Jedrzejczyk, L., Mancini, C., Corapi, D., Price, B., Bandara, A., Nuseibeh, B.: Learning from context: A field study of privacy awareness system for mobile devices (2011)
8. Kahneman, D., Krueger, A., Schkade, D., Schwarz, N., Stone, A.: A Survey Method for Characterizing Daily Life Experience: The Day Reconstruction Method (2004)
9. Khalil, A., Connelly, K.: Context-aware telephony: privacy preferences and sharing patterns. In: Proceedings of the 2006 20th Anniversary Conference on Computer Supported Cooperative Work, CSCW 2006, pp. 469–478. ACM (2006)
10. Larson, R., Csikszentmihalyi, M.: The experience sampling method. New Directions for Methodology of Social and Behavioral Science 15, 41–56 (1983)
11. Mancini, C., Thomas, K., Rogers, Y., Price, B., Jedrzejczyk, L., Bandara, A., Joinson, A., Nuseibeh, B.: From spaces to places: emerging contexts in mobile privacy. In: Proceedings of the 11th International Conference on Ubiquitous Computing, pp. 1–10 (2009)
12. Patil, S., Lai, J.: Who gets to know what when: configuring privacy permissions in an awareness application. In: Proceedings of the SIGCHI Conference on Human Factors in Computing Systems, CHI 2005, pp. 101–110. ACM (2005)
13. Westin, A., Harris, L. Associates: Equifax-Harris Consumer Privacy Survey. Equifax (1996)

Constructing Positive Influences for User Security Decisions to Counter Corporate or State Sponsored Computer Espionage Threats

Martyn Styles

University of South Wales Pontypridd, Glamorgan, CF37 1DL, UK
03157210@glam.ac.uk, martyn.styles@ntlworld.com

Abstract. This paper presents an analysis of employees' security behavior, which focuses upon improving user awareness to counter computer espionage attempts by corporate or state sponsored activity. The author examines existing literature, presents the results from initial experiments in security awareness and proposes further work.

Keywords: Security awareness, user behavior, APT, corporate espionage, employee psychology, social engineering.

1 Introduction

Already, 2013 is shaping up to be another significant year for computer security breaches. Apple, Microsoft, Facebook, The New York Times, NBC and Evernote have all succumbed to computer hacking in the first months of this year. Almost universally, they appear to be the result of weaknesses in employee security behavior. Since 2007, the perceived rise in state or corporate espionage (as designated by the modern term 'Advanced Persistent Threats' or APTs) has caused many firms to consider the type of activities they are engaged in and the likelihood of them being a target for long-term malicious activity. A significant proportion of current academic literature ignores the psychological aspects of computer security. This research paper has been undertaken in part to address this shortfall with the aim of reducing the risks of corporate espionage. Why is it that most computer users feel an overwhelming urge to open suspicious email, access a URL sent to them by an unknown 'friend', open the attachment that they were not expecting but which appealed to their curiosity, or to click on a pop-up message telling them to "Update your anti-virus software now!" when they open a web page? Research into this kind of human 'herd mentality' has been clearly shown to affect social networks (Onnela and Reed-Tsochas, 2010). Onnela and Reed Tsochas analyzed Facebook applications from 2007 during a period when the site allowed friends to alert each other when they installed an application. Their research clearly highlighted a pattern of social influence that compelled users to follow their friends in tendency of installing common applications. When a Facebook

L. Marinos and I. Askoxylakis (Eds.): HAS/HCII 2013, LNCS 8030, pp. 197–206, 2013.

user generated an alert to their friends by installing an application, there was an implied endorsement of the application's features and benefits which tended to lead recipients of the alert to install the application themselves; even though their friend may have already uninstalled the application after finding it unsuitable or worthless. Similarly, computer hackers have begun utilizing methods that imply recommendation from others to persuade targets to install rogue software such as malicious imitation anti-virus programs (FakeAV), which attempt to fool users into fraudulent purchases. Cognitive dissonance causes the subjects confusion when faced with on-screen choices that imply required obedience, by the implication that installing an application is mandatory behavior that is expected of them. Obedience and a willingness to conform help to re-enforce that behavior to the benefit of the criminals who manufactured the fake software.

Corporate security officers may rely on technology to secure their network infrastructure, but this ignores the fundamental issue of human vulnerabilities, which exist in every organization. The focus of this research on analyzing end-user security behavior in order to address the growing number of corporate or state sponsored computer espionage threats. The U.K government office of the Centre for Protection of National Infrastructure (CPNI), a commercial subset of the intelligence service M.I.5, has recently provided advice to professional services firms for recognizing APT-type behavior since they recognize that these businesses are increasingly likely targets of state sponsored espionage. This is because it is recognized that finance and government organizations generally spend large amounts of budget on security measures, whereas professional services firms may be lacking the necessary resources and inclination for comprehensive security controls. The author of this research paper is employed by an international law firm, as an information security professional. Both in the U.S and in U.K, since 2011, there have been regular meetings with InfoSec representatives from all the major law firms together with security professionals from financial and international corporate organizations, in response to the rise in global corporate hacks. This is an attempt to address the human weaknesses in corporate data security.

2   Research Hypothesis

The proposition of this research is that through critical analysis and modeling of employee computer security behavior, security professionals will be able to identify and positively influence user security decisions to counter the threats of corporate or state sponsored computer espionage.

Do end-users really care about information security? In most industries, end-users often subscribe to the view that information security is 'someone else's problem'. This can lead to somewhat reckless behaviour – for example when surfing the Internet. The information security industry needs to understand its users much more if they are ever going to be in a position to dramatically reduce human-aspect security incidents. Examining corporate or state sponsored computer espionage is a challenge to researchers because proving the hacker's origin and motivation is inherently difficult. Hackers commonly utilise multiple jump-box hosts and encrypted VPN tunnels (such as the notorious Tor network) to hide their geo-location. Hackers may work alone or with others and may be motivated by money, a quest for fame or allegiance to a business or country. This research project examines hacker activity through the analysis of employee workstations that have been subject to attack and by investigations of infection patterns through corporate anti-malware technologies. Contacts with other corporate information security officers will enable comparisons to be made across industries and co-operative research with a major anti-malware vendor is planned. Global firms with international offices in Russia, China and France have the potential, according to meetings held with the U.S & U.K security services, to be compromised by state or corporate sponsored espionage.

3   Psychological Factors Influencing User Security Behavior

People often believe that they are in full control of the computer that sits in front of them. However, although the computer system may appear to function at the behest of the user, many aspects of computer activity may be beyond the user's control or cognitive understanding. Current research into computer user behaviour, particularly by Eirik Albrechtsen (Albrechtsen, 2007) and Jeffrey Stanton (Stanton et al., 2005), indicates that there is still a long way to go to improve end user security behaviour. Corporate or state sponsored criminal activity is extremely difficult to detect if users are not motivated to identify and stop it. This is because technological protections are quite often far too restrictive towards genuine business activity, leading to a condition in which security systems, which may have been used to prevent data egress, are simply either turned off or put into audit or monitor-only mode. Security managers, across different business sectors, have confirmed that installed Data Loss Prevention (DLP) systems are often not used, because to do so would prevent essential routine file movements inside and out of the organisation. Other security managers stated that their DLP systems are permanently set for Data Loss Detection i.e. audit only mode rather than blocking. David Lacey (Lacey, 2009) analysed the security structures of corporate enterprises and found them to be severely lacking in sophistication and effectiveness.

- **Motivation.** Employee motivation towards information security is a key factor in helping to protect corporate assets. Psychological homeostasis, which is when a state of mind is reached where the subject feels that they have attained equilibrium, can also be applied to user security behavior. A lack of homeostasis can cause people to feel be disillusioned if they feel that they are not motivated enough, and in terms of behavior they may feel that security is of no interest to them because they are divorced from the effects of any negligent or naive behavior which may lead to security incidents. Research into computer user behavior by Albrechtsen (Albrechtsen, 2007), (Albrechtsen and Hovden, 2009) and Kruger (Kruger and Kearney, 2006) has stimulated thought on some of the motivational aspects of security awareness. Indeed, Albrechtsen asserts that most 'users consider other work demands as more important than information security tasks in the day-to-day operation of the organization'(Albrechtsen and Hovden, 2009). Other researchers, among them Jeffrey Stanton (Stanton et al., 2005) (Stanton and Stam, 2006) and Donn Parker (Parker, 2002), also consider the motivation of users for computer security through empirical research amongst the information security community. Parker is particularly interested in the relative inequalities of the resources and motivation of hackers, compared with security managers, in the 'cat and mouse' war of control over an organization's information assets. Articles by Angela Sasse et al. (M A Sasse, 2001) (M. Angela Sasse, 2007) (Inglesant, 2010) argue that user motivation for the typical password based security mechanisms that most organizations use for authenticating users to systems needs to be improved because social engineers like Kevin Mitnick (Mitnick and Simon, 2002) commonly exploit user preferences for simplistic password choice.

- **Obedience.** Most organizations define acceptable use policies and best practice guidance to ensure that employees do not abuse the privileges they enjoy when using company equipment. Just how obediently employees follow these rules and regulations is an interesting area for investigation. A number of experiments in the 1960's and 1970's investigated the obedience traits in humans. These experiments provide us with an insight into the way people react to orders, and how in the area of computer security, we can begin to understand why users may cause security incidents through negligent actions. The Milgram experiments (Milgram, 1974) demonstrated that participants willingly administer apparently painful electric shocks to fellow participants if they believe that compliance is required through an order issued by a figure of authority. Similar to Milgram's experiments, the Hofling experiment (Hofling, 1966) studied the effects of authority (an impatient doctor) on nurses in charge of patient drug administration. It was found that 95 percent of nurses would administer dangerous doses of medication when demanded by a doctor. These two sets of experiments emphasize the lengths to which humans may go in order to comply with perceived authority. This also seems to be the case with the example of 'The Third Wave' experiment. In this experiment, school children were inducted into a neo-Nazi movement by their history teacher, as a means of explaining the apparent willingness of the German populace to participate in Nazi atrocities. Although this experiment was performed on school children and was poorly documented (Leler, 1967), it is a valuable commentary on obedience. The six day 1974 Stanford Prison Experiment (SPE) (Zimbardo, 2007) and the BBC Prison Study (Reicher, 2006) showed that group behavior bordering on sadism could be produced by simply arbitrarily designating 'prison guards' and 'prisoners'. The key to understanding computer security behavior may lie in user attitudes to obedience; Do employees willfully open malicious email attachments as a way of defying the obedience required by the organizations IT policies?
- **Cognitive Dissonance.** The theory of cognitive dissonance, which states that the mind becomes confused when trying to assess conflicting ideas, was defined by the psychologist Leon Festinger (Festinger, 1957). Cognitive dissonance can used by social engineers (Hadnagy, 2011) to their advantage and malware writers can

use it to cause target employees confusion and uncertainty which leads to them unwittingly installing malicious software on company computers. This phenomena has been witnessed many times in many organizations when users receive emails which claim to come from genuine individuals or companies, but which turn out to be counterfeit and contain either malware or links to malicious websites. Recipients tend to believe the messages unless the forgery is particularly poor and will execute the attachments and install the malware. Because such messages often zero day executable code, which is unrecognized by anti-virus vendors, the only way to stop them reaching their intended targets is to block all messages containing executable code. Malware analysis websites such as VirusTotal.com and ThreatExpert.com can be used to evaluate unknown code – in the same way as the malware writers, who use these websites to see if AV vendors recognize their code as malicious! Cognitive dissonance, which results from the receipt of a malicious email that claims to contain a genuine security update, is difficult for end users to resolve. Unfortunately, the action of blocking all incoming executable code can have a business impact because genuine emails are also stopped.

- **Automatic Social Behavior.** Automatic social behavior is a relatively new area of psychology that explores the influences that compel individuals to exhibit behaviour that verges on automaton-like actions, through peer pressure inferred by online friends or acquaintances. A number of papers, particularly by John Bargh (Bargh, 1989) (John A. Bargh, 1996) and Ap Dijksterhuis (Dijksterhuis, 2000, Ap Dijksterhuis, 2001) together with Joseph Cesario (Cesario et al., 2006), have established this phenomenon as a valid area of psychological research. Researchers argue that humans use inaccurate mechanisms to justify their self knowledge and identified the presence of automatic behaviour in the misattribution of decisions which would lead them towards a particular objective (Bar-Anan et al., 2010). This is an interesting theory because it is recognised that sometimes users will give inconsistent reasons for errant security behaviour based on their perceived objective. For example, an employee who forwarded confidential information onto a gossip website may justify their actions by claiming that the information is already common knowledge amongst their peers both inside and outside the company rather than admitting that they had done any wrong, even though the document was marked 'Company confidential - Do not forward outside'. The temptation to automatically forward confidential information to personal email accounts, webmail accounts or file-sharing sites is often too much for staff to resist.

- **Probability Neglect.** Jonathan Baron (Baron, 2008) and Cass Sustein (Sunstein, 2002), (Sunstein, 2009) delve into the phenomena exhibited by the human trait of probability neglect which leads individuals to make irrational decisions based on an inability to believe that a series of events will result in a particular outcome, either negative or positive. This is particularly interesting for information security when the number of security incidents is a growing trend – this may explain why users ignore the warning signs leading up to a security incident because they feel immune from security issues. Users may cite a naive "It will never happen here," or "It's someone else's problem" in response to appeals for security vigilance.

- **Risk.** Risk homeostasis (Wilde, 1982), could help to explain the reason for naive or negligent computer security behaviour. Risk homeostasis would apply because users feel they are protected from Internet threats through the organization's security defences, and therefore will take risks such as visiting potentially dangerous parts of the web or wilfully clicking on obviously unsafe website elements. Risk management is a key topic in the information security industry. CISO's and information security officers are increasingly asked to provide management with tangible evidence of security vulnerabilities and capable threat agents before budgets for security solutions are released (Gerber and Vonsolms, 2005).

- **Mistake.** People make mistakes. A number of information security managers and CIO's that were approached agree that a commonly held belief in the fallibility of IT users is expected and that employees are bound to make mistakes that lead to security incidents. Travis and Aronson's book (Tavris, 2007) provides insight into the paradox that users face when accused of mistakes at work. This is a particularly interesting area for information security research because of the link between simple mistakes and security incidents. An unintentional confidential email sent by mistake to an unauthorized third party being a prime example. In April 2010, Gwent police sent a plain text Excel spreadsheet containing over ten thousand names and addresses from a confidential Criminal Records Bureau (CRB) disclosure, which included 863 people who had been in trouble with the police, to the technology website 'The Register' (Williams, 2010). The email address of The Register had been saved in the sender's email address list after The Register had previously been in contact with Gwent police over a Freedom of Information request. In September 2011, an article in WIRED online magazine (Vetter, 2011) indicated that two researchers managed to capture 20 gigabytes of misdirected data via doppelgänger Fortune 500 domain registrations - users had simply mistyped the real domain names and forwarded confidential data to the doppelgänger domains! Clearly, something has to be done to reduce end user mistakes such as these.

- **Self-Control Reserve Depletion.** Preserving an element of self-control is required by employees to counter the conflicting information that they may experience, for example, following the receipt of a malicious email or perhaps the compromise of their work computer by Fake Antivirus infection. Cognitive resource depletion may be experienced by employees as a result of the bombardment of inaccurate information from malicious sources leading to perception corruption and the inability of users to make rational security decisions. In these instances, infiltration of an enterprise by Advanced Persistent Threats is possible. If the method of infection is designed in such a way that recipients are not alerted, and the Trojan code is utilized in a stealth manner, the infiltration of an organization can go unnoticed for months if not years. The 2011 Google (Operation Aurora), Sony PlayStation and RSA hacks were perpetrated through the compromise of the computers of low privilege users. The hackers slowly escalated their privileges through the infection of subsequent computers and user accounts throughout the organizations own internal networks. Those low privilege computer users were targeted as a doorway into a fortified network protected by multiple technological defense systems.

4   Neuro Linguistic Programming and Social Engineering Defense

Neuro Linguistic Programming (NLP), credited to Richard Bandler and John Grinder (Bandler et al., 1990) and based on earlier work by Milton H. Erickson, has been used by some recent authors to explain the uncanny ability of some social engineers to elicit confidential information from targets. Mann (Mann, 2008) and also Brown (Brown, 2006) identify how NLP may be used by talented social engineers to compromise security. It is an interesting challenge to educate employees, particularly reception staff, about the possible use of NLP in the perpetration of social engineering attacks. Few academic and commercial articles currently address social engineering defense strategies, most simply exist to glamorize the life of a social engineer, with Kevin Mitnick (Mitnick and Simon, 2002) and Frank Abagnale Jr. (Abagnale and Redding, 1980) being the most notorious examples. Recent publications by Mann (Mann, 2008) and Hadnagy (Hadnagy, 2011), however, have a number of interesting ideas including sections on interpreting and rejecting attempts by social engineers to use NLP-type techniques on unsuspecting targets.

5   Method and Metrics

Measurements will be made through a combination of online surveys, social engineering experiments and observed end-user behavior (monitored at user workstations and through Internet gateway traffic analysis). Measurements of existing technical solutions will be performed through statistical analysis of data gathered from enterprise anti-malware systems, together with APT analysis through code sandboxing and Command and Control 'phone home' monitoring. The number of virus and Trojan horse infections on machines within a global corporate enterprise are a key metric compared with the number of malicious files received through email and web channels. These statistics help to identify the number of compromised machines on the network.

6   Security Awareness Experiments

Security Questionnaire. As part of an initial experiment, a Survey Monkey (www.surveymonkey.com) questionnaire was designed according to the standards set by the Social Psychology Network (www.socialphychology.org), which is available as an academic resource for online psychological testing. Participants were sought through professional LinkedIn contacts (www.linkedin.com) and links to the survey were published via the Social Psychology Network website and Twitter (www.twitter.com). Over the two-month period that the survey was open, a sample of 73 people started the survey and 49 (67.1%) completed all the questions. All the answers were anonymous and only a log of IP addressed of responds was retained. The participants were mostly a purposeful self-selection biased sample because it was determined that there was a need to test out some of the question formats and the questionnaire design, on a reasonably mature and co-operative audience. The demographic of participants were a cross-section drawn from both senior staff and professional level members of society, together with those participants who arrived at the survey via the Social Psychology Network website and who were interested in taking psychological surveys. An experiment was designed using an online survey website to evaluate user attitudes in relation to some of the security behaviors under investigation. Subject areas investigated included some of the topics identified as areas of interest: Automatic Social Behavior, Motivation for security objectives, Mistake and Cognitive Dissonance. Extensive questionnaires and spear phishing experiments are planned for 2013 to build on the results of the initial test.

Tiger Team Social Engineering Exercise & Results. Given the current industry focus on Advanced Persistent Threats it was decided that an evaluation of employee reaction to unknown/untrusted USB devices was necessary. Tiger (or Red) Team exercises attempt to test the security of an organization by breaching physical barriers through social engineering and other such methods of entry. Custom benign malware was developed which would initiate a 'phone home' event when a USB memory stick was plugged into a corporate workstation. Devices were also posted to staff working in the UK, France and Morocco, along with bogus letters, using office contact details found during Internet reconnaissance. The consultant retrieved target contact details though a fake LinkedIn account linked to the company name. Within days, 17 employees confirmed a connection with the fake id, which demonstrates that people do not routinely check the legitimacy of online curriculum vitaes. The professional social engineer, dressed in business attire, successfully infiltrated the corporate office building and dropped compromised devices in high footfall areas of the building. Three days later, several USB devices containing the custom malware were handed in to the security department as suspicious items. Investigations through the centralized USB device management console reports showed that six employees had attempted to execute the malicious content on the USB sticks, but had been blocked from doing so by the corporate USB device policy which prevents executable code from running from USB. The results of the exercise were reported to the company Risk Committee and actions were planned to improve employee security awareness when dealing with suspicious USB memory sticks.

7   Conclusion

Research carried out to date has demonstrated that there is a clear need for further work in the field of end user security behaviors. Analysis of the current literature available on the security behavior of users has established that there is still much work to be done to reduce the impact of negligent or compromised user activity. The experiments conducted this year have demonstrated that even users who have been schooled in good security behavior may still act in negligent ways, which potentially increase the risks to the organization. There is still much work to be done in the area of user security awareness - since 2010 multiple corporate businesses began identifying long-term and extensive hacking incidents. Technology alone cannot protect organizations because in order to function as a business there is a need for users to maintain some autonomy in the actions they perform on information systems. New and flexible ways of working, including mobile communications, Bring Your Own Computer/Device (BYOC/BYOD) and Cloud applications/data management will undoubtedly require even more considered and appropriate user behavior if information is to be kept confidential. Security-educated employees should be motivated, able to recognize computer espionage attempts, and capable of alerting the presence of anomalous computer activity to their in-house information security or incident response team. This will consequently reduce the possibility of corporate cyber-crime success.

References

1. Abagnale, F.W., Redding, S.: Catch Me If You Can: The Amazing True Story of the Most Extraordinary Liar in the History of Fun and Profit. Edinburgh, Mainstream (1980, 2003)
2. Albrechtsen, E.: A Qualitative Study of Users' View on Information Security. Computers & Security 26, 276–289 (2007)
3. Albrechtsen, E., Hovden, J.: The Information Security Digital Divide Between Information Security Managers and Users. Computers & Security 28, 476–490 (2009)
4. Ap Dijksterhuis, J.A.B.: The Perception-Behavior Expressway: Automatic Effects of Social Perception on Social Behavior. Advances in Experimental Social Psychology 33, 1–40 (2001)
5. Bandler, R., Grinder, J., Andreas, S.: Frogs Into Princes: The Introduction to Neuro-Linguistic Programming. Enfield, Eden Grove (1990)
6. Bar-Anan, Y., Wilson, T.D., Hassin, R.R.: Inaccurate Self-Knowledge Formation as A Result of Automatic Behavior. Journal of Experimental Social Psychology 46, 884–894 (2010)
7. Bargh, J. A.: Conditional Automaticity (1989),
   http://Books.Google.Com/Books?Id=Ht6ddclz6eac&Lpg=Pa3&Ots=Db
   9yj_Q5ai&Dq=CognitionAttention&Lr&Pg=Pr4V=Onepage&Q=Cognitio
   n%20attention&F=False
8. Baron, J.: Thinking and Deciding. Cambridge University Press, Cambridge (2008)
9. Brown, D.: Tricks of the Mind. Channel 4 Books, London (2006)
10. Cesario, J., Plaks, J.E., Higgins, E.T.: Automatic Social Behavior as Motivated Preparation to Interact. J. Pers. Soc. Psychol. 90, 893–910 (2006)
11. Dijksterhuis, A.: On The Relation Between Associative Strength and Automatic Behavior. Journal of Experimental Social Psychology 36, 531–544 (2000)
12. Festinger, L.: A Theory of Cognitive Dissonance. Evenston, Row Peterson (1957)
13. Gerber, M., Vonsolms, R.: Management of Risk in the Information Age. Computers & Security 24, 16–30 (2005)
14. Hadnagy, C.: Social Engineering: The Art of Human Hacking. Wiley (2011)
15. Hofling, C.: An Experimental Study of Nurse-Physician Relationships. Journal of Nervous and Mental Disease, 171–180 (1966)
16. Inglesant, P.S., Angela, M.: The True Cost of Unusable Password Policies (2010)

17. John, A., Bargh, M.C., Burrows, L.: Automaticity of Social Behavior: Direct Effects of Trait Construct and Stereotype Activation on Action. Journal of Personality and Social Psychology 71, 230–244 (1996)
18. Kruger, H., Kearney, W.: A Prototype for Assessing Information Security Awareness. Computers & Security 25, 289–296 (2006)
19. Lacey, D.: Managing the Human Factor in Information Security. John Wiley and Sons, Ltd. (2009)
20. Leler, R., Bernice, S.: Through the Tiger's Eye. The Catamount 11, 2 (1967)
21. Sasse, M.A., Brostoff, S., Weirich, D.: Transforming the 'Weakest Link' — A Human/Computer Interaction Approach to Usable and Effective Security. Bt. Technol. J. 19(3), 122–131 (2001)
22. Angela Sasse, M., Ashenden, D.: Human Vulnerabilities in Security Systems. Cyber Security Ktn White Paper (2007)
23. Mann, I.: Hacking The Human: Social Engineering Techniques and Security Countermeasures. Aldershot, Gower (2008)
24. Milgram, S.: Obedience to Authority: An Experimental View. Pinter & Martin, London (1974, 1997)
25. Mitnick, K., Simon, W.L.: The Art of Deception: Controlling the Human Element of Security. Wiley, New York (2002)
26. Onnela, J.P., Reed-Tsochas, F.: Spontaneous Emergence of Social Influenc in Online Systems. Proceedings of the National Academy of Sciences (2010)
27. Parker, D.B.: Motivating The Workforce to Support Security Objectives: A Long Term View (2002)
28. Reicher, S.D., Haslam, S.A.: Rethinking The Psychology of Tyranny: The Bbc Prison Study. British Journal of Social Psychology, 1–40 (2006)
29. Stanton, J., Stam, K., Mastrangelo, P., Jolton, J.: Analysis of End User Security Behaviors. Computers & Security 24, 124–133 (2005)
30. Stanton, J.M., Stam, K.R.: The Visible Employee: Using Workplace Monitoring and Surveillance to Protect Information Assets-Without Compromising Employee Privacy or Trust. Information Today, Medford (2006)
31. Styles, M., Tryfonas, T.: Using Penetration Testing Feedback to Cultivate An Atmosphere of Proactive Security Amongst End-Users. Information Management & Computer Security 17, 44–52 (2009)
32. Sunstein, C.R.: Probability Neglect: Emotions, Worst Cases and Law (2002)
33. Sunstein, C.R., Richard, A.Z.: Dreadful Possibilities, Neglected Probabilities (2009)
34. Tavris, C., Elliot, A.: Mistakes Were Made (But Not By Me): Why We Justify Foolish Beliefs, Bad Decisions, and Hurtful Acts. Harcourt, Orlando (2007)
35. Vetter, K.: E-Mail Typos Result in 20gb of Stolen Data. Wired (2011)
    http://Edition.Cnn.Com/2011/Tech/Web/09/09/
    Email.Typos.Stolen.Data.Wired/Index.html (accessed September 9, 2011)
36. Wilde, G.: The Theory of Risk Homeostasis: Implications for Safety and Health. Risk Analysis 2, 209–225 (1982)
37. Williams, C.: Police Send Reg Hack Crb Check Database - Massive Security Breach Prompts Investigation. The Register (2010),
    http://www.Theregister.Co.Uk/2010/04/16/Gwent_Police_Data/
    (accessed September 2011)
38. Zimbardo, P.G.: The Lucifer Effect: How Good People Turn Evil. Rider, London (2007)

Part III
Security and Privacy Policies

Strategic Interaction Analysis
of Privacy-Sensitive End-Users of Cloud-Based Mobile
Apps

Kalliopi Anastasopoulou[1], Theo Tryfonas[2], and Spyros Kokolakis[1]

[1] Dept. of Information and Communication Systems Engineering
University of the Aegean, Samos, Greece
[2] Bristol Cryptography Group, Faculty of Engineering, University of Bristol, UK
{sak,k.anastasopoulou}@aegean.gr,
theo.tryfonas@bristol.ac.uk

Abstract. Free mobile applications of cloud computing offer a range of diverse services (e.g. gaming, storage etc.) usally in return for delivering personalized advertising to their consenting end-users. In order to do so they may retain a range of personal information such as location and personal preferences. Thus, privacy-related interactions between service providers and end users are important to be studied as personal data are valuable in a subscription-based cloud system. In this paper, game theory is used as a tool to identify and analyze such interactions in order to understand stakeholder choices, as well as how to improve the quality of the service offered in a cloud computing setting.

Keywords: Privacy, mobile apps, cloud, game theory, strategic interactions.

1 Introduction[1]

There exist many free cloud-based mobile applications (apps), which individuals can use to store their information into a cloud (e.g. Dropbox, Google Drive) and also to make transactions and use related services (navigation, gaming etc.). End users of these usually come to terms with decisions that include a trade off of handing over privacy sensitive information [1]. The term privacy sensitive information refers to any personally identifiable information (e.g. name, address), sensitive information (e.g. religion or race, sexual orientation), usage data (recently visited websites) and also to unique device identities (e.g. IP addresses) [3].

---

[1] This research has been co-financed by the European Union (European Social Fund - ESF) and Greek national funds through the Operational Program "Education and Lifelong Learning" of the National Strategic Reference Framework (NSRF) - Research Funding Program: Heracleitus II Investing in knowledge society through the European Social Fund. The authors would also like to thank the University of Bristol's Systems Centre for kindly hosting the sponsored researcher.

L. Marinos and I. Askoxylakis (Eds.): HAS/HCII 2013, LNCS 8030, pp. 209–216, 2013.
© Springer-Verlag Berlin Heidelberg 2013

Services and applications that make use of privacy information into a cloud-computing context are components that can be implemented and scaled up or down, providing an on-demand utility model. Some of these applications include mobile social networking, real time data processing and content delivery [2]. Outsourcing data hosting functionality to the cloud through a secure platform-as-service is something increasingly utilized and offered at a low price [1]. For example infrastructure services, platform and software applications are provided to end users of cloud computing through pay-as-you-go business models. Their simpler offering can take the form of free service in return for delivery of personalized advertising (that providers then make profit from).

In this paper, we follow a game-theoretical approach to understand and analyze how privacy agents behave when they have to trust, store and share their personal data into a cloud-based service application (such as Google Drive) and how better understanding of their privacy decisions can be used as a tool for companies to create business value. We propose a model where service providers and end users interact with respect to general privacy policies for storing and sharing personal information. End users are expected to be honest in providing personal information in order to be subscribed in cloud services and on the other hand service providers are obligated to obey their privacy policies and do not disclose end users' information to third parties.

In the following section we discuss related work in cloud computing and in section 3 we present and interpret our basic model. In section 4 we discuss the outcomes, which come out of this basic model. The last section contains our conclusions and further research issues are addressed.

2   Related Work

Much of the past and current literature depicts that cloud computing is pretty much connected with human based negotiations for personal data stored and exchanged in internet datacenters.

Data storage at a low cost, flexibility to pass services and better resiliency, are some of the benefits that give to end users a competitive advantage to adopt cloud-based services [5]. Individuals rely increasingly on cloud service providers to cover their computing needs, however, the pace of adoption of upcoming cloud technology is not excessively quick, as individuals and organizations do not migrate critical systems to cloud computing yet. The same happened in the past with technologies like virtualization, where stakeholders started to use them for non-critical systems, and when they became comfortable with the new technology, they used it for all type of systems.

A major inhibiting factor is related to the loss of control over storage of critical data and the service's outsourced nature. The challenge for cloud providers is to identify and understand the concerns of privacy-sensitive users, and adopt security practices that meet their requirements [1]. Ramireddy et al. [11] examine if cloud providers' characteristics influence their decision to adopt security practices for protecting privacy policies and offer a secure platform to end users for storing and processing data.

Their results, based on quantitative analysis, lead to the fact that providers use different information assurance practices in order to offer cloud services. Misunderstanding the privacy concerns of end users may lead to loss of business, as they may either stop using a perceivably insecure or privacy-abusing service, or falsify their provided information – hence minimising the potential for profit via personalised adverting. Riedl et al. [10] mention that strategic decisions and forecasting under uncertainty are considered as essential requirements, during the negotiation process, for establishing players in a cloud market. An end user can give fake data if she believes that the service provider is going to abuse the privacy agreement and sell personal data derived from a cloud–based subscription to a third party.

Game theory in these cases emerges as an interesting tool to explore, as it can be used to interpret stakeholder interactions and interdependencies across the above scenarios. For example, Rajbhandari and Snekkenes [7] implemented a game theory based approach to analyze risks to privacy, in place of the traditional probabilistic risk analysis (PRA). Their scenario is based on an online bookstore where the user has to subscribe in order to have access to a service. Two players take part in this game: the user and the online bookstore. The user could provide either genuine or fake information, whereas the bookstore could sell user's information to a third party or respect it. A mixed strategy Nash equilibrium was chosen for solving the game, with user's negative payoffs, in order to describe quantitatively the level of privacy risk.

Also, according to Hausken [4] the behavioral dimension is a very important factor in order to estimate risk. A conflict behavior which is recorded on individuals' choices can be integrated in a probabilistic risk analysis and analyzed through game theory. Friedman and Resnick [8] worked on providing the use of "cheap pseudonyms" as a way to measure reputation in Internet interaction between stakeholders. This was a game of M players where users provided pseudonyms during an interaction in the Internet world and they had the option either to continue playing with the current pseudonym or fin a new one, at each period of time. A suboptimal equilibria is found, as a repeated prisoner's dilemma type of game, while methods of limiting identity changes are suggested. Kokolakis et al. showed why it is not easy to establish trust when personal information is used in electronic commerce by implementing a game model in an e-transaction between a buyer and a seller [9].

Concluding, game theory research in online privacy-related decision-making has provided some evidence that it can give credible results in understanding privacy-related behavior, however it is still an ongoing and open field in its early stages of maturity.

3   The Basic Model

Our model refers to content delivery/storage applications, where privacy-related decisions for storing and gathering information between the participants are made. Much importance is given in understanding the underlying motivations of their actions and reactions. In these decisions, risk and uncertainty are involved and in this case, economic factors related to costs per processing, costs per unit of memory, costs per unit of storage and costs per unit of used bandwidth have to be taken into account [2]. We develop a basic game model in order to understand how strategic interactions among the rational agents influence their behavior to use or not such cloud services.

Consider a cloud service provider (SP), i.e. a company which provides the ability to end users to store and share their data with others via mobile apps that enable data access and storage in a cloud computing environment. The company's objective is to maintain a platform that can provide secure services to end-users, whilst ensuring at the same time that profit is raised by delivering value for which clients are happy to pay, or at least surrender their personal data, for.

The SP stores personal information of end users in a database server and an application server hosts a number of data reporting and monitoring applications using a remote mobile client over the Internet. A two-tier service is provided: (a) free of charge with personalized advertising based on the retained personal data, or (b) paid for, which is advertising-free and offers greater sharing storage capacity.

The end user reads carefully and checks the privacy policy and decides to proceed with either registering for the free of charge option, consenting to their personal data being used for advertising purposes, or chooses the advertising-free, paid option. SP and end user then have an agreement. But both of them have the option to violate the agreement. The SP may use end users' information in a more profit-making way that violates its privacy policy, e.g. passing the information to advertisers. The end user, on the other hand, may provide false personal information. That means that the end user is protected from privacy violations, but loses any personalization advantages. We assume that the case that someone registers for a paid service under false personal data is of equal payoff to the provider with the one where the data is accurate, as in this case the registered data would not be further used under SP's consent. At that point, each party has to choose a strategy, based on their expectations of the other party's behavior. Therefore, exploring each party's behavior separately would not allow us to understand the dynamics of the SP - End User interaction.

A game with a single end user and a service provider interacting is modeled below. Each player has the following options: to Cooperate (C) or to Defect (D). Cooperation for the end user is equal to providing true personal data, whilst defecting is deciding to fake personal information. Respectively, SP cooperates when she complies with privacy policies, whilst she defects when violates them. Thus, four combinations (strategy profiles) exist, which are presented in the following paragraphs together with our definitions of their corresponding payoffs.

The payoffs are in utility and in each strategy are given by: *payoff = usage for internal purposes + selling information to third parties.*

If both end user and SP decide to defect, the end user receives a minimum benefit, and the SP may get some minimum benefit too, if they manage to trade the false data, albeit inaccurate. We give it a value of one (1) for both in an arbitrary way.

If the end user is the actor who defects, whilst at the same time the SP respects the privacy policy, then the end user again gains the some benefit (1) but the SP will get no benefit from providing the free service plus the cost of maintaining the privacy policy. Thus, we consider the payoff for the SP to be less than in the previous case, so we give it the value of zero (0).

If the end user gives true information about her and the SP mistreats it in some way, then the SP gains a significant profit and the end user suffers a loss, as we indicated that we have a privacy-sensitive end user. A payoff of three (3) is considered for the SP and (0) for the end user.

Finally, if both parties cooperate, then all will have benefits. The end user will receive personalized services according to their preference and the SP may have the chance to use end user's data, within the limits of the privacy policy. A payoff of two (2) is considered appropriate in such case to both players. The game is played in normal form and is being presented in Table 1. As we stated, we use arbitrary values for the payoffs for illustrative reasons. Only the order of payoffs is significant for the analysis that follows and not their exact values.

Table 1. The End user-SP Privacy Game for Clouds

		End User	
		Cooperate (C)	Defect (D)
SP	Cooperate (C)	2,2	0,1
	Defect (D)	3,0	1,1

Defecting is thought to be a dominant strategy for SP as she wins a better payoff regardless of the end user's choice. We are thus going to examine only how the end user would respond to the only remaining SP's strategy (defect), as, from a privacy-concerned perspective, we can eliminate the dominated strategy for SP (cooperate). In this case the end user will also defect. Thus, the equilibrium in the above game - the iterated dominant strategy equilibrium- is equal to {Defect, Defect}. In the equilibrium state the overall payoffs are less than when both players cooperate.

Supposing that this game is played only once, we address the simplest format of the game. In fact, a SP would normally expect the end user to choose again the same SP and make a new subscription for data storage services. So, if the game is repeated there are two more factors to take into account. Firstly, whether there are finite or infinite repetitions and secondly whether SP's policy violation gets detected. If policy violation doesn't get detected, then the iterative version of the game is identical to the one-off game presented above. So, we only examine the case of observable policy violation, i.e. one that gets immediately detected.

Referring to the finite case, the game is designed to be repeated several times and then stops. If we want to find a solution for this game, then we should first examine the last round. We can see that the game played at the last round is identical to the one we presented above. Thus, the end user would think that the SP would violate the policy the last time the game is played. However, for the end user it would be too late to fake her information. So, if the end user expects that at some time in the future the SP will mistreat the information provided, then she will fake her information from the beginning. Thus, the equilibrium of the finite repeated game is the same as in the case of the one-off game.

When an end user respects cloud services policies that considers reliable and makes regular moves, we may model the relevant game as an infinitely repeated game. The case of the infinitely repeated game is more complex. However, we can simplify our analysis, if we consider the act of discontinuing the end user-SP relation as a penalty imposed by the end user to the unreliable SP. The penalty is equivalent to the loss of profit from all future subscription fees or targeted advertising revenue. Whilst formal analysis of the game is left for future research, our preliminary analysis shows that defecting the privacy policy is a dominant strategy for the SP.

Finally the equilibria of the different variations of the end user-SP cloud privacy game are summarized in Table 2.

Table 2. Equilibria in Variations of the End user-SP Privacy Game in Clouds

	One-off	Repeated	Infinitely repeated
Observable violation	D, D	D, D	C, C
Undetectable violation	D, D	D, D	D, D

4   Discussion

In the following paragraphs we will present some preliminary results from the above game model. Where end users have the ability to choose a cloud service provider to match their expectations, their stated privacy policies cannot assure trust. The utilization of cloud computing services, such as in the content delivery domain is growing, however, it is still extremely difficult for many end users to trust service providers and store their personal data in a cloud-based environment, as privacy violation issues may perceivably happen at any time.

When end users adopt cloud-based services and chose to use relevant apps, they do not know in advance, if the service provider is reliable with respect to retention of their personal data. There are many instances where end users provide fake personal information in order to receive services (e.g. cloud-based storage) as they feel more protected. On the other hand, service providers are interested to implement their strategic policies so that end users would remain loyal and pay for premium services. In this case, they should carefully consider giving data to a third party in order to avoid disappointing both their premium and basic end users and salvage their reputation.

Providing a fair solution to assure both end users' loyalty and SP compliance is a necessity. However, since such violations are difficult to be detected by most stakeholders, regulating the use of policies by enforcing audits is rather of a low effectiveness. Enforcing penalties for any violation from SPs, or using reputation systems, is a helpful countermeasure to provide assurance to end-users. SPs might not risk illicitly offending personal data, when they are expected to lose a number of potential end users from such practices

To summarize, we have to note that the above findings are applicable only to stakeholders that care about privacy policies and are sensitive to privacy violation issues. It is notable, that much of the population does not want to pay for protecting their privacy, either because they believe that Internet users cannot protect their privacy in an effective way, or because have the Feeling that the information they reveal is not useful for further use by others, or because they have the perception that there is no effective way to protect your privacy in the Internet.

5   Conclusion and Further Research

A game-theoretic model has been developed in order to show that privacy policies alone are not enough to ensure that no violation would occur, when an end user trusts free mobile apps in clouds. Equilibrium in this game comes when the SP does not adhere to the privacy policy and the end user fakes personal information. Therefore imposing penalties to violating SPs, or employing reputation systems that increase the cost of violation have to be considered in an effort to enforce policies that serve the purpose for which they were designed. It is also clear from our model that it is better for SPs and end users to be honest when they interact as a system.

We should also note that our ongoing study has limitations at this stage, as some potentially significant factors have been excluded from discussion in this paper. We have not presented the formal definition and analysis of our game model in full terms of formal economic theory, as they are left for future research. Limitations therefore are with respect to the analysis of uncertainties underlying the players' preferences. If players think in a different way, they will choose a different strategy and a different equilibrium will occur.

Game theory is regarded as an excellent tool for behavioral analysis [4,6,7], as rational agents interact in many fields of social life. There are many cases where privacy-related incidents obliged organizations to remove their products from the market with considerable financial loss. It would be of value to provide guidance on how to consider such issues during risk analysis, in order to identify this kind of business risk from an SP's perspective. Risk assessment, as a way to predict the likelihood of occurrence of a threat and the scale of its consequences, is not enough to provide much guidance on how to do this well. Game theory can be a suitable complement, as it is compatible with traditional risk management and could be integrated into approaches like PRA. Further work would be focused on matching the ISO/IEC 27005 process [6] with complementary game theory techniques.

References

1. Brunette, G., Mogull, R. (eds.): Security Guidance for Critical Areas of Focus in Cloud Computing V2.1. Cloud Security Alliance (December 2009)
2. Calheiros, R.N., Ranjan, R., Rose, C.A.F.D., Buyya, R.: CloudSim: A Novel Framework for Modeling and Simulation of Cloud Computing Infrastructures and Services. CoRR, vol.abs/0903.2525 (2009)

3. Pearson, S.: Taking account of privacy when designing cloud computing services. In: ICSE Workshop on Software Engineering Challenges of Cloud Computing, Vancouver, Canada, pp. 44–52 (May 2009)
4. Hausken, K.: Probabilistic risk analysis and game theory. Risk Anal 22, 17–27 (2002)
5. Diez, O., Silva, A.: Cloud computing and Critical Infrastructure Systems. In: Proc. of the 2011 6th International Conference on System of Systems Engineering, Albuquerque, New Mexico, USA, June 27-30, pp. 7–12 (2011)
6. Rajbhandari, L., Snekkenes, E.A.: Mapping between Classical Risk Management and Game Theoretical Approaches. In: De Decker, B., Lapon, J., Naessens, V., Uhl, A. (eds.) CMS 2011. LNCS, vol. 7025, pp. 147–154. Springer, Heidelberg (2011)
7. Rajbhandari, L., Snekkenes, E.A.: Using game theory to analyze risk to privacy: An initial insight. In: Fischer-Hübner, S., Duquenoy, P., Hansen, M., Leenes, R., Zhang, G. (eds.) Privacy and Identity Management for Life. IFIP AICT, vol. 352, pp. 41–51. Springer, Heidelberg (2011)
8. Friedman, E.J., Resnick, P.: The Social Cost of Cheap Pseudonyms. Journal of Economics and Management Strategy 10(2), 173–199 (2001)
9. Kokolakis, S., Anastasopoulou, K., Karyda, M.: An Analysis of Privacy-related Strategic Choices of Buyers and Sellers in e-Commerce Transactions. In: Proc. of the 16th Panhellenic Conference on Informatics with International Participation, Pireaus, Greece, October 5-7 (2012)
10. Christoph, R., Stefanie, L., Markus, B., Phillip, Y., Helmut, K.: Competing in the Clouds: A Strategic Challenge for ITSP Ltd. Communications of the Association for Information Systems 27, Article 40 (2010)
11. Srilakshmi, R., Rajarshi, C., Raghu, T.S., Raghav, R.H.: Privacy and Security Practices in the Arena of Cloud Computing - A Research in Progress. In: AMCIS 2010 Proceedings. Paper 574 (2010)

Essential Lessons Still Not Learned? Examining the Password Practices of End-Users and Service Providers

Steven Furnell[1,3] and Nina Bär[2]

[1] Centre for Security Communications and Network Research, Plymouth University,
Plymouth, United Kingdom
[2] Chemnitz University of Technology, Chemnitz, Germany
[3] Security Research Institute, Edith Cowan University, Perth, Western Australia
sfurnell@plymouth.ac.uk, nina.baer@psychologie.tu-chemnitz.de

Abstract. Password authentication remains the dominant form of user authentication for online systems. As such, from a user perspective, it is an approach that they are very much expected to understand and use. However, a survey of 246 users revealed that about one third chose weak passwords, including personal information or dictionary words. To prevent such forms of bad security behavior, service providers should offer support, but the reality of the situation suggests that tangible weaknesses can exist amongst both parties, and thus despite their long-recognised importance, good password practices have yet to become an established part of our security culture. An experimental study was conducted in order to investigate the effect of providing password guidance upon end users' password choices. The findings revealed that the mere presentation of guidance (without any accompanying enforcement of good practice) had a significant effect upon the resulting password quality.

Keywords: Password guidance, authentication, end user, security behavior.

1 Introduction

Passwords continue to be the most common context in which people come into contact with security, representing the de facto authentication method on desktop and laptop computers, as well as the standard mode for requesting authentication on the various websites and other online services that now require it. However, in spite of their long-established and widespread use, the underlying password choices made by end-users continue to exhibit a variety of weaknesses. Put simply, good password selection is not a skill that many users seem to possess by nature, and so they require appropriate awareness and support in order to do things properly. Unfortunately, the extent to which this is provided for them is often insufficient, thus leaving them to perpetuate a problem across multiple systems and accounts.

This paper examines the situation based upon the current practices of end-users and service providers, revealing notable gaps in both cases. It then continues to investigate the improvements in password practices that can result from relatively minor

L. Marinos and I. Askoxylakis (Eds.): HAS/HCII 2013, LNCS 8030, pp. 217–225, 2013.
© Springer-Verlag Berlin Heidelberg 2013

additional efforts on the provider side, by simply ensuring that relevant guidance is presented to users to inform their password choices.

2   A Survey of End-User Practices

In order to assess the degree to which good practices are now embedded within password usage, a series of related questions were incorporated in to a wider survey of end-user security practices (with the full question set also spanning issues such as use of antivirus and Internet security tools, and security of mobile devices).

The overall results are based on a respondent group of 246, of which 108 are classified as 'general public' and 138 were 'IT students'. The public sample was captured during a science and technology showcase event, at which online security was highlighted as one of the key issues. Meanwhile, the 'IT students' were newly commencing the first year study for an undergraduate degree in computing, and were approached to complete the questionnaire during their first week of study, before receiving any specific tuition in relation to security topics. Thus, as a respondent group, they can be considered to have declared an explicit interest in IT (and may therefore be more regular and active users of it), but they should not be assumed to inherently be any more aware in relation to security issues than the wider population. The first notable finding in relation to passwords was that users can potentially have a fair number of them to manage. Respondents were asked how many systems or sites they used that required a password, and the overall results are depicted in Figure 1. Looking within the sub-population, the IT students were (perhaps unsurprisingly) facing more of a password management challenge, with only 8% of them responding in the '1-5' category and 39% reporting to use 16+ password-based systems.

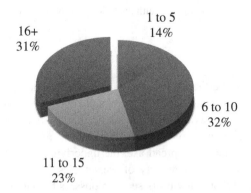

Fig. 1. Number of systems or websites requiring passwords

Of course the number of systems or sites used does not necessarily map onto an equivalent number of distinct passwords, and so the respondents were also asked to broadly indicate their practices in this regard. The majority (54%) indicated that they have a set of passwords that they choose from, while 27% claimed to have a different on for each site, and 17% suggested that they used the same one on every system (the remaining percentage left the question unanswered).

Having established a clear dependency upon password-based approaches, the final segment of password-related questions helped to further demonstrate the extent to which users' practices can be often be less than ideal. Respondents were presented with a series of potential statements about the password used on their most valuable system, and asked to indicate all that applied. The average responses across the whole group are presented in Table 1, and it can be seen that good practice tends to vary.

Table 1. Responses to statements around password usage

Statement	Agreement (n=246)
It is at least 8 characters long	82%
It has alphabetic and numeric characters	84%
It includes other characters (e.g. punctuation symbols)	49%
It uses a word you would find in a dictionary	18%
It is based on personal information about me	26%
I have changed it since I started using it	36%
I change it regularly	21%
I have shared it with other people	6%
I have forgotten it and had to reset/recover it	10%

From these overall findings, the only one that stands out as suggesting the good practice is properly embedded is the fact that only 6% report to have shared their password. This suggests that the vast majority of users understand and accept the premise of the password as being their authentication secret. Beyond this, however, there are tangible proportions of weaker practice in all of the areas considered. While there was no significant difference between the populations in terms of baseline length, there was a tangible difference in how they were reportedly composed. For example, 91% of IT students reported using passwords containing both alphabetic and numeric characters, as opposed to only 76% of the general public group. Even more notably, when asked about the use of punctuation characters, these were incorporated by 59% of the students versus only 36% of the public.

Findings suggest that IT students are marginally better in terms of good practices such as changing their passwords regularly, not sharing, and not having forgotten their details. This sub-group was also significantly better in terms of not using personal information (78% versus 68%), but this still leaves tangible proportions in both cases (and some 26% of the respondent group overall) that were admittedly using passwords based upon personal details. Moreover, largely equal proportions from both groups (averaging 18% of the respondents overall) reported using dictionary words. Thus, assuming that the categories of personal information and dictionary words do not intersect too greatly, this easily represents more than a third of respondents making password choices that would contravene standard guidance, before one even gets to the stage of looking at password composition.

3   Assessing Service Provision

Given that some users clearly exhibit inclinations towards making weaker choices, it is relevant to consider the extent to which they may be supported and guided towards doing things properly. An indication of this can be gained by looking at the password guidance and enforcement offered by leading websites. A prior study from Furnell considered ten leading sites, and discovered that half provided little or no guidance on password selection when users initially registered and set up their accounts [1]. Of the sites that did provide guidance, only two went to the extent of providing links to comprehensive guidance pages covering tips for password selection, use and protection. By contrast, some sites provided no password guidance at all at the point of registration, and most fell somewhere between the extremes, providing some indication of criteria for selecting passwords, but no wider suggestions for protecting them once chosen.

In addition to the variability of guidance, the sites also varied significantly in the degree to which they enforced good password practices. As the summary presented in Table 2 illustrates, the level of support is by no means uniform and (in many cases) is below that which one might consider desirable [1].

Table 2. The varying enforcement of password restrictions on websites

Site	Enforce min length (+max if approp)	Prevents Surname	Prevents User ID	Prevents 'password'	Prevents dictionary words	Enforces composition	Prevents reuse
Amazon	6	✗	✗	✗	✗	✗	✗
eBay	6-20	✗	✓	✓	✗	✓	✓
Facebook	6	✓	✗	✓	~ (1)	✗	✗
Google	8	✗	✓	✓	✓	✗	✓
LinkedIn	6	✗	✗	✓	✗	✗	✗
Twitter	6	✗	✗	✓	✓	✗	✗
Wikipedia	✗	✗	✓	✗	✗	✗	✗
Windows Live	6-16	✓	✓	✓	✗	✓	✗
WordPress	4	✗	✓	✓	✗	✗	✗
Yahoo!	6-32	✓	✓	✓	✗	✗	✗

(1) Provision is only made when the user changes their password.

In view of these findings, it seems fair to suggest that users cannot rely upon the sites they are using to be proactive in safeguarding their interests. At the same time, without the provision of associated guidance, it is difficult for users themselves to ensure that they are using passwords as safely as possible.

4   Assessing Password Selection in Practice

Having critiqued the websites, it was hypothesized that the provision of credible guidance would help to ensure that users made better password choices. In order to test this in practice, an experimental study was mounted that required users to choose passwords as part of a wider set of activities.

Choosing a secure password as a form of security behavior is influenced by a set of factors perceived by the user. Huang et al. [2] suggest a model including knowledge, controllability, awareness, severity and possibility as determinants of a users' intention to follow security practices. The more end users know about the rationale of threats like password cracking and the better their understanding of such threats is, the more likely they will adopt a good security practice. The participants who stated in the survey that their password includes personal information or dictionary words might just not know that passwords can be cracked by dictionary attacks. By implementing password guidance on websites providers can help to explain that issue. When users are shown how to prevent or predict threats they feel much more comfortable and in control of the situation. The use of immediate feedback on their password choice, such as the use of a password strength meter, can enhance awareness that a proposed choice is too weak and help to ensure that even people without knowledge about the topic feel in control to protect their data. However, the compulsion to follow good password practices is nevertheless related to the perceived severity of consequences in case the password might be cracked. End users often indicate that even if their passwords were cracked they would not be concerned because they would not attach much importance to the consequences. That might be the case for passwords on accounts/systems of less personal relevance, but when asked for their most valuable account users should indeed be aware of the severity of negative consequences, especially as people are typically concerned about the privacy of the data they provide to websites. In contradiction to this, however, that concern is often not noticeable in their online actions [3]; mostly because of the immediate benefit of more convenience. Taking into account that users are willing to trade-off concerns about their online security for convenience, it seems likely that the additional influence of the subjective possibility of being a victim of online attacks is by far underestimated. "I know my password is not strong, but I don't think anyone will have any interest in cracking my password and breaking into my computer" is what participants answered when asked for their opinion about password security [4].

4.1   Experimental Design

To investigate the effect of providing security guidance upon the actual quality of passwords two versions of a website were tested in a between-design. Unbeknownst the participants, there were two versions of the site (one that paid attention to usability good practice, and the other which did not – see Figure 2), and they were not aware that they were being assigned to a particular version. The initial task for the users was to register on the site by selecting a username and password. The experimental group was shown one version of the website which paid attention to good security usability including password guidance. They were provided with guidelines how to create a secure password and a password strength meter as immediate feedback on their password choice. The control group was shown a second version of the same website which did not contain any guidance or feedback on passwords.

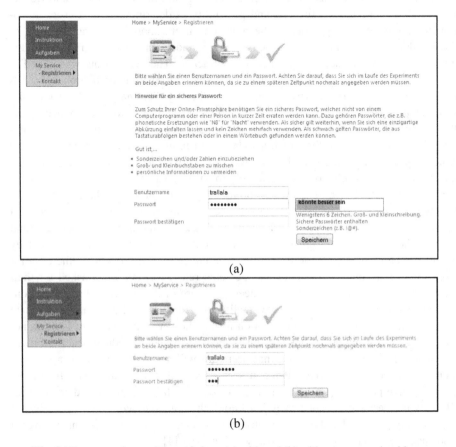

(a)

(b)

Fig. 2. The two variants of the website – (a) with and (b) without password guidance

For the experimental group the password guidance advised them in the following way: "For protecting your online privacy you need a safe password, i.e. one which cannot be easily guessed by a computer program or an individual in a short period of time. This includes passwords with phonetic replacements, e.g. 2nite for tonight. Furthermore, it is advised to create a unique acronym and not to repeat characters. Weak passwords consist of keyboard patterns or can be found in a dictionary. It is good…(1) to include punctuation marks and/or numbers, (2) to mix capital and lowercase letters and (3) to avoid using personal information." Both groups were instructed to create a username and a password which both could be memorized throughout the whole experiment. Neither variant of the website enforced password selection rules, and on the version that included password guidelines there was still no obligation for the participants to read them. As such, any differences in the resulting password behavior would be attributable to the mere provision of guidelines.

4.2   Procedure

The participants were being asked to use a website and assess aspects of its usability. They were not made specifically aware that attention would be given to their password choices, and they were simply advised that they were participating in a website usability study (i.e. from the user perspective, choosing a password was just something they needed to do in order to get started, rather than being a central focus of the task). The users were, however, instructed to select a new password rather than one that they already used elsewhere. The basis for this was to both enable the study to assess their password selection practices, and to reduce the risk of them inadvertently divulging a password that they already used when it came to the later analysis. Having successfully registered, the users were then required to use the password to log in and comment upon the website's usability (the results of which form part of a wider HCI study, which is out of scope for this paper).

4.3   Sample

A total of N=27 participants (17 female, 10 male) were involved in the initial study. The mean age was M = 27.3 years. The experimental group (N=13) and the control group (N=14) did not differ in terms of the time they spent online for private purposes or other control variables such as affinity for technology.

4.4   Results

The resulting password choices were rated using a subset of the prior criteria from Table 1 that could be measured at the point of password creation. Specifically, a point could be scored for a password satisfying each of the following (thus giving a maximum of 5 points for good choice):

- at least 8 characters long
- composed of both alphabetic and numeric characters
- using other characters (such as punctuation symbols)
- not based upon a dictionary word
- not based upon personal information

Table 3. Summary results from study participants

	Used at least 8 characters	Used alphanumeric characters	Used other characters	Used non-dictionary	Avoided personal info
Guided (n=13)	85%	85%	62%	54%	92%
Unguided (n=14)	50%	64%	7%	50%	64%

It is arguable that the 8-character minimum is not a particularly secure baseline, but it was nonetheless the best of the set assessed from the earlier group in Table 2 and so forms a foundation on that basis. The results revealed a significant difference between those receiving guidance and those attempting to select passwords without it (t(25)=3.82, p=.001, d= 1.5). The mean for the former group was M=3.8 out of 5, whereas the unguided users averaged just M=1.9. The qualitative analysis of the individual cases revealed that those without guidance were notably more inclined to use personal information in their passwords, and far less likely to have considered the use of character types beyond alphanumeric. Table 3 summarises the overall performance of the two groups against each of the assessment criteria.

Although the results are only based upon a small sample, they nonetheless appear to offer a clear message in terms of the effectiveness of providing password guidance versus leaving users to their own devices. Although it can be argued that the users may not have been choosing typical passwords because they knew it was only being used in a study, the fact remains that all users were operating in this context and those receiving guidance nonetheless chose better. So, it is notable that the guidance even made a difference in this context (i.e. with a site they would be unlikely to value).

5   Conclusions

The paper has clearly evidenced that, that despite our long-standing use and familiarity with them, some significant problems surrounding passwords have yet to be resolved. Although the sample population in the practical study is currently small, the overall message emerging from the collective findings in the paper remains clear: users readily admit to making weak password choices, websites do not guide on or enforce good practice as well as they could, and yet the experiment clearly suggests that even the basic provision of guidance can help to deliver a tangible improvement. As such, there appear to be clear lessons to be learnt that could help to uplift authentication practices while passwords continue to be retained as a primary method.

Building upon these findings, it is intended that the research to benchmark the effect of providing password guidance will continue with a larger and more diverse sample of users. If the later findings continue to support the same conclusions, then we believe this should represent a persuasive message regarding appropriate baseline standards that websites (and organisations) ought to be following in supporting their users' security practices.

References

1. Furnell, S.M.: Assessing password guidance and enforcement on leading websites. Computer Fraud & Security, 10–18 (December 2011)
2. Huang, D.-L., Rau, P.-L., Salvendy, G.: Perception of information security. Behaviour & Information Technology 29(3), 221–232 (2010), doi:10.1080/01449290701679361
3. Davinson, N., Sillence, E.: It won't happen to me: Promoting secure behaviour among internet users. Computers in Human Behavior 26(6), 1739–1747 (2010), doi:10.1016/j.chb.2010.06.023
4. Huang, D.-L., Rau, P.-L., Salvendy, G., Gao, F., Zhou, J.: Factors affecting perception of information security and their impacts on IT adoption and security practices. International Journal of Human-Computer Studies 69(12), 870–883 (2011), doi:10.1016/j.ijhcs.2011.07.007

Ethical Issues Surrounding the Asymmetric Nature of Workplace Monitoring

John D. Bustard

University of Southampton, Hampshire SO17 1BJ, UK
jdb@ecs.soton.ac.uk

Abstract. Public discussion of the privacy concerns of individuals has focused on protecting them from criminal attacks, government spying and the manipulation of consumers by businesses. While these are important areas of concern, there is also a significant ethical and societal risk from privacy intrusion from other sources, such as employers. Many employers gather extensive and highly personal information on their staff. The availability of this information is often asymmetric, with higher status employees having correspondingly greater access to the personal data of others. This paper examines some of the risks inherent in this asymmetry and discusses to what extent existing legal and social measures are sufficient to protect individuals, organisations and society.

Keywords: Ethics, privacy, workplace monitoring.

1 Introduction

This paper argues for the need to reconsider the ethics of common workplace monitoring practices due to their effects on employees, employers, the economy and society as a whole. Such an examination is particularly important due to the increasing deployment of technology that enables the monitoring of ever greater aspects of employee's lives [Moore(2012)]. The main body of the paper is divided into five sections. The first provides a brief summary of evidence that workplace monitoring is asymmetric. This is followed by an examination of disparities between workplace privacy and privacy in other contexts, such as in police investigations or between individuals. The third section then outlines a number of studies that show how monitoring can lead to psychological and physical harm suggesting that there is an ethical requirement for legislative protection. The paper also examines a common criticism of any restriction on how workplaces function, that of the need to optimise businesses for profitability in a competitive economy [Bork(1991)]. The analysis is also used to evaluate the argument that within many countries, one is free to leave an employer, and thus the potential harm caused by workplace practices has been freely balanced with the benefits the employer provides and thus is inherently ethical. The basis for these anti-legislative arguments is examined, focusing on monitoring effectiveness at increasing productivity and addressing risk. The paper then highlights the additional risks that monitoring bring, specifically in how monitoring can be used to undermine

L. Marinos and I. Askoxylakis (Eds.): HAS/HCII 2013, LNCS 8030, pp. 226–235, 2013.

the investigation of unethical and illegal business practices. Failing to protect against such practices can cause wide reaching economic and social damage. This is highlighted by recent business scandals such as the incidents of phone hacking by journalists in the UK [BBC(2012)] and the misleading sale of sub-prime mortgage investments in the US [Khuzami(2010)]. The paper then examines to what extent unions and professional associations can address workplace privacy issues. The paper concludes by summarising six key points that privacy legislation should include to ensure that the ethical issues outlined in this paper are addressed.

2   Asymmetry

Asymmetries occur from the beginning of employment, where employees provide a detailed CV of their working history and any relevant employment factors. Although there are legal restrictions on what personal information can be requested, it is not uncommon for lifestyle information, such as marital status, to be shared. Most employers keep a record of employee performance along with any information that is deemed relevant, such as days off sick or holidays. Most periods of absence will require some form of permission or justification, particularly for long medical absences. Such highly personal information can then form part of an individual's employment record. This record is typically only visible to more senior staff.

One area of particular concern is the asymmetric working practices of Human Resource (HR) departments [Renwick(2003)]. Kochan [Kochan(2004)] argues that the role of such departments has shifted from personnel administration to a strategic position focused directly on fulfilling the goals of senior management. The concern with such an emphasis is that that it can lead to HR departments attempting to manipulate employment law in favour of employers and against the best interests of employees.

A survey by Vorvorenau et al. [Vorvorenau(2000)] notes that according to several studies in the 1980's, surveillance is most prevalent in clerical fields and low level professional jobs. The authors also suggest that as the technological tools have developed, more low-level jobs are being widely monitored.

3   Legislation and Cultural Norms

Many countries recognise the potential problem of privacy invasion by employers. However, between different countries there is significant variation on the restrictions imposed on employer's use of monitoring technology. A detailed comparison of differences between US and EU privacy legislation has been produced by Mitrou et al. [Mitrou(2006)] This analysis indicates the relatively weak protection provided by US law relative to that in the EU. Although it should be noted that some European governments, such as the UK, have senior political figures who are actively opposed to such policies and have proposed changes to bring their employment legislation closer to that of US practices [Grice(2012)]. Three significant areas of legislation can be identified:

- Non-Work Use of Technology Within the Workplace, such as email, web browsing, printing
- Monitoring and Tracking Employees While They Work, such as security cameras, computer loggers, GPS trackers
- Out of Work Hours Monitoring, such as Facebook, Twitter

3.1 Non-work Use of Technology within the Workplace

Monitoring of employee's personal communication within work has been possible prior to the widespread use of email and web access, with many countries having no protection against employers opening employee postal mail. However such action is difficult to perform secretly. The overt nature of this monitoring may go some way to explaining why it is relatively less common than the monitoring of employee's email [Introna(2000)]. Outside of organisations such monitoring is culturally unacceptable and would be objectionable and illegal for individuals except under the most intimate of personal relationships. However, the violation of such norms by authorities is not uncommon. In the case of police authorities, the legitimacy of such actions is often limited by the need for additional evidence that an individual is likely to be engaged in some form of illegitimate activity [UN(2009)]. There may also be strong limits on how information gathered under such circumstances can be used and for the need for timely communication that an individual has been monitored. In contrast, for some countries, employers may only be required to provide an argument that there is a business need for such monitoring [Mitrou(2006)].

3.2 Monitoring and Tracking Employees While They Work

Over the past forty years, businesses have been steadily increasing the degree to which their organisational activity is recorded and controlled by computers. This technology has the potential to increase automation and help prioritise productive work and thus increase the amount of profitable output per employee. While such technology can be used to monitor the physical mechanisms and processes of a business, it can also be applied to employees themselves, treating them as components within a business machine that can be optimised for profit. Many cultures have expectations that all human beings be treated as individuals and that their feelings and personal preferences be considered in any interaction. To treat them otherwise is to treat them as an object and thus to treat them without respect. One concern with increasing technological monitoring and tracking, particularly when it is performed secretly, is that it encourages dehumanisation of employees. Treating them as statistics that are controlled by rules and computerised processes [Lammers(2009)] rather than individuals that can be inspired by leaders.

3.3 Out of Work Hours Monitoring

There is also concern that monitoring may reduce the degree to which individuals can have a free private life outside of work. Without prior evidence of wrongdoing, some businesses [AMA(2007)] would appear to be secretly tracking and recording employees' personal life in a way that would be unacceptable for individuals, or many government authorities. Similar issues apply to monitoring of employee's behaviour outside of work. Some steps have been taken to provide legal protection against this intrusion [Yahoo(2012)] and recently a number of US states have prevented employers from forcing potential employees to reveal their passwords to social media systems [KnowledgeCenter(2012)]. Monitoring of an employee's personal life in this way runs the risk of employers imposing lifestyle restrictions that may have no bearing on an employee's effectiveness and may be merely unjustified prejudice. Many countries have introduced specific laws to protect against the problem of prejudice, focusing on bias against those with a particular sex, race, religion or sexual orientation. However, these can be seen as simply examples of a more general psychological tendency towards irrational poor treatment of those with identifiable appearance, opinions and behaviour [Tajfel(1982)]. It could be argued that the potential productivity and security gains of out of work-hours communications and social media monitoring do not outweigh the likelihood of prejudiced treatment by employers.

With the growth and popularity of the internet. all individuals have the potential to communicate and influence millions of people. This represents a potential problem for employers as businesses need to maintain corporate secrets and a good reputation with their customers. However, such concerns can lead to a highly autocratic working environments where any criticism of an organisation is seen as being potentially harmful, particularly if such criticism is made public. The rise of social media has intensified this issue. Many users of such services experience them as an extension of existing social comunication with friends and family. Traditionally, during most social interactions, employees would suffer no consequences for speaking openly about their feelings concerning their life, including their workplace, as such communication would remain private. However, when comments are made using social media systems, employers can actively monitor such communications and use them as the basis for disciplinary action including dismissal. Such disciplinary action can occur even if comments are, in reality, only viewed by a small group of friends and family. This can be seen as a breaking of the cultural norms of informal social communication that individuals have come to expect.

4   Physical Harm

Although the breaking of cultural norms of privacy by employers would appear unethical, it could be argued that provided individuals can maintain a free private life outside of the workplace there may not be a need for significant employment privacy legislation. Some have suggested [Bork(1991)] that it is, itself, a cultural norm that employment is not a private activity. However, beyond the ethics of cultural expectations there is also evidence that loss of privacy in and of itself can be harmful, both for the individual and the authority engaged in the monitoring. For example, the dramatic effects of the Stanford Prison Experiment [Zimbardo(2007)] have revealed the ease with which dehumanisation can lead to abusive treatment by otherwise psychologically healthy individuals. This is particularly the case when a controlled group is viewed as a potential threat. The effect of focusing on employees in this way and evaluating their actions remotely and secretly is likely to increase the chances of abusive behaviour.

Thankfully, most workplaces are limited in the degree to which those in power can physically harm individuals. However, psychological harm in the form of workplace bullying remains a major concern, with evidence that it can be sufficiently stressful to create post traumatic stress disorder [Matthiesen(2004)].

In addition, recent research has demonstrated that asymmetries of power cause moral hypocrisy. The study by Lammers et al. [Lammers(2010)] shows that as individuals feel more powerful they are motivated to judge others harshly while simultaneously being motivated to engage in practices they themselves would describe as immoral. Crucially, immoral actions by the powerful are significantly more likely when such actions can be performed in secret. Secretive remote monitoring technology is likely to exacerbate this effect.

Likewise, if monitoring leads to a reduction in an employee's sense of control over the work that they do, they may suffer physical harm. An extensive study of the effects of working practices and health [Marmot(1991)] has shown that such a lack of control within work is one of the strongest factors influencing relative life expectancy, particularly due to the increased risk of heart disease. The potentially alienating effect of having one's work monitored and judged remotely, as opposed to having a close and supportive relationship with a manager, has also been found to increase the risk of mortality from cardiovascular disease [Marmot(1991)]. The magnitude of such an effect suggests that, in addition to privacy legislation, the wider issue of employee control within work is an area that may require governmental protection.

5   Choice and Rights

One argument against legal restrictions on workplace practices is that employees are freely choosing their employment. Thus, any imposed working conditions are inherently ethical as the employee has balanced the costs of such employment with its benefits. To make this choice explicit, some legal jurisdictions require that employees clearly consent to monitoring activity. However, if there is no organisational support for individuals working without monitoring, there is a question as to whether such consent is real; particularly as the consent may form part of an employment contract and be made when an employee is being interviewed. If the alternative to consent is not to be employed, then it would appear that consent is being coerced and thus not providing any real ethical protection.

Even if monitoring consent is not a real choice within a workplace it could be argued that employees are free to chose their employers and thus have implicitly consented, provided they are informed. In cultures where monitoring is widespread, it could even be argued that consent is implicit, as employees have no cultural expectations of workplace privacy. However, most countries see limits to this argument; indeed one of the main roles of ethics is to identify rights that a citizen cannot lose. While there may be some moral absolutist arguments for such rights, they can also be interpreted as a counter balance to some of the harmful workplace practices that may naturally emerge from asymmetries of power and its effects on human psychology.

6   Economic Growth

While there are ethical arguments for minimising harm within the workplace, a number of commentators have suggested that even harmful workplace practices may still be legitimate. Arguments [Hines(2001)] have been made that despite some working environments being highly undesirable, the trickle-down benefits of being a part of a successful company and a growing national economy are such that even oppressed employees are ultimately gaining. However, the actual resulting benefits to employees may well be marginal if there is limited redistribution of wealth; for example, as a result of widespread tax avoidance [Henry(2012)]. For countries with little or no unemployment benefit, the alternative to undesirable working may well be physical harm from deprivation. However, there is concern that the gain to employers from exploitative working environments may be so great that they may actively undermine alternative, more appealing, sources of employment, or self provision, in order to increase the size of their workforce and their relative power over it [Perelman(2000)].

Workplace monitoring practices may also be unnecessarily negative, with unpleasant working environments conveying little commercial benefit but emerging as a result of unjustified fears [Tversky(1973)] or an intrinsic desire by senior staff for greater control over those they manage [Lammers(2010)]. Indeed studies of the effects of surveillance and monitoring on employees have indicated that there can be significant negative effects on morale and productivity if such practices are perceived to be unfair or unreasonable [Vorvoreanu(2000)]. Some workplace privacy legislation contains terms such as 'unjustified', 'excessive' or 'inappropriate', intended to limit these purely negative practices. However, such terms are clearly open to interpretation, so there is a question as to the real degree of protection that they can provide; particularly given the significant asymmetry of resources in pursuing legal claims.

6.1   Motivation and Inequality

Some have suggested that an economy is most productive as a result of having the carrot of relative status, power and wealth and the stick of disrespect, loss of control and destitution. While it is plausible to see how this could be motivating to the small number that succeed in such an environment, psychological studies indicate that there are limits to how effective it is at motivating those at the bottom [Vorvoreanu(2000)]. The most significant example of such a failure is in the treatment of the unemployed. The disrespect shown to the unemployed [Starin(2002)] is likely to trigger depression [Montgomery(1999)] which is highly limiting to motivation [Simon(2001)].

6.2   Asymmetry as a Factor in Unethical Business Practice

With increased monitoring capability it is possible that employers will attempt to identify and stop any perceived threats to an organisation even those that are legitimate. A recent case in America involving the Federal Drugs Administration (FDA) has highlighted this issue [NYTimes(2012/07/15)]. Five scientists working for the FDA were concerned about mismanagement and safety abuses in the review of medical equipment. Following a number of public leaks concerning these issues, FDA officials constructed a list of 'collaborators' that they felt were working together to put out 'defamatory' information about the agency. The affected individuals included congressional officials, academics and journalists. The list was produced as a result of extensive monitoring of all of the employee's emails and documents. The monitoring included confidential letters to congressional offices and oversight committees, drafts of legal filings and grievances. A governmental review of the scientists' medical claims found they had identified "a substantial and specific danger to public safety" [NYTimes(2012/07/15)]. A further press article suggested that one of the scientist's actions was sufficiently provocative that the agency's managers felt they had to resort to these extreme tactics [NYTimes(2012/07/31)]. Unfortunately, due to the asymmetric nature of such monitoring it is not possible to obtain an equivalently detailed account of the actions and motivations of the managers. This highlights how easily monitoring can change from preventative to combative, especially where litigation is involved. It is of particular concern due to the generally high rates of retaliation against whistle blowing employees [Reuters(2012)]. This suggests that the very technology that is being advocated as an aid to economic growth may in fact be contributing to the concealment of unethical or illegal business practices. Such behaviour may result in significant social and economic loses and thus outweigh any productivity gains such technology could provide.

7   Unions and Professional Associations

While, historically, employee groups, such as unions, have played an important role in ensuring protection for their members, their influence has steadily fallen in a number of countries, particularly the UK [Wright(2011)] and USA [Mayer(2004)]. In addition, some unions have adopted a less confrontational approach to collective bargaining, which, in some cases, has resulted in compromises on working conditions to minimise redundancies [Wright(2011)].

Professional associations are also limited in the degree to which they will protect members against unethical workplace practices. For example, while the Association of Computing Machinery has a detailed ethical code [ACM(1992)] which, if followed, could address many of the issues identified within this paper, it also includes terms suggesting that those who follow such principles will not be helped by the organisation. This is evident in the line: "If one decides to violate a law or rule because it is viewed as unethical, or for any other reason, one must fully accept responsibility for one's actions and for the consequences." If one of the consequences of ethical action is unjust treatment by employers it seems reasonable that those imposing such ethical standards should be partially responsible for supporting those that follow them. However, the practical costs of assisting with litigation and the political consequences of such support may prevent any practical action on these ethical issues.

As a result, for many employees it falls to governmental legislation to provide ethical protection. Within Europe at least, there have been a number of new employment laws introduced. These have emerged largely as a result of policies developed to unify employment law across the European Union. However, there has been some political opposition to such laws and even the suggestion that some countries, particularly the UK, may split from the Union, in part, because of objections to such legislation [Cameron(2013)].

8   Conclusions

This paper has identified a number of problems inherent in asymmetric workplace monitoring. These problems can be seen as a practical justification for the need for privacy legislation. These problems could be addressed by ensuring legislation protects the following five privacy needs:

1. The need for monitoring to be obvious as secretive monitoring is a moral hazard that may lead to abuse.
2. The need to restrict monitoring to explicitly commercial factors to minimise the effects of prejudice.
3. The need to treat employees with respect, ensuring that their preferences are acknowledged by providing them with real choices in how their work is performed.
4. The need to minimise asymmetries of control and judgment to ensure that monitoring directly addresses risks and commercial needs, rather than being an intrinsically motivated indulgence of the powerful.
5. The need to ensure that employee monitoring does not lead to a diminished sense of control over employee's work as a loss of control can cause physical harm.

Leading to perhaps the most critical ethical consideration:

- The need to protect open, public discussion of workplace practices by employees to facilitate improvements in working conditions and to ensure they are legal and moral.

A common theme throughout this paper has been the identification of ways in which restrictions on employers are often less than those imposed on business to consumer relationships, individuals or governments. This raises the question as to why such a significant part of the lives of most people is not being held to the same standard. It is hoped that the arguments presented in this paper go some way to highlighting this issue.

References

[ACM(1992)] ACM Code of Ethics and Professional Conduct (1992),
  http://www.acm.org/about/code-of-ethics
[AMA(2007)] Electronic monitoring surveillance survey (2007),
  http://press.amanet.org/press-releases/177/
  2007-electronic-monitoring-surveillance-survey/
[BBC(2012)] Phone Hacking Scandal (2012), http://www.bbc.co.uk/news/
  uk-14045952
[Bork(1991)] Bork, R.H.: The Tempting of America: The Political Seduction of the Law. Sin-
  clair-Stevenson (1991)
[Cameron(2013)] Cameron, D.: UK and the EU (2013),
  http://www.bbc.co.uk/news/uk-politics-21160684
[Glassdoor] Glassdoor and inside look at jobs and companies,
  http://www.glassdoor.com/
[Grice(2012)] Grice, A.: Bosses told they can't 'fire at will' (2012),
  http://www.independent.co.uk/news/uk/politics/bosses-told-
  they-cant-fire-at-will-theyll-have-to-pay-off-staff-instead-
  7836789.html
[Henry(2012)] Henry, J.S.: The Price of Offshore Revisited. Tax Justice Network (2012)
[Hines(2001)] Hines Jr., J.R., Hoynes, H.W., Krueger, A.B.: Another look at whether a rising
  tide lifts all boats. Working Paper 8412, National Bureau of Economic Research (2001)
[Introna(2000)] Introna, L.: Workplace surveillance, privacy and distributive justice. Computers and Society, 33–39 (2000)
[Kanagaretnam(2008)] Kanagaretnam, K., Lobo, G.J., Mohammad, E.: Determinants and consequences of large CEO pay. Int. Jou. Accounting & Finance, 61–82 (2008)
[Khuzami(2010)] Khuzami, R.S., Reisner, L.L., Lench, K.R.: Goldman Sachs to Pay Record
  $550 Million to Settle SEC Charges Related to Subprime Mortgage CDO (2010),
  http://www.sec.gov/news/press/2010/2010-123.htm
[KnowledgeCenter(2012)] Maryland employers cannot ask for facebook passwords,
  http://knowledgecenter.csg.org/kc/content/maryland-employers-
  cannot-ask-facebook-passwords
[Kochan(2004)] Kochan, T.A.: Restoring trust in the Human Resource Management profession.
  Asia Pacific Journal of Human Resources–13 (2004)
[Lammers(2010)] Lammers, J., Stapel, D.A., Galinsky, A.D.: Power increases hypocrisy mora-
  lizing in reasoning, immorality in behavior. Psych. Science 21, 737–744 (2010)
[Lammers(2009)] Lammers, J., Stapel, D.A.: How power influences moral thinking. Personali-
  ty & Social Psychology 1, 61–82 (2009)
[Marmot(1991)] Marmot, M.G., Smith, G.D., Stansfeld, S., Patel, C., North, F., Head, J.,
  White, I., Brunner, E., Feeney, A.: Health inequalities among British civil servants: the Whi-
  tehall II study. Lancet 337(8754), 1387–1393 (1991)
[Matthiesen(2004)] Matthiesen, S.B., Einarsen, S.: Psychiatric distress and symptoms of PTSD
  among victims of bullying at work. British Journal of Guidance & Counseling 32(3), 335–
  356 (2004)
[Mayer(2004)] Mayer, G.: Union Membership Trends in the United States. Congressional
  Research Service (2004)
[Mitrou(2006)] Mitrou, L., Karyda, M.: Employees' privacy vs. employers' security: Can they
  be balanced? Telematics and Informatics 23(3), 164–178 (2006)

[Montgomery(1999)] Montgomery, S.M., Cook, D.G., Bartley, M.J., Wadsworth, M.E.: Unemployment pre-dates symptoms of depression and anxiety resulting in medical consultation in young men. International Journal of Epidemiology 28(1), 95–100 (1999)

[Moore(2012)] Moore, S.: Monitoring Employee Behavior in Digital Environments is Rising (2012), http://www.gartner.com/it/page.jsp?id=2028215

[NYTimes(2012/07/15)] FDA surveillance of scientists spreads to outside critics (2012), http://www.nytimes.com/2012/07/15/us/fda-surveillance-of-scientists-spread-to-outside-critics.html

[NYTimes(2012/07/31)] Dr Robert Smith caustic crusader in FDA spying scandal, http://www.nytimes.com/2012/07/31/us/dr-robert-smith-caustic-crusader-in-fda-spying-scandal.html

[Perelman(2000)] Perelman, M.: The Invention of Capitalism: Classical Political Economy and the Secret History of Primitive Accumulation. Duke University Press (2000)

[Renwick(2003)] Renwick, D.: HR managers. guardians of employee wellbeing? Personnel Review, 341–359 (2003)

[Reuters(2012)] Retaliation rate against us company whistleblowers climbs (2012), http://blogs.reuters.com/financial-regulatory-forum/2012/09/06/retaliation-rate-against-u-s-company-whistleblowers-climbs-senior-staff-affected-survey-finds/

[Simon(2001)] Simon, G.E., Barber, C., Birnbaum, H.G., Frank, R.G., Greenberg, P.E., Rose, R.M., Wang, P.S., Kessler, R.C.: Depression and work productivity: the comparative costs of treatment versus nontreatment. Occup. Environ. Med. 43, 2–9 (2001)

[Starin(2002)] Starrin, B.: Unemployment, poverty and shame: Exploring the field (2002), http://www.humiliationstudies.org/documents/StarrinUnemploymentPovertyShame.pdf

[Tajfel(1982)] Tajfel, H.: Social Identity and Intergroup Relations. CUP (1982)

[Tversky(1973)] Tversky, A., Kahneman, D.: Availability: A heuristic for judging frequency and probability. Cognitive Psychology 5(2), 207–232 (1973)

[UN(2009)] United Nations Office On Drugs and Crime. Current practices in electronic surveillance in the investigation of serious and organized crime (2009)

[Vorvoreanu(2000)] Vorvoreanu, M., Botan, C.H.: Examining electronic surveillance in the workplace: A review of theoretical perspectives and research findings. In: Int. Comm. Assoc. Conf. (2000)

[Wright(2011)] Wright, C.F.: What role for trade unions in future workplace relations? ACAS (2011)

[Yahoo(2012)] Job seekers getting asked for facebook passwords, http://finance.yahoo.com/news/job-seekers-getting-asked-facebook-080920368.html

[Zimbardo(2007)] Zimbardo, P.: The Lucifer Effect: Understanding How Good People Turn Evil. Random House (2007)

A Reasonable Expectation of Privacy?
Secrecy and National Security in a Democracy

Kathleen M. Hogan

University of Maryland University Campus, Largo, Maryland, USA
Kathleen.Hogan@faculty.umuc.edu

Abstract. Citizens do not routinely agree to sacrifice their privacy. When cases come to light that the government has been spying on its citizens, there is outrage. Still, citizens' fierce protection of personal privacy does not obviate their expectation of government to ensure national security. Public support for secret government operations is cyclical, self-interested, influenced by citizens' knowledge of political affairs, and related to the public's level of trust in its leaders and the perception of threats. Polls indicate that citizens are protective of their personal privacy but willing to give up a degree of control to trusted leaders.

Keywords: Secrecy; privacy, public opinion polls about national security, government, public preferences.

1 Introduction

When one works for the government, the phrase "no reasonable expectation of privacy" is part of every information systems security briefing and contract. This pertains to government employees at nearly all levels of seniority. In effect, employees affirm that they understand that every email, telephone conversation, or any other transaction is subject to monitoring and should not be considered private. Public awareness campaign placards tacked up in certain public areas within the company spaces state that "monitoring is for everyone's good." This understanding is considered part of the job.

Private citizens, however, do not routinely agree to sacrifice the privacy of their communications and activities. When cases come to light that the government has been spying on its citizens, people are outraged, watchdog groups spring into action and there is heavy media coverage. Still, citizens' fierce protection of their privacy does not change their expectation for the government to ensure national security by an architecture that is based on secrecy. Public support for secret government operations is cyclical, self-interested, and influenced by the public's level of trust in its leaders and their perception of external threats. Support for secret operations in the WWII years gave way to outrage in the mid-1970s when "allegations of abuse and improper activities" and "great public concern that the Congress take action to bring intelligence agencies under the constitutional framework" (US Congress Final Report of the Select Committee 1976, 94). The Church and Pike Committee reports, published in a multi-volume series, presented a litany of illegal actions taken by the CIA, the FBI,

L. Marinos and I. Askoxylakis (Eds.): HAS/HCII 2013, LNCS 8030, pp. 236–245, 2013.

and other government agencies and departments that included assassination of foreign leaders to spying on and plotting against American civil rights, and anti-war activists (US Congress Final Report of the Select Committee 1976, 101-755). Disclosure of intrusion into citizens' personal lives galvanizes public opinion and illuminates the degree of ambivalence toward secrecy that there is in our society: it is one thing to spy on "enemies" in the interest of national security; it is quite a different matter to spy on Americans!

Despite whistleblowers' accounts of government wrongdoing, public polls indicate that citizens continue to maintain trust in the government's role to safeguard national security despite some tradeoffs in transparency. That leaves one to explore the threshold at which secrecy in government is acceptable. Legal and constitutional institutions address secrecy, however, interpretation and implementation of these measures are dependent on the political environment, the administration's relationship to Congress, foreign policy issues and the tenor of public opinion. This paper discusses the paradox of secrecy in a democracy as a democratic government seeks to maintain national security for its citizens without overstepping the limits of personal privacy. It argues that citizens accept secrecy as a necessary means to protect national security and economic interests as long as personal privacy is sacrosanct, and that citizens maintain the right of oversight and consultation, even when those rights are limited, delegated to representatives, or perhaps not even practicable.

2   Review of the Literature

A survey of the literature about government secrecy and prevention of unlawful intrusion into the private sphere illustrates both the necessity and danger of the practice of secrecy within a democracy. While some quip that "intelligence is the second oldest profession", one could argue that secrecy represents the ubiquitous dilemma a democracy addresses. To ensure strategic advantage, governments protect information and hide vulnerabilities. This creates a Byzantine system of limited accessibility to information, which may be necessary to a nation's viability in a competitive world, but is nonetheless abhorrent to an open society. The next sections explore ideas relevant to various aspects of secrecy.

2.1   The Instrumental Role of Secrecy

Secrecy is part of human life. It allows persons to preserve personal thoughts, interests, and privacy. Our own understanding of why we wish to protect our own private elements makes us suspicious of others' motives. It is natural, then, that citizens expect these same motivations to carry over into public life, especially when there are competitive interests at stake. Secrets are a protective mechanism, imperative for self-preservation, and thereby legitimate as a means to preserve security.

As individuals, we know our own secrets and why we need to hide them. Yet we have a certain discomfort with secrets held by our government. Halperin and Hoffman write that from the beginning of the US' early democratic experience, the framers of the Constitution devoted thought and debate to the issue of secrecy and how much was appropriate. For example, Article I, Section 5 requires that Congress publish journals of their proceedings "except such parts thereof as may in their judgment require secrecy", yet the President was given no such allowance to conceal secrets from Congress (Halperin and Hoffman 1977, 87-91). Still, secrecy of the proceedings of the Convention itself was controversial. While secret meetings were more expedient, members were suspicious of conclusions without days of wrangling and discussion. Members of the Convention were sworn to secrecy and agreed that members would not divulge information from the session journals. (Bok 1984, 183) This duality of thought regarding the place of secrecy highlights the crux of the argument. Debate and open discussion endangers national security by revealing not only practices, intentions, and capabilities, but also our vulnerabilities. Debate can be a messy, time-consuming practice which could result in a loss of initiative and the element of surprise. Yet, our democratic process dictates that, however inefficient, citizens must retain the right to bring complaints, questions, and information to any forum at which government action is carried out on behalf of the people.

Secrecy safeguards economic advantage. This is evident in the modern industry of business intelligence, which uses practices similar to those used in national intelligence to gather information about competitors to gain advantage. Corporate "spying" can be traced back to our own years of "manifest destiny" when clever politicians and leaders used information gathered surreptitiously to political and economic advantage. O'Toole and Miller write that administrations dispatched Army officers to distant ends of the country to collect information about leaders, defense, and public sentiment. Members of Congress benefited from this knowledge to secure lucrative contracts for their constituencies and dividends for themselves (O'Toole 1991; Miller 1989). There is obvious advantage when nations and businesses can cloak their own intentions while ferreting out information about the competitor; in conditions where the competition is close, sensitive information provides an exponential advantage.

2.2 Ethics and Secrecy

Just as it would be capricious for a nation to plan a campaign without knowledge of the enemy's capabilities, it would be negligent for leaders to engage in foreign policy without the best information about intentions, political maneuvering, and domestic conditions. The public depends on its leaders to safeguard security, and expects those in charge of their interests to use the tools at their disposal. That said, polls indicate that citizens are conflicted about what is necessary and what is unethical, especially when their security and economic interests are at stake (Best, Kruger, and Ladewig 2006).

It is useful to consider Bok's "tests "as a baseline for the morality of secrecy. She writes that one should determine if there is an alternative action that achieves the same goals without lying or hiding the truth, then lay out the rationale for choosing secrecy. The final test would be to determine how a reasonable person might respond to the arguments. (Bok 1984, 113) She argues that secrecy goes against the democratic practices of deliberation, discourse, and consideration of other views. A leader who might sometimes need "perfect secrecy and immediate dispatch" to keep sensitive operations intact, could result in a tendency to circumvent the practice of seeking consensus and public approval. (Bok 1984, 171; Gutmann and Thompson 1996)

It is important to note that there are different categories of secrets. For example, when secrecy is employed to safeguard critical national interests, it is defensible. However, if the very act of collecting those secrets violates law or would provoke a public outcry should the details come to light, the act becomes intuitively less defensible. Citizens regularly grapple with the dilemma of secrecy and make value tradeoffs for the advantages that secrecy yields. Citizens also are quick to differentiate that practices employed against potential enemies are thoroughly unacceptable when used at home. By accepting conditional dishonesty against those designated as our enemies, citizens become responsible for the outcomes. There are also nuances between what is acceptable against a commonly perceived enemy (a terrorist, cyber attacker, or an individual or nation who commits a significant economic fraud against the US), and more ambiguous cases. In these instances, citizens would be subject to the influence of the media, their own biases, and incomplete information.

It is important to recognize and acknowledge the motives for keeping secrets because, ultimately, those motives will influence how secrets are used. Warren writes of the connection to trust. One has less "need to know" if parties share interests. A citizen cannot know the facts of every issue so he must place his trust in leaders in whom he has faith to carry out actions on his behalf (Warren 1996, 57). Defensible secrets require that those with authority observe constitutional and legislative guidance, remain responsive to the public trust, and make daily judgments about the importance and utility of secrecy. Being above any possible gain from illegitimate acts is critical, and problematic.

2.3   The Unintentional Consequences of Secrecy

There is no shortage of comprehensive accounts of the history of secrecy, the dangers, and unintended consequences resulting from secrecy and this paper will recap the salient points. First, policies to create and maintain a culture of secrecy within government agencies have been fairly consistent since World War II. Kate Doyle provides a historical summary of events and executive policies from the start of the Cold War through the Clinton administration and makes a clear argument that policymakers have historically used "national security" as an excuse to evade questions and a public justification of their actions. (Doyle 1999, 34) She shares Steven Aftergood's view that the public regularly abrogated right to disclosure because it chose not to question in prevailing security considerations (Aftergood 2009; Aftergood 2010.)

During the Cold War decades, there was considerable public fear of a nuclear attack by the Soviet Union, but even after the fall of the Soviet Union, there were always new events on the horizons to keep the public fearful, and conditioned to trust leaders to act appropriately to maintain national security. The attack on the USS Cole by suicide bombers in a Yemeni port brought a new set of fears to the public. The catastrophic attacks of 9/11 actualized to many people the greatest fears of the Cold

War – that an enemy would attack the US on its own soil. Following these attacks, the public expected results from their leaders and cost was no object.

Second, the proliferation of secrecy by over- or misclassification of information denigrates the ability of government to be transparent and responsive to its citizens, and creates opportunities and plausible deniability for government entities to illegally collect information on US citizen. Advocates for a more open society argue that this "culture of secrecy" must be rehabilitated, and disclosure policies systematically reviewed at every level of government because without greater disclosure of information, citizens are "deprived of a meaningful role in the political process" and the exercise of authority remains "insulated from public oversight" (Aftergood 2011, 399).

Third, secrecy carries its own burdens. By the very nature of hiding information and actions, secrecy requires exclusion and collusion: exclusion to limit the number of people who have access to the information, and collusion to reinforce the pact of secrecy within the membership of the group. The danger of exclusion is that people or agencies that may need to have the information may be prevented from access to it. Many events in our political and military history demonstrate that key members were unable to get critical information and important operations failed as a result. The latest and most glaring instance of the results of exclusion and over classification is documented in the 9/11 Report, which describes the dysfunctional relationship between agencies and their ability to share information (9/11 Report 2006). Collusion also pressures indoctrinated members to conform to the rules of the group or risk expulsion, or worse. Alexander George, the seminal author of the concept on the psychology of group dynamics, explains how members of a group feel compelled to adhere to group objectives. The element of secrecy produces its own momentum for consensus, which is dangerous because there is little room for dialogue in this environment (George 1980)

Last, the proliferation of classified documents devalues the information and creates risks of unintended errors in the handling of the material. The Moynihan Commission concluded that excessive secrecy carries risks. To coin a phrase from the Ellsberg case, the report notes that when "everything is secret, nothing is secret". The best way to "ensure that secrecy is respected, and that the most important secrets remain secret, is for secrecy to be returned to its limited but necessary role." (Secrecy: Report of the Commission on Protecting and Reducing Government Secrecy 1994, 794) Aftergood argues that the proliferation of classified material requires more handling, more attention to rules, and is more prone to error as a result. (Aftergood 2010, 846)

Yet, despite the immense power of the government to collect information and engage in surveillance against both U.S. citizens and foreigners, a degree of risk to personal privacy is still acceptable to many Americans. Best, Kruger, and Ladewig write that trends from polls conducted during the years of 1990 – 2005 indicate that while Americans affirm that privacy is a critical right, they are willing to "support expansion of government investigative powers to combat terrorism…and support specific surveillance measures introduced since 9/11" (Best et al 2006, 383).

Other polls also demonstrate that the public does not believe the government is the biggest culprit when it comes to infringement of personal privacy. Rather, they believe that banks and credit card companies, and entities not associated with the U.S. government at all, but other countries' governments are the entities that create suspicion. A recent poll taken by McAfee in partnership with the National Cyber Security Alliance (**NCSA**) reveals a "substantial disconnect between their respective online security perceptions and their actual practices while on the Internet" (*Newswire Story* "Kickoff of National Cyber Security Month" 2012, accessed October 1, 2012). Reportedly, 90 percent of the citizens surveyed believed that "Americans do not feel completely safe online and believe a safe and secure internet is crucial to U.S. economic security." Respondents replied that "a safe and secure Internet is crucial to our nation's economic security", it was vital to American jobs, and they were worried that their personal economic data had been breached (*Newswire Story* 2012, accessed October 1, 2012).

Given Americans' degree of alarm about cyber security, there is surprisingly little mention of citizens' concern that the government is intruding into their private cyber lives. This leads to a preliminary conclusion that citizens are less concerned about government practices in its efforts to maintain national security. This perception may be attributable to ongoing fears of terrorism and national security, fears that are not lessened in a citizenry that is technologically more sophisticated but yet exposed to breaking news from around the world that contributes to a perception that the world is unstable, unsafe, and threatening to American security. Taken at face value, this seemed a counterintuitive stance, though perhaps it is in line with how people adopt positions and beliefs. The next section explores the basis of public adoption of beliefs and relates the concepts to polls.

3   Zaller's Concept of Reception and Acceptance of Messages

The process by which citizens arrive at their preferences is admittedly mysterious. Therefore, this paper uses John Zaller's explanation of how people come to their beliefs, which in turn shapes the way they vote, who they support, and what they will accept when they have faith in their leadership. Simply, the average citizens, even those who are well-informed and follows political issues cannot own every issue. Therefore, citizens rely on trust and other heuristics to arrive at their opinions about secrecy, national security, and citizens' right to privacy, especially since the event of 9/11 (Zaller 1992). Media and political leaders also shape public perceptions of national security and the degree of transparency in government. First, citizens vary in their attention to politics so have varying exposure to political information and media coverage of political events. Second, people react to information based on their own knowledge of political events. Third, citizens do not carry around fixed notions about every issue that a poll might ask, so their answers are often "top of the head" and perhaps based on their most recent information or attitudes. Finally, citizens formulate their answers to questions from information most readily available to them. (Zaller 1992, 1)

The two most important elements to political preferences are political knowledge and political attitudes. Incoming and available information shapes preferences. In the simplest case, individuals receive information and accept or reject it. However, there are often two-sided information flows in which the dominant message is pushing opinion in one direction as the less intense countervailing message counteracts the effect of the dominant message, especially when discourse is divided along partisan lines. The choice the individual makes is based on the strength of his feelings for the messages, based on the source, degree of interest in the issue, and the most salient beliefs the individuals hold at that particular time. The next section applies these concepts to polls about individuals' belief about secrecy as part of national security and personal privacy.

3.1   The Best, Krueger, and Ladewig Poll

These researchers sought to determine public attitudes about the degree of acceptance of forms of surveillance, the types of abuses that could occur, and under what circumstances individuals believe that collective interests matter more than individual ones (Best et al 2006, 375). This study presented data from a fifteen year period of time from 1990 – 2005 from a variety of opinion polls to capture developments that shifted public attitudes: the emergence of the internet; the war on terrorism; and, the development (and use) of a wide array of surveillance technology (Best et al 2006, 375). The conclusions indicate that citizens believed that privacy was an important right, but they also understood that the government had to institute measures to guard against attacks. The trend toward a more skeptical view indicates reception of a countervailing message and less support for government invasion of privacy.

To summarize, there were five primary conclusions. First, privacy is an important right in the abstract and even after 9/11 this opinion did not change markedly. (Best et al 2006, 377). Second, although few people actually reported government invasion of privacy, concern had grown in recent years. The public reported greater worry over intrusion over the internet, although these worries were not solely targeted against government surveillance but more against fraud by private citizens and corporations (Best et al 2006, 377-8). Third, the public is willing to expand government surveillance capabilities to combat terrorism, but that willingness steadily declined since 9/11 and did not support carte blanche "all means available" even to combat terrorism (Best et al 2006, 379). Fourth, the majority of Americans supported specific surveillance measures introduced since 9/11 but the support for these measures has since steadily declined, especially support for wiretapping (Best et al 2006, 380). Finally, while few people report being victimized by new government powers, many worried that the government would overstep its bounds, especially since the passage of the Patriot Act (Best et al 2006, 381).

3.2   Response to the NSA Spying Case

The breaking of a series of articles in the *New York Times* that "President Bush had authorized the National Security Agency to eavesdrop on Americans and others inside the United States to search for terrorist activity without the court-approved warrants that are required for domestic spying" caused a furor in public outrage (*New York Times* "Bush Lets US Spy" December 16, 2005.) It also touched off a skirmish between entities that argued that the first poll issued by the *Washington* Post which indicated support for the President's actions was skewed by the way the questions were worded. *USAToday*/Gallup and *Newsweek* followed with their own polls which produced results indicating that Americans felt much more negatively about NSA's domestic surveillance program. This indicates that the mood for counter terrorism action remained strong as long as personal privacy (phone conversations, for example) was not monitored. Another key point to make is that respondents with the strongest preferences were in the age group 30-45 and Republican, indicating support for the administration and a level of knowledge and maturity greater than younger and older respondents.

3.3   The Latest Polls on General Satisfaction with the Government

Recent polls indicate that Americans' fear of terrorism is at its lowest point since 2001 and the public is most satisfied with the nation's military strength and preparedness and the nation's security from terrorism and least satisfied with the state of the economy. Fig 1 shows the poll on Americans' fear of terrorism and indicates stable satisfaction rates since 2002.

	Very satisfied	Somewhat satisfied	Somewhat dissatisfied	Very dissatisfied	No opinion
	%	%	%	%	%
2013 Jan 7-10	22	45	16	13	4
2012 Jan 5-8	23	49	14	10	5
2008 Jan 4-6	14	44	20	17	4
2007 Jan 15-18	13	40	26	18	3
2006 Jan 9-12	16	42	23	16	3
2005 Jan 3-5	14	44	22	17	3
2004 Jan 12-15	19	51	16	13	1
2003 Jan 13-16	11	43	26	17	3
2002 Jan 7-9	10	41	27	20	2

GALLUP

Fig. 1. Gallup Poll Results indicating Americans' satisfaction with the nation's security from terrorism (Source: Gallup Poll Jan 10, 2013. Accessed from http: //www.gallup.com/poll/160154/Americans-security-from-terrorism.aspx)

Finally, a Gallup poll in early February 2013 asked about American's particular concerns. The "big five" were as follows:

• The economy
• Jobs and unemployment
• Problems with the way government works
• The federal budget deficit
• Healthcare

The big differences, according to Gallup's Frank Newport, is that terrorism, education, and Medicare were not mentioned very much in the poll. He writes that these are important matters but they were not "top of the mind" issues, or seen as particular problems for this poll (Newport "Polling Matters" Feb 20, 2013). This behavior support Zaller's claim that preferences are based on immediate considerations and the issues that are most prevalent at the time of the question. A respondent might have listed the government's work on counter terrorism as important, but the subject just did not measure as a problem.

4   The Way Forward: The Role of Secrecy in the Government

The thesis of this paper has been that, contrary to a view that average citizens are alarmed about the potential for the government to illegally monitor its citizens, the public generally believes that national security "trumps" personal privacy concerns as long as the breaches are not egregious, public, or signals a movement toward a police state or habitual offenses. As part of the government kit, secrecy has a legitimate role in a democracy as an integral element of national security. By electing officials to act on their wishes to protect collective interests – both security and privacy – citizens are delegating authority to their elected leaders. The nature of secrecy complicates this relationship because citizens do not have access to classified information so must take on faith the need for secrets and faith that their leaders will accomplish their will as effectively in secret as they can in open debate.

Transparency within a democracy and the public availability of information about nearly every facet of government enables citizens to engage in government by the powers of opinion, oversight, and public action. Trust and integrity are enviable resources and democracy must rest on social capital, a shared belief in communities of citizens. Another safeguard within the US system of government is the system of checks and balances and Congressional oversight of the US intelligence community. The Constitution does not seek to infringe upon or grant exclusive powers regarding secrecy and national security; rather, the intent is to forge a cooperative relationship between the Executive branch and Congress. Presidents and their advisers recognize the wisdom of encouraging Congressional participation in matters of secrecy. While Congress might be considered "obstructionist" and "complicating", it provides the forum for debate as the elected representatives of the people. The prospect of justifying secret actions in Congress has a way of keeping imprudent ideas in check.

Americans situate their beliefs about the role of secrecy in national security versus the expectations of personal privacy. Citizens' participation is critical. Democratic authority is based on deliberation and citizens must exercise their right and duty to engage those in authority. Far from weakening national security, debate and judgment enables it. Discourse is a key element of oversight and safeguards privacy. Even if some citizens choose not to exercise their prerogative for discourse with authority, the prospect for interaction allows citizens to suspend judgment and build trust.

Citizens are charged by the Constitution to hold government responsible. Thus, effective and balanced policies require citizens to be knowledgeable, interested, and involved in foreign affairs, ever questioning of actions carried on under the cloak of secrecy. When these responsibilities are borne by the people and government, there is the assurance of a reasonable expectation of privacy.

References

1. The 9/11 Commission Report: Final Report of the National Commission on Terrorist Attacks Upon the United States. W.W. Norton & Company, Inc., New York (2004)
2. Steven, A.: Reducing Government Secrecy: Finding What Works. Yale Law and Policy Review 27(399), 399–416 (Fall 2009)
3. National Security Secrecy: How the Limits Change. Social Research 77(3), 839–852 (Falll 2010)
4. Americans' satisfaction with the nation's security from terrorism. Gallup Poll. (January 10, 2013), http://www.gallup.com/poll/160154/Americans-security-from-terrorism.aspx (accessed)
5. Best, S.J., Krueger, B.S., Ladewig, J.: Poll Trends:Privacy in the Information Age. Public Opinion Quarterly 70(3), 375–401 (Fall 2006)
6. Sissela, B.: Secrets. Vintage Books, New York (1984)
7. Gary, D.: Majority of Americans Do Not Feel Safe Online. 2012. McAfee Blog (2012), http://blogs.mcafee.com/consumer/online-safety-survey2012 (accessed)
8. Kate, D.: U.S. National Security and the Imperative for Openness. World Policy Journal 70(2), 34–50 (Fall 1999)
9. Alexander, G.: Presidential Decisionmaking in Foreign Policy: The Effective Use of Information and Advice. Westview Press, Boulder (1980)
10. Morton, H., Hoffman, D.: Top Secret: National Security and the Right to Know. New Republic Books, Washington (1977)
11. James, R., Lichtblau, E.: Bush Lets U.S. Spy on Callers Without Courts. New York Times (December 16, 2005), http://www.commondreams.org/headlines05/1216-01.htm (accessed)
12. State of the Union and the People's Will Poll. Gallup Poll (February 12, 2013), http://www.gallup.com/poll/160445/economy-dominant-obama-speech-americans-priorities.aspx (accessed)
13. U.S. 1976 U.S Congress, Final Report of the Select Committee to Study Governmental Operations with Respect to Intelligence Activities, 94th Congress. Government Printing Office, Washington, DC (April 26, 1965)
14. Secrecy: Report of the Commission on Protecting and Reducing Government Secrecy. Government Printing Office, Washington, DC (1994)
15. Warren, M.E.: Deliberative Democracy and Authority. American Political Science Review 90(1), 46–60 (1996)
16. Zaller, J.R.: The Nature and Origins of Mass Opinion. Cambridge University Press, Cambridge (1992)

Towards Usable Generation and Enforcement of Trust Evidence from Programmers' Intent

Michael Huth[1], Jim Huan-Pu Kuo[1], Angela Sasse[2], and Iacovos Kirlappos[2]

[1] Department of Computing, Imperial College London
London, SW7 2AZ, United Kingdom
{m.huth,jimhkuo}@imperial.ac.uk
[2] Department of Computer Science, University College London
London, WC1E 6BT, United Kingdom
a.sasse@cs.ucl.ac.uk

Abstract. Programmers develop code with a sense of purpose and with expectations on how units of code should interact with other units of code. But this intent of programmers is typically implicit and undocumented, goes beyond considerations of functional correctness, and may depend on trust assumptions that programmers make. At present, neither programming languages nor development environments offer a means of articulating such intent in a manner that could be used for controlling whether software executions meet such intentions and their associated expectations. We here study how extant research on trust can inform approaches to articulating programmers' intent so that it may help with creating trust evidence for more trustworthy interaction of software units.

We first describe a known model for expressing the mechanics of trust in transactions between two parties. Then we sketch a possible technical approach that allows programmers to capture intent in the form of expectations about method invocations. We then demonstrate how this approach may generate quantitative trust evidence that can form the basis for deciding whether methods should be executed. Finally, we discuss to what extent this technical approach reflects the model of trust mechanics and identify future work in this space.

1 Trust Mechanics

We begin with a discussion of the mechanics of trust in transactions by recalling research in that area from the social sciences and the usability of security.

Trust versus Assurance. In the real world, individuals and organizations cooperate to achieve mutual benefits. But this only works out if both parties fulfill their side of the bargain. As Flechais et al. [2] point out, we can carry out a risk assessment for a specific cooperation, and deploy mechanisms that make it hard for our transaction partner to cheat us; such an assurance strategy does, however, come at a cost, which reduces the benefits we reap from the cooperation.

L. Marinos and I. Askoxylakis (Eds.): HAS/HCII 2013, LNCS 8030, pp. 246–255, 2013.
© Springer-Verlag Berlin Heidelberg 2013

The second strategy allows cooperation partners to save the cost of assurance, by trusting each other to behave as expected. Mayer et al. [8] define trust as: *"... the willingness to be vulnerable, based on positive expectation about the behavior of others."* The idea of *"willingness to be vulnerable"* is the antithesis of the traditional security perspective, whose raison d'être is the creation of mechanisms to prevent exploitation of vulnerabilities.

But even the security community has become aware of the cost of assurance, which sometimes consumes the benefits that can be reaped from the cooperation. Consideration of the economics of security has become a thriving sub-discipline, with the Workshop on Economics of Security (WEIS), founded by Jean Camp and Ross Anderson, now in its 11th year. Trust provides economic benefit to cooperation partners – provided neither of them cheats. If there are too many incidents of cheating, we need to add security mechanisms that make cheating harder, but doing so comes at a cost.

Leading security expert Bruce Schneier calls these cheater *"Liars and Outliers"* in his latest book [12]. In a shift of perspective that must be a shock to many of his devoted audience of security professionals, he argues that – rather than develop costly mechanisms to deter and prevent cheating – we must shift our focus to designing systems that foster and incentivize trustworthy behavior, so modern society can reap the benefits that come with cooperating and trust-based interactions. Without cooperation and trust, individuals and organizations, economies and societies cannot thrive [4].

Disembeddedness. The introduction of modern technology has significant implications for trust. Giddens [3] was the first to point out that the knowledge on who we can trust, when, under which circumstances (something we learn from our parents and other sources of social authority, and though experience) – is very much embedded in a particular space-time context.

Modern technology has enabled collaborations that are *disembedded* from space and time – more and more interactions are now taking place without the transaction parties ever meeting in face-to-face, in the same place. Disembedding makes cheating easier: in a shop, it is unlikely that the shopkeeper will take your money, and then not hand over the goods you just paid for; with online transactions, you don't know for days if the seller in Transaktistan will send the artisan set of nesting dolls you just paid for. And you won't know for weeks, months or maybe even years whether the seller decided to sell your credit card information to someone else.

But our mental models of trust are still very much dominated by the embedded transactions. Kirlappos et al. [5], for instance, found that even experienced Internet users trust websites based on familiarity (*"looks like one I've used before"*), and based on the apparent presence of links to social networking sites and charities – and are unaware of how easily these trust signs can be forged in the online environment. The *Mechanics of Trust* framework by Riegelsberger et al. [11] examines trust signaling online.

Trust-Mediated Interactions. We now consider interactions between two parties, where the interaction is mediated by trust. The two parties are the trustor (who exposes a vulnerability to the other party, in hope for gaining a benefit from this) and the trustee (who may or may not provide such a benefit to the trustor). A schematic of such a transaction is depicted in Figure 1.

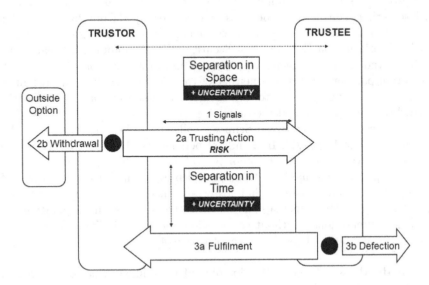

Fig. 1. Trust-Mediated Interaction between Trustor and Trustee who are separated in space and in time, figure reproduced from [11]

During the first phase of a Trust-Mediated Interaction, the trustor and the trustee exchange signals, which are used to assess each other's *ability* and *motivation* to engage in a successful transaction. After the initial signal exchange the trustor has the option to either proceed to the trusting actions (2a), which renders them vulnerable to the trustee's behavior (2b), or withdraw, in which case the transaction ends.

The decision is not solely based on the signal exchange though: trustor's risk propensity, perception of exchanged signals and other external factors (e.g. existence of easy withdrawal) also affect the choice between trusting action and withdrawal. After the trusting action the trustee has full control over the situation and they can choose to either fulfill (3a), by behaving in the way the trustor expects, or defect, having already obtained the benefits of the trustor's trust (e.g. monetary sums or financial details).

The advantageous position in which the trustee is after the trusting action means that fulfillment will occur when the trustee realizes some gain from it; otherwise trustees are better off defecting and reaping the benefits. As a result, fulfillment – which successfully ends the interaction – will occur only when the trustee has *both* the ability and motivation to fulfill. And therefore the trustor needs to be able to 'read' the trustee's trust signals to determine both ability and motivation are present.

Trust Signals and Trust Symbols. In online transactions, the technology is the channel through which trust signaling occurs. Prior to the occurrence of a trusting action, both parties transmit signals, resulting in a perceived level of trustworthiness of each other. By reading those signals, the trustor forms expectations on the behavior of the trustee. There are two types of trust signals: symbols and symptoms

1. *Trust symbols* have arbitrarily assigned meaning, and were designed specifically to signal the presence of trust-warranting properties. Trust seals, for instance, signify that a seller is a member of a scheme, and promises to abide by its rules. There are many problems with trust seals [5]: they can be easily forged, and customers over-interpret the level of protection they offer. Reputation mechanisms (such as the 'star' rating on ebay) can be subverted through the creation of multiple identities, shill bidding, and 'cashing in' established reputations. For instance, a fraudster can buy an existing online shop with a good reputation, offer attractive prices at a busy time of year, and then just take payment without shipping the goods. By the time their actions are discovered, the damage is done.

2. *Trust symptoms*, on the other hand, are signals given off as natural by-products of honest transaction partners going about their business. So a business that takes a certain level of payments for goods has to ship a certain amount of goods. There are a limited number of shipping agents they can use, and transmitting information of their shipping activity incurs no extra cost to an honest seller. But for a fraudster, creating fake shipments would be a considerable cost. Another example of a trust symptom, would be that a commercial website has an easily usable and well thought out user interface with a coherent design look; this creates the impression of professionalism that may be conceived as a symptom of trust.

2 Trust-Mediated Interaction of Units of Code

The trust mechanics described above is based on the notion of a transaction: will it come to a trusted action or not? And this mechanics involves two parties: the trustor who may take the risk of committing to the trusted action, and the trustee who may or may not fulfill the expectations or obligations inherent in the trusted action. We now examine to what degree this model of trust-mediated interaction may be of use in articulating and enforcing programmers' expectations of code and its interaction with other units of code. Let us here consider the scenario where a unit of code is a method (also called a *procedure* or a *function* in various programming languages).

Methods may have parameters and – when invoked by another method – instantiate such parameters with concrete values, execute a method body within these instantiations, and may return a value as result (or may change state as a side effect). An example method name withdraw with its output type and list of parameters is int withdraw(Account acc, int amt). Its method body (not shown here) aims to withdraw the amount amt (an integer) from the account acc and return the new account balance (also an integer).

Programmers will often articulate intent that concerns functional correctness, and they can do this in program documentation, in assert statements that check whether Boolean predicates hold at specific program points, or through other executable program annotations (e.g. as in the Java modeling language [7]). For method withdraw, e.g., a programmer might stipulate that amt has to be non-negative (otherwise, one could potentially withdraw money and increase the account balance at the same time) and greater than the account balance, etc..

But there are other expectations that the programmer is likely to have that cannot be articulated through the aforementioned means. For example, a programmer might know that method withdraw will only ever be called (i.e. invoked) by another method authenticatedWithdraw. Yet this knowledge is at best expressed in program documentation and so cannot be harvested for informing and potentially controlling the execution of such units of code.

A programmer may further expect that certain tasks within a workflow of code may be completed more frequently than others. For example, that over the lifespan of a social network user account there are at least, say, three times as many successful login attempts than requests to recover or change a password.

Another expectation that programmers will have is about the range of data values for program identifiers. For example, a programmer may expect that some input parameter x is what is known as a *safe* prime. One could specify such a requirement as a precondition for input: that the value of x is a prime number of form $2q + 1$ where q is itself a prime. But programmers might still want to execute a method if the value of x is not a safe prime but at least a prime. Yet, this deviation from expectations may decrease the trust in running the method.

Conceptually, we may think of a programmer as collecting expectations on normal method execution. And a run-time system could then determine which of these expectations are true. And this set of observably met expectations would then, ideally *compositionally*, compute the overall trust evidence for executing the method body. We note that it is far from obvious to answer how such evidence should be composed so that its composition be meaningful to the programmer and consistent with the 'sum' of his or her expectations on program behavior. One challenge here is that expectations may be quantitative (e.g. in the login example above) or qualitative (e.g. in the method invocation example above).

Relating Trust Evidence Annotations to Trust Mechanics. We now discuss how such use of annotations for trust evidence generation and enforcement relates to the trust mechanics depicted in Figure 1. We begin by identifying the roles of trustor and trustee.

The trustor seems to be the programmer, whose annotations make it possible to assess the risk of committing to a trusted action – which in this case would be the execution of a method body. We may equally think of the annotated method as the trustor who ponders whether it should be executed. And if we were to implement these annotations by integrating their evaluation within a run-time environment, we may think of the run-time environment (e.g. a modification of the Java Virtual Machine) as the trustor.

In this setting, the trustee is the method calling the annotated method. Interestingly, it would also make sense to think of calling methods as trustors since a called method may return values that calling methods further process and so may need to trust. The above approach is consistent with embracing this view as well. A calling method `foo1` may itself have intent of using another method `foo`, and this intent may lead to annotations within `foo1` that may be used to evaluate whether or not to call `foo`. And the results of `foo`, if called, may then be used to judge whether the interaction met the intent of `foo1`.

Returning to the view where the annotated method is the trustor, its decision to withdraw (2b in Figure 1) comes about when its annotated policy computes as decision value **deny**. If that value computes to **grant** instead, it will take the risk of performing the trusted action that executes its method body.

As for the signals (1 in that figure), the trustor takes the predicates expressed in expectation blocks as trust signals that, when true, trigger the generation of quantitative trust evidence – through the declaration of trust evidence scores, composition operators, and default composition values.

Separation in space, in time, and uncertainty are also relevant in this approach. Calling methods may stem from different machines, different domains, etc.. A process-based program model such as Actor languages [1] would definitely exhibit separation in time as well, due to their asynchronous communication.

Trust Evidence Generation. We now sketch what sort of annotation support might be able to express programmers' expectations, and the composition of the trust evidence that each expectation would generate.

First, let us consider ways of articulating the trust we may have in particular callers or groups of callers for a given method. We may write an annotation block and place it in front of the method declaration, as in

```
@expect[max] default 0.1 {
  if (calledBy foo1) setTrustEvidenceTo 0.9;
  if (calledBy foo2) setTrustEvidenceTo 0.3;
  if (sameDomain(@caller)) setTrustEvidenceTo 0.8;
}
method foo(...) { ... } // body of method foo(...)
```

This defines an expectation block with three statements that each capture expectations on executing method `foo`. The first statement specifies that the trust evidence for executing method `foo` is 0.9 if the caller of that method is method `foo1`. In contrast, if the caller is method `foo2` that trust evidence is only 0.3. Finally, the predicate `sameDomain(@caller)` may express that the method that invokes `foo` is from the same system domain as method `foo`, in which case the trust evidence would be 0.8.

The annotation [max] directs to compute the maximal such trust evidence, whereas default 0.1 says that the composed trust evidence is 0.1 if all three predicates are false (i.e. when the method that calls foo is not from the same domain and different from foo1 and foo2). For example, if the method that calls foo is foo1 and if foo1 happens to be from the same system domain as foo, the composed trust evidence would be 0.9 since max is used for composition.

The composition operator max takes an *optimistic* view of trust evidence: take the most trustworthy evidence as basis for assessing the risk of committing to a trusted action (here: executing the method body). Of course, we may also want to write expectation blocks that are composed through min and so take a *pessimistic* view on trust evidence, by considering the least trustworthy evidence as a basis of decision making. Alternatively, a block @expect[+] {...} may additively *accumulate* trust evidence (with composition +): the sum of all the evidence becomes the baseline for assessing risk of committing to a trusted action.

And we may even conceive that programmers may want to specify several such blocks with different composition operators, and then also specify how the composed evidence of each block should be composed to an overall evidence. For example, we may consider the minimum of the evidence computed from a pessimistic, an optimistic, and an additive expectation block to compute the trust for executing the method body in question.

Usability Issues. Whatever an approach to capturing programmers' intent of method interaction may be, it needs to be simple enough so that programmers can reliably capture their expectations in it. It also needs to be expressive enough so that key expectations can be formulated in it. This suggests that such a language should be *extensible* as we cannot anticipate the needs and intents of programmers for general code development.

Furthermore, a critical issue is that the semantics of *evidence composition* is both natural and intuitive enough for programmers and also consistent with the intent that programmers had in mind. We believe that techniques from program analysis [10] can be transferred to such annotation support in order to generate diagnostic information that can help programmers to validate that their @expect annotations are consistent with their actual intent. To illustrate this on a very simple example, we may edit the above expectation block to

```
@expect[max] default 1.0 {
    if (calledBy foo1) setTrustEvidenceTo 0.9;
    if (calledBy foo2) setTrustEvidenceTo 0.3;
    if (sameDomain(@caller)) setTrustEvidenceTo 0.8;
}
method foo(...) { ... }  // body of method foo(...)
```

which changes the default value to 1.0, a numerical indication of complete trust. This seems inconsistent in the following sense: the block formulates three observables that, when true, might constitute trust evidence. But if all observables are false, this results in a higher trust evidence 1.0 than the one we would assign, say, when foo1 is the caller of this method.

Put in another way, this seems to trust callers that are not in the same domain and different from the two named methods in the block more than any other callers! In particular, this would apply to some unknown method from another system domain. One sensible integrity constraint for the default value for `max` composition may thus be that it be equal to the minimal trust evidence value in that expectation block (i.e. 0.3 in this case). Semantically, this would make the default value redundant, but having it explicitly in the syntax may help with better comprehending these annotations and their meaning.

Trust Evidence Enforcement. We do not suggest that this approach to trust evidence generation is the only feasible one or one that can work *as is*. But whatever programmatic means are used for generating quantitative trust evidence of method invocations, it raises the question of how to enforce such evidence.

We suggest to use simple policies for articulating contextual and other circumstances under which a method should be executed. Let the programming language have a reserved keyword `localTrust` in which we store the composed trust evidence, computed as above. Then a very simple policy may be of form

```
@policy{
  grant if (localTrust > threshold)
  deny otherwise
}
```

where `threshold` is some value chosen by the programmer, e.g., 0.6. In that case, the method would be executed if the composed trust evidence is greater than 0.6; and this execution would be blocked if this evidence is ≤ 0.6.

It is attractive to have such a simple and uniform policy pattern. But, in a way, such simplicity just shifts the complexity into understanding the circumstances in which the value of `localTrust` exceeds 0.6, say. Ideally, we would want static analysis support that can inform us about the scenarios in which there is sufficient trust evidence. And such diagnostic information may lead the programmer to revising his or her expectation specifications or it may confirm that these specifications meet the programmer's intent.

Some applications may require more complex policies. For example, qualitative evidence is best expressed at the policy level itself, e.g., using rule formats as familiar from the OASIS standard XACML [9]. And so its combination with quantitative evidence may result in other policy composition patterns such as

```
deny if (calledBy evil)
grant if (localTrust > threshold)
deny otherwise
```

which lists rules in a priority ordering so that method execution is certainly blocked when the call comes from a method `evil` and where otherwise the policy evaluates as in the above composition pattern.

We note that policy decisions may not only result in either blocking or allowing a method execution; a policy decision may for example report an inconsistency which may lead to an execution of that method with modified input. Although this has ramifications for language design and usability, we do not present such a more complex enforcement mechanism in this paper.

3   Discussion

Looking at the trustee's options of Fulfillment (3a in the figure) and Defection (3b in the figure), we interpret these terms from the perspective of the trustor (as intended in this trust mechanics). Fulfillment here seems to mean that when the annotated method body is actually executed it turns out that this decision to run that code was beneficial. And Defection seems to suggest that granting that execution leads to some undesirable outcome. Our vague language is not accidental: what 'beneficial' and 'undesirable' mean depends on circumstances.

Another issue is whether these annotations can also model the possible evolution from trust in signals and systems to a reliance on behavior based on past positive interactions. One idea might here be to allow for the update of trust evidence scores in annotations. And there is the issue of how to derive initial trust scores, which may be informed by a programmers' risk posture.

The last two points asked what Fulfillment and Defection might mean and whether trust scores may evolve based on the interpretation of these actions performed by the trustee. We think that these questions are intimately related to the notion of *intent* that the programmer would have when developping or using units of code.

To illustrate this relation on a simple example, let a programmer develop a new sorting algorithm sort that delegates core sorting work to an auxilliary function sort0. The programmer's intent behind this division of labor is that sort0 should only be called by sort and not by any other method. So in this case, the intent and the possible annotation (which may assign trust evidence 1 when the call comes from sort and trust evidence 0 otherwise) are at the same explanatory level.

A more complex example would be when a programmer has the intention that a unit of code only be used with other units of code, *provided* that interaction is strictly about business. So this may rule out interactions with third-party applications, access of certain web pages, and use of an editor if the edited text is not work related, etc. As this suggests, it will be much harder to refine such abstract intentions into annotations that are close enough to the application layer in order to be enforceable. The problem of refining policies to cross semantic layers has been studied in the context of usage control [6], and it would be interested to see whether these techniques may be applicable here.

But we note that a first research problem here is to actually come up with usable languages in which high-level intentions could be captured, before we may consider how to refine such specifications.

4   Conclusions

We have identified that there is currently no adequate support for expressing expectations that programmers may have on the interactions of units of code. Then we described a technical approach that provides a partial solution to this problem and that seems to conform with a standard model for trust mechanics in trust-mediated interactions. We also identified an explanatory gap between *intent* and enforceable programm annotations that needs to be closed so that high-level considerations can be reflected and enforced in low-level programming.

Acknowledgments. We acknowledge the kind support of Intel® Corporation: the first two authors are funded within the Intel® Corporation *Trust Evidence* project; and the last author is funded for a grant *Teaching Security Through Serious Games.*

References

1. Agha, G.A.: ACTORS - a model of concurrent computation in distributed systems. MIT Press series in artificial intelligence. MIT Press (1990)
2. Flechais, I., Riegelsberger, J., Angela Sasse, M.: Divide and conquer: the role of trust and assurance in the design of secure socio-technical systems. In: Proceedings of the 2005 Workshop on New Security Paradigms, NSPW 2005, pp. 33–41. ACM, New York (2005)
3. Giddens, A.: The Consequences of Modernity. Polity, Cambridge (1990)
4. Handy, C.: Trust and the virtual organization. Harvard Business Review 73(3), 40–50 (1995)
5. Kirlappos, I., Angela Sasse, M., Harvey, N.: Why trust seals don't work: A study of user perceptions and behavior. In: Katzenbeisser, S., Weippl, E., Camp, L.J., Volkamer, M., Reiter, M., Zhang, X. (eds.) Trust 2012. LNCS, vol. 7344, pp. 308–324. Springer, Heidelberg (2012)
6. Kumari, P., Pretschner, A.: Model-based usage control policy derivation. In: Jürjens, J., Livshits, B., Scandariato, R. (eds.) ESSoS 2013. LNCS, vol. 7781, pp. 58–74. Springer, Heidelberg (2013)
7. Leavens, G.T., Cheon, Y., Clifton, C., Ruby, C., Cok, D.R.: How the design of JML accommodates both runtime assertion checking and formal verification. In: de Boer, F.S., Bonsangue, M.M., Graf, S., de Roever, W.-P. (eds.) FMCO 2002. LNCS, vol. 2852, pp. 262–284. Springer, Heidelberg (2003)
8. Mayer, R., Davis, J., Schoorman, F.D.: An integrative model of organizational trust. Academy of Management Review 20(3), 709–734 (1995)
9. Moses, T.: eXtensible Access Control Markup Language (XACML) Version 2.0. OASIS Standards Committee (February 2005)
10. Nielson, F., Nielson, H.R., Hankin, C.: Principles of program analysis (2. corr. print). Springer (2005)
11. Riegelsberger, J., Angela Sasse, M., McCarthy, J.D.: The mechanics of trust: A framework for research and design. Int. J. Hum.-Comput. Stud. 62(3), 381–422 (2005)
12. Schneier, B.: Lairs and Outliers: Enabling the Trust and Society Needs to Thrive. John Wiley & Sons (2012)

Modeling Security Policy and the Effect for End-Users

Kevin D. Jones and Kizito Salako

City University London
kevin.jones.1@city.ac.uk, kizito@csr.city.ac.uk

Abstract. Many "good practices" in computer security are based on assumptions and local evidence that do not generalize. There are few quantifiable methods of establishing or refuting the validity of these practices from a user perspective. We propose a formal model of security policies that allows us to evaluate the claimed benefits to the user of the system quantitatively. We illustrate the use of the model by looking at a security policy we all live with daily: The Password Policy.

1 Introduction

There are many myths in the field of computer security that have a daily effect on the users of systems. Since there is little in the way of quantitative evaluation to support or disprove claims about improved security, assumptions are taken as fact, and we accept discomfort in return for supposed benefit. In most other parts of the security space, we have strong systems for reasoning about the strength of the system, but this has not been the case for user level policy. We know that many security vulnerabilities are due to users not complying with stated policy, due to a lack of understanding of the value of that policy. A mathematical model of the security system allows a firm underpinning for discourse with users on the motivation for the policy.

We use a password policy as an example since it illustrates the concept. To address questions about the efficacy of such policies, we develop a probabilistic model which captures the way these policies constrain how people choose passwords, and what this means for system security. Our primary aims with this model are twofold: 1) clarifying and formalising concepts used when discussing password policies and the level of security they engender (some concepts we clarify include *password strength* and the *difficulty* an attacker might have in subverting password security), and 2) exploring new applications of probabilistic modelling approaches already applied in other contexts, with the aim of gaining insight into security evaluation.

The rest of this paper is structured as follows. We begin in Section 2 with details of how we model a password-based security system that is both subject to password policies and open to attack from adversaries. Section 3 develops this further with a discussion of what *password strength* means in our model. In Section 4, user implications of our model are explored.

L. Marinos and I. Askoxylakis (Eds.): HAS/HCII 2013, LNCS 8030, pp. 256–265, 2013.

2   Modelling Password Choices and Attacker Actions

In a *password-based security system*, access to computing resources are controlled as follows: each user of the system has preassigned access rights to the resources – we refer to these access rights as a *user–profile* – and anyone can gain the access granted in a given user–profile by submitting the password for the user–profile to the system for authentication. In practice, the system may be viewed as a collection of software tools that: 1) maintain a database of the one-to-one correspondence between a user-profile and its related password, and 2) grant an entity access to a user profile if and only if the entity submits the password associated with the user-profile.

Naturally, there is a limited amount of computer memory available to the system for storing each password chosen by its users, where these passwords are comprised of symbols from a finite character set. Consequently, the set of all possible passwords, $\mathcal{P}$, is finite and completely defined by the password security system.

A user of the password security system chooses a password, say π, from the typically large set $\mathcal{P}$ according to some probability distribution.

The system is open to attack by an attacker. Here, an **attacker** is any entity that seeks to subvert the password security system by correctly guessing the password for a legitimate user, submitting this guess to the password security system and, thereby, gaining access to those computer resources granted in a legitimate user–profile. An **attack** is the choice and submission of a password to the security system by an attacker. We refer to a collection of attacks by an attacker as an **attack campaign**. In conducting an attack campaign, the attacker chooses a sequence of passwords from $\mathcal{P}$ at random. Suppose the number of attacks (that is, the length of such a sequence) is N. Then the sequence of passwords, which we may refer to as σ, is an ordered N-*tuple* of passwords, say $(\pi_1, \ldots, \pi_N)$. That is, an attack campaign is characterised by some sequence of passwords σ chosen by an attacker so that:

$$\sigma = (\pi_1, \ldots, \pi_N) \in \underbrace{\mathcal{P} \times \mathcal{P} \times \cdots \times \mathcal{P}}_{N \ times},$$

We accept the view that an identical amount of time and effort is expended by the attacker in carrying out each attack in an attack campaign. After all, attackers have no notion of how much closer they have gotten to correctly guessing a password after a succession of failed attacks, and the act of guessing and submitting a password to the system does not significantly change from attack to attack. Formally, therefore, if an attack campaign occurs over regular time-intervals in calendar time, then the length N of an attack campaign is a measure of the time and effort spent by the attacker. For the sake of brevity we shall write the cartesian product above, $\mathcal{P} \times \mathcal{P} \times \cdots \times \mathcal{P}$, as $\mathcal{P}^N$.

An attack is deterministic in its outcome: a correctly guessed password by an attacker compromises the system, while an incorrect guess will not. Therefore, for each pair of user-password π and choice of password an attacker submits to the security system π_i, the indicator function $\nu(\ ,\ )$ tells us if an attack is successful; it is defined as follows

$$\nu(\pi, \pi_i) = \begin{cases} 1, & \text{if } \pi = \pi_i \\ 0, & \text{otherwise} \end{cases}$$

A *user policy* is the set of rules and constraints, imposed on a user of a password-based security system, which limit both how the user chooses a password and the length of time for which such a user-password is valid. So, for instance, a password policy that gives guidance to a legitimate user about how to choose a "*strong*" password would be part of the user policy for any user that follows such guidance. In effect, a user-policy defines a partition of $\mathcal{P}$ into two disjoint subsets – those passwords that a user may choose from, and those passwords that the user will not choose from. A user policy is partly the result of system imposed rules for password choices – imposed on the user to restrict which passwords she can choose – and system imposed time limits for the validity of a chosen password. In addition, user policy is also the result of the preferences a user has about how to construct a password, such as using a combination of letters from the lyrics of a favourite song or the sum of family members birthdays.

In the same vein, there exist (possibly self-imposed) constraints on an attacker which determine both how the attacker chooses passwords and how long the attack campaign may last for. We loosely refer to these constraints as an *attacker policy*. An attacker-policy partitions $\mathcal{P}$ into two disjoint subsets of passwords: those that an attacker may choose from when conducting a campaign of attacks, and those the attacker will not choose from. The partition arises naturally because an attacker policy is partly defined by the attacker's beliefs and preferences: for instance, he might take the view that certain passwords will never be chosen by the user. This limits the potential passwords considered by the attacker. However, this alone may be insufficient for the attacker's needs, given that the typical number of attacks an attacker can carry out is exceedingly small compared with the number of possible passwords a user may have choose from, so that the attacker's beliefs still result in a relatively large subset of passwords to be considered by the attacker. Compound this limitation with the fact that for many practical systems there is a finite amount of time for which a user's password might be valid – so, an attacker has a finite number of attempts to guess the user's password – and we see that an attacker would seek to maximize his probability of correctly guessing a user's password by focusing his attacks only on those passwords that he deems a user most likely to choose. In summary, the attacker policy defines the subset of passwords an attacker might try, but the attacker still needs to optimize which of these passwords he should try – an optimization problem that results in a probability distribution for which passwords the attacker chooses, as we shall see shortly.

A user of the system is required to choose a password, at random, in accordance with the user policy. For a given user and user policy, let Π be the

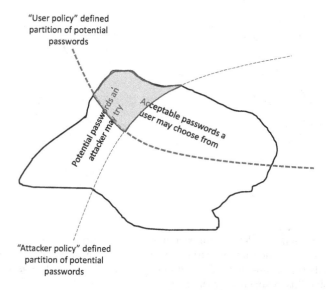

"User policy" defined
partition of potential
passwords

Potential passwords an
attacker may try

Acceptable passwords a
user may choose from

"Attacker policy" defined
partition of potential
passwords

Fig. 1. The overlap of those passwords that may be chosen by a user and those that may be chosen as part of an attack campaign

random variable that models the random choice of a password by the user. Then, $P(\Pi = \pi)$ is the probability that a given password π is chosen by the user from $\mathcal{P}$. This defines the *distribution of user-password choice*, an example of which is depicted in Fig. 2.

On the other hand, an attacker typically has a limited number of tries to guess a password, so he chooses each password in an attack campaign according to his attacker policy and some probability distribution. For a given attacker and attacker policy, let Π_i be the random variable that models the *i*th random choice of password made by the attacker for an attack campaign. Then, the probability that a given potential password, π_i, is used in an attack is $P(\Pi_i = \pi_i)$. This is a *distribution of attacker-password choice*, an example of which is depicted in Fig. 3. Actually, more interesting is the probability that a given sequence of potential passwords, say $\sigma = (\pi_1, \ldots, \pi_N)$, is chosen by the attacker to use in a campaign. In general, this is given by the discrete joint probability distribution of the random vector $\Sigma = (\Pi_1, \ldots, \Pi_N)$,

$$P(\Sigma = \sigma) = P(\Pi_1 = \pi_1, \ldots, \Pi_N = \pi_N) . \tag{1}$$

This defines the *distribution of the attacker's attack-campaign choice*.

For the campaign to be successful it is sufficient that at least one of the passwords tried by the attacker is a correct guess; where exactly in the sequence such a correct guess occurs is unimportant for now. In particular, the probability that an attack-campaign successfully compromises the system by guessing the legitimate password π being used by a given user

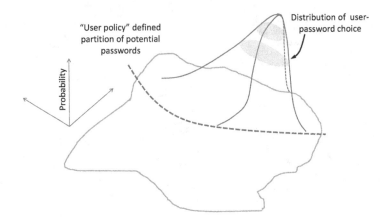

Fig. 2. A distribution that defines, for each password, the probability that the password is chosen by the user. The random variable is defined on the space of passwords $\mathcal{P}$, and those passwords that a user will never choose from (according to the user-policy) will have zero probability associated with them.

is given as:

$$P\Big(\nu\big(\pi,\Sigma\big) = 1\Big) = \mathbb{E}\Big[\nu\big(\pi,\Sigma\big)\Big] = \sum_{\sigma \in \mathcal{P}^N} \nu\big(\pi,\sigma\big) P\left(\Sigma = \sigma\right). \qquad (2)$$

In practice, the precise form of Eq. (2) is influenced by different factors. For instance, many password-based systems have a maximum placed on the number of consecutive failed authentication attempts on a user profile. When this number is reached the user profile is made unavailable for authentication for a period of time. This limits the length of an attack-campaign carried out by an attacker. Another example is how some websites use so-called "Captchas" to determine if a human being is attempting to access the material they contain, as these also hinder an attackers ability to perform a brute-force attack, thus significantly reducing the length of an attack-campaign and increasing the effort required by an attacker.

While our focus is on passwords, the model does not ignore the utility of a *username* which, in conjunction with a password, may be viewed as a unique identifier for a legitimate user of the security system.

The model allows for an asymmetry between a system administrator and an attacker in what each can learn from a failed login attempt. Usually, failed attempted logins are not informative in indicating to an attacker just how "close" the attacker's wrongly guessed password is to the true password. On the other hand, a system administrator can compare the incorrect password that was submitted with the actual password to determine if the two passwords differ by an insignificant number of characters.

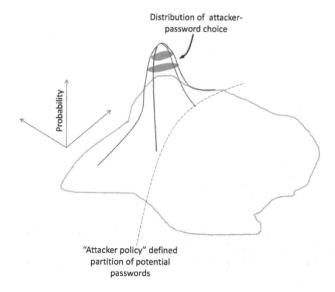

Fig. 3. A distribution that defines, for each password, the probability that the password is chosen by an attacker in an attack. The random variable is defined on the space of passwords $\mathcal{P}$, and those passwords that an attacker will never choose from (according to the attacker-policy) will have zero probability associated with them.

For clarity it has been indicated that a single attacker carries out an attack-campaign. However, this simplification is not necessary and the model generalizes easily to cater for multiple attackers.

3   Password Simplicity

When is a password chosen by a user a *simple password*? A user-password could be simple for any of the following reasons:

1. The password is chosen from a set of related passwords, where an attacker armed with some knowledge about this set can deduce what the underlying relationship between the passwords is. For instance, a symmetrical relationship between the passwords (e.g. they all comprise of some permutation of the same vowels, consonants and symbols), or a set of simple transformation rules that gives another password in the set once one of the passwords in the set is known (e.g. a rule that replaces all 's' characters with the '$' symbol).
2. The password is one of many common passwords known to attackers (e.g. common phrases such as *"password"* or *"123456"*).

A user choosing simple passwords potentially increases the probability of an attacker correctly guessing the user's password. We can make this notion precise as follows. For an attacker carrying out a randomly chosen attack-campaign aimed at accessing a given user-profile, we define *the simplicity of a given user-password*

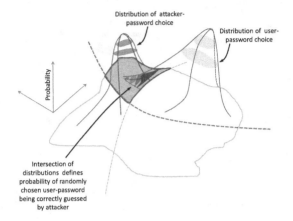

Fig. 4. The overlap of the distributions in Fig.'s 2 and 3 defines the probability that a randomly chosen user-password is correctly guessed by an attacker. A simple password would be one for which such an overlap implies an attacker is likely to guess the password.

for the attacker as the probability that the attacker correctly guesses the password in a random attack-campaign, if the password is the one associated with the user-profile. That is, for a user-password π and a random variable Σ that models an attacker's choice of attacks in an attack-campaign (where the length of the campaign is N), the simplicity of π for the attacker is computed by Eq. (2) Let us consider a particular case of this formula. Suppose further that the attacks in an attack-campaign are independently and identically distributed password choices made by the attacker, where Π_a is the random variable that models the choice of an attack by an attacker. Then, the simplicity of the password π for this attacker is:

$$
\begin{aligned}
\mathbb{E}\left[\nu\left(\pi, \Sigma\right)\right] &= \sum_{\sigma \in \mathcal{P}^N} \nu\left(\pi, \sigma\right) P\left(\Sigma = \sigma\right) \\
&= \sum_{\left(\pi_1, \ldots, \pi_N\right) \in \mathcal{P}^N} \left(1 - \prod_{i=1}^{N}\left(1 - \nu\left(\pi, \pi_i\right)\right)\right) P\left(\Pi_a = \pi_1, \ldots, \Pi_a = \pi_N\right) \\
&= \sum_{\pi_N \in \mathcal{P}} \cdots \sum_{\pi_1 \in \mathcal{P}} \left(1 - \prod_{i=1}^{N}\left(1 - \nu\left(\pi, \pi_i\right)\right)\right) P\left(\Pi_a = \pi_1\right) \ldots P\left(\Pi_a = \pi_N\right)
\end{aligned}
$$

$$(3)$$

Note that we can make the following expansion:

$$
1 - \prod_{i=1}^{N}\left(1 - \nu\left(\pi, \pi_i\right)\right) = \sum_{i=1}^{N} \nu\left(\pi, \pi_i\right) - \sum_{i_1 < i_2}^{N} \nu\left(\pi, \pi_{i_1}\right) \nu\left(\pi, \pi_{i_2}\right) + \ldots
$$
$$
+ (-1)^{N} \sum_{i_1 < \ldots < i_{N-1}}^{N} \prod_{j=1}^{N-1} \nu\left(\pi, \pi_{i_j}\right) + (-1)^{N+1} \prod_{i=1}^{N} \nu\left(\pi, \pi_i\right).
$$

Therefore, upon using this expansion in Eq. (3), the linearity of mathematical expectation $\mathbb{E}\left[\bullet\right]$, and the notation $\phi_a\left(\pi\right) := \mathbb{E}\left[\nu\left(\pi, \Pi_a\right)\right]$, we have:

$$\mathbb{E}\left[\nu\left(\pi, \Sigma\right)\right]$$

$$= \binom{N}{1}\mathbb{E}\left[\nu\left(\pi, \Pi_a\right)\right] - \binom{N}{2}\mathbb{E}\left[\nu\left(\pi, \Pi_a\right)\right]^2 + \ldots + (-1)^{N+1}\mathbb{E}\left[\nu\left(\pi, \Pi_a\right)\right]^N$$

$$= \binom{N}{1}\phi_a\left(\pi\right) - \binom{N}{2}\left(\phi_a\left(\pi\right)\right)^2 + \ldots + (-1)^{N+1}\left(\phi_a\left(\pi\right)\right)^N$$

$$= 1 - \left(1 - \phi_a\left(\pi\right)\right)^N \tag{4}$$

as the expression for the simplicity of the password π for the attacker. By examining this form of password simplicity we make the following observations:

1. *Password simplicity is affected by the length of the attack-campaign*: for $0 < \phi_a\left(\pi\right) < 1$ the longer the attack-campaign the more likely the attacker is in being successful. This follows from the function $1 - \left(1 - \phi_a\left(\pi\right)\right)^N$ being a strictly monotonically increasing function of N, and the following limit.

$$1 - \left(1 - \phi_a\left(\pi\right)\right)^N \to 1 \quad \text{as} \quad N \to \infty.$$

   Consequently, if the security system limits the number of tries an attacker has to validate password guesses this, in turn, limits the length of an attacker's attack-campaign. Many online password-based security systems implement this sort of limitation, but a significant number still do not.
2. *The probability of an attack succeeding affects password simplicity*: the more likely an attacker is at guessing the password in a single attack, the more likely the attacker is at being successful in a random attack-campaign. For, if $1 \geq x \geq \phi_a\left(\pi\right) \geq 0$, then the following inequality holds.

$$1 - \left(1 - x\right)^N \geq 1 - \left(1 - \phi_a\left(\pi\right)\right)^N.$$

   The probability $\phi_a\left(\pi\right)$ takes into account the knowledge an attacker has, as well as the method by which the attacker chooses a password to be used in an attack.
3. *Password Strength*: Given the distribution for an attacker's password-choice, the Shannon-entropy

$$-N\log_2\left[1 - \phi_a\left(\pi\right)\right].$$

By definition, each password π chosen by a user has an associated simplicity, $\mathbb{E}\left[\nu\left(\pi, \Sigma\right)\right]$, for a given attacker. Consequently, there is a natural notion of a *simplicity function* for the attacker: for each password π, the simplicity function $\theta\left(\pi\right)$ gives the probability that the attacker successfully guesses the password in a random attack-campaign.

$$\theta\left(\pi\right) := \mathbb{E}\left[\nu\left(\pi, \Sigma\right)\right] \tag{5}$$

The simplicity function makes apparent the idea that some passwords are easier to guess than others for a given attacker. There is also a dual relationship: a given password chosen by a user could be easy for some attackers to guess but difficult for other attackers. So, different attackers have different simplicities.

Since $\theta\left(\pi\right)$ is defined on $\mathcal{P}$, the user-policy and attacker-policy have the following implications for password simplicity:

1. Those passwords that a user will not choose from will be of no use to the attacker, even if those passwords are very simple for an attacker to guess had they been chosen by the user.
2. Those passwords that an attacker will not choose from have associated simplicity of 0, and hence are the best passwords for a user to choose from.
3. Simple passwords that a user may choose from hold the most potential for the attacker being successful.

4   Password Policy and Its Effects on Users

Password policies have a clear effect on users. For example, some password-based security systems implement a user-policy that puts a time limit on the validity of a password chosen by a user. In effect, for a user to continue to access computing resources, the user has to choose a new password after a fixed amount of calender time has elapsed. Rationale for such a policy include:

1. Limit the time an attacker has to penetrate the system
2. Limiting the time a successful attacker has "unauthorised" access to computing resources.

We all live with such expiration policies, and many of us complain about having to change our passwords "too often". We are generally told that we have to live with this for "added security" but there is rarely any quantitative evidence that security is added. The models we have proposed can be instantiated for any given situation to establish whether or not there is value in such a policy. Unsurprisingly, whether there is additional security or not depends on the assumptions made about the relationship between the user and attacker profiles. To illustrate this point consider the following counterexample to claims of password expiration being beneficial. Let Φ_i be the random variable $\left(1 - \phi_a\left(\Pi_i\right)\right)^N$ that models an attacker failing to guess a user password Π_i in N independent consecutive attacks (we defined the function $\phi_a\left(\pi\right)$ when proving Eq. (4)). Suppose that upon being required to renew her password a user is increasingly more likely to choose a simpler password with each new choice. So formally, given $m - 1$ successive password choices $\pi_{m-1}, \ldots, \pi_1$ made by a user, the user being more likely to choose a weak password in her m^{th} choice, compared with her 1st choice, is modelled by the following inequality.

$$\mathbb{E}\left[\Phi_m | \pi_{m-1}, \ldots, \pi_1\right] \ll \mathbb{E}\left[\Phi_1\right] .$$

The rationale for this inequality is that in such a situation an attacker can expect the passwords chosen to become simpler. As a consequence of this, the **probability that an attacker will fail to guess a users password after m password choices by the user** is much less than it would be if the user chose only one password over the same time period. That is

$$\mathbb{E}\left[\Phi_m \Phi_m \ldots \Phi_2 \Phi_1\right] \ll \left(\mathbb{E}\left[\Phi_1\right]\right)^m \leq \mathbb{E}\left[\Phi_1{}^m\right] .$$

5 Conclusion

Much of what we assume to be true in security is not, particularly when we involve users! Our assumptions about policy improving security often turn out to be untrue. We need a system of quantifiable reasoning, that allows us to make informed decisions about the validity of policy choice, to ensure that we do get the right balance of security and convenience. In particular, we have shown that policies based only on one dimensional assumptions are likely to be erroneous. For our simple case, we show it is necessary to take both user and attacker choices into account to get a true understanding of vulnerability. We have proposed a probabilistic framework for reasoning about policy, which allows such discourse. In the future, we propose to extend this work to allow reasoning about more aspects of security policy and the environment, including multiple attacker profiles. We also intend to develop user studies, allowing accurate instantiation of the user based variables, leading to better overall understanding of the validity of security policy change.

The next time your IT department says "we have changed our password policy to increase security", you can legitimately say "prove it".

Legal Protection for Personal Information Privacy

Yinan Liu

School of Economy and Law
University of Science and Technology Liaoning
Anshan City, China
liu_anna@hotmail.com

Abstract. While the privacy concerns raised by advances in information technologies are widely recognized, recent developments have led to a convergence of these technologies in many situations, presenting new challenges to the right to privacy. This paper examines the information technologies and its potential impact on individual privacy interests. The paper first discusses the right to privacy, personal information and information privacy separately, noting ways that new technologies create privacy concerns. The paper then examines the legislation in U.S., E.U. Finally, the paper examines existing protections for privacy in China, considers why they are insufficient, and proposes measures to enhance the legal protection of privacy interests to address these new technologies.

Keywords: personal information, right to privacy, information privacy, legal protection.

1 Introduction

With the technological advancement, personal information is readily available because of the widespread usage of the Internet and of cloud computing, the availability of inexpensive computer storage, and increased disclosures of personal information by Internet users in participatory Web 2.0 technologies. For example, Web 2.0 involves more voices than previous Internet technologies. With more voices online, there is a wider scope for privacy invasion. With more recording technologies readily at hand—such as cell phone cameras and text messaging services like Twitter—there is a wider scope for incidental gathering of details of people's private lives that can be uploaded and disseminated globally at the push of a button. [1] The advent of computers required the adoption of specific means to safeguard personal information. One of the most discussed and worried-about aspects of today's information age is the subject of privacy. There is a new social relationship, human and computers, in the information age.

2 Personal Information and Privacy

2.1 Personal Information

Information about individual can be divided into three categories—personal information, sensitive information, and personally identifiable information. [2]

L. Marinos and I. Askoxylakis (Eds.): HAS/HCII 2013, LNCS 8030, pp. 266–275, 2013.
© Springer-Verlag Berlin Heidelberg 2013

Personal information can be regarded as the set of all data that is associated with a specific individual, e.g., date of birth, gender, address, name of first pet, favorite chocolate, high school of graduation, geographical location at 3:14 p.m. on March 30, 2005, and on and on and on.

- Personal information is the set of all information that is associated with a specific person X. Personal information is thus defined in a technical or objective sense.
- Sensitive information is the set of personal information that some party believes should be kept private. If the party is the person associated with that information (call that person X), the set is defined by personal preferences of X, and X's definition of private (which may be highly context dependent and linked to particular cultural standards regarding the revelation or withholding of information). [3]
- Personally identifiable information (PII) refers to any information that identifies or can be used to identify, contact, or locate the person to whom such information pertains. This includes information that is used in a way that is personally identifiable, including linking it with identifiable information from other sources, or from which other personally identifiable information can easily be derived, including, but not limited to, name, address, phone number, fax number, e-mail address, financial profiles, Social Security number, and credit card information.

2.2   Privacy

As we all know today, right to privacy is one of the most important civil rights. The story of the "right to privacy" starts at the end of the eighteenths century. In the 1890 Warren and Brandeis published in the Harvard Law Review an essay titled "The Right to Privacy" defining this new right as "the right to be let alone" [4]. The article was written in response to invasions of personal privacy caused by the technological innovations of mass printing (newspapers) and the portable camera (photographs). With the late 20th century technological innovations of the Internet and the World Wide Web, the collection, use, and dissemination of electronic personal information is potentially much more invasive. [5] As noted above, the right to privacy has long been characterized as the "the right to be let alone." And yet, today the more practical view may be that "[i]n the digital era, privacy is no longer about being 'let alone.' Privacy is about knowing what data is being collected and what is happening to it, having choices about how it is collected and used, and being confident that it is secure." [6]

3   Information Privacy

3.1   What Is Information Privacy?

Technological advances are changing the face of our society dramatically. New technology affects individuals countless ways, including the manner in which they interact with each other, with businesses, and with the government. While technology makes it possible to accomplish many tasks more efficiently, and even to accomplish tasks previously not possible, these accomplishments do not come without costs. Even though they provide solutions to current problems, many technological developments often create new, sometimes unforeseen, problems. One area in which new technology currently is creating such problems is the right to privacy.

A more recent concern regarding privacy rights is information privacy. Information privacy is a component of the fundamental right to privacy. Information privacy involves an individual's personal information and his ability to control that information. Personal information includes data assigned to an individual, such as a social security number, address, or telephone number. Other personal information is generated on a day-to-day basis, such as records of bank transactions, credit card purchases, phone calls, and medical treatments. The "assigned" personal information may be used primarily to identify a subject; the "generated" information may be used to track the subject's activities and habits. This information then can be used, unbeknownst to the subject, by government, businesses, and individuals for any number of purposes." As society becomes more dependent on computer databases and electronic record-keeping, an individual's ability to control that has access to his personal information becomes more tenuous. [7] This inability to control the use of personal viewed no differently than other commodities in the market gives rise to the issue of information privacy.

3.2   Information Technology and Information Privacy Concerns

Technological advancements, coupled with changes in other areas, combine to make the privacy challenge particularly vexing. Technological change is, of course, not new. The printing press has been described as a precursor to the World Wide Web; e-mail and cell phone text messaging have revolutionized interpersonal and group correspondence. Affordability and advances in sensor technologies have broadened the volume and scope of information that can be practically acquired. The privacy debate itself has part of its roots in the technological changes involving the press and technology for photography Warren and Brandeis, in their landmark 1890 Harvard Law Review paper, were responding to, as they put it, "recent inventions and business methods." [8]

What makes information special is that it is reproducible. In digital form, information can be copied an infinite number of times without losing fidelity. Digitized information is also easy to distribute at low cost. Today, in the information age, the sheer quantity of information; the ability to collect unobtrusively, aggregate, and analyze it; the ability to store it cheaply; the ubiquity of interconnectedness; and the magnitude and speed of all aspects of the way we think about, use, characterize, manipulate, and represent information are fundamentally and continuously changing.

With the technological advancement, the growing use of personal information in society by both the government and private actors threatens to diminish further the right to privacy. As technological advances increase the amount of daily activities that generate personal information, an individual's ability to control his personal information decreases. This information reveals much about one's habits and routine, and a lack of control over one's "data image" diminishes one's privacy. In the other hand, a person whose privacy has been breached is likely to be concerned about the negative consequences that might flow from the breach, and those kinds of psychological concerns constitute a type of actual though intangible harm entirely apart from the other kinds of tangible harm that the law typically recognizes. Therefore, the right to information privacy in the information age needs more legal protection.

4   Information Privacy Protection in U.S. and E.U.

Throughout the world, there are several modes of legislation to protect information privacy. The two typical modes are American self-discipline and the European Union's legislative regulation.

4.1   U.S. Model

There is no comprehensive federal privacy statute that protects personal information. Instead, a patchwork of federal laws and regulations govern the collection and disclosure of personal information and has been addressed by Congress on a sector-by-sector basis.

Legislative protections of privacy appear in a variety of statutes aimed at both government and private actors. The Fair Credit Reporting Act of 1970 was one of the first attempts to protect individuals' interest in information privacy from private actors, while the Privacy Act of 1974 was among the earliest statutory protections against governmental misuse of personal information. Congress has enacted a wide variety of other statutes in an effort to protect. information privacy, including the Bank Secrecy Act, the Cable Communications Policy Act, the Computer Matching and Privacy Protection Act, the Driver's Privacy Protection Act, the Electronic Communications Privacy Act, the Electronic Fund Transfer Act, Title III of the Omnibus Crime Control and Safe Streets Act (also known as the Wiretap Act), the Right to Financial Privacy Act,''' and the Video Privacy Protection Act.

The US adopted this model for two reasons.

- The US-American legal culture focuses on individualism and the function of the constitution and the basic position of the right to privacy in protecting people's rights. The government should not intervene if existing regulations can settle matters.
- There exists the tense imbalance between individualism and public interests in the society. The US model chases the maxim of both the individual and public interests. It tends to use the minimum cost to achieve the best balance between both the personal protection and public interests.

4.2   E.U. Model

The US legal system was the first to elaborate on the right to privacy: it surfaced and developed by means of several cases and finally came to be codified in statutory rules.

Meanwhile, in Europe, to respond to these fears, enforceable laws throughout Europe have been formulated. The Swedish Data Act was the first national privacy act in the world; other countries framed their own national legislation successively by the end of 1980s. Many international initiatives have been adopted to protect privacy and personal data, which yield many agreements binding on many nations. Many international organizations such as The Council of Europe (CoE), the Organization for Economic Cooperation and Development (OECD) and the United Nations (UN) has adopted regulations and policies.

Since 1995, the European Union has enacted its own acts, including [9]:

- Directive 95/46/EC of the European Parliament and the Council of 24 October 1995 on the Protection of individuals with regard to the processing of personal data and on the free movement of such data;
- Directive 97/66/EC of the European Parliament and of the Council of 15 December 1997 concerning the processing of personal data and the protection of privacy in the telecommunications sector;
- Directive 2002/58/EC of the European Parliament and the Council of 12 July 2002 concerning the processing of personal data and the protection of privacy in the electronic communications sector (Directive on privacy and electronic communications), abrogating directive of 1997.

4.3   Comparing with the Two Models

The United States and the European Union select different privacy protection mode, which relates not only with the legal developing path and history of protection for right to privacy, also with the social and economic, political tradition.

1) The main differences between the US model and the EU model are as follows:.

a) Supervisory measures: The EU model may also be called the "unitary" model, in which a special organization, which has an independent investigative power, is established. The US model may also be called a "decentralization" model, in which the supervising organizations are scattered in various relevant bodies. For example, medical information and financial information are supervised by relevant bodies.

b) Supervisory model and manner of personal data protection by the commercial organization and the public organization: In order to balance the protection and the flow of data, the emphasis of the US model and the EU model are placed particularly in different fields. More emphasis is placed on data protection in the EU, but in America the emphasis is on self-discipline in the commercial organization and on regulating public bodies.

c) Resources of legislation: The United States uses a sectorial approach that relies on a mix of legislation, regulation, and self-regulation. The European Union, however, relies on comprehensive legislation that, for example, requires creation of government data protection agencies, registration of data bases with those agencies, and in some instances prior approval before personal data processing may begin. Regarding the provisions of personal data protection in the US, their scope is not comprehensive, and heavily relies on self-regulatory efforts by the data processors. The EU system, in contrast, relies primarily on a legal framework and statutory controls, with self-regulation being possible as a complementary solution.

2) The two different protection modes have its own advantages and disadvantages

The mode of United States lacks of effective enforcement measures and means of support lacks of coercive power. This pattern which the interests of both sides are consistent can play its role, if the network industry and users of both sides have a interest conflict, its reliability is questionable. Furthermore, the effect of self-regulation is only to the joined websites and enterprises, without any legal binding to those unjoined.

Comparing with the United States, the advantages of European Union's pattern are authority, mandatory and stability. But the disadvantages also exist. The main problem is, the rapid development of information technology which challenges this centralized legislative mode. Relative to the rapid development of science and technology, the legislation often appears lag; even hinder the development of science and technology.

5 Legal Proposal for China

5.1 Current Legal Protection

Comparing with the developed countries, whether theory research, legislative protection or the judicial practice on the right to privacy are very backward in China.

1) Introduction of Chinese law

Generally speaking, the Chinese legal system can be characterized as a civil law system. Therefore, statutory law is main source other than case law. There are generally 6 types of laws in the Chinese legal system. In the order of priorities, they rank as: Constitution, National Law, Administrative Regulations, Local Legislative Regulations, Departmental Regulations and Local Governmental Regulations.

Table I illustrates the rank of these laws. The Constitution is the supreme law of the whole legal system. The National People's Congress is responsible for legislation and for amendment of the Constitution Law as well as other national laws. The State Council is the chief administrative body and has power to enact nation wide Administrative Regulations. It is chaired by the Premier and is composed of the heads of each governmental department and agency. Under the State Council, various ministries are responsible for supervising different sectors. Operating under the State Council are several Commissions that set policies for, and coordinate the related activities of, different administrative organs. In addition, there are several Offices operating under the State Council that deal with matters of ongoing concern. Apart from these, there are also Bureaus and Administrations operating under the State Council but their organizational status is lower than those of the Ministries.

Each of the governmental entities mentioned above makes relevant regulations for matters falling within its jurisdiction. It is common practice for administrative organs to provide more detailed regulations for the application of National Laws. Local government can also enact laws in areas where they have jurisdiction. But such legislation cannot conflict with the Constitutional Law, National Laws, and the law made by the State Council.

Table 1. The ranks of law and regulations

Constitution promulgated by The National People's Congress

↓

National Law promulgated by The National People's Congress and Standing Congress

↓

Administrative Regulations promulgated by State Council

↓

Local Legislative Regulations promulgated by   local People's Congress

↓

Departmental Regulations and Local Governmental Regulations promulgated by agencies under the State Council and local governments

2) The Constitution guarantees the protection to the right to privacy

The Constitution of PRC stipulates that the freedom and privacy of correspondence of citizens should be protected. Article 38 of Constitution of PRC states: "The personal dignity of citizens of the People's Republic of China is inviolable." Article 39 states that the residences of citizens of PRC are inviolable. Unlawful search of or intrusion into, a citizen's residence is prohibited. Constitution Article 40: "Freedom and privacy of correspondence of citizens of the People's Republic of China are protected by law. No organization or individual may, on any ground, infringe citizens' freedom and privacy of correspondence, except in cases where, to meet the needs of State security or of criminal investigation, public security or procuratorial agencies are permitted to censor correspondence in accordance with the procedures prescribed by law.

3) Other laws and administrative regulations and the decisions of the Standing Committee

- Civil Liability law enacted in 2010 firstly stipulated right to privacy is a separate right of personality.
- Law of the People's Republic of China on Resident Identity Cards stipulates that Public security organs and people's police shall keep confidential citizen's personal information gained through making, issuing, examining or seizing resident identity cards. (Article 6(3)) The Law Article 19 states that Police must not disclose personal information obtained through examining identity cards.
- Postal Law guarantees the protection of freedom and privacy of correspondence and safety of the email. Law of the PRC on the Protection of Minors provides the special group with protection against the breaching of privacy. The State Council also formulated the law that no person may disclose information identifying AIDS sufferers.
- The Regulation on Management of the Administration of Internet Electronic Messaging Services issued by Ministry of Information Industry on 8 October 2000, in which Article 12 states that Electronic Messaging Service providers shall maintain the confidentiality of personal information concerning online subscribers and may not disclose the same to third parties without the subscribers' consent.
- The People's Bank of China made the regulation that banks must keep secret individuals' credit information.

As is obviously observed from the existed provisions in Chinese legal framework, the laws and the administrative regulations demonstrated above do cover data protection to a limited degree. Without a comprehensive data protection law, the existing provisions only give static, rather than expected dynamic, protection to personal data in different aspects and in different areas.

5.2   Legal Proposal for China

1) Adoption of the EU and the US Model

It is suggested by most of the jurist experts that China should adopt the model combining the both the EU and the US model. Chinese legislation model on data protection should absorb both of their essences while in accordance to China's basic social and political situation. Judging from China's current legal and social environment, it appears more reasonable and feasible to base a personal data protection regime on EU approaches to data protection – with necessary modifications accommodating for China's specifics in law and administration, and also to allow for Europe's experiences with implementation of its provisions over the past decades. In particular, Chinese data legislation model would go more towards the EU model .[10]

Since there is no existing legal system to protect personal data, a fully-fledged EU framework will be set as a comprehensive good model. Relatively speaking, this solution has provided the highest level of protection to personal data and received the vast popularity. Seen from economic angle, as the biggest trading partner of the EU, China must pay attention to meet the international norms, especially EU "adequacy" level for the protection of personal data so as not to be restrained by the flaws in the handling of international data flows. The equal guarantee of data protection will benefit the growth of bi-lateral or multi-lateral trade and economic activities.

In addition, China is also a country whose legislation is based on laws and statues instead of cases and self-regulations. China is under the same regime as European civil law, rather than case law. The legislation, enactment and compliance of the law in China all need discreet and precise statutes and code. Consequently, the EU model constitutes a fairly reasonable model of legal reference regardless of some deficiencies.

Moreover, there is not yet a strong tradition in China of entrusting industry and professional organizations with self-regulatory tasks and the necessary authority to assume responsibility from the government. In the specific case of data processing industries, it appears that industry associations do not yet have the necessary capacity to establish and implement this kind of self or co-regulatory system.

2) Personal Information Privacy Law

There is no such thing as a perfect solution to the matter of privacy protection of such complexity. Even if the EU directive is significant, it is far from being an exact model of legislation to follow but sets a common standard for the protection of personal data. Having heavier international pressure on personal information protection, China should take the initiative to reform and establish personal information protection law, rather than wait to be forced to change its current system.

3) Executive Mechanism

It is practical to construct a comprehensive government information resources department on the basis of government reform and restructuring. The department needs to take the comprehensive responsibilities of the management of the information and the use of the technologies involved. Under that circumstance, some measures can be adopted to enhance the efficiency of the enforcement. A case in point is that Germany as well as each province has authority with distinct responsibilities. A further feature of the German law is that the organizations in some cases are permitted to appoint some officials to carry out certain function of protecting data. [11] Independent of the organizations they work with, the officials are required to assist to solve the problem, record the organizational work and make public hearings of the questions. It has been regarded as a quite successful example of the cooperating work with the relevant supervisory authority, which has been followed by some other states like France, Luxembourg, the Netherlands and Sweden.

Likewise, inspired by the above German practice, it is sensible for the corresponding Chinese government agency to invite some interior information protection officers or experts to ensure the agency's compliance with the information protection regulations. The Chinese government information resources may establish a special information committee of interior officers or other related experts to handle the reconsideration of some case thus acting some of the management as well as enforcement. In such a case, the compliance with the law, also the transparency of the agency work will be hugely promoted.

References

1. Lipton, J.D.: Mapping Online Privacy. 140 N.W. U. L Rev. 477, 481–482 (2010)
2. Marx, G.T.: Varieties of Personal Information as Influences on Attitudes towards Surveillance. In: Ericson, R., Haggerty, K. (eds.) The New Politics of Surveillance and Visibility. University of Toronto Press (2006)
3. Sweeney, L.: Uniqueness of Simple Demographics in the U.S. Population, LIDAP-WP4, Laboratory for International Data Privacy. Carnegie Mellon University, Pittsburgh (2000)
4. Warren, S.D., Brandeis, L.D.: The Right to Privacy. Harvard Law Review 4, 193 (1890)
5. Elder, D.A.: The Law of Privacy. Lawyers Cooperative Publishing, Rochester (1991)
6. Anderson, E.: Deputy General Counsel of Microsoft Corporation, The State of Online Consumer Privacy, Hearing before S. Comm. on Commerce, Science, and Transportation, 112th Cong. (2011) (hereinafter Microsoft testimony), http://commerce.senate.gov/public/?a=Files.Serve&File_id=f8e b430d-c017-4ca1-b7e7-c2f7ec240c67
7. Reidenberg, J.R.: Privacy in the Information Economy: A Fortress or Frontier for Individual Rights? Fed. Comm. L.J. 44, 95 (1992)
8. Warren, S.D., Brandeis, L.D.: The Right to Privacy. Harvard Law Review 4, 195 (1890)
9. Pascuzzi, Il diritto dell'era digitale, cit., 40 ff.;PARDOLESI (edited by), Diritto alla riservatezza e circolazione dei dati personali, cit., 14 ff
10. Yang, L.: Discussion on Law of Personality Rights. Higher Education Press (2005)
11. Zhang, X.: EU-China Information Society Project, http://www.eu-chinainfso.org/UserFiles/File/Access%20to%20Go vernment%20Information%20report.pdf(accessed October 20, 2009)

"The Four Most-Used Passwords Are Love, Sex, Secret, and God": Password Security and Training in Different User Groups

Birgy Lorenz[1], Kaido Kikkas[1,2], and Aare Klooster[1]

[1] Institute of Informatics, Tallinn University, Narva Road 25, 10120 Tallinn, Estonia
[2] Estonian Information Technology College, Raja St 4C, 12616 Tallinn, Estonia
{Birgy.Lorenz,Kaido.Kikkas,Aare.Klooster}@tlu.ee

Abstract. Picking good passwords is a cornerstone of computer security. Yet already since the early days (e.g. *The Stockings Were Hung by the Chimney with Care* from 1973; we have also borrowed our title from the 1995 movie *Hackers*), insecure passwords have been a major liability. Ordinary users want simple and fast solutions – they either choose a trivial (to remember and to guess) password, or pick a good one, write it down and stick the paper under the mouse pad, inside the pocket book or to the monitor. They are also prone to reflecting their personal preferences in their password choices, providing telling hints online and giving them out on just a simple social engineering attack. Kevin Mitnick has said that security is not a product that can be purchased off the shelf, but consists of policies, people, processes, and technology. This applies fully to password security as well. We studied several different groups (students, educators, ICT specialists etc – more than 300 people in total) and their password usage. The methods included password practices survey, password training sessions, discussions and also simulated social engineering attacks (the victims were informed immediately about their mistakes).

We suggest that password training should be adjusted for different focus groups. For example, we found that schoolchildren tend to grasp new concepts faster – often, a simple explanation is enough to improve the password remarkably. Thus, we would stress the people and process aspects of the Mitnick formula mentioned above.At the same time, many officials and specialists tend to react to password training with dismissal and scorn (our study suggests that 'you cannot guess my password' is an alarmingly common mindset). Examples like 'admin', 'Password', '123456' etc have occurred even at qualified security professionals, more so at educators. Yet, as Estonia is increasingly relying on the E-School system, these passwords are becoming a prime target. Therefore, for most adult users we suggest putting the emphasis on policy and technology aspects (strict, software-enforced lower limits of acceptable password length, character variability checks, but also clearly written rulesets etc).

Keywords: passwords, security awareness, training, privacy, user behavior.

1   Background

Finding good passwords has been an important issue since the early days of computing [11]. Two decades later, things were still the same [2] – passwords were

L. Marinos and I. Askoxylakis (Eds.): HAS/HCII 2013, LNCS 8030, pp. 276–283, 2013.
© Springer-Verlag Berlin Heidelberg 2013

short and ways to produce good passwords were complicated. The well-meaning attempt to add security by forcing frequent password changes resulted in users starting to write them down [1]. Nowadays, after two more decades, most passwords tend to be hard to remember but easy to crack.

A major security risk results from user-generated passwords, as among common users, comfort prevails over security [5]. At present, best passwords are considered to be at least 15 characters long and containing at least two numbers and one special character, making them practically impossible to crack due to the processing power needed [4]. However, getting the users to comply has presented a challenge [6] and without actual understanding the effect would be negligible [7]. Some researchers also suggest that a way to add contextual security it is safer to avoid passwords in common, internationally used languages. Native words are easier to remember and, with some tweaks, can result in passwords resistant to dictionary-based attacks [10].

Another issue is the exponential growth of password-using environments, making it very difficult to generate unique yet user-friendly passwords for all of them – even if some algorithm is used, and its pattern is usually easily distinguishable [8]. Various frameworks involving password testing or user training has been suggested [9], another way would be to use biometrics [12] or independent one-time passwords [13]. In Estonian context, using the national ID card infrastructure can be considered a good approach.

Several studies (e.g. Brown, 2004) point out two central flaws of user-generated passwords – personal origins and password reuse [3]. Our current study confirms most features outlined by Brown.

2   Methods

Our study consisted of two main stages. Stage I consisted of a survey among different groups with 341 respondents in total: 44 high school students, 51 vocational school students, 78 university students, 26 teachers/trainers, 35 ICT specialists, and 107 other adults (the „average Joe" comparison group). The survey was carried out in May 2012 for some groups and in September and October 2012 for others.

The survey used the snowball method with the 'seed' for each group being students of Pelgulinna Gymnasium (the high school group), Tallinn School of Economics (vocational school) and Master students of various ICT-related programs at Tallinn University (university), teachers and instructors (teachers) and ICT staff (ICT instructors, educational technologists, network administrators; ICT professionals) from the same facilities. Respondents from these groups were then asked to forward the questionnaire to other would-be respondents. The comparison group of 'other adults' was compiled purely on random personal contacts who then distributed the survey further on.

The 28-point survey was divided into four sections – current password use, personal password policy, e-safety awareness and the respondent's background. Response types included Likert scale, multiple choice as well as open-ended questions.

The second stage involved Internet safety training and discussion of the Stage I results among different groups, including primary school students. Password training events included discussion about common password models, testing current password strength, learning about safe password storage options and ICT safety suggestions based "simple safety rules" or 12 easy steps model provided at the Arvutikaitse.ee (SafeComputer) website – e.g. using antivirus and firewall, regular software updates and backups, account types and policies, selective downloading, password security, caution with unknown e-mail attachments or web links, using authentication based on the national ID card, and also some behavioral tips (e.g. asking for help when needed, avoiding using computers when tired etc).

3   Results

The results from the Stage I survey reveal that the overall situation in password security and related awareness has plenty of room for improvement. While the groups and their presumed knowledge about the issue was chosen to be remarkably different (e.g. high school students versus people working as ICT professionals; this was also a reason to include the large 'other adults' group to represent a supposedly average level), the differences were notably smaller than anticipated.

More than 50 per cent of the respondents claimed to use only 4 or less different passwords, with most groups having the percentage over 75 and even among the ICT professionals they accounted for a small majority (only 46% used more than 4). 50% of university students, 65% of teachers and 62% of the generic 'other adults' group claimed to use shorter passwords than 9 characters. There was a visible correlation between using longer passwords and different passwords in different places (likely reflecting the overall security awareness or lack thereof). Teachers and ICT professionals were notably different – while professionals used stronger and variable passwords (they were also the only group making wider use of special characters), teachers rather fell to the opposite side (e.g. 81% using just 2-4 passwords).

Most passwords still consisted of letters and numbers (although change of case is widely used) – the only notable exception in this was ICT professionals. Special characters were not used by 3 of every 4, and those who did use them, mostly confined themselves to a small subset (notably period, again favored by ICT professionals). Overall, the most used components for passwords are one's birth date or a date of special meaning, either one's or his/her close person's nickname, one's favorite animal and 1-4 random numbers – only the last one of which could be recommended as a good practice. Random numbers were most favored by ICT professionals and the youngest group of students – this suggests that the awareness may be slowly rising.

Another often-recurring feature is the password model of "Room1000" (starting with capital letter and ending with numbers or vice versa) – the model is used by a strong majority (70-80%) of all groups. For comparison, the so-called CamelCaps model (a multi-word sentence, every word capitalized) was used relatively less, ranging from one third to half of the respondents in different groups.

Password storage practices also varied but widespread neglect was visible here as well. While a strong majority of the respondents picked the option „only in my memory", this was likely exaggerated and a more realistic picture was revealed by studying other options.

While storing passwords on paper seems to be declining, it is still done by about one third of respondents (inside a notebook, hidden e.g. under the keyboard, locked up somewhere etc). About half of the respondents uses an electronic means but tend to neglect safer options like encrypted 'password safe' software (used by just 0-4 people in each group), rather storing passwords in a generic file or in a web browser.

Solutions when losing one's password show the overall preference towards password reminder (2/3 to 3/4). An intriguing point is that those who should know best – teachers and ICT professionals – do not like to use password reminders and secret phrases, using more controversial techniques instead. A sizable share of teachers (10 out of 26) favors their notebook as password storage, while about half of the ICT staff would just 'hack' (try different passwords, attempt bypass etc).

Using secret questions to retrieve/change passwords reflects some of the same lack of imagination seen at the password choice. The most popular options for the question seems to be 'favorite animal' for younger people (around 40%) and 'something personal' (also about 40%), ICT professionals also use the 'my first (teacher, car)' rather often. Given that knowing the person would provide a lot of clues for the question (as the 'personal' question is often also limited to a couple of generic options by the service provider), the situation is worrisome.

Further into password safety, it seems to be a common practice to share passwords with one's life partner (among adults, 30-50%) or a family member (20-25%). Sharing is especially common among the 'other adults' group (the 'general public'). Students usually share their password also with friends and sometimes with ICT support staff.

The survey also contained some questions about general awareness of computer security. While different aspects varied, the differences between groups were not substantial. On the one hand, most laptops (around 60%) and wireless networks (around 70%) had passwords and the majority of home computers had antivirus and firewall installed and updated. On the other hand, most home desktops did not use passwords, were mostly used with administrative (and in most cases, one common) account and the operating system was not regularly updated. A troubling notion: while the situation looked a little better for ICT professionals, the difference was not substantial – e.g. 26% of them did not update the operating system regularly either.

Some more observations about the lack of security awareness include:

- the majority of home computers were very weakly protected, at the same time only 1/3 of the respondents said that the computer was not used by people outside the family;
- slightly more than a half of the respondents use a PIN/screen lock on their cell phones (among teachers, the percentage was even lower at 38%), at the same time a visible minority uses the same device to store their passwords;
- less than 10% would lock their account or log out before leaving the computer for a longer period.

When asked to describe a good password, the common consensus clearly preferred the length of '7-14' to 'over 15' – the latter was given preference by less than 10%. While the importance of having symbols in different cases was acknowledged (60-70%) as well as using a mix of letters and numbers (about 70-80%), using special characters and refraining from using dictionary words were given very low priority (10-30%; here, the ICT professionals stood out as a group). Given a choice between a short but complicated and a long but simple password the latter got a little more votes, but the percentage ratio was just around 45 to 55.

The password training and discussion sessions at the Stage II of the study focused on finding out different attitudes and solutions for using passwords in a networked environment. We found that although there have been discussions about the need for media literacy training already at the kindergarten [14] privacy awareness is very low among younger students. Although the sites used for 'my first password' are mostly recreative and thus often considered 'unimportant' from the adults' point of view, this is where later password habits are rooted at.

Different user groups need different approaches. For example, working with different student grades showed that:

- grades 1-2 typically visit children's gaming sites and use simple 4-6 character passwords. They are however quick learners and develop healthy password habits when taught properly;
- grades 3-4 are typically already more involved on the Net – even on gaming sites, they understand the need to protect their virtual assets well and have often also had their first negative experiences with strangers online. Yet these students still trust adults and tend to reveal their passwords to them when asked (especially by teachers or ICT professionals). They also wrote passwords down to their notebooks (which then occasionally got lost or stolen). At the same time, they were probably the most receptive audience and quick adopters of better security practices;
- while Grades 5-6 were mostly similar in attitudes with their younger peers, notable change occurs at Grade 7, after which the attitudes fell more in line with high school students (more diversity, less trust in authority, more confidence in one's own knowledge);
- among the high school students and all adults, there was clear correlation between interest in security issues and the person's overall ICT skills. At the same time, we noted an unpleasant tendency of overconfidence in one's skills, especially among ICT professionals, teachers and Master students. In many cases, they were reluctant to believe that they need to improve. For example, some considered using password tools like storage software 'weak', instead proposing that they will remember all password (which, according to Stage I findings, is not always true). Some were genuinely amazed when some recurring patterns in password creation were shown to them.

In conclusion we see that it is important to understand background and behavioral patterns, learning ability before conducting any awareness training in this matter.

4 Discussion

Today's average Internet user faces a lot of passwords in his/her online life – several e-mail accounts, social networks, various e-services and workplace solutions would all need different passwords. In reality, people are lax and use at most four passwords that get rotated in different environments. Only a few consider the possibility of break-in as they think their password is 'good enough'. Passwords may be elaborate but they tend to be short – perhaps hard to guess but easy to crack by today's technical means. And if they are forced to be longer, the users start relying on easy-to-remember combos stemming from their personal life. Using special characters is rare – even if adding just one greatly improves the password's quality. Most importantly, if admins start to enforce stricter password policies without a thorough explanation and user training, this has almost no effect – at best, users will use their former short password mechanically doubled or tripled.

Most users at least attempt to memorize their passwords, but in our study, a lot of people used notebooks or similar places, the rest made heavy use of password reminders with generic secret questions (maiden name, favorite teacher or country etc) whose answers are rather easy to find online. Therefore, training users specifically on password storage security becomes essential.

The main aim of our study was to understand how people with different age and background create and store their passwords. We saw a lot of similarities, but the follow-up training sessions also revealed different issues and stances in different groups. For example, small children do not grasp the idea of secrecy – the understanding of proper password use tends to grow by time as some passwords get forgotten and some accounts broken in. At the same time, the youngest users were also the easiest to train – the change in password models resulting from the training was radical. Adults, especially with ICT background, often were the most reluctant trainees who needed 'proof' of their incompetence (anecdotal evidence also includes a meeting of ICT professionals during which everyone's password was cracked and presented to the owner afterwards).

Another common problem is password sharing with friends and partners. On the one hand, it is understandable that besides common home, children and finances, online resources are also shared. Yet actual cases suggest that following break-up, it is much easier to change a door lock or block a bank account than even remember all the online accounts that were used together; the situation grows worse if the ex-partner also knows the password models of the other side.

Studying the result of the current and also earlier surveys, one has to wonder why this issue has only but little approached from the angle of social engineering. There are no simple solutions for managing human behavior, and 'the problem between the keyboard and the chair' remains - but people can be trained and informed. While technical aids (tokens, ID card) can be beneficial, they are effective only where they are ubiquitous (e.g. education or public sector). With the border between work and home dissolving (e.g. BYOD or Bring Your Own Device), extra stress is put on corporate security as well (a part of which is that users create 'comfortable' passwords also at their workplace) – the Mitnick formula of policies, people, processes and technology remains of prime importance.

5   Conclusion

While the topic is as old as first secrets hidden behind closed doors, the only valid solutions are still policies and training. We tend to have policies, but as long as users do not understand them thoroughly, passwords will stay easy to deduce and/or easy to intercept. Training works, but has to overcome many misconceptions – awareness training must be down-to-earth, sometimes also using 'shock therapy' by demonstrating the vulnerability in a direct manner (care must be taken not to violate any legal rights though).

Passwords that keep pace with today's technology should be at least 15 characters long and contain at least two numbers and one special character – in our study, 2% complied with the rule. Therefore constant and repeated reminders and awareness raising campaigns are needed.

Next steps in this area involve developing training units and exercises as well demo environment where people can test out their knowledge. It should not only be done thru survey testing, but also include real life situations, games and videos.

Acknowledgements. This research was supported by European Social Fund's Doctoral Studies and Internationalisation Programme DoRa, which is carried out by Foundation Archimedes and also by Estonian Information Technology Foundation.

References

1. Adams, A., Sasse, M.A., Lunt, P.: Making passwords secure and usable. People and Computers, 1–20 (1997)
2. Belgers, W.: UNIX password security (1993) (retrieved July 1, 2009)
3. Brown, A.S., Bracken, E., Zoccoli, S., Douglas, K.: Generating and remembering passwords. Applied Cognitive Psychology 18(6), 641–651 (2004)
4. Burnett, M.: Ten Windows Password Myths. Online Document (2002), http://www.securityfocus.com/infocus/1554
5. Cazier, J., Medlin, D.: Password Security: An Empirical Investigation into E-Commerce Passwords and Their Crack Times. Information Systems Security (1065-898X) 15(6), 45 (2006)
6. Charoen, D., Raman, M., Olfman, L.: Improving End User Behaviour in Password Utilization: An Action Research Initiative. Systemic Practice and Action Research 21(1), 55–72 (2008)
7. Chaumont, S.: Security Awareness Training: Passwords. Illinois banker (0019-185X) 97(11), 13 (2012)
8. King, D.: Unforgettable Passwords. American libraries (Chicago, Ill.) (0002-9769) 43(11/12), 57 (2012)

9. Kulkarni, D.: A Novel Web-based Approach for Balancing Usability and Security Requirements of Text Passwords. International Journal of Network Security & its Applications (0975-2307) 2(3), 1 (2010)
10. Malempati, S., Mogalla, S.: Enhanced Authentication Schemes for Intrusion Prevention using Native Language Passwords. International Journal of Computer Science Issues (IJCSI) (1694-0784) 8(4), 356 (2011)
11. Metcalfe, B.: The Stockings Were Hung by the Chimney with Care. RFC 602 (1973), http://tools.ietf.org/html/rfc602
12. O'Gorman, L.: Comparing passwords, tokens, and biometrics for user authentication. Proceedings of the IEEE 91(12), 2021–2040 (2003)
13. Rubin, A.D.: Independent one-time passwords. Computing Systems 9(1), 15–27 (1996)
14. Vinter, K., Siibak, A., Kruuse, K.: Meedia mõjud ja meediakasvatus eelkoolieas. Haridus 4, 11 (2010)

The Privacy Paradox between Users' Attitudes, Stringent Legal Framework and (the Lack of) Adequate Implementation Tools

Shara Monteleone

EC, JRC-IPTS, Seville, Spain
sc0563@gmail.com, shara.monteleone@ec.europa.eu

Abstract. This paper discusses the phenomenon, typical of our Digital Age, called as the 'privacy paradox': although users are aware of the threats to their privacy, the analysis of their online behavior seemingly shows a lack of interest in their privacy, as they keep using online services and products, and even if they know their privacy rights and the existing legal measures to protect them, they appear unwilling of using available protection tools. This paper will show that the reason of this (apparent) paradox is not necessarily the users' neglectful attitude towards their privacy but should be found in the lack of effective implementation tools, at both legal and technical level (e.g. privacy policies).

Keywords: privacy paradox, European DP legal framework, privacy policies.

1 Introduction

This paper will, firstly, discuss the phenomenon called as 'privacy paradox': although users are aware of the threats to their privacy, the analysis of their online behavior seemingly shows a lack of interest in their privacy, as they keep using online services and products and even if they know their privacy rights and the existing legal measures to protect them, they appear neglecting protection tools. Secondly, it will sustain that the reason of this (apparent) paradox is not necessarily the users' neglectful attitude towards their privacy (youngsters are often accused of 'not caring' about their privacy) but should be rather found in the lack of effective implementation tools, at both legal and technical level. One of the persisting issues regarding data protection rights is the fact that, despite their the fact they are acknowledged in numerous legal acts, their practical implementation is often not feasible. This situation makes difficult for the users to fully exercise their data protection rights (the only alternative would be to quit the digital environment); meanwhile, it allows those who have the burden of providing information on the data processing they carry out and of safeguarding users' data, to easily bypass the stringent data protection rules (e.g. ISPs that provide incomplete information, or do not require users' consent while collecting their data, or create and sell profiles of unaware users). Often, the inapplicability of certain legal measures neutralizes the legal strength of the principle that stays behind them. Leaving aside the economic/ political reasons that may play a relevant role in these implementation

L. Marinos and I. Askoxylakis (Eds.): HAS/HCII 2013, LNCS 8030, pp. 284–294, 2013.
© Springer-Verlag Berlin Heidelberg 2013

hurdles, this paper focuses on the legal and technical shortfalls of the existing data protection system, as the main problem seem still lying in the separate approaches through which the legal and technical issues, as regards privacy, are addressed.

Some scholars have already pointed out the need to achieve also in the privacy domain a more integrated legal-technical approach (Poullet 2005), and to adopt ad hoc measures, like 'Transparency Enhancing Technologies' (Hildebrandt 2008). This paper claims that the adoption of this approach is even more urgent in a developed Information Society, taking as case study the online privacy policies and their level of effectiveness as privacy-enhancing tools. Some examples of experiments and good practices are also illustrated. Finally, the opportunities/limitations of the new European Proposal for a Regulation on Data Protection, as regards the achievement of a more effective legal-technical framework, will be briefly considered.

2 Data Disclosure *vs* New Privacy Perception: The Eurobarometer's Results

In June 2011, as a result of a three years study, the European Commission published the Special Eurobarometer 359 (EB), the largest survey ever conducted in Europe on the attitudes of the European citizens regarding data protection and Electronic identity.[1] From this EB interesting data emerge about users' perceived control over their personal data, about awareness of privacy risks, expectations and disclosure habits that not necessary correspond to the common idea about people's behaviour with regard privacy protection. A general consideration that can be inferred is that the majority of people in Europe are aware of the risks raised by the use of digital technologies, but, nonetheless, they continue to disclose their personal data in their daily online activities, e.g., on social networks (SN)[2]. This 'privacy paradox' may be rethought in the light of the Eurobarometer and re-assessed as an *apparent* paradox: in other words, there is not necessarily a contradiction in the Internet users' behaviours. What might be contradictory or inadequate are, instead, the available legal and technical instruments to safeguard users' privacy and to allow them, meanwhile, to fully enjoy the advantages of innovation and technology.

In order to understand this 'apparent' paradox some example may help. The majority of Europeans see disclosing personal information as an increasing part of modern life and the social networking users are more likely to disclose their personal information. However, when we look at the reasons of disclosure, the most important

---

[1] See European Commission, Special Eurobarometer 359 (2011), http://ec.europa.eu/public_opinion/archives/ebs/ebs_359_en.pdf. and W. Lusoli, et al. *Pan-European Survey of practices, attitudes & policy preferences as regard personal identity data management*. EC JRC Institute for Prospective Technological Studies EUR- Scientific and Technical Research series, Luxemburg: Luxemburg Publications Office (2012).

[2] Similar considerations emerge from previous studies on users' privacy concerns conducted in U.S. See J. Tsai, L. Cranor, A. Acquisti, C. Fong, What's it to you? A survey of online privacy concerns and risks, Preliminary Progress Report 2006, *NET Institute Working Papers n. 06-29.*

one seems to be to access an online service (61%). From the Eurobarometer it appears that, though Internet users are commonly concerned about their privacy, they feel that it is necessary (when not mandatory) to provide personal information in order to obtain a service and almost a half of Internet users in Europe say they have been asked for more personal data than necessary when they tried to access or use an online service. A large number of Europeans (70%) are concerned that their personal data held by companies may be used for a purpose other than that for which it was collected.

Data protection Laws in Europe and elsewhere have been strengthened against the indiscriminate practices of online companies to collect personal data and create detailed profiles over users[3]. As a response to privacy concerns, information notices (so-called privacy policies) started to be imposed by mandatory regulation (like in EU) or adopted, as self-regulation practices, by businesses (like in U.S.). The majority of Internet users report to read privacy statements. Most of them say to be informed about the data collection conditions when registering for a service online (in Europe, the 54%), appearing to have a good perception of control. However, people do not act according to their statements as they show not to read the privacy policies entirely or to find difficult to obtain information about a website's data protection practices[4].

From the point of view of the accountability, most users feels responsible themselves for the safe processing of their personal data. As for the strategies used to protect their privacy on Internet, the usual strategies are technical or procedural, like tools and mechanisms to limit spam, or checking whether a website has a safety logo that ensures a protected transaction.[5] When asked what type of regulation should be introduced to prevent companies from using people personal data without their knowledge, most Europeans think that such companies should be fined, banned from using such data, or compelled to compensate the victims. The inference is that, when users are provided with adequate privacy protective tools, or when they dispose mechanisms to better know how to avoid privacy risks, they make use of them.

Data from the Eurobarometer point out also some discrepancies in the behaviour of older and younger users, so called Digital Natives[6], with as regards a number of rele-

---

[3] See the European Commission Proposal for a DP Regulation of the 25 January 2012, Art 20 ("Every natural person shall have the right not to be subject to a measure which produces legal effects concerning this natural person or significantly affects this natural person, and which is based solely on automated processing intended to evaluate certain personal aspects relating to this natural person or to analyse or predict in particular the natural person's performance at work, economic situation, location, health, personal preferences, reliability or behaviour.") in which few exceptions are contemplated. For a first analysis of the text see P de Hert, and V Papakonstantinou, 'The proposed data protection Regulation replacing the Directive 95/45/EC: a sound system for the protection of individuals', Computer Law and Security Review 28 (2012).

[4] J. Tsai, L. Cranor, A. Acquisti, C. Fong, What's it to you? A survey of online privacy concerns and risks, Preliminary Progress Report 2006, *NET Institute Working Papers* n. 06-29, accessible at
http://papers.ssrn.com/sol3/papers.cfm?abstract_id=941708.

[5] This emerges from the Eurobarometer 359 (2011).

[6] In literature a difference is made between Digital Immigrants and Digital Natives, the latter being, the youngsters, born and raised with digital technology (M Prensky, 'Digital Natives, Digital Immigrants', On The Horizon. 6 MCB University Press (2001). In the EB 359 (2011) they are Europeans aged 15-24.

vant issues[7]. Around 94% of the users aged 15-24 use the Internet; 84% of them use social networking sites and a large majority of them use websites to share pictures or videos. Digital Natives are also most likely to disclose various types of personal data on social networking sites; they usually do not read privacy statements/policies on the Internet but they feel sufficiently informed about the conditions for data collection and the further uses of their data when accessing a social networking site or registering for a service online. They are also more likely to feel that they have control over the information disclosed on social networking or sharing sites (84%) and they are the *least* likely to mention the risk that their data may be used to send them unwanted commercial offers or that the websites will not respect the privacy policies[8].

3   Reasons of This (apparent) Paradox

Knowing the behaviours as regards privacy, especially of young people, is important, first of all, for online companies, in particular for those like social networks that provide most of the services to teens and to advertisers (often their partners).

The way Digital Natives behave through the different services and applications existing online is, to some extent, a barometer and a driver of the success of Internet companies and the services they offer. A SN as Facebook knows it very well as it was able to progressively adapt its platform to new trends (e.g., introducing FB messanger) or to users' criticisms (changing its privacy policies) more than it did to regulators' warnings (it took FB a couple of years to disable, as ordered by the EU Data Protection Authorities, the automatic tagging relying on facial recognition features)[9].

The attitudes of young people (they are the target for many commercial companies) is also taken into account when, on the opposite, they demonstrate a changing behaviour, such as a decreased interest in a service or in the whole functioning of a SN. Behavioural studies are being run in the last years to investigate the users' response to the online tracking practices[10], as well as the response to the available privacy protection tools from which policy considerations are drawn. More recently, research pays attention also to the users' response to the personal information overload. At first, the success of SN was accompanied, especially among teenagers, with an over-disclosure trend (in contrast with the legal requirement and good practice of data minimization).

---

[7] Similar survey conducted outside Europe is that of: Hoofnagle et al., *How different are Young adults from older adults when it comes to information privacy attitudes and policies* Survey, April 14, 2010.

[8] See the Eurobarometer 359, p. 7; 204.

[9] See S. Monteleone, Privacy and Data Protection at the time of facial recognition: towards a new right to digital identity?, European Journal of Law and Technology, Vol 3, n 3, 2012. N. Andrade, A. Martin, S. Monteleone, "All the Better to See You with, My Dear": Facial Recognition and Privacy in Online Social Networks, in *IEEE, Security and Privacy*, 99 2013.

[10] A. Acquisti, J Grossklags, What Can Behavioral Economics Teach Us About Privacy? In *Digital Privacy: Theory, Technologies and Practices*, Taylor and Francis Group, 2007; N. King, P. Wegner Jessen, Profiling the mobile customer – Privacy concerns when behavioural advertisers target mobile phones, *Computer Law and Security Review*, 25, 2010.

A SN like FB has been, so far, the place where to share pictures, tell stories about oneself, look at the others' profiles and 'brag' about one's everyday little achievements. However, the euphoria of the first moment seems to be replaced by a colder attitude towards the over-sharing social networking system. Though few data exist at the moment[11], it is possible that "the age of overshare...the age of brag is over".[12] Knowing what is the favorite SN of contemporary users is not the aim of this paper; however, what these new trends testify is that users start to prioritize privacy to data disclosure.

Not only DN have shown a different behaviour in terms of privacy online if compared to their parents, revealing in many case a different privacy perception[13]rather than a disregard for their personal data. They seem to have changed their same preferences as regards SN or other on-line services but more important the web community is changing and perhaps privacy need starts to be more important for young people.

This would also explain why a very popular social network like FB, as today's press reports[14], is starting to lose appeal among young people bored of the information overload and the over-exposition of themselves and friends; on the opposite, younger users seem to be more projected towards new Apps or sites (like Tumblr) that offer them a more intimate way to communicate or share (e.g., only with few, trusted people). It appears not only a question of social trends among youngsters (looking for the coolest apps) but also a question of privacy preference and identity construction. They simply may want more privacy[15].

Though young people may ignore (and it is not always the case) the risks of being tracked, of the data usage made by their favorite website, of the profiling for marketing purposes, they seem however to have started to naturally move towards "contextual social networks", more restricted platforms apt to truly shared interests[16], as well as to prefer privacy protective websites (like Tumblr, with its simple privacy

---

[11] See the Pew Internet Report on a survey conducted by the Pew Research Center that shows, if not a mass abandon to FaceBook but more a fragmentation and a shift in the behaviour of FB users, who have taken breaks from using the site in the last years (61%) and who plan to spend less time on the SN during the 2013 (an almost 40% of young users). Notable numbers point to a decreasing value and a decline in usage over the past year. The report contains also data about the Tumblr's success: http://www.pewinternet.org/~/media//Files/Reports/2013/PIP_Coming_and_going_on_facebook.pdf

[12] E. Hamburger, The age of the brag is over: why Facebook might be losing teens, The Verge, 1/03/2013.

[13] S. Monteleone, N. Andrade, Digital Native and the metamorphosis of the European Information Society, The Emerging Behavioural Trends Regarding Privacy and Their Legal Implications in S. Gutwirth et al. Data Protection: Coming of Age, pp 119-144.

[14] See V. Luckerson, "Is facebook losing its cool? Some teens think so" Time, Business & Money, 7 March 2013.

[15] The reasons for the success of a social network like Tumblr seems to lie, in fact, in the possibilities it offers to build/create two or more digital identities, as opposed to FB's one (and often real) identity.

[16] As it has been observed, companies like Facebook and Twitter "have turned their focus away from users and toward shareholders to get bigger, not better", this being also the reason why they are anymore in the list of the most innovative companies, see D. Lidsky, Fastcompany.com http://www.fastcompany.com/most-innovative-companies/2013/why-facebook-and-twitter-are-not-most-innovative-companies

policies). The private sharing seems also to be at the basis of the success of a mobile App like Snapchat and its temporary service (where photos last about only 10 seconds): as it has been observed, in our age, "where a sense of online privacy is very sacred, being able to communicate without leaving a permanent record is empowering".[17]

4   Legal and Technical Issues: Different Approaches

FB and like are called to be more agile and to adapt to the new trends; but the change is not only on this side. The new trends and changing attitudes of users with regards to their data protection are also relevant for law-makers, first, because the users' behavior (e.g., reading or ignoring the privacy policies) may impact the implementation degree of a legal requirement, such as the information obligation borne by the service provider; but also because users' behaviour, especially of DN, tell us a lot of the evolving needs of users, that cannot be ignored by a DP regulation that wants to keep pace with the times, and it obliges us to (re-)think about legal-technical responses.

The law should be attentive to the techno and socio-economic trends regarding information and communication technologies and flexible enough to adapt to new relevant changes that occur in the society (more and more merely 'Information' society), to support the technological development and (not less important) to allow the users to be more free in their preferences as regards privacy protection, at least in situations in which the rigid intervention of the law risks to result in an excess of paternalism, being sometimes dangerous instead of beneficial for the users' rights.

If the Law cannot precisely anticipate the technological trends it should at least become able to have a prospective vision of the users' attitudes and needs as regards their data protection and identity management[18]. It should be able not to fossilize itself in outdated mindsets and requirements but evolving with the technologies as the users' rights are to be benefited through the technology; it should be able to forecast what it is opportune to strictly regulate and what not, also according to what users and in particular DN manifest. Meanwhile, regulation should be firm on sensitive legal issues concerning data protection, like the unauthorized re-use of personal data, illicit data access, sensitive data processing and accountability issues.

5   The Case of the Privacy Policies

As previous studies pointed out[19], by lowering the barriers to finding privacy information, i.e., to making the access to privacy policies easier, simpler, agile and therefore more effective, users may be able to take more informed decisions regarding the usage of their personal information online. The current existing privacy policies are not effective, as surveys demonstrated, though allow companies to easily demonstrate they are compliant with privacy regulations.

---

[17] E. Hamburger, The age of the brag is over: why Facebook might be losing teens, The Verge, 1 March 2013.

[18] See S Muller, S Zouridis, M Frishman and L Kistemaker, The Law of the future and the future of Law, TOAEP, 2012.

[19] J. Tsai, L. Cranor, A. Acquisti, C. Fong, What's it to you? A survey of online privacy concerns and risks, Preliminary Progress Report 2006, *NET Institute Working Papers* n. 06-29.

The new European Proposal for Data Protection Regulation aims at strengthening the individual rights also imposing the transparency principle as a rule[20]. How to make these privacy notices more effective? Should the law impose stricter requirements for privacy policies of online providers? A similar approach might probably help users to be more aware of the usage that third parties make of their data and to be able to protect better their privacy (i.e. to limit the data disclosure); nevertheless, stricter legal requirements on how a privacy notice should appear/should what contain, would probably be countered by companies that would see them a further burden (unless they receive incentives to adopt them and the technology proposes simple and cheap solutions). Without counting the fact that those who have at the end to pay the price of this burden will be probably the same end-users, in a way or another.[21]

However, as it emerges from recent press[22], online privacy is not only imposed by regulators and urged by privacy advocates, but it became an achievement to purse for business, an asset to flaunt in competition with each other that can make the market advantage. Given that people are more and more concerned about their privacy as technology becomes an essential part of their daily life, the race among companies to convince the consumers that their data are safe is, in some ways, proving to be an effective competition driver, fruitful not only for the market but for the same privacy goals. This is especially true in the U.S. [23], where there is not a general DP Law and

---

[20] See Art 11 of the European Proposal for a general DP Regulation: "1.The controller shall have transparent and easily accessible policies with regard to the processing of personal data and for the exercise of data subjects' rights. 2. The controller shall provide any information and any communication relating to the processing of personal data to the data subject in an intelligible form, using clear and plain language, adapted to the data subject, in particular for any information addressed specifically to a child."

[21] A different issue is that related to the nature and level of regulation that would better suit with the aim of imposing precise information notices in view of protecting users' privacy. Would this role be better played at national or supranational level in order to regulate data processing, ensuring the safeguard of individual privacy rights and meanwhile the economic growth (increasingly relying in data-intensive business models)? Would a state-mandatory regulation be the best choice for this purpose or self-regulation mechanism or co-regulation strategies would better serve this scope? Lively debates around these issues take place in legal and non legal environments.

[22] S. Sengupta, 'Web privacy becomes a business imperative', *TheNewYorkTimes*, March 3, 2013.

[23] For instance, Apple started to require applications in its operating system to get permission from users before tracking their location; Microsoft turned on an anti-tracking signal in its browser, Internet Explorer, and Mozilla more recently announced that it will soon allow its users to disable third parties tracking software; moreover, the businesses have also started to provide some specific mechanisms that allow users to better control their data, like Google Plus's 'Circles', a way to keep separate sharing spaces and a context-sensitive social network. See on this: S. Sengupta,'Web privacy becomes a business imperative', *TheNewYorkTimes*, March 3, 2013. However, Google had also recently faced the strong reactions of EU Data protection Authorities after its decision to shift its privacy policies, to integrate all its products/services so to be able to collect, combine and store users data across all its online services; see on this: L. Essers, EU privacy taskforce plans to take action against Google before the summer, *Infoworld* 28 February 2013 (CNIL press release at: http://www.cnil.fr/english/ news-and-events/news/article/googles-privacy-policy-g29-ready- for-coordinated-enforcement-actions/)

where the recent attempts to curb online companies with binding privacy rules did not seem to be so far particularly successful[24]. In these conditions, the fact that companies develop privacy protecting services is also a way for companies to avoid state strict regulation. However, proposing more effective privacy-friendly mechanisms is a competitive plus for a company and fosters the development of more privacy protective tools. Said that, a question that may rise is whether the online companies should be left free to decide how to shape their privacy policies, according to a self-regulation model, instead of imposing them government restrictions on privacy[25].

What if it is, on the opposite, a mere technical problem? In this case, would the designers of technical privacy-enhancing solutions be the sole accountable for the protection/breach of individual privacy?

6   Joint Responses: Towards a Renewed Legal-Technical Approach

The right approach is not easy to seek, but it does not seem to have a unidirectional nature[26]. In particular, the EU policy challenge in this field will be to conciliate its classical fundamental rights approach with a more technological or market-driven one[27]. Probably the reasons of inadequate responses available so far are to be found in the fact that legal and technical issues have been addressed as two completely separate fields, though a legal-technical approach to privacy problems has been urged

---

[24] The reference is in particular to the Do Not Track systems launched a couple of years ago in the U.S. DNT is a browser setting that would allow Internet users indicate that they do not want their activities to be tracked, but no consensus has been reached among privacy advocates, Internet companies and online advertisers. See J Melvin, Do not Track Internet spat risks legislative crackdown, *Business News*, 24/07/2012. However, a new bill, aimed to ensure that web browsers and online companies provide users with opt-out options of being tracked by advertisers, has been recently introduced in the U.S. Senate, See D. Kerr, Do Not track privacy bill reintroduced in Senate, CNET News, 28/02/2013.

[25] This kind of question arose for instance in the occasion of the recent launch of the 'privacy lockers'. The underlying principles are in line with a propriety rights approach of personal data, as they assume that a data-subject is the 'owner' of her data-assets, who can decide (and transact) about their use. A market of personal data management tools is already emerging. These start-up companies, that promise to work as data lockers are Azigo, Mydex, the Data Banker, Personel.com, Connect.me. They work as cyber-lockers that would allow users to store own personal data and meanwhile as personal digital assistant.

[26] See Y. Welinder. A Face Tells More than a Thousand Posts: Developing Face Recognition Privacy in Social Networks. *Harvard Journal of Law and Technology*, 26(1):165-239, 2012, who stressed that even good market-based solutions should to be considered possible only in combination with legal (i.e. consent and information notice requirements) and technological ones (i.e., privacy-by-design/notices).

[27] Legal studies have already demonstrated that the adoption of a property-oriented vision of personal data also in Europe is not only formally possible, but that offers also advantages in solving data protection issues, see: N. Purtova, *Property Rights in Personal Data. A European perspective*, Kluwer Law International 2012.

since years[28]. Several scholars stressed that many privacy concerns may be addressed through a good design that embeds fundamental privacy principles[29].

Some good examples of experiments and studies are not missing as mentioned below. However, political resistances or practical difficulties prevent their adoption. Examples of the implementation of a legal-technical approach, better called as privacy by design[30], are, for instance, the privacy agents studied for online environments or for the more concealed data processing carried out in ubiquitous computing (Ambient Intelligence)[31]. Similar to these agents are the tools ideated to make privacy policies more accessible[32] or more effective by increasing their interactive nature (like the 'visceral notices')[33]. Other studies, for instance in behavioural economics, propose the introduction of (tested) tools like 'privacy nudges' for behavioural advertising, location sharing and social networks.[34] An example of techno-legal mechanism, introduced recently in Europe, that has also an economic impact, is the 'privacy seal'.[35]

The problem with many of these solutions is that their implementation may be difficult in practice and burdensome for businesses.

---

[28] Y. Poullet (2005). Pour une troisième génération de réglementations de protection de données, *Jusletter*, 3 (22); M. Hildebrandt (2008c), Legal and technological normativity: more (and less) than twin sisters, *Techné: research in philosophy and Technology,* 12, 3, who sustains, however, that technological devices should be regulated by the law, "precisely because they are able to regulate and constitute our interactions".

[29] T Olsen, and T Mahler, 'Identity management and data protection law: Risk, responsibility and compliance in 'Circles of Trust''. Computer Law and Security Report, *23,* (4&5) 2007; A Murray, Information Technology Law. The Law and Society, Oxford University Press (2010); on the concepts of 'Transparency Enhancing Technologies' (allowing citizens to anticipate how they will be profiled and the consequence of that) see M. Hildebrandt (2012). Hull, G, Lipford, HR and Latulipe C (2011), 'Contextual Gaps: Privacy issues on Facebook', Ethics and Information Technology, 4; S. Monteleone, 'Privacy and Data Protection at the time of Facial Recognition: towards a new right to Digital Identity?' European Journal of Law and Technology, 3/3, http://ejlt.org//article/view/168/257

[30] See A. Cavukian, Privacy by design and the emerging personal data ecosystem, October 2012. http://www.ipc.on.ca/images/Resources/pbd-pde.pdf

[31] D Le Métayer, S Monteleone. Automated consent through privacy agents: Legal requirements and technical architecture. *Computer Law & Security Review,* Elsevier, 25(2), 2009. L. F. Cranor, User Interface for privacy agents in *ACM TOCHI,* vol 13, 2, 2006.

[32] See for instance, the Privacy Finder (a privacy-enhanced search engine) described in J. Tsai, L. Cranor, A. Acquisti, C. Fong, What's it to you? A survey of online privacy concerns and risks, Preliminary Progress Report 2006, *NET Institute Working Papers n. 06-29.* The ability of this privacy-enhanced search engine (a P3P tool) to provide information that address privacy concerns is explored by Tsai et al., who conclude that privacy concerns and risks may be mitigated through the design of tools that make online privacy notices more accessible and easy to find.

[33] R. Calo, Against notice scepticism in privacy (and elsewhere), *87 Notre Dame Law Review* (2012).

[34] A. Acquisti, From the Economics to the Behavioral Economics of Privacy: A Note, in *Ethics and Policy of Biometrics,* 6005, Springer, 2010.

[35] See for instance the IXquick search engine, the first to receive the EU privacy seal https://www.ixquick.com/eng/protect-privacy.html

If we look at the adequacy of the European legal framework, especially in view of the criticisms received by online businesses to its ongoing reform, we should consider what the Art 29 Working Party has affirmed: despite the emergence of new technologies and globalization, the core principles of European data protection are still valid, but "the level of data protection in the EU can benefit from a better application of the existing data protection principles in practice".[36] In other words, what we miss as users are not principles and values but more suitable, interactive and effective privacy tools, able to embed in the same technological design data protection rules, but also capable to keep pace with the times.

With the aim to tackle some of these issues, the study 'Behavioural responses to online tracking and profiling' are being undertaken at the IPTS, JRC of the European Commission[37], the results of which are expected to be published in 2014.

References

1. Acquisti, A.: From the Economics to the Behavioral Economics of Privacy: A Note. In: Kumar, A., Zhang, D. (eds.) ICEB 2010. LNCS, vol. 6005, pp. 23–26. Springer, Heidelberg (2010)
2. Andrade, N., Martin, A., Monteleone, S.: All the Better to See You with, My Dear: Facial Recognition and Privacy in Online Social Networks. In: IEEE, Security and Privacy, vol. 99 (2013)
3. Andrade, N., Monteleone, S.: Digital Native and the metamorphosis of the European Information Society, The Emerging Behavioural Trends Regarding Privacy and Their Legal Implications. In: Gutwirth, S., et al. (eds.) Data Protection: Coming of Age, pp. 119–144
4. Calo, R.: Against notice scepticism in privacy (and elsewhere), 87 Notre Dame Law Review (2012),
   http://cyberlaw.stanford.edu/files/publication/files/ssrn-id1790144.pdf
5. Cavukian, A.: Privacy by design and the emerging personal data ecosystem (October 2012)
6. Cranor, L.F.: User Interface for privacy agents in ACM TOCHI 13(2) (2006)
7. Essers, L.: EU privacy taskforce plans to take action against Google before the summer. Infoworld (February 28, 2013), http://www.infoworld.com/d/security/eu-privacy-taskforce-plans-take-action-against-google-the-summer-213675
8. European Commission, Special Eurobarometer 359 (2011), http://ec.europa.eu/public_opinion/archives/ebs/ebs_359_en.pdf
9. Hildebrandt, M.: Legal and technological normativity: more (and less) than twin sisters. Techné: Research in Philosophy and Technology 12(3) (2008c)
10. Hoofnagle, et al.: How different are Young adults from older adults when it comes to information privacy attitudes and policies Survey (April 14, 2010), http://www.ftc.gov/os/comments/privacyroundtable/544506-00125.pdf

---

[36] Article 29 WP, "The Future of Privacy. Joint contribution to the Consultation of the European Commission on the legal framework for the fundamental right to protection of personal data", 2009a.

[37] http://is.jrc.ec.europa.eu/pages/Mission.html

11. Le Métayer, D., Monteleone, S.: Automated consent through privacy agents: Legal requirements and technical architecture. Computer Law & Security Review 25(2) (2009)
12. Melvin, J.: Do not Track Internet spat risks legislative crackdown. Business News (July 24, 2012)
13. Monteleone, S.: Privacy and Data Protection at the time of Facial Recognition: towards a new right to Digital Identity? European Journal of Law and Technology 3(3), http://ejlt.org//article/view/168/257
14. Muller, S., Zouridis, S., Frishman, M., Kistemaker, L.: The Law of the future and the future of Law. TOAEP (2012)
15. Murray, A.: Information Technology Law. The Law and Society. Oxford University Press (2010); Hildebrandt, M.: (2012); Hull, G., Lipford, H.R., Latulipe, C.: Contextual Gaps: Privacy issues on Facebook. Ethics and Information Technology 4 (2011), http://ssrn.com/abstract=1427546
16. Olsen, T., Mahler, T.: Identity management and data protection law: Risk, responsibility and compliance in Circles of Trust. Computer Law and Security Report 23(4&5) (2007), http://dx.doi.org/10.1016/j.clsr.2007.05.009
17. Poullet, Y.: Pour une troisième génération de réglementations de protection de données. Jusletter 3(22) (2005)
18. Purtova, N.: Property Rights in Personal Data. A European perspective. Kluwer Law International (2012)
19. Sengupta, S.: Web privacy becomes a business imperative. TheNewYorkTimes (March 3, 2013), http://www.nytimes.com/2013/03/04/technology/amid-do-not-track-effort-web-companies-race-to-look-privacy-friendly.html?pagewanted=all&goback=%2Egde_4255573_member_219668331&_r=0
20. Tsai, J., Cranor, L., Acquisti, A., Fong, C.: What's it to you? A survey of online privacy concerns and risks, Preliminary Progress Report 2006, NET Institute Working Papers n. 06-29, accessible at http://papers.ssrn.com/sol3/papers.cfm?abstract_id=941708
21. Welinder, Y.: A Face Tells More than a Thousand Posts: Developing Face Recognition Privacy in Social Networks. Harvard Journal of Law and Technology 26(1), 165–239 (2012)

Part IV
User Centric Security and Privacy

Addressing User Privacy and Experience in Distributed Long Lifetime Systems

Scott W. Cadzow

Cadzow Communications Consulting Ltd.
(as partner to European Research projects i-Tour and i-SCOPE)
scott@cadzow.com

Abstract. Very large distributed systems that aim to offer natural interaction with their human users fail to address the everyday nature of trust and its establishment at their peril. In human interactions trust builds slowly, it builds contextually, and it builds by association. In contrast most software systems make assumptions regarding user behaviour and do little to learn at the natural pace of the user, this leads to an unnatural relationship between the user and the software, system or service they are using. The claims of social networking to address this only go so far as in many cases the objectives of the service and those of the user do not align or one melds to the other – treating a person as a social network entity quite distinct from that same person as a natural person. What this paper intends to show is how the privacy and security problem is being addressed across the smart city projects in Europe with particular emphasis placed on material from case studies taken from the i-Tour and i-SCOPE projects.

1   Introduction

Colouring almost all of human interaction is trust. This assertion covers every aspect of human endeavour whether that be in work, sport, parenting, …, in fact it is difficult to identify a single relationship that does not depend to some extent on trust. As we move our lives to an increasingly virtual world and to greater reliance on software and machines we need to also re-evaluate trust and how to engage our human instincts for trust in the machine world. Trust, by colouring human interaction, also determines to some extent how we experience an event as trust and confidence become synonymous.

2   i-Tour and i-SCOPE Project Goals

A very simple list of *i-Tour*'s functional goals are the following:

- Multi-modal personalised urban route planning and route maintenance
- Goal based rewards for using the system and thus the public transport resources of the host
- Point of interest recommender engine

.. Marinos and I. Askoxylakis (Eds.): HAS/HCII 2013, LNCS 8030, pp. 297–305, 2013.
© Springer-Verlag Berlin Heidelberg 2013

i-SCOPE extends this list by adding capabilities of individuals to upload noise maps and the routing model is extended with detail architectural models written in cityGML to enable, in particular, multi-modal routing for wheelchair users and to address solar potential of the host city.

3   Challenges

The challenge for both privacy and security is in both the conflict between privacy and security and in the conflict in managing privacy and security with the personalisation at the core of *i-Tour*'s and *i-SCOPE*'s functionality.

The core model in i-Tour and i-SCOPE for security and privacy is based on the simple access control model: *Entity "A" allows entity "B" to process data from "A" only under the agreed constraints "C"*. This introduces another problem for design as stated by Donald Rumsfeld "*... there are known knowns ... there are known unknowns ... there are also unknown unknowns ...*" which whilst being unwieldy political speak points to a key problem in security work, that of establishing (and proving) a security and privacy boundary. As systems become more complex, and interactions with them become more developed over time, the establishment of that boundary become increasingly crucial in establishing the security, privacy and trust relationship.

The role of privacy as an attribute in trust is well understood in human relationships. However much of the technical work in protecting privacy has been addressed from a security standpoint, i.e. assuring confidentiality of data or providing complex access control models. Trust and privacy are in practice softer technologies that provide reinforcement that privileged information given is enacted on within the bounds of a mutually agreed policy (the "C" in the generic access control statement). The approach of developing non-repudiation of consent structures within a policy driven processing engine allows for contraction and expansion of the allowed policy as the relationship evolves allowing a more natural development of a relationship.

The human model of trust is complex, slow, and expensive, but it is also ultimately resilient. This compares quite badly to the normal trust models used in computing systems where the model is often reduced to trust for a single transaction with third parties brought into the loop to give validation. In human terms this is like saying "you can trust Angela, David does, and you trust David", so trusting David establishes the model for trusting Angela. The problem here is that you may trust David on a tennis court as a reliable partner but may not trust his financial judgement and you are asking Angela for financial advice. It is this very contextual nature of trust that is natural in human interactions but that is notoriously difficult to make work for machine interactions.

There are specific privacy issues raised by i-Tour that need care in handling to ensure i-Tour is acceptable both from a regulatory viewpoint and from a user viewpoint. An example is taken from the "bootstrapping" sequence in the "trust based recommender system" in which the initial hypothesis is that the system "doesn't know what I like, but does know where I live, where I work, when I travel and how (e.g. from Oyster card data)". The privacy challenge is to ensure that the hypothesis can build communities and make recommendations without allowing unauthorized parties to make assertions related to the person.

4   Developing Contextual Trust

In the i-Tour project contextual trust in recommender systems and in the privacy model has been key to the basic design. For example when reading reviews and recommendations for hotels you may be more likely to trust the opinions of real travellers who have actually stayed at the hotel than employees of the hotel or competitors to the hotel. We understand trust as incremental, contextual and relationship centred. In building a framework built from conventional asymmetric and symmetric cryptographic security modules to meet the requirement of incremental, contextual and relationship centred trust one of the keys is to develop policy as testable statements. In itself this step is still in development by taking TPlan as a candidate language and extending it to the new language ExTRA.

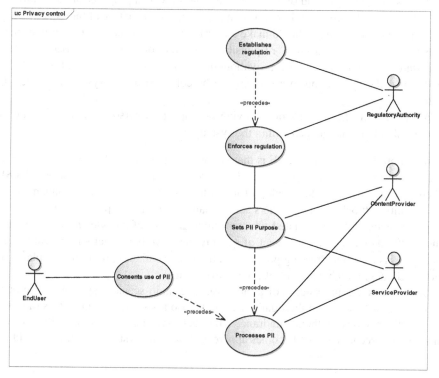

Fig. 1. Use cases for use of Personal Identifiable Information (PII)

It is important to note that privacy is a protected right and there is a significant body of legislation in Europe that applies to organisations seeking to gather personal data with consequences including criminal prosecution for failure to properly maintain the right to privacy of those they interact with. This is a very "hot" topic in society with high stakes in both the protection of the rights to privacy and the use of the same data to build business. In approaching this topic i-Tour is taking the view that it has to be open about the risks and impacts of its design on privacy and security.

Many of the privacy concerns raised by consumers regarding the use and deployment of any new technology surround the uncertainty of the system design, its operation and its intent. An increasingly prevalent privacy concern is that of the system's capability to track individuals. For i-Tour tracking is core as this is required to make routing decisions and to offer recommendations to users, thus it is essential that such tracking information is not open to exploit of the i-Tour users.

i-Tour and i-SCOPE when deployed have to meet the expectations of privacy established in the Organisation for Economic Co-operation and Development (OECD) Declaration of Human Rights, the EU Data Protection laws, and the EU Convention on human rights and which can be summarised as defining the following top level objectives for the system.

— Access to services should only be granted to users with appropriate authorization;
— The identity of a user should not be compromised by any action of the system;
— No action of the system should make a user liable to be the target of identity crime;
— No change in the ownership, responsibility, content or collection of personal data pertaining to a user should occur without that user's consent or knowledge;
— Personal data pertaining to a user should be collected by the system using legitimate means only;
— An audit trail of all transactions having an impact on personal data pertaining to users should be maintained within the system.

Core to both i-Tour and i-SCOPE is that an increasing amount of people are living in cities and, by 2030, the number will be close to 5 billion (United Nations 2008). Therefore, it is essential to develop efficient techniques to assist the management of modern cities. It behoves researchers across many disciplines to pay attention to smart cities, as technologies associated to smart cities are part of knowledge-based economies with a key being development of socially inclusive but socially responsible services. In this regard addressing privacy and trust is essential in providing the platform for social integration by citizens of future smart cities.

Smart cities are an example of a multi-variable multi-scenario system whose purpose is to assist citizens in their daily life and to also assist the administrators of cities to run their cities without hindrance. In such systems the complexity of the trust/privacy/security model becomes apparent. Smart city systems and their providers

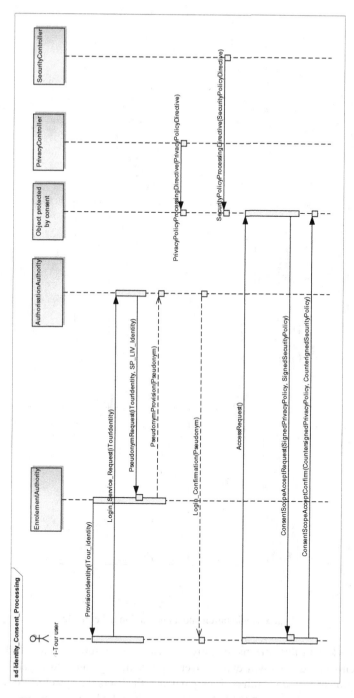

Fig. 2. Simplified processing to allow non-repudiation of consent

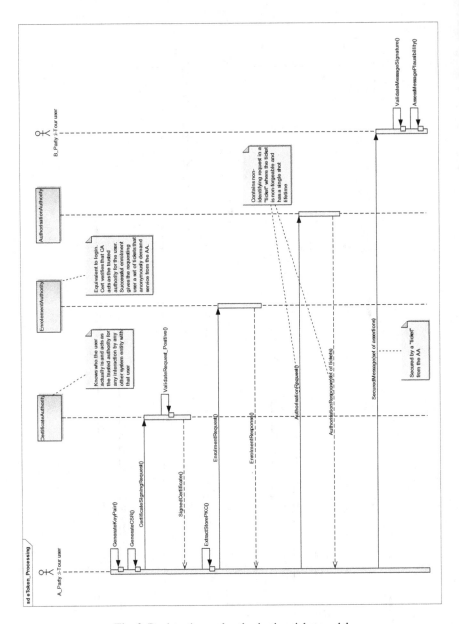

Fig. 3. Registration and authorisation ticket model

have to work with the citizens, employers, visitors to ensure they all work together. The systems themselves will evolve over time gathering data and capability as they grow. If growth is unconstrained it may damage the users the systems are intended to serve therefore we have to be able to bring growth and education into the lifecycle of our systems. Without intending to anthropomorphize systems lending them some of the characteristics of human nature regarding relationships with their users is part of the path to make systems that appear as partners. As trust is established over a long period of time in normal human relationships, and where introductions form part of normal relationship establishments, so should the relationships of users and systems. As an example using a mobile phone as a sensor in gathering noise data may use the mobile phone operator as the party that introduces the user to the noise measurement agency, but once the initial introduction is achieved and the new relationship established there is no need for details of the relationships to be shared. Whilst this form of introduction and use of trusted third parties has been used to underpin much of the public key cryptography at the heart of digital signature it has not been developed to assist in the business and social interactions at the heart of smart cities.

What i-Tour and i-SCOPE have introduced is an extension of non-repudiation to consent. The aim in general is that policy has to be properly machine processable and in i-Tour and i-SCOPE we are taking the step of extending the test notation TPlan to cover assertions and requirements.

5 Summary and Conclusions

In summary the role of privacy as an attribute in trust is well understood in human relationships. However much of the technical work in protecting privacy has been addressed from a security standpoint, i.e. assuring confidentiality of data or providing complex access control models. Trust and privacy are however considered in this work as softer edged to provide reinforcement that privileged information given is enacted on within the bounds of a mutually agreed policy. The approach allows for contraction and expansion of the allowed policy as the relationship evolves allowing a more natural development of a relationship.

6 Definitions and Abbreviations

Confidentiality: The process of ensuring that information is accessible only to those authorized to have access

Privacy: Right of the individual to have his identity, agency and action protected from any unwanted scrutiny and interference

NOTE: Privacy reinforces the individual's right to decisional autonomy and self-determination which are fundamental rights accorded to individuals within Europe.

References

1. ETSI EG 201 940: Human Factors (HF); User Identification solutions in converging networks
2. ETSI EG 202 067: Universal Communications Identifier (UCI); System framework

3. ETSI TR 187 011: Telecommunications and Internet converged Services and Protocols for Advanced Networking (TISPAN); NGN Security; Application of ISO-15408-2 requirements to ETSI standards - guide, method and application with examples

4. ETSI TR 187 020: Radio Frequency Identification (RFID); Coordinated ESO response to Phase 1 of EU Mandate M436

5. ETSI TS 102 165-1: Telecommunications and Internet converged Services and Protocols for Advanced Networking (TISPAN); Methods and protocols; Part 1: Method and proforma for Threat, Risk, Vulnerability Analysis

6. ETSI TS 187 001 Telecommunications and Internet converged Services and Protocols for Advanced Networking (TISPAN); NGN SECurity (SEC); Requirements

7. Clark, R.V.: UK Home Office; Hot Products: understanding, anticipating and reducing demand for stolen goods, ISBN 1-84082-278-3

8. ITU-T Recommendation X.509 (11/2008): Information technology – Open Systems Interconnection – The Directory: Public-key and attribute certificate frameworks

9. ISO/IEC 15408-1: Information technology - Security techniques - Evaluation criteria for IT security - Part 1: Introduction and general model

10. SO/IEC 15408-2: Information technology - Security techniques - Evaluation criteria for IT security - Part 2: Security functional requirements

11. ISO/IEC 17799 2005: Information technology - Security techniques - Code of practice for information security management

12. Directive 95/46/EC of the European Parliament and of the Council of 24 October 1995 on the protection of individuals with regard to the processing of personal data and on the free movement of such data

13. Directive 2002/58/EC of the European Parliament and of the council of 12 July 2002 concerning the processing of personal data and the protection of privacy in the electronic communications sector (Directive on privacy and electronic communications)

14. Recommendation of the OECD Council in 1980 concerning guidelines governing the protection of privacy and transborder flows of personal data (the OECD guidelines for personal data protection

15. European Convention on Human Rights (ECHR) (long title: Convention for the Protection of Human Rights and Fundamental Freedoms)

16. Universal Declaration of Human Rights

17. David, C.: Blind signatures for untraceable payments. Advances in Cryptology Proceedings of Crypto 82(3), 199–203 (1983)

18. Article 29 of Directive 95/46/EC Working group (an independent European advisory body on data protection and privacy. Its tasks are described in Article 30 of Directive 95/46/EC and Article 15 of Directive 2002/58/EC): Opinion 15/2011 on the definition of consent (adopted on July 13, 2011)

19. Article 29 of Directive 95/46/EC Working group Opinion 13/2011 on Geolocation services on smart mobile devices (adopted on 16 May 2011)

20. Privacy Impact Assessment Handbook,
http://www.ico.gov.uk/upload/documents/pia_handbook_html_v2/files/PIAhandbookV2.pdf

21. Fletcher, G.: Identity in practice blog: Privacy across Social Network aggregation,
http://practicalid.blogspot.com/2010/09/privacy-across-social-network.html

22. Shannon, C.E.: A Mathematical Theory of Communication. Bell System Technical Journal 27, 379–423, 623–656 (1948)

23. ISO/IEC 15408: Information technology - Security techniques - Evaluation Criteria for IT security
24. ISO/IEC 10181-3: Information technology - Open Systems Interconnection - Security frameworks for open systems: Access control framework
25. ISO 14977: Extended Backus-Naur Form (EBNF) syntactic meta-language
26. Kerckhoffs, A.: La cryptographiemilitaire. Journal des Sciences Militaires IX, 5–38, 161–191 (1883)
27. Computer Misuse Act 1990: An Act to make provision for securing computer material against unauthorised access or modification; and for connected purposes, http://www.legislation.gov.uk/ukpga/1990/18/contents

Secure and Energy-Efficient Life-Logging in Wireless Pervasive Environments

Alexandros Fragkiadakis*, Ioannis Askoxylakis, and Elias Tragos

Institute of Computer Science, Foundation for Research and Technology - Hellas
(FORTH)
P.O. Box 1385, GR 711 10 Heraklion, Crete, Greece
{alfrag,asko,etragos}@ics.forth.gr

Abstract. The current proliferation of ubiquitous networking (e.g. WiFi, bluetooth) along with the high penetration of the pervasive devices (smart phones, tablets) have provided a substantial boost to life-logging; a framework for the every-day recording of sensitive and personal data of individuals. Life-logging systems usually consist of resource-constrained devices (sensors). Moreover, as for every emerging technology, life-logging is susceptible to a number of security threats. In this paper, we implement and evaluate a joint encryption and compression scheme using the current advances in compressed sensing theory. The evaluation shows that the reconstruction error is kept low even for high compression ratios, and the power consumption of the life-logging system significantly reduces.

1 Introduction

The current advances in technology and especially the penetration of the pervasive devices (smart phones, tablets) along with the proliferation of ubiquitous networking (WiFi, WiMAX, blueetooth) have provided a substantial boost to the convenient recording of the every-day life activities. This is called as life-logging (LL) and includes all sort of personal activities like diaries, storage of photographs, etc.

As every emerging technology, LL faces a number of security threats. Typical LL systems employ a number of sensors, either contained within the pervasive devices, or in a form of dedicated and independent devices (e.g [1]) grouped and forming a wireless sensor network (WSN). WSNs and pervasive devices face unique threats, and a vast number of algorithms has been proposed to combat these threats. Adversaries usually try to steal very sensitive data, therefore encryption is required in a LL system. However, as the LL systems are mainly based on severe resource constrained devices (often battery-operated), lightweight encryption schemes are of paramount importance in order to prolong LL lifetime.

In this work, we perform joint encryption and compression in a WSN using the relatively new theory of compressed sensing (CS). Using CS, data are compressed and encrypted concurrently without any extra overhead, offering a very

---

* Corresponding author.

L. Marinos and I. Askoxylakis (Eds.): HAS/HCII 2013, LNCS 8030, pp. 306–315, 2013.

high secrecy and decryption fidelity. We provide performance evaluation results in terms of the power consumption and the reconstruction error for different compression ratios. Several related contributions include physical-layer security using CS ([2,3]). Others consider CS for image or speech encryption [4,5].

The rest of this paper is organized as follows. Section 2 describes the general idea behind the LL systems. In Section 3 we discuss the privacy and security considerations. Section 4 described energy considerations for LL. The CS-based encryption scheme is presented in Section 5. Section 6 presents the performance evaluation while the conclusions appear in Section 7.

2 Life-Logging

Life-logging refers to the collection, storage, interpretation, and sharing of information related to an individuals' personal life. LL is not a totally new concept as V. Bush described his vision for life recording back in 1945 ([6]). He envisioned *memex*, a device having the role of an enlarged intimate supplement to one's memory, used by individuals for the compression and storage of records, books, communications, etc. Some primitive forms of LL are the handwritten diaries, and the storage of personal photograph into photo albums. Nowadays, people more frequently store and share personal data with their relatives, friends, and colleagues due to the high penetration of pervasive devices (smart phones, computers) and associated technologies (bluetooth, IEEE 802.11).

Typical LL applications include:

- **Personal archiving**. Current technology advancements have made feasible to individuals the possession of high-volume storage devices in a relatively low cost. Given this ability, people can now store on a very frequent basis personal data on smart phones, laptops, etc. These data comprise parts of their everyday life that are recorded and archived. Emerging LL implementations (e.g [7,8,9]) enhance LL by automating the data collection and storage operations, thus off-loading users and providing a convenient use of the LL services.

- **Emergency response and disaster relief**. As LL systems are mainly based on sensors for data collection, they can be used for emergency response and disaster relief. Smart LL systems that can measure vital information (e.g. heart beat) along with an appropriate backhaul communication network ([10]) can be used to detect and provide immediate medical assistance to victims after a disaster has occurred.

- **Tele-medicine**. Tele-medicine is another area where LL systems can be employed. Micro-sensor networks can monitor, record, and transmit to a central node several information such as blood pressure, heartbeat, etc., forming a tele-medicine infrastructure for the provision of clinical care to people located at a distance ([11]).

- **Human memory augmentation**. Memory is a key human facility for supporting life activities (social interactions, life management, problem solving, etc). As human memory is not perfect, memory problems can arise for normal people occasionally. A LL memory augmenting framework can significantly assist people as it logs their everyday activities ([12]). Such a LL system can provide valuable help in case of more serious memory problems like the episodic memory impairment ([13]).

– **Law enforcement.** Often people are involved in serious crimes. In many cases the law enforcement agencies fail to locate and prosecute the offenders, and justice cannot be served due to the lack of evidence. At this direction, LL becomes a useful tool (e.g. audio and video footage collection from a crime scene) for the authorities and for the fight against crime.

3   Privacy and Security Considerations

Both users and society can benefit from the LL systems. However, as these systems record, store, and share very personal information, there is always the risk for users of loosing privacy. A number of major risks have been identified [14]: (i) **surveillance**: individuals are monitored by governmental agencies, business organizations, etc., without their desire, (ii) **memory hazards**: LL can cause rumination for unipolar and bipolar depression as it can remind people of their past bad experiences, (iii) **long term availability of personal information**: LL can be a permanent record of peoples' mistakes, and (iv) **stealing LL information**: as LL records very sensitive data, the chance of loss or theft is increased.

In general, a LL process has tree stages [14]: (i) data sensing, (ii) data collection, and (iii) data browsing by the users. In practice, LL systems become feasible through the use of sensors that can be of different types: (i) desktop applications ([15]), (ii) pervasive devices such as cameras and smart phones ([7]), and (iii) dedicated sensors in motes ([1]). The last two types of sensors is expected to be heavily utilized in LL, given the proliferation of the pervasive devices (especially the smart phones), and the advances in ubiquitous networking (IEEE 802.11, IEEE 802.15.4, bluetooth).

Often sensors are grouped into WSNs. Several attacks and at different layers can be launched against a WSN. Jamming attacks at the physical layer; collision, exhaustion and unfairness at the medium access layer; sybil attacks and acknowledgment spoofing at the network layer; and flooding and synchronization attacks at the transport layer can cause severe security breaches and performance degradation [16].

A security breach in a LL system can cause loss or theft of very personal and sensitive data of individuals. This in turn could have several negative effects in those individuals: (i) lack of trust in technology, (ii) identity theft, (iii) unauthorized surveillance, and (iv) harm to their reputation.

4   Energy-Efficiency for Security Operations

Typical LL systems are realized using sensors (e.g. [7,9]) and WSNs. Fig. 1 shows such a system employing two WSNs with sensors that can perform operations such as location tracking ([17]), pervasive devices such as smart phones ([7]) and tablets that can monitor user-sensitive data like location, emails, incoming calls, etc., and a LL repository where all these data are collected. A backhaul network with technologies like WiFi, WiMAX, and 4G is used to interconnect the WSNs and the pervasive devices with the LL repository. It is obvious that sensors are fundamental elements of a LL system, and as they are severe resource-constrained devices, energy efficiency is of paramount importance. Sensors are usually battery-operated devices (e.g. smart phones) and therefore a resilient and secure framework for LL should employ lightweight algorithms that substantially prolong their lifetime. Moreover, such a framework should meet the following requirements [16]: (i) resiliency, having the ability to maintain an acceptable level of security in case of attacks, (ii) scalability, as LL systems use a large number of sensors, (iii) robustness: to operate despite abnormalities such as node failures and attacks, (iv) assurance: having the ability to discriminate different information at different assurance levels to the users. In the next section, we propose and evaluate a security algorithm for joint encryption and compression in a WSN for LL purposes.

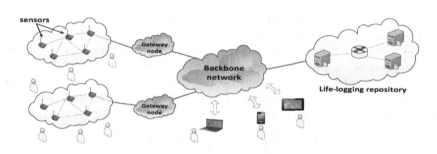

Fig. 1. A typical life-logging framework

5 Joint Encryption and Compression Using Compressed Sensing Techniques

There are several contributions in the area of security and especially for encryption in WSNs (e.g. [18,19]). Most of these works either perform encryption only, without considering compression, or use encryption and compression separately. In this work, we use the compressed sensing (CS) principles in order to apply joint compression and encryption.

5.1 Background on Compressed Sensing

The recently proposed theory of compressed sensing (CS) ([20]) unifies compression and encryption in order to minimize the overhead for data acquisition and sampling in a WSN. CS exploits the signal structure in order to enable a significant reduction in the sampling and computation costs at a central unit. The key principles in the development of CS theory are *sparsity* and *incoherence*. A signal $x \in \mathbb{R}^N$ is called sparse if most of its elements are zero in a specific transformation basis. Incoherence satisfies the fact that the sampling/sensing waveforms have an extremely dense representation in the basis. Assuming signal $x \in \mathbb{R}^N$ is sparse in a basis Ψ, it can be written as $x = \Psi b$, where $b \in \mathbb{R}^N$ is a sparse vector with S non-zero components ($\|b\|_0 = S$). CS theory proves that an S-sparse signal x can be reconstructed exactly with high probability from M randomized linear projections of the signal x into a measurement matrix $\Phi \in \mathbb{R}^{M \times N}$. The general measurement model is expressed as follows:

$$y = \Phi x = \Phi \Psi b = \Theta b \tag{1}$$

where $\Theta = \Psi \Phi$.

The original vector b and consequently the sparse signal x, is estimated by solving the following ℓ_0-norm constrained optimization problem:

$$\hat{b} = \arg\min \|b\|_0 \quad s.t. \quad y = \Theta b \tag{2}$$

where the $\|b\|_0$ norm counts the number of non-zero components of b. Note that the formulation of the optimization problem in (2) uses an l_0 norm that measures signal sparsity instead than the traditionally used in signal processing applications l_2 norm, which measures signal energy. However, solving (2) is both numerically unstable and NP-complete. For this reason, the ℓ_0 norm can be replaced by the ℓ_1 norm and problem (2) can be rephrased as the following ℓ_1 norm convex relaxation problem:

$$\hat{b} = \arg\min \|b\|_1 \quad s.t. \quad y = \Theta b. \tag{3}$$

The ℓ_1 norm ($\|b\|_1 := \sum_i |b_i|$) can exactly recover the S-sparse signal with high probability using only $M \geq CS \log(N/S)$ measurements ($C \in R^+$) [20]. Finally, the reconstructed signal is given by $\hat{x} = \Psi \hat{b}$. A variety of reconstruction algorithms based on linear programming, convex relaxation, and greedy strategies have been proposed to solve (3). Among them, greedy strategies such as the Orthogonal Matching Pursuit (OMP) [21] are computationally efficient when the signal of interest is highly sparse.

5.2   The Secrecy and Robustness of Compressed Sensing

The vast majority of the related contributions in encryption and/or compression schemes for WSNs (e.g. [22,23]) consider encryption and compression as two separate and distinct operations. This increases the computation overhead, and encryption is usually carried out before compression. Fig. 2a shows a conventional scheme where data are collected, then compression follows and finally, encryption is performed using a secret key, prior to transmission through the communication channel (e.g a wireless network). On the other hand, CS can be used for joint compression and encryption (Fig. 2b). This has the inherent advantage that encryption and compression occur concurrently with no extra overhead.

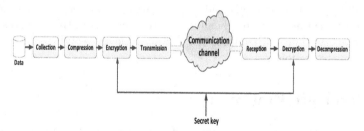

(a) Conventional scheme with separate encryption/compression and decryption/decompression operations

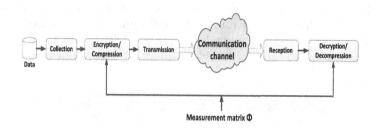

(b) Compressed sensing scheme for joint encryption/compression and decryption/decompression operations

Fig. 2. Conventional and Compressed sensing schemes for encryption/compression and decryption/decompression

Assuming the collected data (plaintext) have the form of a signal $x \in \mathbb{R}^N$, the ciphertext ($y \in \mathbb{R}^M$) is generated applying CS using (1); therefore, the secret key in this case is the measurement matrix $\Phi \in \mathbb{R}^{M \times N}$. As $M < N$, compression is concurrently performed with the compression ratio controlled by the value of M. Joint decryption and decompression, referred as reconstruction in CS terminology, can be performed using algorithms such as the OMP [21].

The encryption/decryption process for CS uses the matrix Φ as a shared secret between two communicating entities. Very often in CS, Φ is generated using a Gaussian distribution. It has been shown ([20]) that this type of matrix allows for a very accurate reconstruction. Moreover, Φ affects CS secrecy as adversaries usually try to exploit the secret key used. Orsdemir et al. [24] show that the CS-based encryption scheme: (i) although it does not achieve a perfect secrecy, its secrecy is very high, and (ii) it is resilient to noise, thus immune to adversaries that try to create noise on purpose. Furthermore, they study two types of attacks against such a scheme. The first one is a brute force attack where an adversary tries to guess matrix $\mathbf{\Phi}$. The authors show that this type of attack has a very high computational complexity that makes it practically infeasible. The second type of attack considers an adversary that tries to estimate matrix $\mathbf{\Phi}$ and a sparse signal $\mathbf{x} \in \mathbb{R}^N$ with S non-zero coefficients, given the ciphertext $\mathbf{y} \in \mathbb{R}^M$, such that $\mathbf{\Phi}\mathbf{x} = \mathbf{y}$. As shown, also this type of attack is of very high complexity. Hence, a CS-based encryption scheme has three very attractive features: (i) it offers joint encryption and compression, (ii) it achieves very high secrecy, and (iii) it is resilient to noise.

6   Performance Evaluation

In order to investigate the performance of joint encryption/compression using CS, we consider the WSN topology shown in Fig. 3. This consists of 16 Z1 sensors [1] and a single sink (having the id:1). We emulate the WSN testbed using Contiki [25], an open source operating system for WSNs, and Cooja; its simulator/emulator. The distance between the sensors is 40 meters, their transmission power is set at 0 dbM, and for routing the RPL protocol [26] is used. Also, all sensors periodically (every 15 seconds) transmit UDP packets to the sink. We run each simulation 20 times, with a duration of 20 minutes for each run.

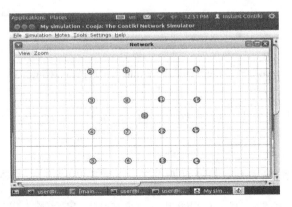

Fig. 3. Wireless sensor network topology

We begin by investigating the reconstruction error for different compression ratios. Each sensor performs joint encryption-compression and decryption-decompression as shown in Fig. 2b. Initially, each sensor creates a measurement matrix $\mathbf{\Phi} \in \mathbb{R}^{M \times N}$ using a Gaussian distribution. Plaintext $\mathbf{x} \in \mathbb{R}^N$ consists of ambient temperature measurements provided by [27]. As we have verified, this set of values is highly sparse in the frequency domain, therefore we select the FFT transformation as the $\mathbf{\Psi}$ matrix. This could also be the case for real life-logging data, as long as they are sparse in the FFT domain. Then, ciphertext $\mathbf{y} \in \mathbb{R}^M$

is computed using (1) and transmitted to the sink over a UDP connection. We control the compression ratio through M, and compute the reconstruction error (at the sink using the OMP algorithm) that is defined as $e = \frac{||x-\hat{x}||_2}{||x||_2}$, where x and $\hat{x}$ are the original and reconstructed signals, respectively. Essentially, the smaller the reconstruction error, the higher the fidelity of the reconstructed signal. Fig. 4 shows the cumulative density function (CDF) of the reconstruction error for all sensors and for different compression ratios of the original signal (plaintext $\mathbf{x}$). As the compression ratio increases, error e increases. However, observe that even for a large compression ratio (80%), 73% of sensors experience a reconstruction error smaller than 0.075, thus achieving a 92.5% fidelity. This shows that encryption along with CS can be successfully combined with a high compression ratio, achieving a high fidelity of the decrypted data.

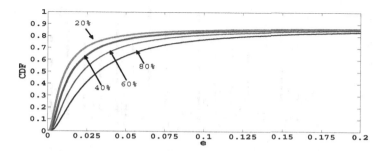

Fig. 4. Reconstruction error for different compression ratios

In Fig. 5 we show the overall (averaged in all runs) power consumption of the simulated WSN, when no CS is used, and for the case where CS is applied with different compression ratios. The error bars show the 95% confidence intervals. Observe that as the compression ratio increases, network's total power consumption significantly decreases. This is because less packets are transmitted into the network, hence less power is consumed. In general, power consumption is of four types within a WSN: (i) CPU, that is the power consumed by sensor's CPU, (ii) LPM, the power consumed during the low power mode, (iii) transmit, the power spent for packet transmission, and (iv) listen, the power consumed for the packet decoding operations. Fig. 6 shows the average power consumption for each of the sensors when the compression ratio is 20%. Note that most of the power is consumed for the listening operations. This is because every sensor, and for every packet transmitted by each neighbor, even if this packet is not destined to it, this sensor has to spend resources in order to decode it and further accept or reject it. Hence, joint encryption and compression saves significant resources of the power-constrained sensors as less packets have to be transmitted into the network.

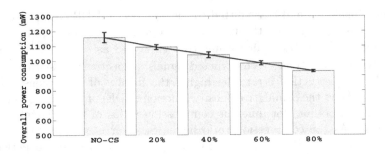

Fig. 5. Overall power consumption of the wireless sensor network for the various compression ratios

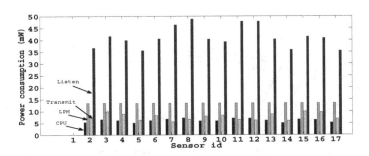

Fig. 6. Power consumption for the different sensor operations

7   Conclusions

In this paper we presented a CS-based scheme for joint encryption and compression in life-logging systems, implemented in Contiki OS. The performance evaluation results show that the reconstruction error is kept low even for large compression ratios. Moreover, power consumption significantly decreases for these compression ratios, prolonging network's lifetime substantially.

References

1. Zolertia z1 platform, http://www.zolertia.com/products/z1
2. Agrawal, S., Vishwanath, S.: Secrecy using compressive sensing. In: ITW, pp. 563–567 (2011)
3. Barcelo-Llado, J., Morell, A., Seco-Granados, G.: Amplify-and-forward compressed sensing as a phy-layer secrecy solution in wireless sensor networks. In: SAM, pp. 113–116 (2012)
4. Kumar, A., Makur, A.: Lossy compression of encrypted image by compressive sensing technique. In: TENCON, pp. 1–5 (2009)
5. Zeng, L., Zhang, X., Chen, L., Fan, Z., Wang, Y.: Scrambling-based speech encryption via compressed sensing. EURASIP Journal on Advances in Signal Processing 2012, 1–27 (2012)

6. Bush, V.: As we think. The Atlantic Monthly 176, 101–108 (1945)
7. Rawassizadeh, R., Tomitsch, M., Wac, K., Tjoa, A.: Ubiqlog: a generic mobile phone-based life-log framework. In: Personal and Ubiquitous Computing, pp. 1–17 (2012)
8. Lu, H., Liu, Z., Lane, N., Choudhury, T., Campbell, A.: The jigsaw continuous sensing engine for mobile phone applications. In: Proc. of SensSys, pp. 71–84 (2010)
9. Belimpasakis, P., Roimela, K., You, Y.: Experience explorer: a life-logging platform based on mobile context collection. In: Proc. of Third International Conference on Next Generation Mobile Applications, Services and Technologies, pp. 77–80 (2009)
10. Tatomir, B., Klapwijk, P., Rothkrantz, L.: Topology based infrastructure for medical emergency coordination. International Journal of Intelligent Control and Systems 11, 228–237 (2006)
11. Hu, F., Wang, Y., Wu, H.: Mobile telemedicine sensor networks with low-energy data query and network lifetime considerations. IEEE Transactions on Mobile Computing 5, 404–417 (2006)
12. Chen, Y., Jones, G.: Augmenting human memory using personal lifelogs. In: Proc. of the 1st Augmented Human International Conference, pp. 1–9 (2010)
13. Lee, M., Dey, A.: Using lifelogging to support recollection for people with episodic memory impairment and their caregivers. In: Proc. of HealthNet, pp. 1–14 (2008)
14. Rawassizadeh, R., Tjoa, A.: Securing shareable life-logs. In: Proc. of SocialCom, pp. 1105–1110 (2010)
15. Gemmell, J., Bell, G., Lueder, R.: Mylifebits: A personal database for everything. Communications of the ACM 49, 88–95 (2006)
16. Chen, X., Makki, K., Yen, K., Pissinou, N.: Sensor network security: A survey. IEEE Communications Surveys and Tutorials 11, 52–73 (2009)
17. Ramesh, M., Lekshmi, G.: Intruder tracking using wireless sensor network. In: ICCIC, pp. 1–5 (2010)
18. Chu, C., Liu, J., Zhou, J., Bao, F., Deng, R.: Practical id-based encryption for wireless sensor network. In: ASIACCS, pp. 337–340 (2010)
19. Wang, W., Hempel, M., Peng, D., Wang, H., Sharif, H., Chen, H.: On energy efficient encryption for video streaming in wireless sensor networks. IEEE Transactions on Multimedia 12, 417–426 (2010)
20. Candes, E., Wakin, M.: An introduction to compressive sampling. IEEE Signal Processing Magazine 25(2), 21–30 (2008)
21. Tropp, J., Gilbert, A.: Signal recovery from random measurements via orthogonal matching pursuit. IEEE Transactions on Information Theory 53, 4655–4666 (2007)
22. Haleem, M., Mathur, C., Subbalakshmi, K.: Joint distributed compression and encryption of correlated data in sensor networks. In: MILCOM, pp. 1–7 (2006)
23. Mancill, T., Pilskalns, O.: Combining encryption and compression in wireless sensor networks. International Journal of Wireless Information Networks 18, 39–49 (2011)
24. Chu, C., Liu, J., Zhou, J., Bao, F., Deng, R.: On the security and robustness of encryption via compressed sensing. In: MILCOM, pp. 1–7 (2008)
25. The open source os for the internet of things, http://www.contiki-os.org
26. Accentura, N., Grieco, L., Boggia, G., Camarda, P.: Performance analysis of the rpl routing protocol. In: ICM, pp. 767–772 (2011)
27. Sensorscope: Sensor networks for environmental monitoring, http://lcav.epfl.ch/sensorscope-en

Supporting Human Decision-Making Online Using Information-Trustworthiness Metrics

Jason R.C. Nurse, Sadie Creese, Michael Goldsmith,
and Syed Sadiqur Rahman

Cyber Security Centre, Department of Computer Science,
University of Oxford, Oxford, UK
{firstname.lastname}@cs.ox.ac.uk

Abstract. The vast amount of information available online places decision makers wishing to use this content in an advantageous but also very difficult position. The advantages stem from the volume of content from a variety of sources that is readily available; the difficulties arise because of the often unknown quality and trustworthiness of the information – is it fact, opinion or purely meant to deceive? In this paper we reflect on and extend current work on information trust and quality metrics which can be used to address this difficulty. Specifically, we propose new metrics as worthy of consideration and the new combinatorics required to take measurements of the various trust factors into a single score. These feed into our existing overarching policy-based approach that uses trustworthiness metrics to support decision-making online.

Keywords: information trustworthiness, information quality, metrics, human decision-making, open-source content, social-media, online risks.

1 Introduction

The Web is the largest source of information in the world as well as the largest open marketplace and social/political forum. A key challenge with its use as an information source for supporting human decision-making, however, is that the resources that sites and services introduce us to are often unknown to us, so raising questions about their quality and trustworthiness. This is especially true in today's world, where anyone anywhere can share content online, some useful and some meant actively to deceive; crisis situations exemplify this perfectly [1,2]. As a result of these concerns and the potential utility of online content in a range of cases, there is an increasingly acute need to provide information-confidence and trust measures to users of online (and particularly social-media) information, to support them in making informed decisions, in light of risk.

In this paper, therefore, we reflect on some of the trust metrics currently available and those being researched, with two objectives in mind. Firstly, we aim briefly to review the state-of-the-art, identifying what trustworthiness factors can feasibly be measured and potentially utilised. This review pulls together several seminal papers (e.g., [3,4,5,6]) which introduce techniques for measuring information quality, credibility and trustworthiness. Secondly, we extend this existing

L. Marinos and I. Askoxylakis (Eds.): HAS/HCII 2013, LNCS 8030, pp. 316–325, 2013.
© Springer-Verlag Berlin Heidelberg 2013

work on metrics and our overarching policy-based approach [7] by proposing new metrics as worthy of consideration and the new combinatorics required to take measurements of the various factors into a single score.

This paper is structured as follows. In Section 2 we review factors that influence trustworthiness and the proposals for measuring them; this builds on our initial work in [8]. Section 3 broadens the scope beyond intrinsic trust factors to consider how to metricise the potential impact of infrastructure vulnerability upon the trustworthiness of the information being communicated over it. In Section 4 we recap our novel policy-based methodology for assigning trustworthiness measures to openly-sourced information. As part of our overall methodology presentation, we also discuss the important problem of how to combine factor measurements/scores appropriately so as to arrive at a single information-trustworthiness score (Section 5); it is this score that is typically (first) presented to a decision-maker. Finally, Section 6 reports on the practical assessment and validation that we have conducted to date on existing and proposed metrics, before concluding and presenting future work in Section 7.

2   State-of-the-Art in Information-Trustworthiness Metrics

The complexity of trust is well-known, and undoubtedly derives from its social origins. To elucidate its use for our purposes, in previous work [8] we conducted a state-of-the-art review focusing on which factors influence an individual's perception of information trustworthiness online. The outcome of that study was the definition of some high-level influences, namely the provenance of information and its intrinsic quality, but also a plethora of specific trust factors within these categories. It is these specific factors that are most useful to our research now, as they are candidate properties through which trustworthiness might be measured. The remainder of this section presents several of these trust factors, and reviews proposals for their measurement; we concentrate on techniques that might be automated, and on social-media content, given its increasing prevalence. This presentation is intended to overview the state-of-the-art as it pertains to metrics and set the foundation for our work building on this baseline.

One of the most fundamental trustworthiness factors is the timeliness of the information. This factor operates on the basis that the closer information is published to a specified time, the more likely it is up-to-date and potentially accurate. Overall, the metric (a calculation of the time elapsed) has been seen to work quite well ([3,9]) and is simple enough to be applied in most domains. Other factors that influence quality and trust include, information's completeness, complexity and relevance. To measure completeness, approaches typically conduct assessments based on expected text/features within the content (e.g., number of internal links on a Wikipedia article [3] or absence of appropriate data [10]) but there is also work that has proposed content length [11]. While not ideal techniques as they fail at judging completeness from a semantic perspective, as those articles have shown, they can be quite useful as a quick initial indicator of trustworthiness in some domains. Complexity/ease-of-understanding is also popular in the literature (e.g., [4,6]), undoubtedly because of its link to well-understood readability metrics (e.g., Flesch-Kincaid) which allow automated analysis based on sentences, words and syllables in content. Grammar and spelling may feed into this textual analysis as an indicator of trustworthiness [9,12] as well. Although useful, these factors should be treated circumspectly considering that the nature of content in some social-media services lends itself to jargon or small snippets of information (e.g., Twitter), which inhibit its proper analysis. Approaches to measuring the relevance of content to the problem at hand have thus far been centred around matching topic keywords to words that appear often and/or are in notable positions in the information items [13]. This is a sensible technique, and indeed is one that search engines apply. Its weakness, however, is that because it only matches words, the semantics and context is overlooked, meaning that irrelevant information may actually be rated as relevant.

Source-related factors such as authority/reputation, recommendation and popularity can influence the trustworthiness of the information as well. To measure reputation, approaches have considered the number of edits made by other authors on a specific author's contributions [14], link analysis and ranking techniques focusing on social relationships [15] and those adapted from Web search [4], and on assessing basic features such as amount of content contributed and number of associates (followers/friends on Twitter) [5]. The metrics for recommendation may overlap with those for reputation, particularly in the social domain, where feedback on input is encouraged. For example, in the question-answer domain (e.g., Yahoo! Answers), highlighting an answer to a question as a 'best answer' affects the author's reputation as well as recommending them and the answer itself. Other work on Twitter has sought to assess retweeting, mentioning and 'favouriting' as indications of trust [16], i.e., as a form of recommendation. These approaches all provide useful techniques for measuring the factor. Finally, metrics for popularity vary across contexts, but largely the aim is to determine how frequently cited a source or page is. On the Web at large, this could mean assessing the number of times a particular site is mentioned (e.g., [17]), but in more social domains, metrics might be based on number of followers, friends or page likes. Albeit a plausible metric, two caveats with it and a few of the others mentioned above are that data is subject to manipulation in hostile situations (e.g., information warfare) and context is crucially important – a source's high popularity or good reputation in one topic may not transfer to another topic. Both are key points to note if metrics are to be broadly applied. There were several factors that we were unable to find published automatic metrics for, including: objectivity, accuracy, believability, corroboration, and location of source. In upcoming sections, we will follow up on some of these.

3   Accounting for Information Infrastructure Vulnerability

In addition to assessing intrinsic trustworthiness factors, we hypothesise that trustworthiness of information may be impacted by attempts to damage its integrity, as enabled by vulnerabilities in the technology of the infrastructure over which it travels. Further, that assessing exposure to such risk might be a useful component of an information-trustworthiness measure, although we recognise that such a metric is likely to be context-dependent in its utility, probably only useful in cases where there is a perception of real, present threat that could target an exploitable vulnerability in the information infrastructure.

To assess the extent to which vulnerability in technologies could result in information corruption, we start by outlining an exposure model: *Exposure = Threat × Vulnerability*. Exposure in this context reflects the possibility that a piece of information has been corrupted, and is considered as resulting from the presence of a motivated *threat* combined with an exploitable *vulnerability*. This is based on current practice in information-risk assessment and is inspired by [18]. The Information Infrastructure Vulnerability (IIV) factor measure is this generic Exposure value detailed with the following factors.

Threats are those entities that perpetrate attacks and, in the context of our work, this means entities that deliberately seek to corrupt information or are reckless as to whether it is corrupted as 'collateral damage' in a broader attack. In general, we can gather evidence on the presence of threat by monitoring various open sources (e.g., CERT announcements, BlackHat discussion boards and security bulletins). In these cases, it is imperative to establish whether a threat actor is motivated and if they have the capability to attack. Given that we are interested in exploitable technology *vulnerabilities*, the factors to be measured by this metric should be driven by an understanding of attacks as well as nature of vulnerability. Literature has proposed several taxonomies of attacks and related vulnerabilities (see [19]). From these, we have identified particularly relevant areas for our vulnerability factor measurement to be: applications; system architectures and platforms; communication networks; and hardware aspects. Establishing the presence of vulnerabilities in these domains (and indeed, specified technology infrastructures) would then be based on a (likely automated) check against existing data stores (e.g., CERT Vulnerability Notes Database, Common Vulnerabilities and Exposures, National Vulnerability Database, BUGTRAQ).

Our general metric for IIV is therefore based on the following. Firstly, a user organisation or individual tool user will need to maintain a general threat table, which they probably already do as part of ongoing risk-management activities, which defines types of threat (t) (e.g., state-sponsored action, hackers, untargeted and opportunistic attackers) and the probability (p_t) of them being motivated to attack. This table of values is defined as p_t as t varies over threats.

Now, assume a new infrastructure vulnerability V_i is published online and has been picked up by the user's vulnerability monitoring tools: **Step 1:** Determine the likelihood that the vulnerability V_i exists within their local technology infrastructure. This can be determined by automated or manual checks against current infrastructure and configurations; the resulting value defined as $v_i : 0 < v_i < 1$. **Step 2:** Estimate which threats that can exploit V_i and their probabilities of exploiting it. This value is defined as e_{it}. **Step 3:** Calculate the probability that V_i will be exploited by the defined threats in order to conduct an attack against the tool user. This value is approximated as a_i with the formula $a_i = v_i.(1 - \prod_t(1 - e_{it}.p_t))$; this treats the threats as independent and so may overestimate a_i. **Step 4**: Calculate the IIV score based on an aggregation of a_i values, i.e., one for each of the vulnerabilities identified. As such: $IIV = 1 - \prod_i(1 - a_i)$. This IIV score can then be applied to amplify/attenuate the other core trustworthiness elements; in fact, we consider the complement, Information Infrastructure Integrity (III): $III = 1 - IIV$, so as less vulnerable situations score higher. We conclude our discussion here due to space limitations but further detail is available in [19].

4   Policy-Based Approach to Factor Application

To be able to appropriately apply the range of metrics discussed above to support decision-making, there is a need for a broad approach that incorporates the differing importance of factors to users, decision context and, crucially, the combinatorics behind how factors' metrics are combined into a single trustworthiness score. In previous work [7], we have introduced such a methodology based on policies by which this could be achieved. Below we briefly recap that approach and then focus on the newly detailed aspect, i.e., the factor combinatorics.

In the first instance, we assume that there is a set of information from online sources (e.g., news feeds, Twitter or Facebook posts) to be used in making a decision. The first level of processing therefore takes this information and applies a high-level policy to it to filter unwanted sources and to ensure that content from trusted sources is included. Next, users or organisations can once more specify through policy what specific provenance, quality and generally, trustworthiness factors (e.g., the competence or reputation of the source, information's recency) are to be considered. This policy also sets a basic scoring scheme defining the importance (weightings) to be given to each factor. Selection of factors will depend upon context, since their reliability as a trustworthiness indicator may vary according to their perceived inherent value (such as location in a disaster situation) as well as their vulnerability to compromise and the likelihood of a compromise (malicious or accidental) taking place. A user's own decision-making policy also impacts factors. This is a third policy level that is intended to allow the decision maker to amplify or attenuate one or more factors that may appear to be more or less important, in their opinion, by increasing or decreasing the weight given to the corresponding score amongst all information. These policies could be based on a user's experience and intuitions, but we allow for the definition of preset templates which can be shared and refined over time.

5   Factor Combinatorics

A part of properly applying the factors is considering how to appropriately combine their measurements/scores to arrive at a single trustworthiness value. For example, if we have scores for recency, popularity and III of 0.13, 0.22 and 0.88 respectively, how do we produce one value which represents the overall trustworthiness of the associated information item? Some articles in the literature have considered this problem, but most (see [10]) seem to opt for simple weighted means, without due consideration of other approaches. Our exploration of this problem consisted of a theoretical evaluation of several methods by which values could be combined and averaged or a single representative value obtained. We considered 6 methods: Arithmetic mean (AM) ($\frac{1}{n}\sum_{i=1}^{n}x_i$), Geometric mean (GM) (($\Pi_{i=1}^{n}x_i$)$^{\frac{1}{n}}$), Quadratic mean (QM) (($\frac{1}{n}\sum_{i=1}^{n}x_i^2$)$^{\frac{1}{2}}$), Harmonic mean (HM) ($n/\sum_{i=1}^{n}\frac{1}{x_i}$), Square-Mean-Root (SMR) (($\frac{1}{n}\sum_{i=1}^{n}\sqrt{x_i}$)^2), Conjugated Root-Mean-Squared (CRMS) ($1-(\frac{1}{n}\sum_{i=1}^{n}(1-x_i)^2)^{\frac{1}{2}}$). These cover a number of popular techniques applied to similar mathematical combination problems. Simple product ($\prod_{i=1}^{n}x_i$, as used for *III*) is rejected as antitonic in n.

The criteria used for assessing these approaches included fairness (i.e., lack of bias towards higher or lower scores), rigour (working well across ranges of values while behaving in a consistent manner, e.g., in terms of ordering compared to other methods), and the ability to add weights to factors (thus allowing users to (de)emphasise factor importance in the calculation of the overall trustworthiness score). We are also interested in 0-cases (i.e., how a 0 score for a factor impacts the calculation of the overall score). We present our key findings below; readers should note that we assume normalised values ([0, 1]) for trustworthiness factors, as it is easier to provide homogeneous transformations on this space.

Several noteworthy points arose from our evaluation. Firstly, there were some methods that violated the fairness requirement in that they placed too great an emphasis on higher values (as compared to lower ones) or lower values (as compared to higher ones). An example of the former case is QM (emphasises higher input scores), and of the latter case is HM (emphasises lower scores compared to the other means). In terms of consistency and predictability of output, all the means did quite well. We knew from existing work [20] of the ordering of four of these techniques (i.e., $HM \leq GM \leq AM \leq QM$), but to find that the SMR tended to fit between the GM and AM was advantageous considering fairness (i.e., getting a truly representative mean score). The CRMS method did appear to give predictable preliminary results particularly in ordering (typically between GM and AM) but then produced peaks and troughs very dependent on the input data that was fed into it. For example, for some high values (0.9,0.8,1.0) it produced a mean even lower than HM.

Relating to weights, all the formulae performed in line with expectations; a range of simple weights were properly handled and increases in a weight did cause means to gravitate towards the respective input value. One observation is that calculation of Weighted GM can result in numeric underflow at high weights (e.g., greater than ~500), thus producing an output mean of 0.0. Finally to comment on the 0-case criterion, we found that the HM was unable to gracefully handle factor scores of 0 (resulting in a divide-by-zero error). This meant that the criteria for rigour and 0 case could not be met by this method. The GM function also evaluated to 0 if there were any 0 scores present. This might or might not be preferred by users, depending on whether a terrible score in one factor meant that the values for other factors was irrelevant or compromised.

In general, it is our opinion that the choice of combination method applied should be the user's, as they may have their own perspectives or contexts. A pessimistic user, for example, may always prefer that final trustworthiness scores (i.e., mean values) are underestimated, whereas an optimist, or someone who is not especially sensitive may not be concerned about an overestimation of the trustworthiness scores. With this understanding, we summarise below cases where particular approaches may be most appropriate.

As it relates to fairness, the SMR appears the most suitable as it typically produces a value in the middle of the means considered. This positioning also makes SMR predictable and not sporadic (like CRMS which can at times result in a mean below the HM and GM). If there is a desire for underestimating trustworthiness, users could select either the HM or GM. These generally perform in a consistent manner (ordering) and cover a range of inputs. Users should however be aware of their nuances relating to 0 cases and high weights, as discussed previously. For cases where users prefer to overestimate mean values (or mask lower values), the AM and QM methods may be most appropriate. Furthermore, they stand the test of rigour and appreciation of ranges of factor weights.

Sometimes there may be cases where there are missing factor values. For example, a piece of information may lack a timestamp or there may be insufficient details to determine the *III* measure. For such situations, we allow users to specify a list of 'must have' factors, and if these are not present, we set the factor's value to 0 and assign a high weight to those information items. This allows calculations to be made as before, but ensures that a penalty is paid for missing that value; higher weighting on the 0 value pulls down the final mean. Conversely, if the factor's value is missing and it is not a required factor, it could be ignored by setting a weight of 0.

6   Experimentation and Validation

We engaged in a practical assessment and critical reflection on some trust-factor metrics. Here we discuss four of these, focusing especially on our proposed metrics (see [19] for others). For our experimentation, we used a 2011 London Riots dataset consisting of a broad range of public tweets and news reports.

Competence of Source refers to the level of expertise of an information source [21]. To measure competence, we drew on contributions from partners in the project and their approach to compare the usage of words by the unknown sources to that of a core and predefined set of competent sources. The unique perspective taken by our metric is based on the assumption that competent authors use words that are measured and appropriate in their information contributions, thus it might be possible to count the number of words from the unknown author that match words from the competent author set. A competence score is obtained by normalising the count with respect to total word count, thereby resulting in a value [0, 1]. The metric was set up, implemented and deployed against the dataset. Based on the initial results, it performed reasonably well at identifying the more competent sources.

To reflect critically on this metric, although it did work well there are reservations, including: (i) reliance on a core set of competent authors/texts for a topic – this would be difficult to define and challenging to prove that a word-set persists as complete; (ii) difficulty of defining the confines and granularity for a 'competent' word set per topic/field/sub-field; and (iii) simply mentioning words may not be in itself indicative of how competent a source is –an author may be constantly re-tweeting other people's content or publishing highly biased opinions. Moreover, such an approach might also fall victim to keyword stuffing attacks. Future metric refinement will need to address these concerns.

Corroboration – captures the extent to which the same information originates from various unrelated sources [22]. For our purposes, we abstracted this factor to be built on an approach that required that 'similar' information be found across different content items. To do this, we chose to apply a clustering algorithm, via the *Carrot²* [23] clustering engine. This engine parses content items and creates and automatically labels clusters. We then use the labels as the comparison key to obtain similarity counts (e.g., how many other items are within the 'looting and riots in London' label), which are then normalised to provide the factor's corroboration score $[0, 1]$ for each item. From the metric's implementation and testing we were able to gather some descriptive and promising topic clusters.

There were two key weaknesses of this clustering approach to assess corroboration. Firstly, clustering does not natively accommodate negation (words like 'no', 'not') therefore proper checks should be conducted to ensure that negative words/sentiment are adequately handled and that conflicting pieces of information are not clustered together. Secondly, this approach does not conduct checks to verify that information originates from different sources. This is a problem as corroboration of information from the same or closely related sources introduces the possibility of bias therefore negatively impacting the metric.

Social-Media Jargon – this factor posits that excessive use of social-media jargon, especially emoticons and shouting (words fully and inappropriately uppercased), might indicate a lack of information trustworthiness, similar to [9]. Our algorithm emphasises simplicity and thus compares the number of characters used on jargon as opposed to real and potentially useful content. As such, the implemented metric measures two aspects, first, the percentage of characters within the content used for emoticons (assessed using regular expressions) and second the percentage of words fully capitalised (excluding well-known abbreviations). These two values are then averaged to deduce a score, which is then subtracted from 1 to get the 'goodness' score for the factor.

By this simple metric, one is able to conduct a very basic assessment of information. When we evaluated it with the dataset, the findings were encouraging but not conclusive. The issues that arose included, the dependence on an up-to-date emoticon list to compare against, in what is a fast-moving social landscape. Furthermore, there was the occasional inability to recognise the legitimate use of uppercase letters both in unknown and specialist/topic-specific fields (e.g.,

CH3CH2OH is not inappropriate excessive use of capital letters, it is the chemical formula for Alcohol). Future work should address these issues.

Location of a Source – this algorithm is based on the hypothesis that sources closer to an event (e.g., eye-witnesses) may know more accurate/up-to-date information about it. The metric calculates the distance between two geographical coordinates (typically, the location of the event of interest and location of a source publishing event-related content) using earth geometry and then heuristically assigns values $[0, 1]$ based on their proximity, higher values for closer proximity. Unfortunately, we were unable to thoroughly evaluate this metric because of a lack of availability of geo-tagged content. A broader investigation of the field highlighted that only a small percentage of tweets are geo-tagged [24]—this is an interesting finding in itself as it suggests that application of this factor might be limited unless novel techniques of source/content positioning are applied.

7   Conclusions and Future Work

In this paper, we have reflected on the existing research on trust and quality metrics as it specifically pertains to using them to support decision-making online. We uncovered numerous measurement techniques which advance the field, but arguably much more needs to be done to allow for a greater degree of automated trust assessment and higher quality of the factor scores output. To further progress the goal of decision-support online, this paper extended previous work on metrics to incorporate the consideration of loss of information integrity due to infrastructure compromise, and also contributed a few new factor metrics and combinatorics. The initial findings from the metrics assessment was positive but as mentioned, further refinement is needed to enhance their ultimate utility at measuring and indicating trustworthiness to users online.

Future work will focus on further development of the proposed metrics, and other techniques that may assist in measurement. This will draw from the weaknesses discovered from our metrics experimentation and ensuring they are adequately addressed. Additionally, we will seek to conduct a case-study evaluation of the III metric with real data on attacks, threats and vulnerabilities. This will be interesting as it will combine live data from online monitoring sites towards the definition of an impact score. Finally, an assessment will be done on the overall utility of the policy-based methodology in enabling users to assimilate significant amounts of online content and make well-conceived decisions in an effective and timely manner. This will interact with our other research towards optimising the communication of risk and trustworthiness in interfaces [25].

References

1. Yin, J., Lampert, A., Cameron, M., Robinson, B., Power, R.: Using social media to enhance emergency situation awareness. IEEE Intelligent Systems 99 (2012)
2. Guardian News: How riot rumours spread on twitter (2012),
   http://www.guardian.co.uk/uk/interactive/2011/dec/07/
   london-riots-twitter

3. Stvilia, B., Gasser, L., Twidale, M., Smith, L.: A framework for information quality assessment. Journal of ASIST 58(12), 1720–1733 (2007)
4. Agichtein, E., Castillo, C., Donato, D., Gionis, A., Mishne, G.: Finding high-quality content in social media. In: Web Search and Web Data Mining Conference (2008)
5. Castillo, C., Mendoza, M., Poblete, B.: Information credibility on twitter. In: 20th International Conference on World Wide Web, pp. 675–684 (2011)
6. O'Mahony, M., Smyth, B.: Using readability tests to predict helpful product reviews. In: Adaptivity, Personalization, Fusion Heterogeneous Information (2010)
7. Rahman, S.S., Creese, S., Goldsmith, M.: Accepting information with a pinch of salt: handling untrusted information sources. In: Meadows, C., Fernandez-Gago, C. (eds.) STM 2011. LNCS, vol. 7170, pp. 223–238. Springer, Heidelberg (2012)
8. Nurse, J.R.C., Rahman, S.S., Creese, S., Goldsmith, M., Lamberts, K.: Information quality and trustworthiness: A topical state-of-the-art review. In: International Conference on Computer Applications & Network Security, pp. 492–500. IEEE (2011)
9. Weerkamp, W., de Rijke, M.: Credibility improves topical blog post retrieval. In: 46th Annual Meeting of the Assoc. for Computational Linguistics, pp. 923–931 (2008)
10. Helfert, M., Foley, O., Ge, M., Cappiello, C.: Limitations of weighted sum measures for information quality. In: 15th Americas Conf. on Information Systems (2009)
11. Blumenstock, J.: Size matters: word count as a measure of quality on Wikipedia. In: 17th International Conference on World Wide Web, pp. 1095–1096 (2008)
12. Mosquera, A., Moreda, P.: Smile: An informality classification tool for helping to assess quality and credibility in web 2.0 texts. In: 6th International AAAI Conference on Weblogs and Social Media (2012)
13. Naumann, F.: From databases to information systems-information quality makes the difference. IBM Almaden Research Center (2001)
14. Adler, B.T., Chatterjee, K., de Alfaro, L., Faella, M., Pye, I., Raman, V.: Assigning trust to Wikipedia content. In: 4th International Symposium on Wikis (2008)
15. Al-Oufi, S., Kim, H.N., Saddik, A.E.: A group trust metric for identifying people of trust in online social networks. Expert Systems with Applications 39(18) (2012)
16. Lumbreras, A., Gavalda, R.: Applying trust metrics based on user interactions to recommendation in social networks. In: International Workshop of Social Knowledge Discovery and Utilization (2012)
17. Ramachandran, S., Paulraj, S., Joseph, S., Ramaraj, V.: Enhanced trustworthy and high-quality information retrieval system for web search engines. International Journal of Computer Science (5) (2009)
18. Ward, J., Leach, J., Creese, S.: Measuring internet threat exposure scoping out a practical approach, metrics special interest group KTN. Technical report (2008)
19. Nurse, J.R.C., Creese, S., Goldsmith, M., Rahman, S.S., Lund, D., Mourikas, G., Price, D.: TEASE Project Deliverable D3.6: Consolidated report on trustworthiness measures and overlay design. Technical report (2013)
20. Agarwal, B.: Programmed Statistics. New Age International Ltd. (2007)
21. Grandison, T., Sloman, M.: A survey of trust in internet applications. IEEE Communications Surveys and Tutorials, 2–16 (2000)
22. Gil, Y., Artz, D.: Towards content trust of web resources. Journal of Web Semantics: Science, Services and Agents on the World Wide Web 5(4), 227–239 (2007)
23. Carrot2: Open Source Search Results Clustering Engine, http://project.carrot2.org
24. Graham, M.: Big data and the end of theory, Guardian News (2012), http://www.guardian.co.uk/news/datablog/2012/mar/09/big-data-theory
25. Nurse, J.R.C., Creese, S., Goldsmith, M., Lamberts, K.: Using information trustworthiness advice in decision-making. In: Socio-Technical Aspects in Security and Trust (STAST) Workshop at 25th IEEE CSF Symposium, pp. 35–42. IEEE (2012)

On the Secure and Safe Data Synchronization

Pavel Ocenasek and Jaromir Karmazin

Brno University of Technology, Faculty of Information Technology, Brno, Czech Republic
ocenaspa@fit.vutbr.cz, xkarma06@stud.fit.vutbr.cz

Abstract. This paper deals the aspects of data synchronization. The first part focuses on existing technologies and their features. We follow with the proposal of application that can be used as an alternative to the existing solutions. The proposed peer-to-peer application includes several safety improvements as well as it supports secure communication and data storage.

Keywords: Synchrnozation, security, safety, cloud, networking.

1 Introduction

Data synchronization becomes popular way how to share documents, personal information and program data between computers and also mobile devices. Dropbox is one of such program. This program is server-based and therefore we have to connect the synchronized computer to the internet (with access to the Dropbox central server). The situation is similar with the other available programs (SkyDrive, SugarSync etc.) Furthermore, these programs do not provide secure data storage. The data is stored usually in an unencrypted form, available to the server owners.

To allow for such an alternative, we have designed a synchronization tool whose network model is peer-to-peer rather than client-server. This allows the user to interconnect their devices in a way they see fit, be it a star topology with the user's own server, or a fully meshed topology of laptops and smartphones [3], none of which is permanently online.

2 Dropbox

Dropbox [6] is a popular cloud synchronization tool with client implementations available for Windows, Linux, Mac OS, Android [3], iOS, BlackBerry and Kindle Fire. To the user, it presents itself as a special type of folder (a „Dropbox") whose contents are automatically mirrored to the Dropbox server and all other devices.

2.1 Introduction

The Dropbox service uses a centralized client-server model [6], requiring the user to create an account on the Dropbox server before they may synchronize their files. To

L. Marinos and I. Askoxylakis (Eds.): HAS/HCII 2013, LNCS 8030, pp. 326–331, 2013.
© Springer-Verlag Berlin Heidelberg 2013

create an account, the user supplies their first and last name, e-mail address, and password of choice. With the default free plan, they receive 2.5 gigabytes of usable space after signing up.

The user can then install a client application on any of the supported platforms [3] and link it to their user account. The client application will then run a background service that watches for changes on the server and downloads them to the client, and that also watches for changes on the client and uploads them to the server. When the service starts up, it also checks for any changes that may have happened during the time it was stopped [6].

2.2   Features

Aside from synchronization, Dropbox allows viewing and downloading stored files using a web interface, sharing files with other users, using an API [6] to support third-party applications, and other additional functions.

When two devices linked to the same amount discover each other's presence in the LAN (using broadcast messages), they may begin a so-called "LAN Sync", which allows one client to download data from another client instead of the server, potentially gaining speed. Both client still need Internet connection to coordinate. The change-originating client still needs to upload its version of the data to the server, so only the download process is accelerated using LAN Sync. [6]

The user can choose specific subfolders of the Dropbox folder to synchronize. This affects only downloads, not uploads. The mobile versions do not download whole directories; instead, they only download files that are marked as "favorites" to save storage space. [6]

2.3   Security

To secure a user's account, Dropbox provides the following services that are available in the account settings [6]:

- Password changing. Obligatory and self-explanatory.
- Two-step verification. This extends user authentication to include one-time codes, either random numbers sent to a mobile phone using text messages or Time-based One-Time Passwords (TOTP) generated by a mobile application. The one-time codes are required for web sign-ins and for linking new devices.
- Notifications. The user may choose to receive notifications by e-mail whenever a new device is linked to their account, and/or whenever a new third-party application is connected to their account.
- Device management. The user may review the devices linked to their account, and unlink those deemed to be illegitimate.

The web interface, as well as the network connections from the various client applications to the server, are secured using the standard SSL protocol with AES-256 encryption, using a certificate signed by Thawte, Inc. (as of 2013). This serves to secure the user credentials and file data in transit. [2]

Dropbox claims to "use modern encryption methods to store [the users'] data" , using what is assumed to be AES-256 encryption, though the encryption key cannot be specified by the user ; in fact, we can assume there exists a single global key for decrypting all users' files, since all files can be shared with other users. Dropbox, Inc. even states that they "have a small number of employees who must be able to access user data". Therefore, one can have good faith that the Dropbox, Inc. employees will not look at one's files, but the security model does not protect the files from law enforcement officials or malicious hackers. [6]

On 19th June 2011, a bug affecting the authentication mechanism caused all Dropbox accounts to be accessible without a correct password. The bug was fixed in about 4 hours. User data that did not use client-side encryption could be readable to anyone during that time period.

To encrypt one's data in a way that even Dropbox, Inc.'s employees or law enforcement officials will not be able to read it, one can add a layer of encryption to one's client system, though this is not officially supported by Dropbox. The list of third-party encryption layers includes EncFS, BoxCryptor, Viivo,

The client application stores all downloaded files as they are, inside the folder designated to Dropbox. If the user wishes to encrypt the Dropbox directory, they have to use a lower-level tool, such as TrueCrypt or dm-crypt, to encrypt the storage partition where the Dropbox directory resides. [6]

2.4   Summary

Dropbox is a user-friendly service that is well suited for synchronizing and sharing non-sensitive data. For sensitive data, one can rely on transfer security somewhat, but the storage security of Dropbox is dubious.

3   Peer-to-Peer Sync

While Dropbox or similar cloud-based synchronization tools [1] may be a suitable choice for the average user who values ease of use more than full control, a more skilled user might desire a tool that can be set up in different configurations, perhaps not requiring a company to store the user's data or even not requiring an Internet connection at all.

The target users of our application are people with moderate computer skills who own multiple electronic devices capable of storing data and connecting to IP networks (such as desktop and laptop computers, tablets, and smartphones). We make no assumptions about the uptime of each device or the stability of their IP addresses. In other words, the application should support not-always-on and mobile devices.

3.1   Challenges

Because there might not be a central element in our peer-to-peer system, we cannot assume the presence of any central authority. This means that modification times, for example, cannot be reliably used for comparing file age because there might be a difference in the devices' internal clocks. Conflict resolution also becomes complicated because of this – first, when a file is modified differently on two devices, it cannot be reliably told which change happened later, and second, devices might clash when trying to resolve the same conflict on both ends. Lastly, a device can easily become out-of-date if it does not connect to the network for a long time, or if during a device's uptime, no other device is online to synchronize with. [1]

3.2 Inspiration

The main inspiration for this project comes from Git [5], the distributed version control system that could, from a certain point of view, be seen as a peer-to-peer synchronization tool for source code. A typical Git project consists of several repositories scattered over different computers, exchanging information with each other using push/pull operations. All repositories appear equal to Git and any repository can generally transmit data to any other, although software projects usually provide policies that restrict the directions data can be transferred. These policies also usually determine where and how conflicts should be resolved. [5]

To allow easy transfer of information between repositories, Git stores all its information as "objects" in a content-addressable database whose keys are SHA-1 hash values of the data stored. All objects in the database are permanent and non-modifiable. Because the collision of two SHA-1 hashes is extremely improbable, the hash value is all that needs to be known to retrieve an object from the database. [5]

There are three types of objects in a Git repository [5]:

- "blobs", containing only data,
- "trees", containing file names, directories and references to blobs, and
- "commits", containing version information, references to previous versions and to a tree.

The references (which are mere SHA-1 hashes of the objects referenced) allow the object database to be represented using a directional acyclic graph (DAG). This mitigates the need of synchronized system clocks – the age of two file versions can be compared using their parent-child relations.

By using object references, changes in files can be stored by creating new objects that reference the old ones as their predecessors. This means that synchronizing two Git repositories consists of very little more than copying over the missing objects. On the downside, this means that a Git object database is constantly growing in size. [5]

3.3 Application Design

Our application uses an object database similar to Git [5], with a few key references:

- Objects are identified by UUIDs rather than SHA-1 hashes, in order to make identifier generation faster for large files.
- Storing a copy of a file's data (called "blob" in Git) is optional.

- "Tree" objects are replaced by "metadata" objects which hold information about only one file each, including its name, path, attributes, size and modification time.
- "Commit" objects are replaced by "snapshots" that only contain a list of metadata objects and an optional parent reference.
- Versioning is shifted from the commit level to the metadata level, meaning that each file can be versioned separately.
- Multiple directories in the file system can be made synchronized "volumes", which are synchronized independently of others.
- An instance of the application monitors changes in the file system while it is running, and updates the object database accordingly. When starting up, the application scans the file system for changes that happened while it was shut down.
- Two instances of the application can form a network connection and transfer information in two ways:
- "Bulk sync" – by exchanging the latest snapshot objects, each device learns the state of the other and then iteratively downloads all missing objects.
- "Real-time sync" – when two devices are synchronized, they send each other new objects (metadata) as soon as they are created in their local database.

The network connection can be formed over either IPv4 or IPv6. For secure communication, the TLS session layer protocol is used. [2] We believe most users will not be willing to pay certification authorities for certificates for their own personal use, so the application allows using self-signed certificates, provided that their fingerprints are checked.

It should be possible to use an untrusted peer for secure storage by encrypting the objects sent to them. This would require all the trusted peers to share a common key. The untrusted peer would learn about the number, relationships and approximate sizes of the data stores, but not about the data itself.

3.4   Comparison with Dropbox

Our application has the following advantages over Dropbox:

- No external providers are required. The user's own devices can be used for storage, mitigating the risk of the provider looking at the user's files.
- No device needs to be always powered and online. As long as the devices get to "see" each other often enough, they will bee synchronized.
- Synchronization can be done over LAN without Internet connection, which means full transfer speeds (usually near 100 megabits per second).
- Data can be encrypted in storage, allowing the user to use untrusted storage providers.
- There are also drawbacks that make the application less favorable than Dropbox:
- The application is not as easy to use as Dropbox, mainly because the needs for designing a topology and distributing one's own cryptographic certificates.
- A device may become out of date if it stays long enough without synchronizing with another device.

- Conflicts must be resolved by the user, otherwise two devices trying to resolve the same conflict might clash.
- Large amounts of metadata need to be stored by each device.

Acknowledgements. The research has been supported by Technology Agency of the Czech Republic (TACR) in frame of the project SCADA system for control and monitoring RT processes, TA01010632. This project has been also carried out with a financial support from the Czech Republic through the project no. MSM0021630528: Security-Oriented Research in Information Technology and by the project no. ED1.1.00/02.0070: The IT4Innovations Centre of Excellence; the part of the research has been also supported by the Brno University of Technology, Faculty of Information Technology through the specific research grants no. FIT-S-11-1 and by the project MPO CR, FR-TI1/037.

References

1. Tridgell, A., Mackerras, P.: The rsync algorithm (1998),
   http://rsync.samba.org/techreport/
2. Stallings, W.: Cryptography and network security: principles and practice. Prentice Hall (1998)
3. Android Developers: Android SDK (2013),
   http://developer.android.com/sdk/index.html
4. Tridgell, A., Mackerras, P.: The rsync algorithm (1998),
   http://rsync.samba.org/techreport/
5. Chacon, S.: Pro Git. Apress (2009) ISBN 978-1430218333
6. Dropbox. Core API Development kits and documentation (2013),
   https://www.dropbox.com/developers/core/sdk

The Practice of Global Internet Filtering

Pavel Ocenasek

Brno University of Technology, Faculty of Information Technology, Brno, Czech Republic
ocenaspa@fit.vutbr.cz

Abstract. This paper deals with Global Internet Filtering.. Various technical solutions for Internet filtering are presented together with filtering analysis options. Several possibilities for blocked content access and filtering circumvention in general are discussed.

Keywords: Internet filtering, filtering circumvention, surveillance, blocking, firewall.

1 Introduction

The expansion of the Internet let many people access very useful information without any limitations. But the Internet itself does not contain relevant and useful information only. It's available to everybody without any difference and it's not possible to prevent users from becoming the victims of malicious behavior of the other users. The need for controlling the way people use the Internet is based on all the positives and negatives that the Internet has adopted over the years from the real world. The main reason for this control is to protect children against explicit adult and inappropriate content. This article deals with Internet censorship in People's Republic of China.

2 Internet Censorship

Internet censorship and surveillance are very often interconnected in modern computer networks, such as the Internet. Many Internet Service Providers (ISP) are monitoring their users due to the accounting issues and spam protection. Once you are not using security tools for keeping your communication anonymous, it is very easy for your ISP to save and control the communication of its users. This is the basic prerequisite for technical censorship [1].

2.1 Censorship Methods

One of the basic methods of blocking the access to the information on the specific websites is based on the URL, IP address or specific keywords. Another way is to block access based on DNS (Domain Name System). Once the web browser sends a request for URL lookup for website that is blocked, DNS server sends a response with the incorrect or no information [2].

L. Marinos and I. Askoxylakis (Eds.): HAS/HCII 2013, LNCS 8030, pp. 332–337, 2013.
© Springer-Verlag Berlin Heidelberg 2013

Other methods include blocking according to the TCP/UDP port, traffic shaping rules in VoIP (Voice over IP) or Internet shutdown. This may occur in case of political events, such as revolutions.

2.2   Analysis Methods

Nowadays, analysis of Internet censorship is simple thanks to the projects that want to warn the rest of the world about the situation in the specific countries. The OpenNet Initiative is a project whose goal is to monitor and report on internet filtering and surveillance practices by nations. The reports are aimed for the public (more information is available on http://opennet.net/).

Another project is WatchMouse which provides simple service for testing the availability of a particular website. The services use the infrastructure of 62 stations in 26 countries (details can be found on http://www.watchmouse.com).

Chinese Firewall Checker is a product that enables users to find out if the given website is available in five different locations in China. List of most checked website is available as well. The Chinese Firewall Checker can be found on http://bestvpnservice.com/.

2.3   Circumvention Methods

There are several techniques how to circumvent Internet censorship. One of the most common way to access blocked content is to use HTTPS protocol or technologies as proxy servers, VPN (Virtual Private Network) and TOR (The Onion Router) [1].

Special versions of the websites might also lead to the desired content without being blocked. Modified websites for smartphones using URL starting with "m" or "mobile" can allow you to access the content that is not available on the parent website.

Another way to circumvent Internet censorship is to use services like Google Cache, RSS aggregators, website translators (Google Translate, Bing Translator, ...) or web archives (Wayback Engine).

3   Practical Results

In order to verify the Internet censorship in a certain country, first we have to have a direct access to the Internet from within that location. For the testing purposes in China, we have an access to the remote PC station physically located in Hangzhou. All results presented in this paper are based on tests performed from that PC station. Different results might be obtained from different locations in China.

3.1   DNS Cache Poisoning

First method of the Internet censorship identified in China is DNS cache poisoning. When trying to resolve the URL of a given website the obtained IP address differs from the one obtained from locations outside of Mainland China. This might be an issue of a different server location, technique like anycast etc. The other explanation for this might be that the DNS response has been poisoned. It means that IP address does not belong to the website the user is trying to access. This is the case that happens in China. Let us look at the results of the dig command from Czech Republic.

```
$ dig www.youtube.com +short A
youtube-ui.1.google.com.
173.194.39.142
173.194.39.128
173.194.39.129
<output-omitted>
```

According to the output one of the IP addresses for YouTube is 173.194.39.142. The given IP address is owned by Google as we can see in the following output (lookup in the Whois database).

```
$ telnet whois.arin.net 43
Trying 199.71.0.47... Connected to whois.arin.net. Escape
character is  '^]'.
173.194.39.142
<output-omitted>
OrgName: Google   Inc. OrgId: GOGL
Address: 1600  Amphitheatre  Parkway
City: Mountain  View
StateProv: CA PostalCode: 94043
Country: US
<output-omitted>
```

Now let's perform the same test from within the Mainland China. The results are different as we can see in the outputs below.

```
$ dig www.youtube.com +short A
59.24.3.173
$ telnet whois.apnic.net 43
Trying 202.12.29.220... Connected to whois.apnic.net. Es-
cape  character is  '^]'.
<output-omitted>
59.24.3.173
inetnum: 59.0.0.0  - 59.31.255.255 netname:KORNET
descr: KOREA  TELECOM
descr: Network Management  Center country: KR
<output-omitted>
```

Based on the results the resolved IP address is not only different but also owned by the organization outside the People's Republic of China. The result of such test is not always the same. Obtained IP addresses differ for a various websites. Results for a certain websites differ over time as well. Websites where DNS cache poisoning was identified are Facebook, Twitter and YouTube. Table 1 contains IP addresses with their owners that were identified during the testing period. The previous results might seem a little bit confusing. Questions like "Why are poisoned IP addresses not registered by Chinese government?" or "Why are big telecommunication companies involved in Internet censorship?" can be answered with simple words "They might not know". When trying to connect to these IP addresses on HTTP port 80 the connection always fails on timeout. Deeper analysis of the IP addresses reveals that no port is open. Even ping fails with timeout. Simple conclusion is that the stations with the IP addresses are down or the IP addresses are not assigned to anybody. These IP addresses are within the registered range of a certain organizations but might not be used at all. The IP addresses might have been identified by Chinese government as those with no usage and were assigned just to simulate valid results. Visible output for a user when accessing blocked website is conclusive. The website is not available.

Table 1. Poisoned IP addresses and their owners

IP address	Location	Owner
8.7.198.45	USA	ARIN
37.61.54.158	Azerbaijan	Baktelekom
46.82.174.68	Germany	Deutsche Telecom
59.24.3.173	Korea	Korea Telecom
78.16.49.15	Ireland	Esat Telecommunications Limited
93.46.8.89	Italy	Fastweb
159.106.121.75	USA	DoD Network Information Center
203.98.7.65	New Zealand	Telstra Clear
243.185.187.39	USA	Internet Assigned Numbers Authority

Table 2. Examples of blocked keywords and expressions

Keyword Expression	Search engine		URL/keyword
	www.google.com	search.yahoo.com	en.wikipedia.org
Falun	Conn Reset	Conn Reset	Conn Reset
Peacehall	Conn Reset	Conn Reset	Conn Reset
Liu Xiaobo	Conn Reset	OK	Conn Reset
Great FW of China	Conn Reset	OK	OK
Free Tibet	OK	OK	Conn Reset

3.2   Connection Reset

Another way of the Internet censorship in China is a "Connection Reset by Peer" result when accessing the blocked website. The result is immediate and several reasons for this approach has been identified. First, the blocked keyword occurs in the URL. Second, the content of the website is not permitted within the Mainland China.

No keyword is always blocked. It always depends on the do- main. Some keywords are blocked   as a content of a search parameters   of search engines (Google, Yahoo, ...). Some keywords are blocked as a part of URL etc. Results of this kind of analysis should be interpreted very carefully because e.g. Google is quite often redirected to it's Hong Kong version which is much less restrictive.   Table 2 contains several keywords with the associated censorship reaction.

According to the [3] the so-called "Great Firewall of China" operates, in part, by inspecting TCP packets for keywords that are to be blocked.   If the keyword is present, TCP reset packets (with the RST flag set) are sent to both endpoints of the connection, which then close. However,   because the original packets are passed through the firewall   unscathed, if the endpoints completely ignore the firewall's resets, then the connection will proceed unhindered.   Once one connection has been blocked, the firewall makes further easy-to-evade attempts to block further connec- tions from the same machine. This latter behavior can be leveraged into a denial-of- service attack on third-party machines.

The way the TCP reset packets can be ignored includes `iptables` installed within Linux. With to following command:

```
iptables -A  INPUT  -p tcp --tcp-flags  RST RST -j DROP
```

which specifies that incoming TCP packets with the RST flag set are to be discarded. Once the TCP resets are discarded the website transfer will occur without any block- ing [3].

4   Conclusion

Results presented in this paper were performed using remote PC station physically located in China. The station used is one particular PC located at one place (Hangzhou) therefore results are strongly dependent on that location.   Results from other locations could be different.

Internet censorship in China is very widespread and used techniques falls into two cat- egories: DNS cache poisoning and Connection   Reset. There are several ways how to circumvent Internet censor- ship. One of them is to ignore RST packets.   Other ways to circumvent censorship could be using technologies as proxy servers, VPN or TOR.

Future analysis of the Internet censorship could be based on the PC station where root account would be available.   We could not perform deep tests of the censorship due to these limitations.

Acknowledgements. The research has been supported by Technology Agency of the Czech Republic (TACR) in frame of the project SCADA system for control and monitoring RT processes, TA01010632. This project has been also carried out with a financial support from the Czech Republic through the project no. MSM0021630528: Security-Oriented Research in Information Technology and by the project no. ED1.1.00/02.0070: The IT4Innovations Centre of Excellence; the part of the research has been also supported by the Brno University of Technology, Faculty of Informa- tion Technology through the specific research grants no. FIT-S-11-1 and by the project MPO CR, FR-TI1/037.

References

1. Deibert, R.J., Palfrey, J.G., Rohozinski, R., Zittrain, J.: Access Denied – ThePractice and Policy of Global Internet Filtering. The MIT Press (2008)
2. Stallings, W.: Cryptography and network security: principles and practice. Prentice Hall (1998)
3. Clayton, R., Murdoch, S.J., Watson, R.: Ignoring the Great Firewall of China. University of Cambridge, http://www.cl.cam.ac.uk/~rnc1/ignoring.pdf

A Privacy-Level Model of User-Centric Cyber-Physical Systems

Nikolaos E. Petroulakis[1], Ioannis G. Askoxylakis[1], Apostolos Traganitis[1], and George Spanoudakis[2]

[1] Institute of Computer Science, Foundation for Research and Technology - Hellas, Heraklion, Greece
{npetro,asko,tragani}@ics.forth.gr
[2] School of Informatics, City University London, London, UK
g.e.spanoudakis@city.ac.uk

Abstract. In an interconnected cyber-world, Cyber-Physical Systems (CPSs) appear to play an increasingly important role in smart ecosystems. A variety of resource-constrained thin clients, such as sensors, RFIDs, actuators and smart devices, are included in the list of CPS. These devices can be used in a number of medical, vehicular, aviation, military and smart cities applications. A plethora of sensitive data is transmitted in insecure wireless or wired environments whilst adversaries are eager to eavesdrop, modify or destroy sensed data invading the privacy of user-centric CPSs. This work presents an overview and analysis of the most effective attacks, privacy challenges and mitigation techniques for preserving the privacy of users and their interconnected devices. In order to preserve privacy, a privacy-level model is proposed in which users have the capability of assigning different privacy levels based on the variety and severity of privacy challenges and devices' capabilities. Finally, we evaluate the performance of specific CPSs at different privacy-levels in terms of time and consumed energy in an experimental test-bed that we have developed.

Keywords: Privacy, Privacy-level model, Security, Cyber-Physical Systems.

1 Introduction

Cyber-Physical System (CPS) is a term used to describe integrations of computation, networking and physical processes [1]. These embedded computers and networks may monitor and control devices that are taking measurements from sensors or RFIDs. One of the most important issues of embedded systems is the small amount of theoretical work to describe how to design computer-based control systems and the work in [2] addresses this problem. Although CPS and the Internet of Things (IoT) both aim to increase the interconnection of constrained devices in cyber-space and the physical world, the term CPS is commonly used in the USA and the National Science Foundation (NFS) [3] while the European Commission refers IoT in a variety of FP7 Calls [4]. The most important

L. Marinos and I. Askoxylakis (Eds.): HAS/HCII 2013, LNCS 8030, pp. 338–347, 2013.

difference is that the main target of IoT is to develop an open platform and infrastructure for communication between smart objects such as sensors whereas CPS focuses on the exchange and feedback of information in order to control devices in the physical world [5].

CPS are small ubiquitous devices, such as sensors, actuators, RFID tags, smart phones and embedded systems able to interact and interconnect with physical elements. They can be used to vehicular networks, medical systems, the aviation industry, defense, environmental monitoring, entertainment, robotic manufacturing, electricity generation and distribution, etc. [1]. They can be categorized into three categories: monitor and detection, process and evaluation, actuation and prevention. An extensive preview of CPS in the aerospace industry perspective is presented by Boeing in [6]. They have declared that CPS investments should include industry-critical mass and multiple technology domains to acquire the required results. Authors in [7] present a human factor-aware service scheduling in vehicular CPS that depends on how drivers could benefit from such systems. Security and privacy in smart ecosystems are both critical for public safety. The large development of interconnected cities, in which humans and devices interact, generates large-scale security threats, especially for public security. CPS face many privacy challenges because of the requirements for real-time interaction and the lack of appropriate physical security due to geographical dispersion [8] and the limited resources and capabilities of thin clients.

In this paper, we extend our previous work in [9–11] by investigating attacks, challenges and methods to preserve privacy in user-centric thin clients such as CPSs. We analyze the most severe privacy challenges occurred from passive attacks, such as eavesdropping and traffic analysis, and from active attacks, such as impersonation and jamming. Suitable countermeasures are described to protect data and identity, location and routing paths. To define the privacy-level model, we group the described mitigation mechanisms into three categories according to the utilized parameters: standard parameters, fake parameters and changing parameters. Based on these categories a privacy-level model is proposed, consisting of three different levels of privacy corresponding to different privacy challenges and attacks. This model can be applied in a variety of CPSs independently of device's capabilities and operating systems. Furthermore, the privacy-level model developed here is evaluated in an experimental test-bed.

The remainder of this paper is organized as follows. In section 2, we describe the most critical attacks and privacy threats whilst in section 3, we construct the privacy-level model to mitigate the previously described privacy threats. In Section 4, we evaluate the privacy-level model using an experimental setup evaluating the trade-off between privacy and energy. Finally, we conclude this paper in Section 5.

2 Privacy Challenges and Attacks on CPSs

The massive production and transfer of sensitive data exposes the danger of privacy violation in user-centric CPSs. The vast amount of transmitted data from devices such as sensors, RFID and embedded systems, may reveal information about location and routing paths or other sensitive details such as private data and identities. CPSs are usually located in uncontrolled environments where physical attacks might occur [12]. Furthermore, their limited ability to securely store key fingerprints, their tiny computation capabilities and their limitations in power and energy make them vulnerable to adversaries. Security and privacy attacks include physical and cyber tampering or compromising devices. In the following approach we concentrate mainly on passive or active attacks that invade the privacy of user-centric CPSs.

2.1   Passive Attacks

Passive are the attacks in which an adversary monitors traffic without interacting with the victim or modifying transmitted data. The most common passive attacks are eavesdropping and traffic analysis. Eavesdropping occurs when an adversary monitors and listens to the exchanged data with the intention to extract private data. The disclosure of sensitive information such as identities and message payload, are severe privacy violations from eavesdropping. For example, the disclosure of sensed medical data such as patient's personal data, blood pressure, vital signs or sugar level, transmitted to a remote hospital or to a doctor's office, may reveal the patient's identity and condition. On the other hand, traffic analysis attacks can be applied by adversaries who do not have the ability to decrypt data payload, but they can obtain private information such as data sources, the location of devices and data routes, by the use of sniffers and packet analyzers on the wireless data transmission for tracking the traffic flow information hop-by-hop [12]. The problem of the panda and the hunter describes the situation in which scientists attempt to locate the position of a panda but they have to hide its location from panda hunters as well [13]. Revealing the topology, nature and routing paths of a transmission could be used by adversaries to track, destroy interrupt and invade the privacy of a CPS. Moreover, the danger of a compromised relay node is a result of location disclosure.

2.2   Active Attacks

An active attack occurs when an adversary attempts to modify exchanged messages, destroy the communication or replay transmitted data. The most severe active attacks which invade the privacy of CPSs are impersonation and denial of service. Impersonation attacks involve the interaction of an adversary with the human user. The adversary acts either as a man in the middle or as a masquerade, pretending to be a legal node in the network to apply spoofing attacks. These kinds of attacks appear to be not only critical for a user's privacy but also the consequences of such attacks could be extremely dangerous. For instance, an impersonation attack on a CPS, interconnected with a patient, may cause false alarms to doctor's office. And the modification of medical data can put patient's life in danger. Denial of Service (DoS) can characterize any kind of attack, which attempts to make the network resources unavailable. An active adversary applies DoS attacks by destroying or modifying the communication channel. The preservation of privacy is disrupted when an attacker applies collisions or jamming attacks creating electromagnetic interference. The lack of channel availability has a severe influence on the privacy of CPS. An adversary, causing interference in a channel in which users interchange sensitive or critical messages, may cause reportable privacy violations, such as data destruction or infinite retransmission of messages, exhausting the batteries of resource constrained CPS. Furthermore, the delayed transmission of critical information, such as private medical data of a patient to the doctors database, means the patients safety might be endangered.

3   The Privacy-Level Model

In this section, we define a privacy-level model based on the aforementioned attacks and challenges to preserve privacy in CPS. Other works, such as [14–16], focus on location privacy and route protection, providing partial privacy protection. Authors in [17] propose a full network and level privacy solution for WSN consisting of three schemes. In the first scheme, anonymity of source node's identity and location assures that path will reach their destination through trusted intermediate nodes. Forwarding packets from multiple secure paths is described in the second scheme. Finally, data secrecy and packet authentication in the presence of identity anonymity is proposed in the third scheme.

In our approach, we present a privacy-level model combining different privacy countermeasures for mitigating critical privacy dangers and attacks as described in the previous section. The main concept of this approach is that a user will be able to assign the suitable privacy level of a network, consisting of CPSs, depending on the security challenges and privacy risks. And as the level is increased we assume the protection becomes stronger. The advantage of our privacy model is that we use generic countermeasures, which can applied in a variety of CPS running different operation systems and having different capabilities. To construct the privacy-level model, we group in one model effective mitigation mechanisms to protect identity, data, routing paths and location protection. Based on our research, we can categorize countermeasures into three categories. The first category includes standard privacy countermeasures, such as encryption. In the second category, fake parameters, such as dummy data and fake paths, are assigned to protect data transmission from adversaries. Finally, the last category includes countermeasures which change frequently such as multi-paths and frequency hopping. More precisely, the three privacy-levels are described as follows.

3.1   Level 1 - Standard Parameters

In the first level, standard parameters have been assigned to mitigate attacks. When cryptographic algorithms are not used, an attacker can compromise the transmitted data easily. In order to protect the payload of transmitted data, encryption mechanisms should be used for encrypting data and prevent adversaries from passive listening and data falsification. To protect the identity of

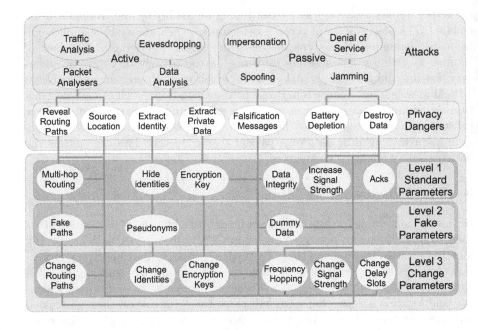

Fig. 1. The Privacy-level Model

CPS, identities of messages should be hidden either encrypted or not being assigned [17]. Furthermore, if a packet has reached the range of radio waves then it
is difficult to locate the source [18]. This can be applied by the use of multi-hop
routing which can also prevent adversaries from identifying the source and the
routing paths of transmissions. Data integrity confirms that data has not been
modified. Integrity is achieved by the use of Message Integrity Codes (MICs)
or Message Authentication Codes (MACs). Furthermore, the increase of signal
strength could mitigate weak jamming attacks [19]. Even though acknowledgment mechanisms do not guarantee data integrity, the use of them can ensure
valid packet reception.

3.2   Level 2 - Fake Parameters

The second privacy level is defined by using fake parameters. Pseudonyms can
be an effective way to hide the real identity of a node. Although pseudonyms
seem to be an effective solution, fixed pseudonyms cannot prevent adversaries
from deducing the topology of the network through traffic analysis [18]. When
actual encrypted data are not exchanged, dummy messages can be send to mask
the channel, hiding the actual data transmission. This mechanism can keep the
bandwidth constant and hide the traffic to confuse passive listeners from effective eavesdropping and traffic analysis [12, 15]. Finally, the creation of fake
paths could potentially prevent an adversary from tracking the routing path and
destroying the transmission [15, 20].

3.3   Level 3 - Change Parameters

In the third layer, stronger privacy attacks can be prevented by changing parameters frequently. As described in the first level, encryption can be an effective way to protect data. However, an adversary knowing the password may decrypt ciphered data. To avoid the danger of revealing the encryption key, a predefined set of anonymous keys changing frequently could protect the encrypted transmission between CPS. Furthermore, changing identities frequently may thwart attackers from identity disclosure. The received signal strength and the time interval appear to be one of the most major factors in locating the position of a CPS [21]. Therefore, the signal strength and the time interval of the transmission should be changed frequently. Thus, random delay slots can used for collision avoidance. Frequency hopping can prevent not only continuous impersonation or passive listening attacks but also anomaly and jamming attacks [22], protecting source location and routing paths, and assuring data transmission [19]. Finally, changing routing paths may thwart adversaries from jamming attacks [14]. In Figure 1 we depict the proposed privacy-level model corresponding to the described attacks, privacy challenges and suitable countermeasures.

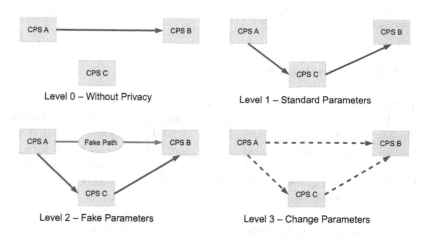

Fig. 2. Topology of the Privacy-level Scenarios

4   Evaluation of the Privacy-Level Model

In this section, we evaluate the proposed privacy-level model investigating the trade-off between energy consumption and privacy protection of each privacy level. The energy needed for computation of each level will increase along with the increase of the security level. Moreover, the time needed to execute some of the more time-consuming procedures, affects the consumed energy as well. The topology of the model consists of three nodes, CPS A, CPS B and CPS C. CPS A acts as the transmitter and CPS B acts as the receiver. The main target of

CPS A is to send a specific number of packets to CPS B. CPS C acts as a relay node to forward transmitted messages from CPS A to CPS B when multi-hop routing is applied. In Figure 2, we depict the topology of the applied scenarios based on the three described privacy levels and level zero which is assigned when privacy protection is not required or not applied.

4.1   Test-Bed Setup

To investigate the energy consumption of the different levels of privacy model, we extend our previously developed test-bed setup [10, 11]. The experimental test-bed consists of three Digi XBee Pro 802.15.4 devices which correspond to CPS A, CPS B and CPS C. All devices are connected through their serial cable with Matlab. Suitable algorithms have been developed in order to evaluate the performance and the consumed energy for each of the described privacy-levels. In the following experiments CPS A sends to CPS B 1000 packets of 100 bytes each. We conduct four different experiments comparing the results of the three privacy levels with level 0, which is the level without any privacy protection. In all four scenarios, we measure the electric current of CPS. To do this, we used a True-RMS polymeter with USB output that enabled us to store the measurements of each experiment in Matlab as well.

4.2   Performance Evaluation

In this part, a description of the conducted experiments is presented. In the first scenario, CPS A sends the specific number of packets to CPS B. Both devices assign similar configuration parameters such as minimum power level and the same channel. In the second scenario, a relay node CPS C is added to forward the traffic from CPS A to CPS B. To avoid weak jamming attacks, the power level of each device is increased at the maximum. Data transmission is assured by the use of acknowledgments, and Maxstream header MAC of XBee sensors enable data integrity. To prevent passive listeners, data privacy is ensured by the use of AES encryption. To protect identity of transmitted messages, we do not assign any identity in their header of messages. In the third scenario, fake data is transmitted in fake paths. Two types of transmissions are applied, a fake and an actual one. In our experiment, CPS A sends 10 actual packets through the relay node CPS C and then 10 fake unencrypted messages directly to CPS B. This procedure is repeated until 1000 actual data are received by CPS B. Finally, in the fourth scenario, parameters are changed frequently. To hide the location of the transmitter, variations in signal strength and in time delay are employed. Frequency hopping is also used to avoid jamming attacks. Multi-path and multi-hop routing is applied to protect the topology of routing paths. To hide the identity of the transmission, CPS A changes its id frequently. Finally, data encryption is assured by the use of a set of predefined encryption keys. The procedure is completed when 1000 messages are received by CPS B.

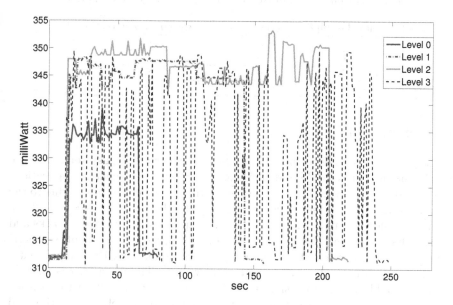

Fig. 3. Energy Consumption of the different Privacy levels

4.3   A Comparison of the Experimental Results

In the last part of this section, we present the results of the conducted experiments. The consumed energy of the experiments, which correspond the four different privacy levels, is depicted in Figure 3. The consumed energy of Level 1 is 142% higher compared to consumed energy of Level 0. This can be explained because of the multi-hop routing, the encryption and the increase of signal strength. In the Level 2, the consumed energy is about 235% higher compared to Level 0 and 46% higher compared to Level 1. The transmission of fake data in Level 2 is the main factor of the increase in consumed energy. The frequent changing parameters affect the needed energy in Level 3. The consumed energy is increased by 297% compared to Level 0, by 64% compared to Level 1 and by 12% compared to Level 2. Finally, a comparison of the consumed energy and time needed of the four different scenarios is presented in Table 1.

The experimental evaluation of the privacy-level model has shown many interesting results. The trade-off between energy and privacy appears to be an important factor for preserving privacy in CPS. The chosen method, measuring the electric current, proved to be an effective way to measure the energy consumption. Single measurements such as monitoring the CPU usage or memory use cannot reflect exactly the total consumed energy of the modules. Therefore, the employed setup was appropriate. This research work has verified our prior assumption concerning the impact on energy consumption in CPS due to different privacy challenges, evaluating the performance of the proposed privacy-level model.

Table 1. Comparison of Needed Time and Energy Consumption

Privacy Level	Time (seconds)	Energy (milliWatt-Hour)
Level 0	50.1	5.35
Level 1	127.8	12.98
Level 2	190.0	18.99
Level 3	224.7	21.29

5 Conclusion

In this paper a privacy-level model of user-centic cyber-physical systems was proposed. The plethora of CPS and their connection with user-centric applications have raised new issues and privacy threats. Privacy challenges appear due to the lack of suitable privacy mechanisms because of the limited resources of CPS. In order to define this privacy model a brief description of a variety of attacks and privacy challenges, was described. The proposed privacy-model applies generic privacy countermeasures which can applied in a number of CPS independently of their capabilities and running operating systems. The main idea is that an operator would be able to assign a specific privacy level based on the privacy challenges of a network. To evaluate this privacy-level model, an experimental investigation of the energy consumption of this privacy-level model in CPS was conducted which indicated that the energy and time needed for computation of each level was increased with the increase of level. The investigation of the trade-off between energy and privacy of each different level completed this work.

References

1. Edward, A.L.: Cyber Physical Systems: Design Challenges. In: 2008 11th IEEE International Symposium on Object and Component-Oriented Real-Time Distributed Computing (ISORC), pp. 363–369 (May 2008)
2. Wolf, W.: Cyber-physical systems. In: Embedded Computing, pp. 88–89 (2009)
3. Program Solicitation. Cyber-Physical Systems (CPS) Program Solicitation NSF 13-502 Replaces Document (S), pp. 1–13 (2013)
4. Frederixand, F.: D Sector. Internet of Things policy of the European Commission Content IoT Policy IoT in Framework 7 R & D (2010)
5. Ma, H.D.: Internet of things: Objectives and scientific challenges. Journal of Computer Science and Technology 26, 919–924 (2011)
6. Winter, D.: Cyber Physical Systems - An Aerospace Industry Perspective. Boeing, 1–18 (2008)
7. Li, X., Yu, X., Wagh, A., Qiao, C.: Human factors-aware service scheduling in vehicular cyber-physical systems. In: 2011 Proceedings of the INFOCOM, pp. 2174–2182 (April 2011)
8. Neuman, C.: Challenges in security for cyber-physical systems. In: ...Future Directions in Cyber-physical Systems Security (2009)
9. Petroulakis, N.E., Askoxylakis, I., Tryfonas, T.: Life-logging in Smart Environments: Challenges and Security Threats. In: The 2nd IEEE ICC Workshop on Convergence among Heterogeneous Wireless Systems in Future Internet (ConWire), Ottava, Canada (June 2012)

10. Petroulakis, N.E., Tragos, E.Z., Askoxylakis, I.G.: An Experimental Investigation on Energy Consumption for Secure Life-logging in Smart Environments. In: The 17th IEEE International Workshop on Computer-Aided Modeling Analysis and Design of Communication Links and Networks (CAMAD), Barcelona, Spain (September 2012)

11. Petroulakis, N.E., Tragos, E.Z., Fragkiadakis, A.G., Spanoudakis, G.: A lightweight framework for secure life-logging in smart environments. In: Elsevier Information Security Technical Report (2012)

12. Li, N., Zhang, N., Das, S.K., Thuraisingham, B.: Privacy preservation in wireless sensor networks: A state-of-the-art survey. Ad Hoc Networks 7(8), 1501–1514 (2009)

13. Ozturk, C., Zhang, Y., Trappe, W.: Source-location privacy in energy-constrained sensor network routing. In: Proceedings of the 2nd ACM Workshop on Security of Ad Hoc and Sensor Networks, SASN 2004, p. 88 (2004)

14. Gruteser, M., Schelle, G., Jain, A.: Privacy-aware location sensor networks. In: Proceedings of the 9th ... (2003)

15. Luo, X., Ji, X., Park, M.-S.: Location Privacy against Traffic Analysis Attacks in Wireless Sensor Networks. In: 2010 International Conference on Information Science and Applications, pp. 1–6 (2010)

16. Kamat, P., Zhang, Y., Trappe, W., Ozturk, C.: Enhancing Source-Location Privacy in Sensor Network Routing. In: 25th IEEE International Conference on Distributed Computing Systems, ICDCS 2005, pp. 599–608 (2005)

17. Shaikh, R.A., Jameel, H., D'Auriol, B.J., Lee, H., Lee, S., Song, Y.-J.: Achieving network level privacy in Wireless Sensor Networks. Sensors (Basel, Switzerland) 10(3), 1447–1472 (2010)

18. Veeranna, M., Krishna, V.R., Jamuna, D.: Enhancement of Privacy Level in Wireless Sensor Network. ijecse.com 1, 1024–1029 (2012)

19. Xing, K., Sundhar, S., Srinivasan, R., Rivera, M.: Attacks and Countermeasures in Sensor Networks: A Survey A wireless sensor network (WSN) is comprised of a large number of sensors that, pp. 1–28 (2005)

20. Sen, J.: A Survey on Wireless Sensor Network Security. International Journal of Communication Networks and Information Security (IJCNIS) 1(2), 55–78 (2009)

21. Hu, Y.-C., Wang, H.J.: A framework for location privacy in wireless networks. In: ACM SIGCOMM Asia Workshop (2005)

22. Chan, H., Perrig, A.: Security in Networks. IEEE Computer 36(10), 103–105 (2003)

High-Level Design for a Secure Mobile Device Management System

Keunwoo Rhee[1,*], Sun-Ki Eun[1], Mi-Ri Joo[1],
Jihoon Jeong[1], and Dongho Won[2]

[1] The Attached Institute of ETRI,
P.O. Box 1, Yuseong, Daejeon, 305-600, Korea
{kwrhee,eunsunki,mrjoo,jihoon}@ensec.re.kr
http://www.etri.re.kr
[2] College of Information and Communication Engineering,
Sungkyunkwan University,
2066, Seobu-ro, Jangan-gu, Suwon, Gyeonggi-do, 440-746, Korea
dhwon@security.re.kr
http://www.skku.edu

Abstract. Corporate security is threatened by Bring-Your-Own-Device trend. As mobile devices that provide high computing and wireless communication capabilities are increasingly being used in business, leakage of personal information and confidential data stored in a mobile device increases and bypass routes to corporate internal network are created by the mobile devices. A mobile device management system is a security solution to cope with these problems. This paper proposes platform-independent mobile device management system with using the Common Criteria for Information Technology Security Evaluation. As a result, the proposed design improves the security of the mobile device management system and guarantees high usability.

Keywords: mobile device management system, high-level design, Security Target, Common Criteria.

1 Introduction

ISO/IEC 15408 - The Common Criteria for Information Technology Security Evaluation (CC) is widely accepted as a framework in which computer users can specify their security functionalities and assurance requirements, developers can then implement and/or make claims about the security attributes of their products, and testing laboratories can evaluate the products to determine if they actually meet the claims [1]. Especially, The Security Target (ST) of the CC, an implementation-dependent statement of security needs for a specific identified Target Of Evaluation (TOE) [2], can be a basis for development method since it entails a systematic way of conforming security requirements. Therefore, in

---

* Corresponding author.

L. Marinos and I. Askoxylakis (Eds.): HAS/HCII 2013, LNCS 8030, pp. 348–356, 2013.

this paper we specify the proposed Mobile Device Management (MDM) system based on the structure of the ST.

The structure of this paper reflects the overall structure of the ST. The remainder of this section, we give an overview of an MDM system. Section 2 summarizes security objectives and Security Functional Requirements (SFRs) to design a secure MDM system. Section 3 shows core modules and describe their functionalities. Section 4 presents the relationship between SFRs and the proposed system. Finally, Section 5 shows the significance and applicability of this paper.

1.1   Mobile Device Management Systems

An MDM system comprehensively manages mobile devices by monitoring their status and controlling their functions remotely using wireless communication technology such as cellular network or Wi-Fi, as well as managing the required business resources.

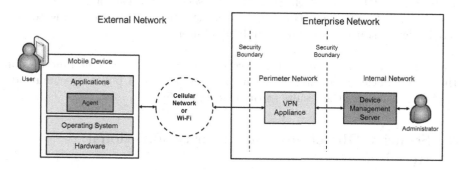

Fig. 1. The Operational Environment of an MDM System. The proposed MDM system is composed of an agent and a device management server. The security boundary includes firewall, IPS, web application firewall and so on.

The proposed MDM System consists of two main components, as shown in Fig. 1. We assume that an administrator connects to the DM server and manages the system via web browser:

An agent collects mobile device status data and sends them to the device management server [3]. It also applies policies received from the device management server to the mobile device and transmits the result back to the device management server [3]. The agent is installed on the mobile device as an application [3].

A Device Management (DM) server manages the data of registered mobile devices and users. In addition, it distributes the MDM policies and applications [3].

In the operational environment, a VPN appliance also plays a key role although it is not a component of the proposed MDM system. The VPN appliance authenticates incoming connection requests and securely relays the traffic between the agents and the DM server. Instead of a VPN, we can use validated cryptographic module [4] and communication protocol (e.g. IPSec, SSH, TLS, TLS/HTTPS) to establish a secure channel

In this system, data flows between the components are as follows.

Enrollment and Configuration (Administrator → DM server). The mobile device data and user data of the organization are registered in the DM system and the policy to be applied to each mobile device is configured [5].

Authentication (Agent → DM server). When an agent is run after installation, certain mobile device data (e.g. IMIE, IP/MAC address, phone number, etc.) are sent to the DM server to verify whether they match the data registered in the system [5].

Instruction (DM server → Agent). The DM server sends each agent the mobile device control policy, and commands such as 'remote wipe, according to the mobile device status data and the individual user [5].

Control and Report (Agent → DM server). The agent controls the functions of the mobile device according to the mobile device control policy or command. And then it reports the results to the DM server [5].

2   Security Objectives and Security Functional Requirements

At first, SFRs should be defined to design a secure system. The SFRs have been already defined in Rhee's researches [5,6]. Rhee's researches are based on the structure of the Protection Profile (PP) [2] to define SFRs. Thus, the security problems are identified by analyzing threats, organizational security policies, and assumptions and then the security objectives are provided as high-level solutions to the identified security problems.

The proposed system cannot directly comply some of the SFRs defined in the Rhee's researches since the proposed system is a part of the system as defined in Rhee's researches. However, some other components such as a VPN appliance in the operational environment satisfy the SFRs which cannot directly be complied. This can be permitted if the components in the operational environment are certified and integrated with the proposed system. For example, Mobiledesk VPN v1.0 (KECS-NISS-0356-2011) [7] is a CC certified product.

The full description of the security objectives and SFRs can be found in [5,6].

3   System Design and Security Functions

In this section, we design the system architecture. Since the proposed system consists of an agent and a DM server, we describe their logical modules and data flow between them.

3.1   Agent

An agent is composed of six logical modules. They are application management, audit and report, communication, device control, policy management, and security management. Fig. 2 describes the architecture of an agent.

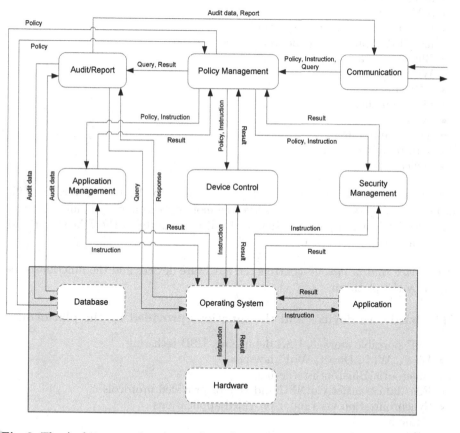

Fig. 2. The Architecture of an Agent. Actually, the applications and hardware modules are controlled by the operating system. For instance, the operating system controls the camera module of the mobile device according to the instruction from the device control module.

The application management module controls installation and execution of applications, updates applications, prevents uninstallation of enterprise applications, and removes unauthorized applications.

The audit and report module collects information of a mobile device and result of the instruction. And then it sends the audit data and the report to the communication module. When the communication module loses connection to the server, it stores the audit data in the database or as a file until the connection module reconnects to ensure that audit data are generated and stored in the DM server-side database.

[The information of a mobile device]

- assigned IP address
- SIM state
- version of the operating system
- installed application name/version/permission
- Bluetooth status
- Wi-Fi status
- GPS status
- phone number
- IMEI
- hardware resource
- data roaming setting
- device type

The communication module provides connections to the DM server. For efficiency, the agents and the DM server cannot make connections all the time. Therefore, when the push message arrived, it connects to the DM server and downloads policy and data.

The device control module controls the hardware devices and the functions provided by the platform.

[The hardware devices and the functions provided by the platform]

- USB portable storage, USB debugging, USB tethering
- Wi-Fi, Wi-Fi Direct, Wi-Fi hotspot
- Bluetooth, Bluetooth tethering
- File/data transfer via NFC and vendor provided protocols
- Synchronization via vendor provided applications
- Camera
- GPS
- Microphone
- External memory such as a SD card.
- Screen capture
- Screen lock
- Data reset or wipe

The policy management module manages configurations related to the application management, device control, and security management. It sends the policies or instructions to the application management module, device control module, and security management module. In addition, it verifies the integrity of the policy to prevent unauthorized modification.

The security management module sets authentication policy such as password, pin, and so on. In addition, it detects the modification of the platform and protects itself from the unauthorized deletion or stop.

3.2   Device Management Server

A DM server is composed of five logical modules. They are application management, audit and report, communication, identification and authentication, and policy management. Fig. 3 describes the architecture of a DM server.

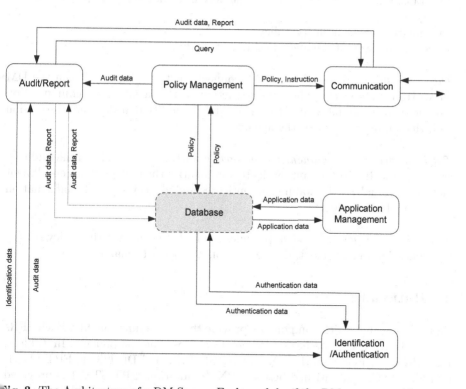

Fig. 3. The Architecture of a DM Server. Each module of the DM server provides user interface for administrator's management.

The application management module manages the list of permitted applications (whitelist) or the list of unpermitted applications (blacklist) with the hash values or digital signatures of applications.

The audit and report module manages audit data from the agents and administrative events (e.g. administrators login, policy change, etc.). In addition, it provides methods to search a specific audit event, a registered user or a mobile device.

[Audit events]

- Administrator's login
- Failure of login attempts (with the number of attempt)
- Session locking or termination
- Duplicate login attempts (with the ID)
- Registration of a user
- Modification of the information of an administrator, a registered user, and a mobile device
- Modification of the security policy
- Transfer a security policy or an instruction to the agents, response from the agents
- Violation of the security policy
- Start and stop of the audit and report module

The communication module provides connections to the agents. When the DM server transmits a new policy or instruction to the agent, the communication module sends push message to the agent first. In addition, it manages the session with the administrator and the agents.

The identification and authentication module authenticates and identifies administrator, user. In order to authenticate and identify them, it provides enrollment methods. Actually, this module authenticates and identifies users by information of their mobile devices.

The policy management module provides methods to configure the policy related to application management, device control, and security management.

4   Rationale

Table 1 indicates which components provide the SFR's functionality. Each SFRs claimed in Rhee's researches trace back to at least one components. In Table 1, FCS_CKM.1ã, FCS_COP.1, FDP_IFC.1, FDP_IFF.1, FDP_ITC.1, FPT_ITC.1, and FTP_ITC.1 are satisfied by the VPN. In addition, FPT_STM.1 is provided by the operating system. The operating system gets the trusted time from an NTP server, a base station, or a GPS satellite.

Table 1. The completeness of SFRs. Some functionality to satisfy the SFRs claimed in PP is provided by the operational environment. The letter indicates where the functionality to satisfy the SFRs is provided. 'A' means that the agent provides the functionality. 'S' means that the DM server provides the functionality. The letter 'E' means that the IT environment provides the functionality.

SFRs	Components	SFRs	Components
FAU_ARP.1	A, S	FDP_SDI.2	A
FAU_GEN.1	A, S	FDP_UCT.1	A, S
FAU_GEN.2	S	FDP_UIT.1	A, S
FAU_SAA.1	S	FDP_ERA_EXT.1	A
FAU_SAR.1	S	FIA_AFL.1	A, S
FAU_SAR.2	S	FIA_ATD.1	A
FAU_SAR.3	S	FIA_SOS.1	A, S
FAU_STG.1	S	FIA_UAU.2	A, S
FAU_STG.3	S	FIA_UAU.4	S
FAU_STG.4	S	FIA_UAU.7	A, S
FCS_CKM.1	E	FIA_UID.2	S
FCS_CKM.2	E	FMT_MOF.1	S
FCS_CKM.3	E	FMT_MSA.1	S
FCS_CKM.4	E	FMT_MSA.2	S
FCS_COP.1	E	FMT_MSA.3	S
FDP_ACC.1	A	FMT_SMF.1	S
FDP_ACF.1	A, S	FMT_SMR.1	S
FDP_APP_EXT.1	A	FPT_ITC.1	E
FDP_ETC.1	A, S	FPT_ITT.1	A, S
FDP_IFC.1	A, S, E	FPT_ITT.2	A, S
FDP_IFF.1	A, S, E	FPT_STM.1	E
FDP_ITC.1	A, S, E	FTA_CTL_EXT.1	A
FDP_LOC_EXT.1	A	FTA_MCS.1	S
FDP_MDC_EXT.1	A	FTA_SSL.1	A, S
FDP_RIP.1	A	FTA_SSL.2	A, S
FDP_SDC_EXT.1	A	FTA_SSL.3	S
FDP_SDI.1	A	FTP_ITC.1	E

5   Conclusion

In this paper, we use the structure of the ST to design a secure MDM system. Our approach is similar to the researches by Pedersen et al., 2006 [8] and Vetterling et al., 2002 [9]. It is very useful way to assure the security functionality. However, the TOE and the version of the CC are different. Besides, we focus on the more detailed modules and their relationship. The framework of the proposed platform-independent design may guarantee high usability.

References

1. Lee, K.: A Study on the Design of Secure Multi Function Printer conforming to the Korea Evaluation and Certification Scheme. Ph. D. Dissertation, Sungkyunkwan University, Suwon (2011)

2. CCMB: Common Criteria for Information Technology Security Evaluation Part 1: Introduction and general model Version 3.1 Revision 4 (2012)
3. Rhee, K., Won, D., Jang, S.W., Chae, S., Park, S.: Threat Modeling of a Mobile Device Management System for Secure Smart Work. Electron. Commer. Res. (to be appeared)
4. Module Validation List, Computer Security Resource Center, National Institute of Standard and Technology, http://csrc.nist.gov/groups/STM/cmvp/validation.html
5. Rhee, K., Jeon, W., Won, D.: Security Requirements of a Mobile Device Management System. International Journal of Security and Its Applications 6, 353–358 (2012)
6. Rhee, K.: A Study on the Security Evaluation of a Mobile Device Management System. Ph. D. Dissertation, Sungkyunkwan University, Suwon (2012)
7. Mobiledesk, Samsung SDS, http://www.sdsems.co.kr/WebContent/product/vpn.jsp
8. Pedersen, A., Hedegaard, A., Sharp, R.: Designing a Secure Point-of-Sale System. In: 4th IEEE International Workshop on Information Assurance, pp. 51–65. IEEE Computer Society Press, Washington, DC (2006)
9. Vetterling, M., Wimmel, G., Wisspeintner, A.: Secure Systems Development based on the Common Criteria: The PalME Project. SIGSOFT Softw. Eng. Notes 27, 129–138 (2002)

Factors Influencing Adoption of Encryption to Secure Data in the Cloud

Kenneth E. Stavinoha

Cisco Systems, San Jose, California
kestavin@cisco.com

Abstract. This research measured factors that influence the adoption of encryption to secure data in the cloud and provided guidance on when encryption might be most appropriate. Additionally, the study investigated the important elements necessary to develop a framework for a secure cloud computing environment. The objective of this research was to provide normative guidance and empirical data that assists both cloud service providers and users of cloud technology in selecting the best mitigation, or suite of mitigations, that most effectively protect data in the cloud. This research helps to fill a gap by examining issues affecting cloud consumers, the elements that play a role in the decision to use a cloud service, and the influencing factors in the decision to use encryption to secure data in the cloud.

1 Introduction

As organizations contemplate the adoption of cloud computing, concerns regarding security and control over client data are being brought to the forefront, as are issues of responsibility between consumers and providers. An IDC (2008) survey and two Avanade (2009a, b) surveys found that while an increasing number of organizations are viewing cloud computing as a viable technology, the most prevalent factor inhibiting the adoption of cloud computing is security. A Ponemon (2011) survey of cloud service providers found that the vast majority did not view cloud security as their responsibility but instead pointed the finger at the cloud consumer. Furthermore, the providers did not perceive a competitive advantage over the competition in offering secure cloud solutions. Research performed by the Queen Mary University of London School of Law found that for a majority of off-the-shelf cloud services, the service contracts were typically written to absolve the cloud service provider of any responsibility for security failures, except where legislation dictated otherwise (Bradshaw, Millard, & Walden, 2011).

Three primary aspects covered in this study were concerns over the security of data in the cloud, the factors in the decision to adopt a new technology, and recommendations on the use of encryption to secure data. The literature has consistently shown that concerns over security, governance, and privacy rank highly in the minds of consumers when considering the use of cloud computing services (Avanade, 2009a; Avanade, 2009b; Blum & Krikken, 2009; CSA, 2009; Chichester, 2009; Chow et al.,

L. Marinos and I. Askoxylakis (Eds.): HAS/HCII 2013, LNCS 8030, pp. 357–365, 2013.
© Springer-Verlag Berlin Heidelberg 2013

2009; ENISA, 2009; Fischmann, 2008; Forsheit, 2009; Kaufman, 2009; Mowbray & Pearson, 2009). Research by Dynes, Brechbuhl, and Johnson (2005), Fichman (1992), and Johnson and Goetz (2007) and suggests that the decision to adopt a technology – particularly information security – is a complex process and that information technology (IT) and information assurance (IA) professionals were most often relied upon for their expertise when organizations considered adopting new IT tools and/or technologies. Finally, encryption is a frequently recommended solution for protecting data as found in standards, guidance, and legislation (21 CMR 17.00, 2010; CSA, 2010; ENISA, 2009; HIPAA HHS, 2006; ISO/IEC 27002, 2005; McCallister et al., 2010; NRS 603A, 2010; PCI DSS, 2009).

However, there are practical limits to encryption as a "cure-all" solution for securing data. As cited by CSA "encryption itself does not necessarily prevent data loss" (CSA, 2009, p.60) because there are vulnerabilities – such as weak authentication – and failures of process – such as poor key management – which can adversely affect the security which encryption is meant to provide. If the cloud service provider performs the encryption and key management (CSA, 2009; Blum & Krikken, 2010; ENISA, 2009), this may weaken protection of the data because a third party has control over, and potentially access to, the data (Couillard, 2010; Gellman, 2009). There is also the challenge of encrypting data at rest versus data in transit which are typically separate actions requiring different sets of encryption keys, additional key management, and separate processing. The largest gap in cryptography is the inability to effectively and efficiently maintain encryption on data in use. Homomorphic encryption – which could enable some processing of data while it remains encrypted - is being offered as a potential solution (Chow et. al, 2009; Fischmann, 2008; Lauter, Naehrig, & Vaikuntanathan, 2011; Naone, 2011), but it will require further research and testing, which may take many years, to bring homomorphic encryption into play as a realistic business solution (Blum & Krikken, 2009; ENISA, 2009; Schneier, 2009).

2   Experiments

Based on research by Dynes, Brechbuhl and Johnson, (2005), Fichman (1992), Johnson and Goetz (2007), and prior willingness to adopt technology research by Cole (2008), Comings (2008), Lease (2005), Ting (2008), and Turek, (2011), it was deemed relevant to solicit the perceptions of IT/IA professionals on their willingness to adopt encryption to secure data in the cloud. The four independent variables for this research - security effectiveness, organizational need, reliability, and cost-effectiveness – have been identified by a number of researchers as factors in the decision to adopt a technology (Ettlie, 2006; Lease, 2005; Roberts & Pick, 2004; Soliman & Janz, 2004; Tobin & Bidoli, 2006; VarShney et al., 2002) and yielded the four research questions posed in this study:

Question 1: Is an IT/IA professional's willingness to adopt encryption to secure data in the cloud dependent on his/her perception of its security effectiveness?

Question 2: Is an IT/IA professional's willingness to adopt encryption to secure data in the cloud dependent on his/her perceived need for security technologies?

Question 3: Is an IT/IA professional's willingness to adopt encryption to secure data in the cloud dependent on his/her perception of its reliability?

Question 4: Is an IT/IA professional's willingness to adopt encryption to secure data in the cloud dependent on his/her perception of its cost effectiveness?

To measure the dependent variable – willingness to adopt encryption to secure data in the cloud – participants were asked about their willingness to adopt encryption and if they believed that encryption uses proven technology. To measure security effectiveness, participants were asked if they would adopt encryption to secure data in the cloud and consider that the use of encryption is secure, if they considered encryption more secure than other data protection methods, whether they had concerns about the technology of encryption, and if they were willing to adopt encryption to secure data in the cloud. For the measurement of organizational need, participants were asked if they perceived that their organization needed to improve the security of its IT assets in the cloud, if they perceived that their organization needed encryption to secure its IT assets in the cloud, and if they perceived that encryption of data in the cloud provided significant benefit to their organization. To measure reliability, participants were asked if they perceived encryption to be reliable, and if they perceived it to be more reliable than other IT security methods. Cost effectiveness was measured by asking respondents if they perceived encryption to provide a good value for the cost, if they perceived that maintenance costs for encryption were lower than other IT security methods, and if they perceived that encryption offered cost savings as compared to other IT security methods.

3   Results

In the hypothesis testing, it was shown that all four of the hypotheses were supported via analysis of the Chi-Square Test for Independence. IT/IA professionals' willingness to adopt encryption to secure data in the cloud is dependent on their perception of its security effectiveness, reliability, cost effectiveness, and the needs of their organizations. The results in this study align with those of previous researchers and guidance in the literature in noting the influence of these four independent variables in the decision to adopt a security technology.

Once it was established that there was a relationship between the dependent variable and each of the independent variables, further statistical analysis was performed to evaluate the strength of those relationships. Pearson's Product Moment Correlation showed that the strongest relationships between dependent and independent variables were, in descending order, security effectiveness ($r =.563$), organizational need ($r = .453$), cost effectiveness ($r = .333$), and reliability ($r = .324$). All of these relationships were statistically significant ($n = 172$, $p = .001$).

Table 1. Pearson Correlation for Dependent and Independent Variables

		Dependent Variable	Need	Reliable	Cost	Security
DV	Pearson Correlation	1	.453**	.324**	.333**	.563**
	Sig (2 tailed)		.000	000	.000	.000
	N	172	172	172	172	.172
N	Pearson Correlation	.453**	1	.087	.356**	.236**
	Sig (2 tailed)	.000		.259	.000	.002
	N	172	172	172	172	172
R	Pearson Correlation	.324**	.087	1	.215**	.392**
	Sig (2 tailed)	.000	.259		.005	.000
	N	172	172	172	172	172
C	Pearson Correlation	.333**	.356**	.215**	1	.268**
	Sig (2 tailed)	.000	.000	.005		.000
	N	172	172	172	172	172
S	Pearson Correlation	.563**	.236	.392**	.268**	1
	Sig (2 tailed)	.000	.002	.000	000	
	N	172	172	172	172	172

** Correlation is significant at the 0.01 level (2-tailed).

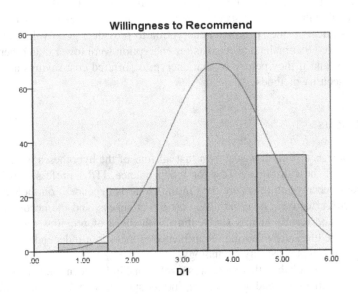

Fig. 1. Histogram: Willingness to Recommend Encryption

While the survey focused on IT/IA professionals, 31.4% of participants identified themselves as being in an IT/IA management role. The results of additional statistical analysis showed that the perceptions of the management respondents the adoption of encryption to secure data in the cloud were largely similar to those of the entire sample population. For this study, the alignment of perceptions for IT/IA management and IT/IA professionals reflects results in the research of Dynes, Brechbuhl, and Johnson (2005) in that IT/IA management often relies on the advice of IT/IA professionals when considering the adoption of security technology.

3.1   Alternatives to Encryption

One item in the survey asked respondents to choose a course of action if encryption was not available as an option to secure data in the cloud. The vast majority of respondents (56.4%) indicated that they would not use a cloud service for this data if encryption was not an option to protect it, while the next highest percentage of respondents (26.4%) replied that access controls would be relied upon if encryption were not available. Only 9.2% of respondents felt that anonymization of the data was a suitable choice if encryption were not available and the lowest number of respondents (8%) felt that relying on the contract with the cloud provider to protect the data was an acceptable option.

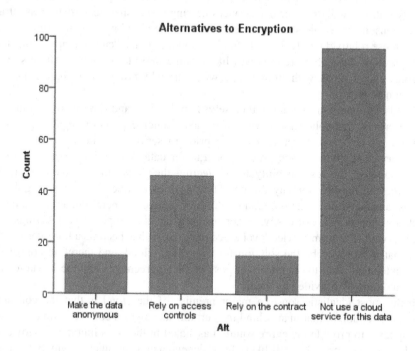

Fig. 2. Survey results for encryption alternatives query

The management subset was even more adamant: 62.96% chose not to use a cloud service for data if encryption was not an option. Only 3.7% of the management respondents chose to use anonymization as an option, and the percentages for the other two options were largely similar to those stated above.

4   Conclusions

The information provided in this research is valuable to both those considering using a cloud service as well as those developing and/or providing cloud services. The results of this research align with earlier studies cited heretofore in that, clearly, users of cloud services feel a strong need to protect their data. Encryption is an often-recommended solution which IT/IA professionals have years of experience in, and a large percentage of those professionals prefer not to use a cloud service if encryption is not an option to protect their data. This need becomes a critical factor in the decision to utilize one cloud offering versus another and it benefits both cloud consumer and provider if encryption is an option.

Implications for practitioners are clear – users of cloud services expect that there will be reasonable options for securing their data. Cloud service providers that feel security is not an important factor in the decision to use a cloud service, or believe that it is not beholden on the cloud service provider (CSP) to provide reasonable data security options, will discover that services lacking this desired feature are less attractive to consumers. While such providers may be able to enjoy some measure of success in these relatively early days of cloud computing with a "caveat emptor" mentality, the law of diminishing returns will likely come into play as more mature service offerings evolve along with an increased willingness by providers to share risks with cloud consumers.

Cloud consumers must educate themselves on the risks and rewards of various service offerings, and solicit the advice of subject matter experts on legal, regulatory, security, privacy, and governance issues prior to serious consideration of using a cloud service to create, store, process, or transfer data. While data owners can outsource some of the responsibility for protecting their data, they cannot effectively outsource the liability for any failure. The penalties of fines, sanctions, regulatory actions, and possible litigation, along with the negative financial impact of damaged reputation and brand, can easily render insignificant the proposed cost savings of a cloud service. The term service level agreement (SLA) has become a buzzword to the point that it seems to be the solution for everything cloud, and therefore consumers must understand well the intended purpose of such agreements and the limitations in scope and remedy provided by them.

In the most idealistic sense, a major premise of the cloud is that the consumer "pays no attention to that man behind the curtain" and signs a contract with a provider who appears to provide the entire solution as stated in the sales literature. However, the cloud service provider will likely have dependencies on other providers (storage, network, application, processing, etc.) – none of which are necessarily contractually obligated directly back to the consumer. Further, these dependencies may change frequently and suddenly without the knowledge of the consumer – especially when cloud service providers are trying to meet elasticity requirements - and it can become a challenge for the consumer to know where their data is and how/if it is being appropriately protected. This daisy chain of trust may well pose risks over which the cloud consumer has no direct legal remedy, and the contract with the provider may not afford such. Increased levels of due diligence and due care are required by policy makers to ensure that cloud service agreements sufficiently identify and address all pertinent risks to the organization, that responsibilities are clearly delineated among all parties, and that remedies are explicitly understood in the case of performance failure and/or breach of contract.

Any organization contemplating using a cloud service should perform thorough due diligence around sensitivity of their data, vulnerabilities of the environment, reputation of the cloud service provider(s), and terms of the contract. While benefits of cloud computing in terms of efficiencies, flexibility, productivity, and cost savings have been shown both in empirical research and more frequently in white papers and case studies, not all of these benefits can be generalized across the vast spectrum of cloud services, infrastructures, and platforms to provide useful data for comparison and study. Hopefully, in the longer term, cloud standards, taxonomies, and ontologies will provide the foundation for a clear understanding of the risks and rewards of cloud computing which transcend current boundaries. In the current environment and for the near future, cloud consumers should entrust their data only to those providers whose platforms and services clearly meet the needs of their organization and do not introduce unacceptable levels of risk.

References

1. Avanade (January 2009a) global survey of cloud computing. Retrieved from the Avanade website:
   `http://avanade.dk/_uploaded/pdf/`
   `avanadethoughtleadershipcloudsurveyexecutivesumma-`
   `ry833173.pdf`
2. Avanade (September 2009b) global survey of cloud computing. Retrieved from the Avanade website:
   `http://www.avanade.com/Documents/Research%20and%20Insights/`
   `fy10cloudcomputingexecutivesummaryfinal314006.pdf`
3. Blum, D., Krikken, R.: Using encryption to protect sensitive data in cloud computing environments (2010), Retrieved from The Burton Group website:
   `http://www.burtongroup.com/Client/Research/`
   `Document.aspx?cid=1904&contentView=FullContent`
4. Bradshaw, S., Millard, C., Walden, I.: Contracts for clouds: Comparison and analysis of the terms and conditions of cloud computing services. Information Journal of Law and Information Technology 19, 187–223 (2011), doi:10.1093/ijlit
5. Cloud Security Alliance (CSA), Security guidance for critical areas of focus in cloud computing v2.1. (2009) Retrieved from Cloud Security Alliance website:
   `http://www.cloudsecurityalliance.org/guidance/csaguide.v2.1.`
   `pdf`

6. Chichester, R.: Litigating on the clouds. Retrieved from the Texas Bar CLE Online Library (2009), http://www.texasbarcle.com/CLE/OLSearchResults.asp?ViewProgr am=25231&searchtype=VA&sCalledFrom=OLSEARCH.ASP&FreeOnly=
7. Chow, R., Golle, P., Jakobsson, M., Shi, E., Staddon, J., Masuoka, R., Molina, J.: Controlling data in the cloud: Outsourcing computation without outsourcing control. In: Proceedings of the 2009 ACM Workshop on Cloud Computing Security (CCSW 2009), pp. 85–90. ACM, Chicago (November 13, 2009), doi:10.1145/1655008.1655020
8. Cole, S.: Adopting Biometrics: factors that influence decision-making managers (unpublished doctoral dissertation). University of Fairfax, Vienna, Virginia (2008)
9. Comings, D.: Factors influencing the development of COTS information security products that meet federal requirements for national security systems (unpublished doctoral dissertation). University of Fairfax, Vienna, Virginia (2008)
10. Couillard, D.: Defogging the cloud: Applying fourth amendment principles to evolving privacy expectations in cloud computing. Minnesota Law Review 93, 2205–2239 (2010), http://ssrn.com/abstract=1832982 (retrieved)
11. Dynes, S., Brechbuhl, H., Johnson, M.E.: Information security in the extended enterprise: Some initial results from a field study of an industrial firm (Working Paper Series 05-1). Glassmeyer/McNamee Center for Digital Strategies, Tuck School of Business at Dartmouth. (2005), http://www.tuck.dartmouth.edu/ cds-uploads/publications/pdf/Paper_InfoSecurityExtended.pdf (retrieved)
12. Ettlie, J.: Managing innovation. Elsevier Butterworth-Heinemann, Burlington (2006)
13. European Network and Information Security Agency (ENISA), Cloud computing: Benefits, risks and recommendations for information security. Retrieved ENISA website (2009), http://www.enisa.europa.eu/act/rm/files/deliverables/ cloud-computing-risk-assessment
14. Fichman, R.: Information technology diffusion: A review of empirical research. In: DeGross, J.I., Becker, J.D., Elam, J.J. (eds.) Proceedings of the Thirteenth International Conference on Information Systems, ICIS 1992, pp. 195–206 (1992)
15. Fischmann, M.: Data confidentiality and reputation schemes in distributed information systems, Humboldt University, Berlin, Germany. Doctoral thesis (2008), http://edoc.hu-berlin.de/dissertationen/ fischmann-matthias-2008-05-23/PDF/fischmann.pdf (retrieved)
16. Forsheit, T.: Legal implications of cloud computing – part four (2009), Retrieved from the Information Law Group web site: http://www.infolawgroup.com/2009/11/articles/ cloud-computing-1/legal-implications-of-cloud-computing- part-four-ediscovery-and-digital-evidence/
17. Department of Health and Human Services (HHS), Health insurance portability and accountability act (HIPAA) administration simplification. Regulation Text 45 CFR Parts 160, 162, and 164 (Unofficial Version, as amended through February 16 2006, Retrieved from the HHS website (2006), http://www.hhs.gov/ocr/privacy/hipaa/administrative/ privacyrule/adminsimpregtext.pdf
18. International Standards Organization/International Electrotechnical Commission (ISO/IEC), Information technology - Security techniques - Code of practice for information security management. ISO/IEC, Geneva (2005)

19. Johnson, M., Goetz, E.: Embedding information security into the organization. IEEE Security and Privacy 5(3), 16–24 (2007), doi:10.1109/MSP.2007.59
20. Kaufman, L.: Data security in the world of cloud computing. IEEE Security and Privacy 7(4), 61–64 (2009), doi:10.1109/MSP.2009.87
21. Lauter, K., Naehrig, M., Vaikuntanathan, V.: Can homomorphic encryption be practical? In: Proceedings of the 3rd ACM Workshop on Cloud Computing Security Workshop, CCSW 2011. ACM, New York (2011), http://dx.doi.org/10.1145/2046660.2046682
22. Lease, D.: Factors influencing the adoption of biometric security technologies by decision making information technology and security managers (2005), http://drdavidlease.com/uploads/David_Lease_UMI_Dissertation.pdf (retrieved)
23. Mass. Gen. Laws § 17 Standards for the Protection of Personal Information. 201 CMR 17.00
24. McCallister, E., Grance, T., Scarfone, A.: Guide to protecting the confidentiality of personally identifiable information. Retrieved from the National Institute of Standards and Technology (NIST) website (2010), http://www.nist.gov/manuscript-publication-search.cfm?pub_id=904990
25. Mowbray, M., Pearson, S.: A client-based privacy manager for cloud computing. In: Proceedings of the Fourth International ICST Conference on Communication System Software and Middleware, pp. 1–8. ACM, New York (2009), doi:10.1145/1621890.1621897
26. Naone, E.: Homomorphic encryption. Technology Review (May/June 2011), http://www.technologyreview.com/computing/37197/ (retrieved)
27. Nevada Gen. Laws NRS 603A: Security of Personal Information (2010)
28. Payment Card Industry, PCI, Data security standard requirements and assessment procedures v1.2.1. (2009) Retrieved from the PCI website: https://www.pcisecuritystandards.org/security_standards/pci_dss_download.html
29. Ponemon Institute, Security of cloud computing providers study (2011), Retrieved from the Computer Associates website: http://www.ca.com/~/media/Files/IndustryResearch/security-of-cloud-computing-providers-final-april-2011.pdf
30. Roberts, G., Pick, J.: Technology factors in corporate adoption of mobile cell phones: A case study analysis. In: Proceedings of the 37th Annual Hawaii International Conference on System Sciences (HICSS 2004 - Track 9) (2004), doi:10.1109/HICSS.2004.1265678
31. Soliman, K., Janz, B.: Interorganizational information systems: Exploring an internet-based approach. Information and Management 41, 697–706 (2004), http://dx.doi.org/10.1016/j.im.2003.06.001
32. Ting, W.: Factors influencing the adoption of enterprise wide information security metrics by decision making managers (unpublished doctoral dissertation), University of Fairfax, Vienna, Virginia (2008)
33. Tobin, P.K.J., Bidoli, M.: Factors Affecting the Adoption of Voice over Internet Protocol (VoIP) and other Converged IP services in South Africa. South African Journal of Business Management 37(1), 31–40 (2006)
34. Turek, J.: Factors That Influence Security Executives to Recommend Unified Threat Management (unpublished doctoral dissertation), University of Fairfax, Vienna, Virginia (2011)
35. VarShney, U., Snow, A., McGivern, M., Howard, C.: Voice Over IP. Communications of the ACM 45(1), 89–95 (2002), doi:10.1145/502269.502271

Cloudopsy: An Autopsy of Data Flows in the Cloud

Angeliki Zavou[1], Vasilis Pappas[1], Vasileios P. Kemerlis[1],
Michalis Polychronakis[1], Georgios Portokalidis[2], and Angelos D. Keromytis[1]

[1] Columbia University, New York, NY, USA
{azavou,vpappas,vpk,mikepo,angelos}@cs.columbia.edu
[2] Stevens Institute of Technology, Hoboken, NJ, USA
gportoka@stevens.edu

Abstract. Despite the apparent advantages of cloud computing, the fear of unauthorized exposure of sensitive user data [3, 4, 8, 13] and non-compliance to privacy restrictions impedes its adoption for security-sensitive tasks. For the common setting in which the cloud infrastructure provider and the online service provider are different, end users have to trust the efforts of both of these parties for properly handling their private data as intended. To address this challenge, in this work, we take a step towards elevating the confidence of users for the safety of their cloud-resident data by introducing Cloudopsy, a service with the goal to provide a visual *autopsy* of the exchange of user data in the cloud premises. Cloudopsy offers a user-friendly interface to the customers of the cloud-hosted services to *independently* monitor and get a better understanding of the handling of their cloud-resident sensitive data by the third-party cloud-hosted services. While the framework is targeted mostly towards the end users, Cloudopsy provides also the service providers with an additional layer of protection against illegitimate data flows, *e.g.,* inadvertent data leaks, by offering a graphical more meaningful representation of the overall service dependencies and the relationships with third-parties outside the cloud premises, as they derive from the collected audit logs. The novelty of Cloudopsy lies in the fact that it leverages the power of *visualization* when presenting the final audit information to the end users (and the service providers), which adds significant benefits to the understanding of rich but ever-increasing audit trails. One of the most obvious benefits of the resulting visualization is the ability to better understand ongoing events, detect anomalies, and reduce decision latency, which can be particularly valuable in real-time environments.

1 Introduction

The benefits of cloud computing for service providers and end users have led to a rapid increase of online services and applications. As businesses and individuals rely on the cloud for most of their everyday tasks, it is inevitable that *personally identifiable information* (PII) will also be stored and processed on third parties premises, like the cloud, outside the administrative control of its owners. Credit

L. Marinos and I. Askoxylakis (Eds.): HAS/HCII 2013, LNCS 8030, pp. 366–375, 2013.

card numbers, private files, and other kinds of sensitive data are temporarily or permanently stored in back-end databases and file systems, beyond user control. In this setting, data confidentiality becomes one of the primary concerns for users of these cloud-hosted services, especially when taking into account the recent security incidents and data breaches [1,5,15,16], witnessed even on major and reputable online services. Customer lack of confidence is actually one of the most highly cited concerns regarding the use of cloud-hosted services [7]. In lack of an alternative option (other than not using the service at all), most users eventually share their data with cloud services, and rely on legal agreements and trust the efforts of service providers in securely handling and protecting their data.

However, even when service providers are considered trusted and follow best security practices, unauthorized access to sensitive data remains a plausible threat, e.g., due to software vulnerabilities, improper access permissions to third-party services, misconfigurations, or incorrect assumptions. Although, there has been a large body of work on the prevention, detection, and mitigation of such incidents, they still pose an tangible threat. From the data owner's perspective, users wish to have a better understanding on how their data is being handled by the cloud-hosted online services, and ensure that their data is not being abused or leaked, or at least have an indication that such an event has occurred.

Auditing has been long employed with success as an added security measure in alleviating user security concerns in domains like banking, where information security is mission critical. Unlike other privacy protection technologies that are built on enforcing policies and preventing data flows, auditing focuses on keeping data usage *transparent* and *trackable*. Thorough, efficient auditing in cloud computing remains a challenge even for straightforward web services, but more research is directed towards this goal [2,10,12,18]. However, even when auditing mechanisms are implemented successfully, services continuously increasing in size (*i.e.*, number of users, components, *etc.*), create massive numbers of audit logs and trails of information. In consequence, their usefulness is limited because the task of interpreting logs and identifying interesting details becomes extremely challenging for end users. Therefore, it is easy to conclude that the audit information collected must be structured in a way that is comprehensible by end users.

To address this privacy challenge, we take a step towards increasing cloud transparency with respect to the handling of sensitive user data by introducing Cloudopsy, a service with the goal of providing *secure* and *comprehensible* data auditing capabilities to both the service providers and their clients for user data collected in the realm of these cloud-hosted services. Even though information flow auditing and enforcement techniques use similar mechanisms, we focus our efforts in *auditing*, due to the concerns that enforcement could have adverse effects like breaking parts of services. Cloudopsy operates together with our cloud-wide data tracking framework [14] and "it" enhances with the power of *visualization*, when presenting the final audit information to data owners and service providers. This novel feature of Cloudopsy significantly reinforces

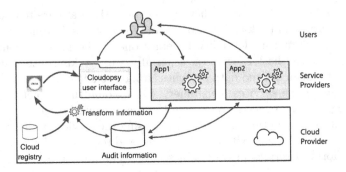

Fig. 1. High-level overview of Cloudopsy's architecture and how it integrates with our cloud-wide data tracking framework

end-user awareness regarding the use and exposure of their sensitive data by the cloud-hosted applications. In a few words, we claim that audit visualization is a necessary feature in the analysis of audit logs, as it helps in recognizing events and associations recorded in the logs that might have otherwise remained unnoticed or would have taken longer to realize.

To truly support this vision, we envision cloud providers offering the Cloudopsy auditing service in addition to their existing hosting environment, to both service providers and data owners. A large, reputable cloud provider can help leverage user confidence much more effectively. Cloudopsy platform architecture could dramatically reduce the per-application development effort required to offer data protection, while still allowing rapid development and maintenance.

The remainder of this paper is organized as follows: Section 2 discusses our goals and key assumptions. We present Cloudopsy and elaborate on its components in sections 3 and 4. In Section 4, we demonstrate Cloudopsy with a real-world application and conclude the paper in Section 5.

2   Cloudopsy

A high-level overview of Cloudopsy's architecture is illustrated in Fig. 1. The participating entities are: the *cloud provider*, who offers the cloud infrastructure or platform, the *service providers* deploying the online service, and the *end users* or *data owners*, who are the clients of the online service. Cloudopsy is an enhanced auditing service offered by the cloud provider to the service providers it hosts on its premises, as well as the end users of these services.

The providers of the cloud-hosted services need to define the boundaries of their *data flow domain*, *i.e.*, the component applications of their *composite* service (*e.g.*, web server, back-end database *etc.*). On the other hand, the users of the cloud-hosted services are assigned a *unique ID*, which will be their unique cloud-wide identification. Each end user has to register/sign in with this ID every time he uses one of the services hosted by the cloud provider, if he wishes to have his sensitive data audited for the services hosted on the same cloud provider. (*e.g.*, Google Apps).

The rest of Cloudopsy's mechanism can be divided in three main components: (a) the generation of the audit trails, (b) the transformation of the audit logs for efficient processing, and (c) the visualization of the resulting audit trails.

2.1   Audit Logs Generation

To generate audit logs, Cloudopsy relies on information flow tracking techniques to track the entire flow of information in the realm of participating services hosted on the same cloud provider [14]. Separate audit logs are created for each cloud-hosted service and they are later correlated and filtered for creating the different audit logs that will be presented to data owner or the service provider requesting the audit. From a high level view, after one user's data enter the service, they are colored with a unique ID bound to that particular user, and audit information is generated every time it crosses the defined boundary of the data flow domain of the service, *e.g.*, when colored data is about to be send to a cloud storage device or host inside or outside of the cloud, that does not belong to the defined components of the service. These events are recorded in an audit back-end database in an "append-only" fashion. Each component of the online service hosted on the cloud provider premises pushes audit messages to the audit database. Note that the auditing mechanism of Cloudopsy is designed to generate "verbose" and detailed audit logs. Although the same audit trails will be used to provide audit information to both service providers and end users, the final information displayed to them will be different. The end user sees information regarding his own data, whereas the service provider has access to the audit logs of all user data handled by his service.

In addition to identifying individual user's data, the colors that are assigned to user data can also reflect their type. That can be accomplished by assigning them a second ID or sacrificing some bits of information, previously part of the user ID, and using them for indicating their type or class. For instance, possible classes of data could refer to credit card numbers, e-mails, social security numbers (SSN), *etc.* The class of user data can be assigned by the service provider, or would be automatically determined by content scanners [6] that identify known patterns of PII like SSNs.

2.2   Audit Trails Processing

The audit logs produced from the auditing component include raw log data in a textual form and need further processing before reaching the visualization component. The necessary transformations include: (a) mapping of the applications that comprise the cloud-hosted services, (b) filtering of the information from the "verbose" audit logs and transforming them to a format understood by the visualization component, and (c) correlating relevant information stored in several log files and generated by different cloud applications exchanging user data.

More specifically, Cloudopsy maintains a global registry of the active connections for the cloud-wide domain that it monitors. In order to transform the audit logs in an appropriate format for the next phase, technical details are used from this registry, and through automated procedures combined to create a more appropriate presentation of the collected audit information for input to the visualization component. Several other mechanisms are applied to the "verbose" audit logs to extract only the necessary segments for final log information that will be presented to the end users. For example, information unrelated to "suspicious" flows of user data will not be extracted for the next phase.

2.3   Audit Trails Visualization

The visualization mechanism of Cloudopsy is a significant enhancement to previous auditing mechanisms as the power of images will offer to both service providers and end users, a better understanding as well as deeper insights in the real flows of user data. It remains a challenge though to choose the appropriate and meaningful graphical representation of the collected audit data, which we discuss in more details in Sec. 4. In a few words, the visualization component receives the transformed audit logs and process them according to a set of different parameters and represents the graphic results in a circular layout representing the cloud on Cloudopsy's web interface. The services monitored by Cloudopsy are included in the final graphical representation and the recorded transfers of the colored user data will be represented by links between them as well, colored and directed according to the information from the audit logs. As expected, the generated output from the visualization component differs not only between users but also between the data owners and the providers of the online service.

3   Cloud-Wide Auditing Mechanism

In previous work we implemented a cloud-wide fine-grained data flow tracking framework [14] for cloud-hosted services. This DFT framework is used for the auditing of the data flows and the generation of the raw audit logs that will be analyzed by Cloudopsy. We assume that the service providers have integrated this mechanism in their applications to enhance the security of the provided services and leverage the generic facility offered by the cloud provider.

From a high-level perspective, the auditing mechanism is built on top of a user-level data flow tracking framework libdft [9], based on runtime instrumentation and is integrated into the components of the service and works as follows: the data that is "tagged" as *sensitive* is tracked across all local files, host-wide IPC mechanisms, and selected network sockets. Audit information selected by the auditing component is kept in a back-end database located outside the vicinity of the service providers, and more importantly operates in an append-only fashion for preventing tampering of the archived audit trails. The audit information collected by the DFT component captures leakage events that result from writing the marked data into files or remote endpoints. Each entry of the audit log will include information about the time, the running application, the action, the destination stream (a network address or a file path) and the tagged data.

Our first prototype of the auditing component is implemented using Intel's binary instrumentation tool Pin 2.10, and works with unmodified applications running on x86-64 Linux. It performs byte-level data flow tracking and supports 32-bits tags, allowing support for 2^{32} different tags values (colors) per byte – consequently, the same number of different users. In a newest version of the auditing mechanism we used the last two digits of the tag to represent different classes of user's sensitive data. The auditing component provides a transparent, fine-grained and domain-wide data flow tracking mechanism suitable for our target cloud environment.

4   Visualization

Our decision on enhancing our audit log analysis mechanism with visualization techniques was influenced by user studies comparing the effectiveness of visual presentations, in comparison to linear textual presentations of similar results to the ones we are handling in our audit logs analysis. In particular, in our case, since we wanted to represent the relationships and flow patterns of user data within the services in and outside of the cloud, Circos [11] seemed as a good candidate. Although Circos was originally developed to provide a better display of the chromosomal relationship between various species, it has been successfully used also for the graphical representations of other types of data, *i.e.*, network traffic. We chose Circos also due to its support for a circular data domain layout (resembles the cloud) and its multiple customizations opportunities, and finally due to its competence of smoothly partitioning the final image into any number of disjoint regions, drawing attention to multiple different events in a single display. Circos uses a circular ideogram layout to facilitate the display of relationships between pairs of services running on the cloud by the use of links (straight lines or Bezier curves), which can visually encode the position, size, and orientation of interacting elements.

Circos requires a specific format for the input data, which we generate through the transformations described in Sec. 2. In addition to our transformed audit log files, we also created configuration files including the necessary parameters for correctly generating the output required. The goal was to effectively present, in the final output, the monitored data flows within the cloud, as well as the ones "leaking" information out of the cloud premises, faithfully matching what is described in the initial audit files.

We provide two types of visual representations of data flows. For end users, we present a graphical display of the flow of their sensitive data that the cloud-hosted online service obtained as the result of their interactions with this service, *e.g.*, a purchase from an online store would result into the storage of a user's credit card number in the service's back-end database. Cloudopsy in this case summarizes the transfers of this data in a circular graph, representing each data exchange as a link between the involved services. This can help users gain a deeper understanding of how their data are handled in a facile way.

On the other hand, Cloudopsy's output for the provider of the service is a much "richer" graph of the audited transmissions entailing information for *all* clients' sensitive data collected. In particular, since the service provider needs

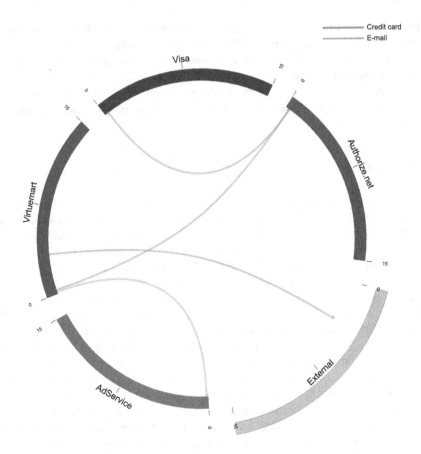

Fig. 2. A user's view of a transaction

to analyze the very large and usually complex audit log files, the visualization of the audited events is extremely beneficial for him as he can immediately verify legitimate operations or identify unexpected "suspicious" transmission patterns that might have otherwise remained opaque in the reams of the audit logs. Furthermore, the service provider can also see the flow of data between components of his service that could help him identify internal errors.

Sample results of this process can be seen in figures 2 and 3. Figure 2 displays the movement of a single user's "marked" sensitive data, *i.e.*, credit card number and email address, as they move in time between the audit-enabled applications. On the other hand, Fig. 3, which is aimed for the provider of the service, is a much "richer" image showing at a first glance patterns in the data flows. In general, the final audit images presented on Cloudopsy's web interface include the communicating applications of the composite cloud-hosted services running over the Cloudopsy mechanism, as well as hosts outside the cloud which according to the logs participated in sensitive data transmissions. In general, the final circular graphs consist of an outer ring representing the cloud-hosted applications

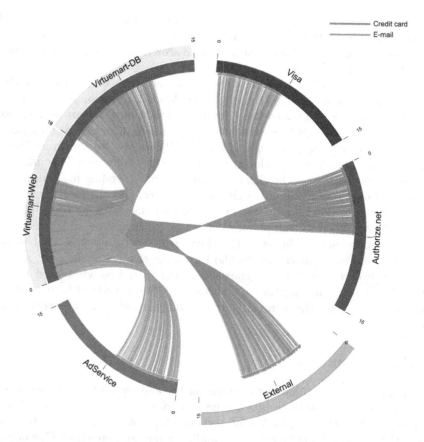

Fig. 3. A service provider's view of user transactions

(colored blocks) running over the auditing infrastructure, whereas the colored arcs depict the recorded transmissions of monitored user data. More specifically, in these two figures the blue and orange colored directed links represent different classes of sensitive data. In particular, in Fig. 3, the different colors could also represent the different users of the service. It is on the provider's discretion to customize the parameters on Cloudopsy's web interface, in respect to the information he is interested in on different occasions.

Scenario: Testing Cloudopsy with an E-Store

To test Cloudopsy we chose an e-store application, namely VirtueMart [17], hosted on a cloud-based infrastructure. We configured VirtueMart to accept only payments with credit card, and set up actual electronic payments through the Authorize.Net service using test accounts. Typically during a purchase transaction, users enter their personal data, credit card, email *etc.*, through the web front end of the application, which then are transmitted to the back-end database

374 A. Zavou et al.

of the e-store, and to the payment processor. After their credit card is verified, the e-store approves the purchase and the transaction completes successfully. The personal data that the user enters remain stored (as is frequently the case) in the database of the e-store.

Figure 2 depicts the movement of the credit card number for one user that completed a successful purchase through VirtueMart. It also represents the email of this user also stored in the backend database of the e-store. Apart from the exchanged data though, this figure shows also the time that each event took place. (For each segment time progresses clockwise). Therefore, we can immediately identify two events. First, that the email is sent to the AdService. This might be a legitimate action in case the client did not opt out of sending his information for advertising reasons while using the online service. But the most interesting event presented in this figure is that credit card number seems to transfer to an unknown IP outside the cloud premises at a later point in time, which definitely looks suspicious and should be further investigated as a possible inadvertent data leak. Note that this cannot be the legitimate channel of the user, as this was known from the start of the transaction and should be whitelisted by the auditing mechanism as a legitimate flow and therefore would not be part of the audit logs. Even with this simple figure this unexpected event was very easily identified.

5 Conclusion

In this paper, we argue that the concerns of the end users of cloud-hosted services about the usage of their data can be a major deterrent for users looking to embrace cloud-hosted services. We focused our efforts on enhancing the effectiveness of the information collected in the audit log files and presented Cloudopsy, a framework that through visualization and automated analysis of the results and based on the graphs produced with the Circos visualization tool, remediates cloud users security concerns and enables even users without any particular technical background to get a better understanding of the treatment of their data by third-part cloud-hosted services.

Acknowledgements. This work was supported by DARPA and the National Science Foundation through Contract FA8650-11-C-7190 and Grant CNS-12-28748, respectively, with additional support from Google. Any opinions, findings, conclusions or recommendations expressed herein are those of the authors, and do not necessarily reflect those of the US Government, DARPA, NSF or Google.

References

1. Berghel, H.: Identity theft and financial fraud: Some strangeness in the proportions. Computer 45(1), 86–89 (2012)
2. Chen, Y.Y., Jamkhedkar, P.A., Lee, R.B.: A software-hardware architecture for self-protecting data. In: Proceedings of the 2012 ACM Conference on Computer and Communications Security, CCS 2012, pp. 14–27 (2012)

3. Chow, R., Golle, P., Jakobsson, M., Shi, E., Staddon, J., Masuoka, R., Molina, J.: Controlling data in the cloud: outsourcing computation without outsourcing control. In: Proceedings of the 2009 ACM Workshop on Cloud Computing Security, CCSW 2009, pp. 85–90 (2009)
4. Cloud Security Alliance: Security guidance for critical areas of focus in cloud computing v2.1 (December 2009), https://cloudsecurityalliance.org/csaguide.pdf
5. Computerworld: Microsoft BPOS cloud service hit with data breach (December 2010), http://www.computerworld.com/s/article/9202078/Microsoft_BPOS_cloud_service_hit_with_data_breach
6. Cornell University: Open-source Forensics Tools for Network and System Administrators – Spider (February 2010), http://www2.cit.cornell.edu/security/tools/
7. Gens, F.: IT Cloud Services User Survey, pt.2: Top Benefits & Challenges. IDC (October 2008), http://blogs.idc.com/ie/?p=210
8. Kaufman, L.: Data security in the world of cloud computing. IEEE Security Privacy 7(4), 61–64 (2009)
9. Kemerlis, V.P., Portokalidis, G., Jee, K., Keromytis, A.D.: libdft: Practical Dynamic Data Flow Tracking for Commodity Systems. In: Proc. of VEE (2012)
10. Ko, R., Jagadpramana, P., Mowbray, M., Pearson, S., Kirchberg, M., Liang, Q., Lee, B.S.: TrustCloud: A framework for accountability and trust in cloud computing. In: 2011 IEEE World Congress on Services (SERVICES), pp. 584–588 (July 2011)
11. Krzywinski, M.I., Schein, J.E., Birol, I., Connors, J., Gascoyne, R., Horsman, D., Jones, S.J., Marra, M.A.: Circos: An information aesthetic for comparative genomics. Genome Research (2009)
12. Massonet, P., Naqvi, S., Ponsard, C., Latanicki, J., Rochwerger, B., Villari, M.: A monitoring and audit logging architecture for data location compliance in federated cloud infrastructures. In: 2011 IEEE International Symposium on Parallel and Distributed Processing Workshops and Phd Forum (IPDPSW), pp. 1510–1517 (May 2011)
13. Molnar, D., Schechter, S.: Self hosting vs. cloud hosting: Accounting for the security impact of hosting in the cloud. In: Proceedings of the 9th Workshop on the Economics of Information Security, WEIS 2010, pp. 1–18 (2010)
14. Pappas, V., Kemerlis, V., Zavou, A., Polychronakis, M., Keromytis, A.D.: CloudFence: Enabling Users to Audit the Use of their Cloud-Resident Data. Tech. Rep. CUCS-002-12, CS Department, Columbia University (2012), http://hdl.handle.net/10022/AC:P:12821
15. Sophos: Groupon subsidiary leaks 300k logins, fixes fail, fails again (June 2011), http://nakedsecurity.sophos.com/2011/06/30/groupon-subsidiary-leaks-300k-logins-fixes-fail-fails-again/
16. The Wall Street Journal: Google Discloses Privacy Glitch (March 2009), http://blogs.wsj.com/digits/2009/03/08/1214/
17. VirtueMart eCommerce Solution: VirtueMart shopping cart software, http://virtuemart.net
18. Wang, C., Wang, Q., Ren, K., Lou, W.: Privacy-preserving public auditing for data storage security in cloud computing. In: 2010 Proceedings IEEE INFOCOM (March 2010)

Author Index